BURT FRANKLIN: RESEARCH & SOURCE WORKS SERIES 650
Geography and Discovery 10

EARLY TRAVELLERS IN SCOTLAND

EARLY TRAVELLERS

IN SCOTLAND

EDITED BY

P. HUME BROWN

BURT FRANKLIN
NEW YORK

Published by LENOX HILL Pub. & Dist. Co. (Burt Franklin)
235 East 44th St., New York, N.Y. 10017
Originally Published: 1891
Reprinted: 1970
Printed in the U.S.A.

S.B.N.: 8337-03846
Library of Congress Card Catalog No.: 73-147148
Burt Franklin: Research and Source Works Series 650
Geography and Discovery 10

PREFACE.

THE present volume contains a collection, as complete as I have been able to make it, of all the accounts of Scotland published by travellers who visited the country before 1700. Although I have spared no pains to find them, there are doubtless other narratives which have eluded my search, and which would have been an interesting addition to this collection. I specially regret that in my list there is only one traveller from Denmark, and that there are none from Norway or Sweden. It is by the standard of these three countries that Scotland before the eighteenth century can alone be fairly judged; to measure her by the standard of England and France, as the travellers from these countries have naturally done, leaves us with impressions which must to a certain degree be misleading. On inquiry at the best sources, however, both in Norway and Sweden, I have been assured that no traveller in Scotland from these countries before 1700 has left any account of his visit.

I here take the opportunity of thanking Mr David Patrick, editor of *Chambers's Encyclopædia*, and Mr F. H. Groome, editor of the *Ordnance Gazetteer of Scotland*, for their kindness in revising my proofs, and for much valuable assistance besides. I am also indebted to Mr Hew Morrison of the Edinburgh Public Library for the solution of certain topographical difficulties which occurred in the course of my work. To Sheriff Mackay I owe assistance on special points, which I have acknowledged in the proper place. The vignette on the title-page has been copied, by the kind permission of Messrs M'Gibbon & Ross, from an oak panel described in their *Castellated and Domestic Architecture from the Twelfth to the Eighteenth Century.*

As the primary object of this collection is to throw light on certain aspects of Scotland and its people, which cannot be presented in ordinary histories, notes have been freely added wherever the text seemed to need correction or illustration. I take the liberty of adding that I should gratefully receive information regarding any narrative which has escaped my search, and which would deserve a place in the series here presented.

P. H. B.

SEPTEMBER 1891.

CONTENTS.

	PAGE
INTRODUCTION, ...	ix–xxvi
TRAVELLERS—	
EDWARD I. (1295), ...	1
JEAN FROISSART (reign of David II.), ...	7
JOHN HARDYNG (reign of James I.), ...	16
ÆNEAS SYLVIUS (reign of James I.), ...	24
JACQUES DE LALAIN (1448), ...	30
PEDRO DE AYALA (1498), ...	39
ANDREA TREVISANO (1498), ...	50
PEDER SWAVE (1535), ...	55
NICANDER NUCIUS (1545), ...	59
JEAN DE BEAUGUÉ (1548), ...	63
ESTIENNE PERLIN (1551), ...	71
FYNES MORYSON (1598), ...	80
HENRI, DUC DE ROHAN (1600), ...	91
SIR ANTHONY WELDON (?) (1617), . . .	96
TAYLOR THE WATER-POET (1618), . . .	104
SIR WILLIAM BRERETON (1636), ...	132

CONTENTS.

TRAVELLERS—*continued*—

PAGE

JAMES HOWELL (1639), ... 159

THOMAS TUCKER (1655), ... 162

RICHARD FRANCK (1656), ... 182

JOREVIN DE ROCHEFORD (1661 ?), ... 217

JOHN RAY (1662), ... 230

JAMES BROME (1669), ... 241

THOMAS KIRKE (1679), ... 251

THOMAS MORER (1689), ... 266

MAPS.

MAP OF SCOTLAND OF THE 13TH CENTURY, WITH KEY.

MAP OF SCOTLAND, BY MATTHEW PARIS, WITH KEY.

MAP OF SCOTLAND FROM MERCATOR'S ATLAS, 1595.

[*To follow Introduction.*]

INTRODUCTION.

O F the value of the following narratives as a contribution to Scottish history there can hardly be any question. They cover four hundred years of the history of Scotland as an independent kingdom, and these the years when the national character and the national fortunes took their defini- tive bent and form. The special value of these narratives is that they supplement the ordinary histories precisely where these histories must of necessity fall short, bringing before us with a vividness beyond the genius of any historian what essentially constitutes a national individuality.

Even to the close of the seventeenth century Scotland was still a kind of *terra incognita*, which men thought of as a half- mythical country, where strange things might exist which it was irrational to look for in any place nearer home. Till past the middle of the sixteenth century it was a common belief on the Continent that Scotland formed a distinct island, that it was considerably larger than England, and that it lay not north and south, but east and west, in the direction of Denmark and Norway.[1] The publication of Mercator's Atlas in 1595 made men more generally acquainted with the earth on which they lived, and Scotland also came to be better known as well as the rest of the world. Yet it still remained a country regarding which travellers' tales were received with a foregone feeling of their intrinsic probability.[2] The remoteness of Scotland, and the nature of

[1] Thus in La Popelinière, *Histoire de France*, i. 172 (1581), we have the expression, " Les Catholiques des deux Isles "—the two islands being England and Scotland. But the vague notions even of educated men regarding the geography of Scotland will sufficiently appear in the sequel. See p. xxvi (note).
[2] For an interesting catalogue of the wonders of Scotland, see the elegiac verses prefixed to " Britannia Magna, sive Angliæ, Scotiæ, Hiberniæ et ad- jacentium Insularum Geographico-Historica Descriptio " (Amstelodami, 1661), by Rutgerus Hermannides.

the country itself doubtless in the first place gave rise to these stories ; but the records of the travellers here collected prove that it was the Scottish and English chroniclers who gave them currency. It will be seen that most of the travellers show their acquaintance with these chroniclers, from Geoffrey of Monmouth downwards. To those who came after 1527 [1] Hector Boece's *History of Scotland* seems to have been the guide-book from which they derived their knowledge of the country. Boece wrote in excellent Latin, then the common language of Europe, and his extraordinary story of the origins of the Scottish nation, the marvellous vicissitudes of its kings, the astounding nature of the country they had ruled for the space of two millenniums, were admirably fitted to interest a public whose best minds took More's *Utopia* for a faithful description of an actual part of the globe.

In the Itinerary of the diarist who accompanied Edward I. into Scotland we seem to have the first notes on the country by one who describes what he actually saw. Of the many saints who came from Ireland at an earlier epoch none have left even jottings that might find a place in the present collection, and none of the English chroniclers who have occasion to mention Scotland speak from personal acquaintance with the country. What we have greater cause to regret, however, is that before 1700 Scotland had many notable visitors, whose reports of what they saw would have been more interesting than any we actually possess. A few remarks on these unrecorded visits will be a fitting supplement to the following narratives.

In 1455, in the reign of James II., Scotland was visited by a personage who far surpassed Froissart in the extent of his wanderings, and who may be fairly regarded as an early specimen of the modern race of tourists. This was a German knight, Georg von Ehingen, whose travels led him to Jerusalem, Damascus, Babylon, Rhodes, Cyprus, Sicily, Africa, France, Navarre, Castille, Granada, Portugal, England, and Scotland. He wrote an account of his travels, but composi-

---

[1] Boece's history was published in that year. It was afterwards translated into French by Nicholas d'Arfeville, royal cosmographer, and presented to Henry II. Bellenden's translation popularized Boece in Scotland, and Hollinshed, making free use of Bellenden's translation, made him known in England.

tion was evidently not such an easy matter for him as for the garrulous Froissart, since his whole published narrative is comprised in a few quarto pages. His visit to Scotland is disposed of in some dozen lines. Both the King and the Queen (Mary of Gueldres) appear to have done their best to give him a favourable impression of Scottish liberality and hospitality. Of the Queen he specially mentions that she spoke Netherlandish Dutch. The king gave him two *zellter* (horses), a cloth of black velvet, and to each of his four servants ten ducats a-piece ; and the Queen presented him with a very fine jewel, thirty ducats, a horse worth a hundred gulden, and, morever, made a very fine banquet, and got up many sports in his honour. To this enumeration of the gifts and honours he received the much-travelled knight confines the narrative of his visit to Scotland.

In the next century Scotland had few visitors of note, though England during the same period has an even shorter list to show.[2] With such narratives as those of the Spaniard Pedro de Ayala (1498), the Venetian Andrea Trevisano (1498), and the Dane Peder Swave (1530), we have, indeed, no good reason to complain. For the reign of James V. we have the curious tract entitled " The Navigation of King James V. round Scotland, the Orkney Isles, and the Hebrides or Western Islands." This tract was drawn up by a Frenchman, Nicholas d'Arfeville, cosmographer to Henri II., who has an additional claim on the memory of Scotsmen as the translator of Hector Boece into French. The " Navigation " is a mere log-book ; but its jottings have a distinct interest as the record of a serious attempt to produce an accurate chart of the coasts of Scotland. As d'Arfeville, however, did not himself accompany James on his voyage, and merely edited the papers put into his hand, his compilation has no place here.[3]

[1] *Historische Beschreibung weilund Hern Georgen von Ehingen Raisens nach der Ritterschaft vor* 150 *Jaren in x verschidliche Königreich verbracht* (Printed from MS. in Fugger's Museum at Augsburg in 1600). The book is in black letter, and contains portraits of the ten kings whose kingdoms Ehingen visited, of James II. among the rest. There is a copy in the National Portrait Gallery, Edinburgh. [2] See Rye, *England as seen by Foreigners* (1865). 3. It is perhaps worth noting that the poet Ronsard, then in his thirteenth year, accompanied James V. on his return from France after his first marriage (1537). Ronsard remained at the Scottish Court for nearly two years in the capacity of a page.

In 1543 a Papal legate came to Scotland, whose visit deserves a passing notice. Curiously enough, though his visit is referred to by several historians, his name and identity are still a disputed point, and he is variously known as Peter Francis Contareno, Mark German, and Marcus Grymanus, Patriarch of Aquileia.[1] Scotland did her very best to give him an exalted opinion of her resources and social refinements, and he was so impressed by the attention shown him, that " after he had been courteously and splendidly entertained at Edinburgh, by persons of the greatest rank, he departed in the beginning of March, and was so well pleased with the reception he had met with, that wherever he went afterwards, he spoke of the magnificent civilities of the Scottish nation." [2] But an incident related by Bishop Lesley in connection with the Legate's visit so well illustrates that jealous pride of country which has ever been the note of the Scottish nation that it deserves to· be quoted in full : "The Earle of Murray makand him the banquet in his house, although he had great store of all kinds of silver wark, yet nottheless, for the greater magnificence, he set forth ane cupboard furnished with all sorts of glasses of the finest chrystal that could be made ; and to make the said patriarch understand that there was great abundance thereof in Scotland, he caused one of his servants, as it had been by sloth and negligence, pull down the cupboard cloth, so that all the whole chrystellings suddenly were cast down to the earth and broken ; wherewith the patriarch was very sorry, but the Earl suddenly caused bring another cupboard, better furnished with fine chrystal nor that was ; which the patriarch praised, as well for the magnificence of the Earl, as for the fineness of the chrystal, affirming that he never did see better in Venice, where he himself was born." [3]

From the Sire Jean de Beaugué's account of the French campaigns in Scotland of 1559–60 we are able to glean some interesting notices of certain of the leading Scottish towns of the period. Of the battle of Pinkie several years before (1546) we have also narratives by a Londoner, George Paton, and by a French Protestant, the Sieur Jean Berteville,

[1] Keith, *Affairs of Church and State in Scotland*, vol. i. p. 96, note (ed. 1845). [2] *Ibid.* [3] Lesley, *History of Scotland*, p. 179 (Ban. Club).

both of whom were present at the scenes they describe.[1] In neither, however, do we find, as in Beaugué, any matter of interest outside the details of the battle which it is their main object to describe. The Italian, Petruccio Ubaldini, who was sometime in the service of Edward VI., and who by his own account also visited Scotland, wrote a book from whose title we should expect something more valuable than any foreign account of Scotland we possess. In translation the title runs as follows :—"Description of the Kingdom of Scotland, and of its adjacent islands, in which are described the boundaries of each province, the places in them, and the things most worthy of memory which are found there, as well natural as marvellous." [2] Ubaldini, however, was an impostor, and his book is a barefaced appropriation of Hector Boece, with scarcely an independent statement which we may regard as the result of his own observation.

In 1552, Scotland and England both were honoured by the visit of one of the most extraordinary personages of the sixteenth century, the half-genius, half-charlatan, Jerome Cardan.[3] Born in 1501, Cardan, by the date of this visit, was known to all Europe for his profound acquirements in medicine, astrology, mathematics, and all the science of the time. Among his admirers was William Cassanate, physician to John Hamilton, the notorious Archbishop of St Andrews. The Archbishop had long been afflicted by a disease which had defied Cassanate's skill; and patient and physician at length agreed that they could do no better than put the case before the great Cardan himself. Induced by the most munificent offers, Cardan proceeded from Italy to Paris, where by arrangement he was to have met the Archbishop. On his arrival he was informed that affairs of state had detained his Grace at home, and still more handsome offers were made to him that, now he was so far on the journey, he would continue it to Scotland. Cardan was not taken with the proposal; but for various reasons he at length consented. Crossing to London, where he spent a

[1] Berteville's narrative is published by the Bannatyne Club, and Paton's by the Society of Antiquaries. [2] Ubaldini's "Description" was published by the Bannatyne Club in 1829. [3] For this account of Cardan's visit to Scotland I am chiefly indebted to Henry Morley's *The Life of Girolamo Cardano, of Milan, Physician* (London, 1854).

few days, he made his way north to Edinburgh, which he
reached on the 29th June, the journey between the two
capitals having taken him only twenty-three days. Among
other things he had expected to see by the way was the
sky much darkened by crows, and sheep watered on morning
dew, neither of which sights, however, was he fortunate
enough to see.

For the first forty days the Archbishop was treated according to a regimen prescribed by the physicians of Paris,
whom Cassanate had also consulted regarding the case. His
Grace, however, lost rather than gained by the new treatment, and he grew impatient with his physicians. Cardan
then explained that it had only been from considerations of
professional etiquette that he had allowed his Grace to be
treated according to the advice of the Paris physicians. On
this explanation Cardan and Cassanate fell out; but
Hamilton was only wroth that so much time had been
wasted on methods which Cardan did not approve. Cardan
was therefore ordered to take the responsibility of the case
entirely in his own hands. In his published writings we
have in fullest detail his diagnosis of Hamilton's disease,
and the regimen he prescribed for its mitigation or cure.
Cardan was regarded by his contemporaries as one of the
safest practitioners of this time, and extraordinary as his
pharmacopœia now seems to us, we can see that he had really
before him the prime conditions of healthy living.[1] However this may be, the Archbishop prospered in his hands,
and they parted on the best of terms, greatly, indeed, against
his Grace's will, who would fain have had Cardan's services

[1] Cardan's medical and hygienic directions for his Grace will be found in
Mr Henry Morley's *Life of Cardan*, vol. ii. pp. 114-122. Among other prescriptions is the following :—Take of goats' or cows' milk and of water, of each
half a pint, mix and dissolve in them two grains of elaterium ; let this be
drawn through the nostrils when the patient has an empty stomach.
Hamilton's ailment was asthma aggravated by a degree of free living not uncommon among the higher clergy of that day. Another rule prescribed for
his lordship's guidance is the following :—De venere. Certe non est bona,
neque utilis ; ubi tamen contingat necessitas debet uti ea inter duos somnos,
scilicet post mediam noctem, et melius est exercere eam ter in sex diebus, pro
exemplo ita ut singulis duobus diebus semel, quam bis in una die. Sir James
Simpson speaks highly of the hygienic rules prescribed by Cardan for his
patient.

for the winter. Hamilton was reputed the wealthiest man in Scotland, and the reward he conferred on Cardan fully confirms the common belief. The fee originally agreed on had been ten gold crowns a day, and as Cardan's stay lasted seventy-five days, the final sum should have been 750 crowns. The Archbishop gave him eighteen hundred gold crowns, a gold chain worth one hundred and fifty, and an ambling horse for his journey through England. As in addition to his Grace's munificence, he also received many gifts from the Scottish nobles, who in great numbers had availed themselves of his skill, Cardan had every reason to be satisfied with his visit. We should have been more grateful to him, however, if instead of his prescriptions for the Archbishop, he had left us some account of the country and its people as a memorial of his sojourn. As it is, only one or two passing remarks indicate that he ever saw the country at all. Of the Highland Scots he says that they were ignorant of fear, that when led to execution they take a piper with them, and that the piper, who is often one of the condemned, plays them up dancing to the place of execution. In another place he incidentally remarks that, continuing to wear the dress he had bought in Edinburgh, he made himself a gazing-stock to his countrymen in Italy. We also gather from him that clocks were unknown in Scotland at the date of his visit. At least, one of his parting advices to Hamilton was that he should procure a clock for the proper regulation of his treatment, adding that every Italian prince was the owner of many good ones.

With Queen Mary on her return to Scotland (August 1561)[1] came a train of followers, certain of whom were very brilliant personages in their own day, but who now move our interest simply as the satellites of her on whom they attended. Among them was her preacher and confessor, Réné Benoit, who, in the serenity of his confidence as a doctor of the Sorbonne, addressed a Latin epistle to " the

---

[1] Thomas Churchyard, an English poet, has left some doggerel verses on the Siege of Leith (1559–60), at which he was present. Churchyard was an original character ; but his poem has no passage of general interest. He had formerly been taken prisoner by the Scots in the campaign of Sir William Drury (1548). Part of Churchyard's *Chippes* was published by George Chalmers in 1817.

most learned" John Knox, in the strange hope of recalling to the fold that reformer and his brother ministers. The courtly Brantôme came also, the sugared vice of whose pages, contrasted with the fierce Hebraism of Knox's *History of the Reformation*, gives us the key to all that was to follow in Scotland till the day of Langside in 1568. In his life of Mary, Brantôme has little, or rather nothing, to say directly of Scotland and its people; but his incidental remarks leave us in no doubt as to his general impression. Scotland, with its gloomy skies, its poverty and squalor, its harsh and rugged aspect, was unfit to have produced the paragon of princesses, and still more unfit to entertain her. As for its people, they were a race of savages, to whom the graces of life were incomprehensible, whose language was "rustic, barbarous, ill-sounding, and uncouth," whose dress was "the barbarous mode of savages," whose citizens were "scoundrels from the town," their music that of "vile violins and little rebecks," their songs "psalms ill-sung and ill-harmonised," who possessed one "fine building,"[1] indeed, but one little in keeping with all else to be seen in the country. As a typical figure in the queen's train Chastellard also should not be forgotten, that "gentle knight," as Brantôme calls him, "excellent at his weapons, and imbued with good letters," who suffered death, as the same chronicler informs us with his delicate sense for shades of conduct, "par son outrecuidance et non pour crime."

A different personage from these was the younger Scaliger, who in 1566 paid what appears to have been a flying visit to Scotland in company with his friend and patron, Louis Chastaigner.[2] A few casual remarks in his reported conversations are unfortunately the sole record of this visit of the greatest of scholars. He came by way of England, where the sight that struck him most was the array of heads on London Bridge,[3] During his stay in Scotland the misunderstandings between

---

[1] Holyrood Palace. The phrases in the text are all taken from Brantôme's *Discours Troisiesme* in his *Dames illustres françaises et étrangères.* [2] By an inadvertence, Dr M'Crie, in his *Life of Andrew Melville* (p. 393, ed. 1856), makes the elder and not the younger Scaliger pay this visit. The father died in 1558, some six years before the date of his son's visit to Scotland. [3] *Scaligerana, sive Excerpta ex ore Josephi Scaligeri*, p. 209 (The Hague, 1668).

Mary and Darnley appear to have been the talk of the country.[1] Mary he appears to have seen, as he describes her as *une belle creature*.[2] Of the Scots he says, what was indeed the common opinion on the Continent, " that they are excellent philosophers." When he was in England, he tells us there were hardly any doctors, and when his brother was in Scotland there was only one in that country, and he the court physician. At the time of his own visit to Scotland, it was the joiners (*menuisiers*), who plied the art of bleeding, while the barbers were restricted to shaving.[3]

In 1587[4] there also came to Scotland the most famous poet of his day in Europe, Guillaume de Salluste du Bartas, author of *The Divine Weeks and Works*, a poem which in six years had passed through thirty editions, and had been translated into Latin, Italian, German, and English, and more than once into each of them. As a maker of verses himself, King James had been dazzled by the prodigious repute of Du Bartas, and it was by the special invitation of his Majesty that the great poet had now come to Scotland. James had already sought to commend himself to Du Bartas by a translation of his *L'Uranie*, accompanied by an egotistically humble preface, in which he expressed his admiration for " the divine and illuster poete," Salluste du Bartas, through " oft reading and perusing " of whom he had been moved "with a restless and lofty desire to preas to attaine to the like virtue." James, it would appear, made it the special reason of his invitation that Du Bartas would be able by word of mouth " to expound his poesie." [5] The only incident connected with Du Bartas' sojourn in Scotland has been narrated in James Melville's *Diary* in a manner that leaves nothing to be desired.

---

[1] *Ibid.*, p. 215. [2] *Ibid.* [3] *Ibid.*, p. 317. Scaliger was also much interested in the Scotch ballads. In a note to his edition of *Ausonius* (ii. 11), he says :— " Vidimus nos in Scotia nutriculas miras harum nugarum (he is speaking of *nœnia*) artifices ad conciliandos pueris somnos, ut eos audire non invenustum mihi ἀκρόαμα fuerit." Like other travellers in Scotland, he was also struck by the use of coal instead of wood in the country. For some interesting remarks on the practice of bleeding in Scotland, see Dr Dickson's Preface to the *Accounts of the Lord High Treasurer of Scotland* (1473–1498). [4] As Claude Nau's visit to Scotland (1575) was purely political, it calls for no special mention here. [5] *Despatches of M. Courcelles* (Ban. Club, 1827), pp. 71–2. Du Bartas bore letters from the King of Navarre with proposals for a marriage between James and the Princess of Navarre.

Moreover, besides its bearing on Du Bartas' visit, the passage throws such a curious light on the characters of the two leading personages that it deserves to be quoted in full.

"That yeir, in the monethe of May, Guiliaum Salust S. Du Bartas cam in Scotland to sie the King, of whom he was receavit according to his worthines, interteined honourablie, and liberalie propyned and dimissed in the hervest, to his Maiesties grait praise sa lange as the French toung is vsed and vnderstuid in the warld.

"About the end of Junie, his Maiestie cam to St Andros, and brought with him the said Du Bartas, and coming first without anie warning to the New Collage, he calles for Mr Andro [Melville], saying he was com with that gentleman to haiff a Lessone. Mr Andro answeres, 'That he haid teatched his ordinar that day in the fornoone.' 'That is all ane,' sayes the King, 'I mon haiff a Lessone, and be heir within an howre for that effect.' And, indeid, within les nor an houre, his Maiestie was in the scholl, and the haill Vniversitie convenit with him, befor whom Mr Andro *ex tempore* intreated maist cleirlie and mightelie of the right government of Chryst, and in effect refuted the haill Actes of Parliament maid against the discipline thereof, to the grait instruction and confort of his auditor, except the King allean, wha was verie angrie all that night.

"Vpon the morn the Bischope haid bathe a prepared Lessone and feast maid for the King. His Lessone was a tichted vpe abregment of all he haid tetched the yeir bypast, namlie anent the corrupt groundes quhilk he haid put in the Kings head contrarie to the trew discipline. To the quhilk lessone Mr Andro went contrar to his custome, and with his awin pen market all his fals grounds and reasones; and without farder caussit ring his bell at twa efternoone the sam day, wharof the King heiring, he send to Mr Andro, desyring him to be moderat, and haiff regard to his presence, vtherwayes he wald discharge him. He answered couragiouslie, that his Maisties ear and tender breist was pitifullie and dangeruslie filled with errours and vntreuthes be that wicked man, the quhilk he could nocht suffer to pas, and bruik a lyff, vtherwayes, except the stopping of the breathe of Gods mouthe, and preiudging of his treuthe, he sould behaiff himselff maist moderatlie and reuerentlie to his Maiestie in all respects. The King send againe to him and me, desyring it sould be sa, and schawin that he wald haiff his four hours in the Collage, and drink with Mr Andro. Sa coming to that Lessone with the Bischope, wha requysted the King for leiue to mak answer instantlie in cais anie thing war spoken against his doctrine. Bot ther Mr Andro, making him as thouche he haid na thing to do but with the Papist, brings out thair works, and reids out of tham all the Bischopes grounds and reasones. The quhilk, when he haid at lainthe and maist cleirlie schawin to be plean papistrie, then he settes against the sam with all his mean, and with inmutible force of reasone, from cleir grounds of Scripture with a mightie parrhesie and fluide of eloquence, he dinges tham sa down, that the bischope was dasht and strukken als dum the stok he satt vpon. Efter the Lessone, the King, in his mother toung, maid sum distingoes, and discursit a whyll thereon, and gaiff certean iniunctiones to the Vniuersitie for reuerencing and obeying of his Bischope; wha fra that day furthe, began to tyre of his teatching, and fall mair and mair in disgrace and confusion. The King, with Monsieur du Bartas, cam to the Collage Hall, wher I causit prepear, and haiff in readines a banquet of wat and dry confectiounes, with all sortes of wyne, wharat his Maiestie camped verie merrelie a guid whyll and thereafter went to his hors. But Mons. du Bartas tarried behind and conferrit with my Vncle and me a wholl houre, and syne followed efter the King: wha inquyring of him that night, as ane tauld me, 'What was his iudgment of the twa he haid herd in St Andros?' He answered the King 'that they war bathe learned men, bot the bischopes were cunned and prepared maters, and Mr Andro haid a grait reddie store of all kynd of lerning within him; and by that, Mr Andro his spreit and courage was far aboue the other.' The quhilk iudgement previously the King approved." [1]

Throughout his stay Du Bartas was treated in princely fashion, and on his departure we are told that "the king,

---

[1] Mr James Melville's *Diary* (Ban. Club, 1829), pp. 170, 171.

besides all his costes which he deffraied, gratefyed du Bartas at his departure with a chain of 1000ᵛ and as much in redie money, made him knight, and accompanyed him to the sea-side, when he made him promise to retourne again."[1] Du Bartas died some three years later (1590), and never returned to Scotland. In requital of James's munificence, however, he did all that a poet could. He translated James's poem on the battle of Lepanto into French, and prefaced it with an introduction, in which he speaks of "the grandeur as well as the admirable spirit, the grave sweetness, the beautiful and artistic *liaison*, the living and speaking description of the Lepanto," "that plant which the Apollo of our time has sown with his own hand, and the Graces have watered with nectar, the most divine which flows from their mouth."

It is a misfortune, not only for Scottish history, but for English literature, that Ben Jonson left no record of his memorable northern journey of 1618. If no more than as a counterpart to his namesake's famous narrative, it would have been one of those interesting things in literature which possess a value independent of their intrinsic quality. The visit of both has the same piquancy of an act in oddest contrast with their general habits and tenor of life. In some respects the earlier traveller would have had the advantage. He remained longer in the country, and he came with no prejudices to distort his impression of what he might hear or see. Moreover, as the picture of a period remoter from our own and less familiar to us from the testimonies of others, the advantage would still have been with the earlier traveller.

As early as June 1617, a month after James had set out for Scotland, Jonson's projected journey is mentioned in the State Papers. The traditional opinion that he went specially to visit Drummond of Hawthornden will not bear examination. Drummond was known to Jonson; but he was not a sufficiently important person to induce the first man of letters in England to trudge the length of a kingdom to see him. We probably do the burly laureate no injustice in supposing that, swashbuckler as he was, the journey was as much a matter of bravado as anything else. His well-

---

[1] *Despatches of M. Courcelles*, p. 80.

known habits and his enormous physical bulk gave his expedition just that character of a wager which brought Ben the notoriety he liked. At the same time, the new relations of the two countries had turned the thoughts of the English more curiously to their enemy of centuries standing. It would appear also, from what he told Drummond, that by his father's descent he looked upon himself as half a Scotsman, so that he had a special interest in seeing the country with his own eyes.[1] Whatever may have been his motives, towards the end of June or the beginning of July 1618, he set out on his journey, to the general amusement of the wits of the city. Lord Bacon told him that " he loved not to see poesy go on other feet than poetical dactyls and spondaes," and there is good reason to believe that Taylor the Water-poet was prompted to his Pennylesse Pilgrimage by way of ironical comment on what was naturally considered a preposterous adventure for one of Ben's habit of mind and body.[2]

Except in the case of one notable episode, we know little of Jonson's doings during his six months' stay in Scotland. Like the Water-poet, he had evidently nothing to complain of Scottish hospitality. In a letter to Drummond after his return to London he speaks, with an evident recollection of jovial meetings, of "the beloved Fentons, the Nisbets, the Scotts, the Livingstones, and all the honest and honoured names with you." We know also that he visited the district of the Lennox, and that he was much impressed by Lochlomond, whose wonders had been celebrated by the chroniclers from Gregory of Monmouth downwards. Leith and Edinburgh, however, would seem to have been his headquarters, and it was in Leith that Taylor met him,[3] and profited by his generosity. His stay at Hawthornden and Drummond's report of him belong to literary history. Among the notes that Drummond took of his conversation there is nothing to indicate his general impressions of the country and people he had put himself to so much trouble to visit, but we are justified in inferring that his impression, like Taylor's, was a kindly one. While in Scotland he had actually made notes

---

[1] See Professor Masson's *Drummond of Hawthornden* (pp. 85–111) on Jonson's visit to Scot d. [2] See p. 104 below. [3] See p. 126 below.

for future use, and from a letter to Drummond we learn that, with the view of at once producing some memorial of his tour, he had asked for further information regarding the things of which he meant to write. "I am arrived safely," he writes, "with a most catholic welcome, and my reports not unacceptable to His Majesty. He professed, I thank God, some joy to see me, and is pleased to hear of the purpose of my book; to which I most earnestly solicit you for your promise of the inscriptions at Pinkie, some things concerning the Loch of Lomond, touching the Government of Edinburgh to urge Mr James Scott, and what else you can procure for me, with all speed. Especially I make it my request that you will enquire for me whether the students' method at St Andrews be the same with that of Edinburgh, and so to assure me, or wherein they differ." From this it would seem that he thought of writing a narrative that should combine topographical with historical matter in a fashion that would make it of solid value to those who really wished to know the true character of the northern kingdom. It was also part of his purpose to write a pastoral poem with Loch Lomond for its subject, but this purpose, like the other, came to nothing. In a poem written on the fire that burnt his lodgings in 1620, he mentions among papers that were destroyed,

> ". . . . . my journey into Scotland
> Sung with all the adventures,"

from which it would seem that his memorials of his Scottish tour had finally taken the form of Horace's account of his journey to Brundisium. As it is, Jonson's visit to Scotland remains one of those picturesque incidents in the life of a man of letters, which owe their interest solely to the individuality of the person to whom they are attached.

From the date of Jonson's visit till the end of the 17th century there is no lack of travellers who left both full and intelligent accounts of Scotland and its people. Brereton, Jorevin, Tucker, Franck, Morer, and Brome cannot be neglected by any one who would know the Scotland of the 17th century. With the narratives of these travellers in our hands, therefore, we have the less reason to regret that the voluminous literature regarding Scotland which sprang from the Cromwellian occupation of the country, contains little or nothing which comes within the scope of our present purpose. Absorbed in their political and ecclesiastical schemes, Cromwell and the other officers of the Parliament in their letters on Scottish affairs never diverge into matter which does not directly bear on the object they have in hand. The same remark holds of one of the most singular personages who ever made his way into Scotland, George Fox, the founder of the Quakers. The pages of Fox's *Journal* which refer to Scotland have certainly an interest of their own, but it is an interest exclusively religious and ecclesiastical. Fox evidently found Scotland no very promising field for his new gospel. The lowland Scots were " a dark, carnal people ; " [1] and as for the Highlanders, he says that they " were so devilish they had like to have spoiled us and our horses ; for they ran at us with pitchforks ; but through the Lord's goodness we escaped them, being preserved by His power." [2] At Edinburgh he was summoned before " Cromwell's Council ; " from Perth he was bodily ejected by its citizens ; and everywhere he seems to have been received with little favour by the bulk of the people, and to have met with special opposition from the clergy of all denominations. He thus closes his record of his Scottish mission ; " When first I set my feet upon the Scottish ground, I felt the seed of God to sparkle about me like innumerable sparks of fire. Not but that there is abundance of thick cloddy earth of hypocrisy and falseness that is a top, and a briarly, brambly nature, which is to be burnt up with God's word, and ploughed up with the spiritual plough, before God's seed brings forth heavenly and spiritual fruit to his glory. But the husbandman is to wait in patience." [3]

Among foreign visitors to Scotland it was hardly to be expected that the number of artists would be either very numerous or very distinguished. Scotland was too poor a country, and led far too precarious a national existence to have leisure or disposition to pay any serious heed to the mere decoration of life. During the period with which we are concerned, some half-a-dozen completes the list of those

[1] Fox's *Journal*, vol. i. p. 412 (edit. 1827). [2] *Ibid.*, p. 411. [3] *Ibid.*, p. 461.

artists who either paid flying visits to the country, or received so much encouragement as to make it their home. In 1503 " au Inglis payntour," variously known as Mynour, De Mayne, and Maynard, came to the court of James IV., bringing with him " ye figures of ye king [Henry VII.], queene, and princes of England, and our queene."[1] It is significant that he was persuaded to remain for two months, and that the king made good use of his skill during his stay. It is not till the reign of James VI., indeed, that we hear of an officially recognised court-painter; and when we first hear of the office, it is a Fleming, Arnold Bronkhorst, who holds it.[2] To Bronkhorst's successor in office, Adrian Vansoum, also a foreigner, we probably owe the well-known portrait of Rollock, the first principal of the University of Edinburgh.[3] It was a Fleming, James de Witt, who, by the order of James, Duke of York, painted that extraordinary series of the " portraits " of the kings of Scotland which adorn the walls of Holyrood Palace. According to the contract he was to paint one hundred and ten portraits in two years, his payment being at the rate of £120 per annum. De Witt bitterly complained that by this arrangement he received less for the whole gallery than Sir Godfrey Kneller did for two full-lengths. But even these hard terms were not kept, for De Witt was eventually dismissed without full payment of the sum that had been pledged to him.[4] David le Grange, the court-limner in Scotland to Charles the Second, seems to have had still stronger reason than De Witt to regret that he had ever come so far north in the exercise of his calling. In a petition he presented to his Majesty he prays for " 76 lib due for work done in Scotland," and urges the pressing necessities of himself and miserable children; his sight and labour failing him in his old age, whereby he is forced to rely on the charity of well-disposed persons.[5] Another foreign artist, however, Sir John de Medina, who came to Scotland after 1686, found more generous patronage than De Witt or Le Grange. Having settled in Edinburgh, he became the favourite portrait-painter of the day, and plied his art so prosperously that " there are few old Scottish

[1] Brydall, *Art in Scotland*, p. 48. [2] *Ibid.*, p. 69. [3] This was David Laing's opinion. [4] *Art in Scotland*, pp. 84, 85. [5] *Ibid.*, p. 100.

houses without a specimen of his work." Both honour and riches came to Medina. He was one of the last Scottish knights made by the Lord High Commissioner before the Parliamentary Union; he was courted by all the best society of the Scottish capital, and he bequeathed to his son and successor in his art both wealth and an assured position.[1]

THE MAPS.

The author of the first map in this volume has not been ascertained. Attention was first drawn to it by Tom Martin, who exhibited it to the Society of Antiquaries in London in 1768. At the sale of Martin's library in 1774 it was purchased by Gough, the author of *British Topography*, with the rest of whose papers it passed to the Bodleian Library. Writing to George Paton, the antiquary, Gough says that it was supposed " to be of the time of one of our Edwards." On the other hand, Cosmo Innes, who reproduced it in the *National Manuscripts of Scotland* (part iii.), is disposed to place it considerably before 1300.[2]

Our second map is that which appears in the chronicle of Matthew Paris, and according to Sir Frederick Madden is by the chronicler's own hand.[3] As Matthew Paris died in 1259, this map must also be referred to the thirteenth century. That the one differs so widely from the other need not surprise us, since, as will abundantly appear throughout this volume, the most conflicting notions regarding the geography of Scotland prevailed till at least the end of the sixteenth century. As the names of the places in both of these maps have been given in full, it is unnecessary to point out their respective peculiarities.

The third map is reproduced from an atlas printed at Dusseldorf in 1595 at the expense of the heirs of Gerard Mercator. As being less known, it is here given in preference

---

[1] There is an interesting account of Medina in the *Scotsman* of June 4, 1884, by Colonel Fergusson. [2] This map was also published in reduced facsimile, with a four-page folio account, by W. B. Sanders of the Ordnance Survey (Southampton, 1875). [3] This map appears in the only MS. of M. Paris's Chronicle that is known to exist. An account of this map will be found in the *National Manuscripts of Scotland*, part ii. It is with the kind permission of Stair Agnew, Esq., of the Register House, Edinburgh, that both of these maps are here reproduced from the National MSS.

to the maps of Scotland in Speed, Camden, and in Blaeu's
Atlas. Though inferior to all these, Mercator's map proves
that by the close of the sixteenth century geographers had
arrived at a fairly accurate conception of the country.
According to Gough the earliest printed map of Scotland is
that of Bishop Lesley,[1] which on a reduced scale appears in
certain copies of his *De Origine, Moribus, et Rebus Gestis
Scotorum,* published at Rome in 1578. Lesley's map marks
a vast improvement on the geographical knowledge of
Scotland, which is shown by such visitors to the country as
Ayala and Estienne Perlin, yet it falls considerably short of that
of Mercator, which appeared only seventeen years afterwards.
In the Atlas of Abraham Ortelius (Plantin, Antwerp, 1592),
we can distinctly trace the advance of geographical science
during the last years of the sixteenth century. While inferior
to that of Mercator, Ortelius's map is in most points clearly
superior to Lesley's. In the map of Scotland given by Speed
(1611) we again mark the improvement made on that of
Mercator, and in Blaeu's map (1662) we have a representa-
tion of Scotland which has been improved upon only in
comparatively recent years.[2]

[1] This map is in the copy of Lesley in the Advocates' Library, Edinburgh.
In many copies it does not appear.   [2] As is well known, in Ptolemy's
map of the British Islands, Scotland is made to trend eastwards towards
Denmark. This error was generally recognised by geographers from at
least early in the sixteenth century. It is pointed out, for example,
in the *Isolario* of Benedetto Bordone (p. 11, Venice, 1533). Bordone
in his Atlas gives two maps of the British Islands, one according to
Ptolemy, the other according to the moderns. In the latter, however,
the whole of Scotland represented is a narrow strip of land completely
detached by an intersecting channel from England. The famous Servetus,
under the name of Michael Villanovanus, published an atlas in 1535,
in which he simply reproduces the British Islands of Ptolemy. In a
subsequent edition (1541), however, he represents Scotland as stretching
directly northwards from England, but with no approach to correctness of
outline. Even till near the close of the sixteenth century atlases continued
to appear in which Scotland was set down according to Ptolemy.

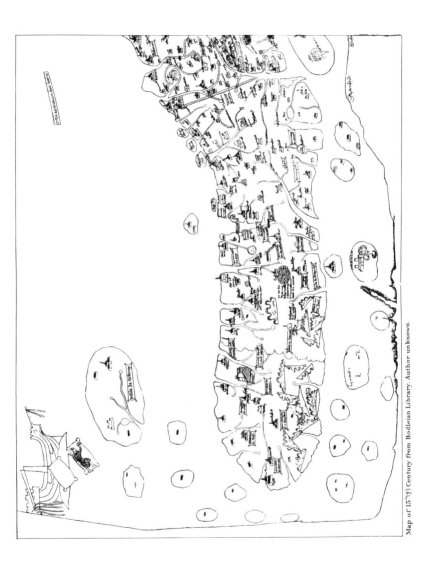

Map of 15 (?) Century from Bodleian Library. Author unknown.

MAP OF 13TH (?) CENTURY. AUTHOR UNKNOWN.

Insula De Orkeney

May

lasse

dunbarr

dentalonne

kyngorn

Sancti Andree

halyngton Celdyngham Berwike

twede

mons chinioth

Wihense [f. Weems] hales

Edenburgh

lawedre mewros [Melrose]

ermitage ffuv. eske

Lomond mons

Thanis Castell hic passagium de drippes

lithcowe streneelyn

ffuv. iedro Pebles Rokesburgh Jedworth

ffuv. tueiot hawyk

Vada de sulway anan

Comitatus, De Fyf

Comitatus de Menteth

Cumbrenald pons Aghmore dunbtane

Byger lanire crowesford locus dictus poloot

fluvius annane

loghmaban

dromfres f. loghnenawe

enderburi [Inverbervie]

dundee

Cas of Goure Couper

Glaumyes S. Johannis florfar

Comitatus De Strathere

Dunkeldyn

aqua clide douglas

Glaskowe Ruglyn Kyle Cammoek fluv. done

Conyngham [Kilwinning]

Comitatus De Carryk

ffuv. Dee

Colly

muuntrosse [Brichen] driglyn

abirluothok fun- data in honore Sancti Thome Cant.

Scone

in isto lacu tria mirabilia, insula natans pisces sine intestinis fretum sine vento

logh tay

Comitatus de Lenenax

dunbretayne Irwyn kynwenyn [Kilwinning]

Are

loghdone Candida Casa

Aberdene

Monthe colli hic vnum passagium

Month Capelle hic vnum pas- sagium

Colgarth hic maxima venacio

dull

Plaga de Bugoire [Balquhidder]

Enuernesse

Kildrony

Murreff Comitatus de Marr

Comitatus De Boghane

Plaga de Baunagd [District of Badenoch]

Plaga que dicitur Loren

Rosse Comitatus de Rosse

Elgyf[u] ternewey Sotherland Comitatus De

Cattesse

Comitatus de Sotherland

hic ha- bundant lupi

Wyke

Comitatus De Cattesse

Les Outiales [The Outer Isles]

Insula de bote

Map of Matthew Paris (13th Century)

Left margin: [hec] pars inter aqui-[lo]nem et austrum [tan]tum mare res [pic]t ubi nil est nisi [mo]nstrorum habi-[ta]tio. Verumtamen ibi [in]uenitur insula . . erum fortissimo.

Right margin: hec pars respicit Norwegiam a boreo

hec pars respicit Daciam ab oriente

Pelagus vastissimum et inuium

patria palustris et inuia peculi-bus et pastoribus apta

Regio montuosa et nemorosa gentem incultam generans et pastomlem propter marisetum et harundinetum

Mai Kalenes   haberleen   Aberbrohot Sutheruelande   Dunde   Orkades Insule

Castrum dinkeuul

Brachium maris   ciuitas sancti andree

Pars maritima et gens montana

SCOCIA VLTRA MARINA
hec et albania dicta est

fif   Insula   Insula

Tyren insula

Dunfermelin   estruelin pons   transitus Regine   transitus comitis   Insula   Insula   edeneburc

Insula columkilli

fluuius faciens Clydesdale   laodonia   Glascu   tuedesdale   Berewic

Regio Scotorum conterminorum
Murus diuidens scotos et pictos olim   Melros abbatia   Rokesburc

Galeweia   Montes chiuieti

Man North Wallia Snaudun   flur-chid

Murus diuidens anglos et pictos olim

MAP OF MATTHEW PARIS (13TH CENTURY).

Left margin: This part, from north to south, looks only towards a sea where there is nought but the abode of monsters. However, an Island exists there.

Right margin: This part looks towards Norway on the north

This part looks towards Dacia on the east.

A boundless and trackless sea

A country marshy and impassable, fit for cattle and shepherds

A mountainous and woody region, producing a people rude and pastoral, by reason of marshes and fens

May   Caithness   Aberdeen   Abirbrohoch   Sutherland   Dundee   Orkney Islands

Castle of Dingwall

Arm of the sea   City of St Andrews

A maritime district and a race of mountaineers

SCOTLAND BEYOND THE SEA
This is also called Albany

Fife   Island   Island

Island of Tyree

Dunfermline   Stirling Bridge   Queensferry   Earlsferry   Island   Island   Edinburgh

Island of Columkille

River making Clydesdale   Lothian   Glasgow   Tweedale   Berwick

Country of the Scots Borderers
Wall dividing the Scots and Picts of old   Melrose Abbey   Roxburgh

Galloway   Cheviot Hills

Man North Wales Snowdon   Riv. Clwyd

Clydesdale

Wall separating the Angles and Picts of old

[1] Only the names in the Scottish section of Matthew Paris's map are given here.

EARLY TRAVELS IN SCOTLAND.

EDWARD I.

(1295).

O F all the visits to Scotland recorded in the present collection this "Voyage of Kynge Edwarde" alone was of
national importance. By the conclusion of that "Voyage,"
Scotland had been deprived of her king, and had been made a
dependency of the English crown. As the narrative refers
to one of the best-known periods of Scottish history, little
is needed by way of introduction. By the support of
Edward I., John Baliol had been crowned King of Scots in
1292, under the express condition of the superiority of
England. As the Scottish nation could never be brought
to recognise this superiority, the opportunity of Edward's
troubles with France and Wales was promptly seized for
throwing off the English yoke. An alliance (memorable as
the beginning of a foreign policy on the part of Scotland)
was formed with Norway and France, and a Scottish army
crossed the border on what proved to be an unsuccessful
invasion of England. This was, in truth, the very occasion
which Edward wanted, as the end of his policy towards
Scotland was that she should have no king to stand between
himself and the country. With an army of 30,000 foot and
4000 heavy-armed horse, therefore, he began his conquering
march through Scotland, and it is of this march, fraught with
such momentous consequences to an entire nation, that the
following narrative is the brief and bald record.

The author of the "Voyage" has not been ascertained;

but the minuteness of his details proves that he attended the army throughout its march. His narrative was first published in 1826, simultaneously and independently, by Nicolas in the *Archæologia* (vol. xxi.), and by Tytler in the *Bannatyne Miscellany* (vol. i.). The text of Nicolas (which is followed here as being the more intelligible to the modern reader) was produced from the collation of three manuscripts in the British Museum, checked by another written in Norman-French. Independently, Tytler had come upon two other manuscripts also in the British Museum, and of earlier date than those discovered by Nicolas, and from a collation of these published a text in the *Bannatyne Miscellany*. In 1834 the Bannatyne Club also published the text of the Norman-French MS., in which the spelling of the proper names differs considerably from that of the texts of Tytler and Nicolas.

As throwing light on one or two points in connection with this momentous expedition of Edward, the narrative has a distinct historical value; but we produce it here for the topographical and even social interest which it also undoubtedly possesses. The occasional comments of its author derive a certain value from the haphazard manner in which he makes them, and the strange disguise in which well-known names appear give a piquancy to his record that make it more than an archæological relic.

HERE FOLLOWETH THE VOYAGE OF KYNGE EDWARDE INTO SCOTLAND, WITH ALL HIS LODGYNGS BRYEFLY EX-PRESSED (*Archæologia*, vol. xxi. p. 478).

IN the xxiiij yer of the raigne of King Edwarde, Ester daie was on the daie of the Annunciation of owre Lady, and on the Wednesdaie in the Ester weke beyng the xxviij day of Marche passed Kynge Edwarde the forenone the Ryver of Twede with v thousand horses coverid and xxx^{ti} thousand fotemen, and laie that nyght in Scotland at the Priori of Calderstreme ;[1] and the Thursdaie at Hatton ;[2] and the Fridaie toke the towne of Barwyk upon Twede by force of

[1] Coldstream.   [2] Now Hutton. In Blaeu's map of Scotland it appears as Hutoun.

armes withought tarieng.[1] The Castell was geven up the
same daie by the Lorde William Dowglas, whiche was in it
and the Kynge in the said Castell all that nyght and his
hoste in the towne, everi man in the house that he hath
gotten and the Kynge taried ther almoste a monthe. And
on Saint Georges daie the xxiij day of Aprill cam newes to
the Kynge that they of Scotland had besegeid the Castell of
Dunbarre that longed to the Erle Patrik[2] the whiche holded
strongly with the Kynge of England. And on the Mundaie,
the Kynge sente his men to areyse the siege but before thei
cam the Castell was geven up the same daie, and the Scottis
wer in it when the Englishmen cam to it and did assige it
with iij hostes on the Wednesdaie that they cam ther; and
the Tuesdaie they that wer within sende owte privyly;
and the Thursdaie and Fridaie cam the hoste of the Scottis
ner (near) them aboute none (noon) to have raysid the siege of
the Englisshmen, and when the Englisshmen se them come
towarde them, then the Englysshmen ran to the Scottis and
discomfitedid them and did overcome them, and the chase
did dure well x myles of waie untill it was evenyng ; and
ther died the Lorde Patrik of Greahm[3] a great lorde and x
thousand and lv by right accompte. And the same Fridaie
cam the Kyng from Barwyk to goo to Dunbarre and laie
that night at Coldynghm;[4] the Saturdaie at Dunbarre ; and
the same daie they of the Castell gave over at the Kynges
pleasure, and ther was in it therle of Acelelles,[5] the erle of
Roos,[6] therle of Monetet,[7] Syr John Comyn of Bedvaasok,[8] the
son of Syr Richard Suard,[9] Syr William Saintler (Sinclair) and
iiij skore men of armes and vij skore fotemen. Ther taried the
Kynge iij daies ; the Wednesdaie Ascencion even the Kynge
went to Hadyngton ; the Sundaie after to Lowedere ;[10] the

---

[1] In the storming of Berwick, the king, mounted on his horse Bayard, was the
first who won the outer dyke ; and the soldiers, animated by the example and
presence of their king, carried all before them. Eight thousand, or according to
Knighton (p. 2480), seventeen thousand, persons were slain in the sack of
Berwick. [2] Patrick, Earl of Dunbar, called Patrick with the black beard, was a
steady partisan of Edward ; but his countess, who hated the English, delivered
the castle to her countrymen. [3] Hemingford (vol. i. p. 96) gives this high
character of Graham, "a valiant knight amongst the wisest in the kingdom,
and noblest among the noble." [4] Coldingham. [5] Athol. [6] Ross. [7] Monteith.
[8] Badenoch.   This was the Comyn afterwards slain by Bruce in the church of
tho Grey Friars at Dumfries. [9] Siward.   [10] Lauder.

Mundaie to Rokesbrough[1] at the Graie Freres, the Kynge lodgeid ther Tuesdaie at the Castell, and the Kynge taried there viiij daies.   And the xv[th] daie went to Gardeford;[2] the Thursdaie to Wiel;[3] the Fridaie to Castelton; the Sundaie bak ageyn to Wiell; the Mundaie to Gaydeford;[4] the Fridaie to Rokesbrough; the Mondaie after to Lowdere; the Tuesdaie to the Abbey of Neubattaill; the Wednesdaie to Edenbrough the abbey, and causid ther to be set up iij engyns castyng into the Castell day and nyght; and the vth daie thei spake of pees; the viij[th] daie the Kynge went to his bedde to Lunsta,[5] the engyns castyng stille before the castell.   The Thursdaie wente to Estrevelyn,[6] and they that were in the castell ran away, and left non but the Porter, which did render the keyes: and theder cam therle of Stradern[7] to the pees; and the Kynge tarried ther v daies. The Wednesdaie before Saint Johns daie the Kynge passed the Scottish se[8] and laid at Entrearde[9] his castell, the Thursdaie to Saynt Johns, a metely goode towne, and ther abode Fridaie, Satordaie, and Sundaie, which was Saint John Baptist daie; the Mundaie went to Kynge Colowen Castell;[10] the Tuesdaie to Clony castell,[11] and ther abidde v daies; the Munday after to Entrecoit Castell;[12] the Tuesday to Forfar castell, a good toune; the Friday after to fernovell;[13] the Saturdaie to Monorous[14] castell and a good toune, and ther abidde Sundaie, Mondai, and Tuesdaie; and ther cam to hym Kynge John of Scotlande to his mercy, and did render quietly the Realme of Scotlande, as he that had done awys.[15]   Also ther cam to merci therle of Marre, therle of Bochan,[16] Syr John Comyn of Badenasshe,[17] and many oder.   The Wednesdaie

---

[1] Roxburgh Castle was surrendered to Edward by James the Steward of Scotland, who swore fealty to England, and abjured the French alliance.
[2] Jedburgh, generally in old writers called Gedworde.   [3] Whitekirk, which in Speed's map of Scotland appears to the south-west of Jedburgh Abbey.   It is in the parish of Castleton.   [4] Jedburgh.   [5] Linlithgow; in an earlier manuscript, viz., that printed by Tytler, this name appears as Linnisca.   [6] Stirling.
[7] Strathearn.   [8] The Firth of Forth.   [9] In other MSS. Lutreard, Outreart, and Cutreard.   The position indicated, and the spelling *Outreart*, prove this place to be Auchterarder.   [10] Kinclavin Castle on the Tay.   For present condition of this castle, see M'Gibbon and Ross's *Architecture*, vol. i. 67.   [11] Cluny.
[12] Inverqueich Castle in parish of Alyth.   In Speed's map it appears as *Interguit*.   [13] Farnell, near Montrose.   [14] Montrose.   [15] Baliol did penance for his insubordination in his churchyard of Stracathro.   [16] Buchan.   [17] Badenoch.

went to Kynge Carden[1] a faiour manour; the Thursdaie to
the mountaigne of Glowberwy;[2] the Wedeninesdaie to a
manour in the Dounes[3] amonge the mountaignes; the Saturdaie to the cyte of Dabberden,[4] a faire castell and a good
towne upon the see, and taried ther v daies; and thedar was
brought the Kynges enemy Syr Thomas Worhne,[5] Sir Hugh
Saint John did take and xij with hym. The Fridaie after
wente to Kyntorn[6] manner; the Saturdaie to Fyuin[7] Castell;
the Sundaie to Banet Castell;[8] the Mundaie to incolan
maner;[9] the Tuesdaie in tentis in Lannoy[10] upon the ryver
to repenathe[11] maner in the counte of Morenue; the Thursdaie to the cite of Deigm,[12] a good Castell and a good towne,
and taried ther ij daies; the Sundaie to Rosers Maner.[13]
The Kynge sente the same daie Syr John Cantelow,[14] Syr
Hugh Spencer and Syr John Hastynges to serche the countrey
of Badenasshe and sente the Bishopp of Dwreysm[15] with his
people over the mountaynes by another way then he wente
hymselfe; the Mundaie he wente into Interkeratche,[16] wher
ther was no more then iij houses in a rowe between too
mountaignes. The Tuesdaie to Kyndroken[17] castell be-
longying to the erle of Marre and ther taried Wednesdaie,
Sainte Peturs daie, the first daie of Auguste; on Thursdaie to the hospitall of Kyncarden in the Marnes;[18]
the Saturdaie to the citie of Breghem;[19] the Sundaie
to the Abbey of Burbro-do-chê,[20] and it was said that the
abbot of that place made the people [of Scotlande] beleve
that there was but women and no men in Englande; the
Mundaie to Dunde; the Tuesdaie to Balygernatthe,[21] the
redde Castell; the Wednesdaie to Saint John of Perte;[22] the

[1] Kincardine. [2] Glenbervie. [3] Durris Castle, near Aberdeen? [4] Aberdeen.
[5] Warham. [6] Kintore. [7] Fyvie. [8] Banff. [9] Invercullen, or Cullen. [10] The
district of Enzie (variously spelled Ainie, Ainzia), to the east of the mouth of
the Spey. The *l* is simply the French article. [11] This may be Balvenie (in
Speed, Bevany). [12] Elgin. In Tytler d'Aigin. [13] Rothes. [14] Cantlow.
[15] Durham. [16] Innerquharanche in the parish of Calbrach in Aberdeenshire.
In Gordon of Straloch's map *Inercherach*. [17] Kildrummy; in Rymer's *Fœdera*
often written Kyndromyn. Speed has a Kindrok, which he places in Mar.
For present condition of this castle, see M'Gibbon and Ross's *Architecture*,
vol. i. 108. [18] The Mearns. Evidently a blunder for Kincardine O Neil,
where there was a hospital. [19] Brechin. [20] Aberbrothock or Arbroath.
[21] Baledgarno in the Carse of Gowrie. [22] St John's Town of Perth. It was at
this time that Edward visited Scone, and gave orders that the "Stone of
Destiny" should be translated to Westminster.

Thursdaie to the Abbey of Loundos,[1] and taried ther the
Fridaie, Seynt Lawrence daie.   Saterdaie to the Cite of
Saint Andrew, a castell and a good towne; the Sundaie to
Merkynch,[2] wher as is but the churche and iij houses.
Mondaie to the abbey of Donffremelyn,[3] ther as all the
moste of the Kynges of Scottes lieth.   The Tuesdaie to
Strevelyn, and taried ther Wednesdaie owre Lady daie; the
Thursdaie to Lansen;[4] the Fridaie to Edenbrough, and
ther taried Saturdaie; Sundaie to Hadyngton; Mundaie to
Pikelton,[5] by Dunbarre; Tuesdaie at Coldyngham; Wednes-
daie at Barwik; and conquerid and serchid the Kyngdom
of Scotland as ys aforesaid in xxj wekys withought any
more.

[1] Lindores in Fife.   [2] Markinch in Fife.   [3] Dunfermline.   [4] In Tytler,
Lunsen, *i.e.*, Linlithgow.   [5] Pinkerton; in Blaeu, *Pynkerton.*

JEAN FROISSART

(REIGN OF DAVID II.).

JEAN FROISSART, priest, canon, and treasurer of the Collegiate Church of Chimay, was born at Valenciennes about 1337. Although intended for the church, all his natural tastes would seem to have suggested a secular calling; for, by his own account, from his earliest years he "loved to see dances, jousts, and late vigils, and fair beds for refreshment, and for my better repose, a night draught of claret or Rochelle wine, mingled with spice." At the age of twenty, by the command of his "dear lord and master, Sir Robert of Namur, Lord of Beaufort," he began his history of the French wars, basing the earlier part of his narrative on the chronicles of Jean le Bel, canon of Liège. With the portion of his history he had written he proceeded to England, and presented it to Philippa of Hainault, the wife of Edward III. After acting for some time as Clerk to the Queen's Chamber, he returned to the Continent; and thenceforth, till within a few years of his death, his life was spent in travelling between France, England, and Italy. His one object in all his wanderings was to make himself acquainted at first hand with the actors and events whose history it was his ambition to chronicle, "to the end that brave men, taking example from them, may be encouraged in their well-doing." About 1390 he settled down in Flanders to the accomplishment of his task, which appears to have engaged him to the close of his life. The exact date of his death is unknown; but as in his chronicles he narrates events that happened in 1400, he must have lived into the fifteenth century.

Froissart himself tells us what opportunities he had of becoming acquainted with the Scots and their country. "In my younger days," he says, "I had been in Scotland as far as the Highlands (*la sauvage Écosse*), and as at that time

I was at the court of King David, I was acquainted with the greater part of the nobility of that country." Elsewhere, he tells us that he was altogether six months in Scotland, that he was for fifteen days the guest of Sir William Douglas[1] at Dalkeith Castle, and that he travelled on horseback, with his portmanteau behind him, and accompanied by a greyhound.

The translation here given is that of Thomas Johnes, which was made the subject of an article on Froissart by Sir Walter Scott in the *Edinburgh Review* (1805). In literary quality the translation of Johnes is far inferior to that of Lord Berners; and in passages of Froissart, which owe their main interest to the manner of the writer, the older translation is always to be preferred. In such extracts as those here given, however, the faithfulness of the translation is the chief point to be considered; and Scott, who does not conceal his preference for Berners, admits that "in a historical point of view there can be no comparison betwixt the usefulness of Mr Johnes's translation and Lord Berners's."

The Scots on their Military Expeditions
(Froissart, *Chronicles*, vol. i. chap. 17).

THE Scots are bold, hardy, and much inured to war. When they make their invasions into England, they march from twenty to four-and-twenty leagues without halting,[2] as well by night as day; for they are all on horseback, except the camp-followers, who are on foot. The knights and esquires are well mounted on large bay horses, the common people on little galloways. They bring no carriages with them, on account of the mountains they have to pass in Northumberland; neither do they carry with them any provisions of bread or wine; for their habits of sobriety are such, in time of war, that they will live for a long time on flesh half sodden, without bread, and drink the river water without wine. They have, therefore, no occasion for pots or pans; for they dress the flesh of their cattle in the skins,

---

[1] Nephew of the good Lord James.   [2] By leagues, both according to Berners and Johnes, we are to understand miles.

after they have taken them off; and, being sure to find
plenty of them in the country which they invade, they carry
none with them. Under the flaps of his saddle, each man
carries a broad plate of metal; behind the saddle, a little
bag of oatmeal: when they have eaten too much of the
sodden flesh, and their stomach appears weak and empty,
they place this plate over the fire, mix with water their oatmeal, and when the plate is heated, they put a little of the
paste upon it, and make a thin cake, like a cracknel or
biscuit, which they eat to warm their stomachs: it is therefore no wonder, that they perform a longer day's march than
other soldiers.

A FRENCH ARMY IN SCOTLAND—THE FRENCH OPINION OF
THE SCOTS (1385) (vol. ii. chaps. 2 and 3).

The French army that was bound for Scotland had very
favourable winds, for it was in the month of May when the
weather is temperate and agreeable. They coasted Flanders,
Holland, Zealand, and Friesland, and advanced until they
approached so near Scotland as to see it; but before they
arrived there, an unfortunate accident befel a knight of
France and an expert man-at-arms, named Sir Aubert
d'Angers. The knight was young and active, and to show
his ability he mounted aloft by the ropes of his ship completely armed; but, his feet slipping, he fell into the sea,
and the weight of his armour, which sunk him instantly,
deprived him of any assistance, for the ship was soon at a
distance from the place where he had fallen. All the
barons were much vexed at this misfortune, but they were
forced to endure it, as they could not any way remedy it.

They continued their voyage until they arrived at Edinburgh, the capital of Scotland, where the king chiefly resides
when he is in that part of the country.[1] The Earls of
Douglas and Moray, from the information they had received,
were waiting for them in Edinburgh; and as soon as they
were come, hastened to meet them at the harbour, and

[1] John Major, in quoting Froissart's remarks regarding Edinburgh, states
that for a hundred years before his own day it had been almost constantly the
residence of the kings of Scotland (*Hist. Maj. Brit.*, lib. i. cap. vi.). Major's
history was published in 1521.

received them most amicably, bidding them welcome to their country. The Scots barons instantly recognised Sir Geoffry de Charny, for he had resided full two months with them last summer in Scotland. Sir Geoffry made them acquainted, as he very well knew how, with the admiral and the barons of France. At that time the king (Robert II.) was not at Edinburgh, but in the Highlands [1] of Scotland : his sons received them handsomely, telling them the king would shortly be there.

They were satisfied with this information, and the lords and their men lodged themselves as well as they could in Edinburgh, and those who could not lodge there were quartered in the different villages thereabout. Edinburgh, notwithstanding it is the residence of the king, and is the Paris of Scotland, is not such a town as Tournay or Valenciennes ; for there are not in the whole town four thousand houses. Several of the French lords were therefore obliged to take up their lodgings in the neighbouring villages, and at Dunfermline, Kelso, Dunbar, Dalkeith, and in other villages.

News was soon spread through Scotland that a large body of men-at-arms from France were arrived in the country. Some began to murmur and say, " What devil has brought them here ? or who has sent for them ? Cannot we carry on our wars with England without their assistance ? We shall never do any effectual good as long as they are with us. Let them be told to return again, for we are sufficiently numerous in Scotland to fight our own quarrels, and do not want their company. We neither understand their language nor they ours, and we cannot converse together. They will very soon eat up and destroy all we have in this country, and will do us more harm, if we allow them to remain amongst us, than the English could in battle. If the English do burn our houses, what consequence is it to us ? We can rebuild them cheap enough, for we only require three days to do so, provided we have five or six poles and boughs to cover them." Such was the conversation of the Scots on the arrival of the French : they did not

---

[1] As Tytler suggests, King Robert was probably at his palace of Stirling, which Froissart would regard as " en la sauvage Écosse."

esteem them, but hated them in their hearts, and abused them with their tongues as much as they could, like rude and worthless people as they are.

I must, however, say that, considering all things, it was not right for so many of the nobility to have come at this season to Scotland: it would have been better to have sent twenty or thirty knights from France, than so large a body as five hundred or a thousand. The reason is clear. In Scotland you will never find a man of worth: they are like savages, who wish not to be acquainted with any one, and are too envious of the good fortune of others, and suspicious of losing anything themselves, for their country is very poor. When the English make inroads thither, as they have very frequently done, they order their provisions, if they wish to live, to follow close at their backs; for nothing is to be had in that country without great difficulty. There is neither iron to shoe horses, nor leather to make harness, saddles, or bridles: all these things come ready made from Flanders by sea; and, should these fail, there is none to be had in the country.

When these barons and knights of France, who had been used to handsome hotels, ornamented apartments, and castles with good soft beds to repose on, saw themselves in such poverty, they began to laugh, and to say before the admiral, "What could have brought us hither? We have never known till now what was meant by poverty and hard living. We now have found the truth of what our fathers and mothers were used to tell us, when they said,—'Go, go, thou shalt have in thy time, should'st thou live long enough, hard beds and poor lodgings;' all this is now come to pass." They said also among themselves,—"Let us hasten the object of our voyage, by advancing towards England: a long stay in Scotland will be neither honourable nor profitable." The knights made remonstrances respecting all these circumstances to Sir John de Vienne, who appeased them as well as he could, saying,—"My fair sirs, it becomes us to wait patiently, and to speak fair, since we are got into such difficulties. We have a long way yet to go, and we cannot return through England. Take in good humour whatever you can get. You cannot always be at Paris, Dijon, Beaune, or Châlons : it is necessary for those who wish to live with honour in this world to endure good and evil.

By such words as these, and others which I do not remember, did Sir John de Vienne pacify his army in Scotland. He made as much acquaintance as he could with the Scottish barons and knights ; but he was visited by so very few it is not worth speaking of ; for, as I have said before, there is not much honour there, and they are people difficult to be acquainted with. The Earls of Douglas and Moray were the principal visitants to the lords of France. These two lords paid them more attention than all the rest of Scotland. But this was not the worst, for the French were hardly dealt with in their purchases ; and whenever they wanted to buy horses, they were asked, for what was worth only ten florins, sixty and a hundred : with difficulty could they be found at that price. When the horse had been bought there was no furniture nor any housings to be met with, unless the respective articles had been brought with them from Flanders. In this situation were the French ; besides, whenever their servants went out to forage, they were indeed permitted to load their horses with as much as they could pack up and carry, but they were waylaid on their return, and villainously beaten, robbed, and sometimes slain, insomuch that no varlet dared go out foraging for fear of death. In one month the French lost upwards of a hundred varlets ; for when three or four went out foraging not one returned, in such a hideous manner were they treated.

The French and Scots marched back[1] the way they had come. When arrived in the lowlands, they found the whole country ruined ; but the people of the country made light of it, saying, that with six or eight stakes they would soon have new houses, and find cattle enow for provision ; for the Scots had driven them for security to the forests. You must however know, that whatever the French wanted to buy, they were made to pay very dear for ; and it was fortunate the French and Scots did not quarrel with each other seriously, as there were frequent riots on account of

[1] From the invasion of England, for the purpose of which the French had come to Scotland.

provision.   The Scots said, the French had done them more
mischief than the English; and when asked, "In what
manner?" they replied, "By riding through their corn, oats,
and barley, on their march, which they trod under foot, not
condescending to follow the roads, for which damages they
would have a recompense before they left Scotland;[1] and
they should neither find vessel nor mariner who would
dare to put to sea without their permission."   Many knights
and squires complained of the timber they had cut down,
and of the waste they had committed to lodge themselves.[2]

When the admiral, with his barons, knights, and squires,
were returned to the neighbourhood of Edinburgh, they
suffered from famine, as they could scarcely procure provision
for their money.   They had but little wine, beer, barley,
bread, or oats: their horses, therefore, perished from hunger,
or were ruined through fatigue; and, when they wished to
dispose of them, they could not find a purchaser who would
give them a groat either for their horses or housings.   These
lords remonstrated with their commander on the manner in
which they were treated, a circumstance well known to himself.   They said, "they could not longer endure such difficulties, for Scotland was not a country to encamp in during
the winter; and that if they were to remain the ensuing
summer, they should soon die of poverty.   If they were to
spread themselves over the country, to better their condition, they were doubtful if the Scots, who had so villainously
treated their foragers, would not murder them in their beds,
when they should be divided."

The admiral, having fully weighed what they said, saw
clearly they were justified in thus remonstrating; notwithstanding, he had intentions of wintering there, and of sending
an account of his situation to the King of France[3] and
Duke of Burgundy, who, as the admiral imagined, would

---

[1] This independence of spirit in the Scottish peasantry must have been
forcibly brought home to the French knights by its contrast with the abject
temper of their own *jacquerie*, whose wrongs issued in the frightful insurrec-
tion of 1358.   [2] As will afterwards be seen, the scarcity of wood in the Low-
lands of Scotland rendered its careful preservation the subject of special
legislation.   It is worth noting that the French brought the same charge of
rapacity against the Scots who served in France (Major, *Hist. Maj. Brit.*,
lib. i. cap. vii.).   [3] Charles VI., then a boy, and under guardians.

hasten to him reinforcements of stores, provision, and money, with which, in the course of summer, he would be enabled to carry on an advantageous war against the English.   But having considered how ill-intentioned the Scots were, and the danger his men were in, as well as himself, he gave permission for all who chose to depart.   But how to depart was the difficulty, for the barons could not obtain any vessels for themselves and men.   The Scots were willing that a few poor knights who had no great command should leave the country, that they might the easier govern the rest. They told the barons of France "that their dependants, when they pleased might depart, but that they themselves should not quit the country until they had made satisfaction for the sums that had been expended for the use of their army."

This declaration was very disagreeable to Sir John Vienne and the other French barons.   The Earls of Douglas and Moray, who pretended to be exasperated at the harsh conduct of their countrymen, remonstrated with them, that they did not act becoming men-at-arms, nor as friends to the kingdom of France, by this behaviour to its knights; and that henceforward no Scots knight would dare to set his foot in France.   These two earls, who were friendly enough to the French barons, pointed out the probable effect their conduct would have on their vassals; but some replied, "Do dissemble with them, for you have lost as much as we." They therefore told the admiral, they could not do anything for him; and, if they were so anxious about quitting Scotland, they must consent to make good their damages.   The admiral seeing nothing better could be done, and unwilling to lose all, for he found himself very uncomfortable, surrounded by the sea, and the Scots of a savage disposition, acceded to their proposals, and had proclaimed through the realm, that all those whom his people had injured, and who could show just cause for amends being made them, should bring them their demands to the admiral of France, when they would be fully paid.   This proclamation softened the minds of the people; and the admiral took every debt on himself, declaring he would never leave the country until everything was completely paid and satisfied.

Upon this many knights and squires obtained a passage
to France, and returned through Flanders, or wherever they
could land, famished, and without arms or horses, cursing
Scotland, and the hour they had set foot there. They said
they had never suffered so much in any expedition, and
wished the King of France would make a truce with the
English for two or three years, and then march to Scotland
and utterly destroy it : for never had they seen such wicked
people, nor such ignorant hypocrites and traitors. The
admiral wrote to the King of France and Duke of Burgundy,
by those who first returned, a full state of his situation,
and how the Scots had acted towards him : that if they
wished to have him back, they must send him the full
amount he had engaged to pay the Scots, and for which
he had bounden himself to the knights and squires of
Scotland : for the Scots had declared, that they had at
this time made war for the King of France and not for
themselves ; and that the damages which the French had
committed must be satisfied before they would be allowed
to return, which he had promised and sworn to perform to
the barons of Scotland.

It was incumbent on the King of France, the Duke of
Burgundy, and their councils, to redeem the admiral, for
they had sent him thither. They had the money instantly
raised, and deposited in the town of Bruges, so that the
whole demand of the Scots was paid to their satisfaction.
The admiral left Scotland when he had thus amicably
settled matters, for otherwise he could not have done it ;
and, taking leave of the king, who was in the highlands,
and of the Earls of Douglas and Moray, was attended by
them to the seashore.

JOHN HARDYNG

(REIGN OF JAMES I.).

THE following quaint itinerary is taken from *The Chronicle of John Hardyng in Metre from the first Begynnyng of Englande unto the reigne of Edward the Fourth.*[1] Hardyng was sent to Scotland by Henry V. and Henry VI. to obtain certain deeds which were supposed to confirm the superiority of England. In his chronicle he tells us that after many toils and dangers, in the course of which he received an incurable wound, he obtained the documents he was in search of on the payment of 450 marks. Sir Francis Palgrave has shown that every one of these instruments is a forgery ; and as Hardyng was a well-informed antiquary, he now stands in a somewhat dubious light. But even if we suppose him to have been guilty of a deliberate forgery, this does not affect the value of his description of Scotland, as in this case he had no reason to say anything besides the simple truth. Indeed, as Hardyng was three years and a half in Scotland, he speaks with fuller knowledge of the country than any other traveller in the present collection. It will be seen that his picture of Scotland during the fifteenth century is much more favourable than that usually presented by the historians. By selecting his authorities in support of a foregone conclusion, Buckle, in his well-known sketch of Scotland during this period, gives the impression that the country was little better than a wilderness. It is remarkable, however, that two observers, Hardyng, and the Spaniard, Pedro de Ayala, should independently have left us a picture of Scotland during the fifteenth

---

[1] In Part ii. of the *National Manuscripts of Scotland* will be found three maps with topographical notes by Hardyng. These notes seem to have been the materials which he afterwards wrought into his chronicle in the verses given above.

century suggestive at once of settled industry and a fair amount of comfort throughout the greater part of the country.

Hardyng thus indicates the object of his report, illustrating with a grim unconsciousness the ceaseless purpose of England to bring Scotland under her supremacy: "How the maker of this booke reporteth the distaunce and miles of the tounes in Scotland, and ye waye how to conveigh an armie as well by lande as water, into the chiefest partes thereof." The precise date when Hardyng visited Scotland cannot be determined; but it must have been early in the reign of Henry V. His chronicle, written in his advanced age, was originally intended for the special behoof of Richard, Duke of York. As it was not completed in its final form, however, till York's death, Hardyng presented it to his son, Edward IV.

THE CHRONICLE OF JOHN HARDYNG (p. 423, Ellis's Edition).

NOWE to expresse unto your noble grace
  The verie waye bothe by sea and land,
With the distaunce of tounes and every myles space,
Through the chefest parte of all Scotland,
To conveigh an armie that ye maye take in hand,
Herafter shall folowe in as good ordre as I maye,
The true discripcion, and distaunce of the waye.

From Berwike to Dombarre twenty miles [1] it is,
And twelfe miles forward unto Haddyngtoune,
And twelfe miles from these to Edenburgh I wisse,
To Lithko twelfe, and so Northwest to Bowne,[2]
Twelfe miles it is unto Sterlyng toune
Besouth Foorth, that ryver principall,
Of right faire waye, and plentifull at all.

Wher y your navy at Leith may rest saufly,
With all your vitayles, a mile from Edenburgh,
And after at the Blacknesse,[3] whiles as ye ly,
At Sterlyng toune, whiche is the kynges burgh,

------

[1] The reader will correct Hardyng's measurements for himself. [2] Bo'ness.
[3] A castle on a headland in Linlithgowshire to the west of Queensferry.

And wynne that shire, all whole out through:
So shall your navy, at your necessitee,
Bee at your hand still, your army to supplie.

From Sterlyng then over the river of Foorth,
Passe alongest the brydge to Camskinelle [1]
And if it bee broken toward the North,
Unto the foorde of Tirps [2] under the fell;
Then spede you westward, thre miles as men tell,
Wher ye maye passe to the downe [3] of Menteth,
Whiche passeth from y[t] Foorth thre miles unneth.[4]

Then frō the downe, a waie ye have right faire,
Throughout Monteth, and eke Clakmannam shire,
And so through Fiffe to Falkeland to repaire,
Thirty long miles, without mosse or myre:
For so it is compted, with horse and carte to hyre,
From Sterlyng eastward, and the highe Oyghylles,[5]
Whiche some mēne call montaignes, and some felles.

From Falkland then to Disert towne, south east,
Twelfe myles it is, of fayre ready waye,
And from Falkland to Saynte Andrewes, east,
But other xii myles, wythouten anye naye,
Wher the byshoppes see is, and castell as thei say,
And at Knagorne,[6] and Disert may ye mete,
You for to uytayle [7] al your Englysh fleete.

Than ride northwest from S. Andrewes towne,
Alongest the South syde of the water of Taye,
Up to the burgh of Saynte Jhons towne,[8]
Right North from Fyfe, a countrie freshe and gay,
And from saynt Androws xxiiii myles they say,
A pleasant grounde and fruitfull countrey
Of corne and cattel, with prosperitie.

Which countrey of Fyfe along the Scottish sea,[9]
And from saynt Androws, to the Oyghles, they say,
Is xliiii myles longe of good countrey,

---

[1] Cambuskenneth.   In Speed, Clamskenar.   [2] Drip, the lowest ford on the
Forth.   [3] Doune, the principal town of Monteith.   [4] Hardly.   [5] Ochills.
[6] Kinghorn.   [7] Victual.   [8] Perth.   [9] Firth of Forth.

And somtyme in bredth vi myles of fayre way,
But from Logh Leven eastward, without nay,
Of ryght good way, briefly to conclude,
Xii myles conteyne it dothe in latitude.

At Ennerkethen[1] and Saynt Margarete,[2] I hope
Your navy maye receave uytayle in that countre,
Alongest the Water of Foorth, as I can grope,
Wyth hulke, and barge, of no smal quantite,
You to supporte in your necessytee,
So that ye maye not in' those countryesfayle,
To have for your armye redye uytayle.

Then to S. Jhons towne, upon the water of Tay,
Within Strathren,[3] that standeth fayre and stronge,
Dytched about syxtene foote depe, I saye,
And xx foote on breadthe overwhart to fonge[4]
Yt is northest xx myles full longe ;
And nere to Scone abbay, within myles thre,
Wher alwayes thei crowne their kinges maieste.

Whyche water of Tay is so navygable,
From the East Sea to Saynt Jhons towne,
For all suche shippes as bee able
Fortie tunne of wyne to carry up and doune,
For vitallyng and keping of the toune ;
Unto the whych so floweth the water of Taye,
That all the dytches it fylleth nighte and daye.

At the whych toune passe over the brydge ye shall
With all your armye, hostyng through that land;
Wher in Angus, that countree pryncypall,
The Kerse of Gowry doth lye I understand,
A plentifull countree, I you warrande,
Of corne and catell, and all commoditees,
You to supporte in your necessytees.

Betwyxt the mounthes[5] and the water of Tay,
Whych some do cal mountaynes in our language,

---

[1] Inverkeithing.   [2] St Margaret's Ferry.   [3] Strathearn.   [4] To measure across.   John Major states that Perth was the only walled town in his day (*Hist. Maj. Brit.*, lib. i. cap. vi.).   Yet in 1450, immediately after the Battle of Sark, Edinburgh was enclosed by walls (Wilson, *Memorials of Edinburgh*, p. 17, ed. 1886).   [5] The Grampians.

Passe eastwarde with your army daye by daye,
From place to place with small cariage,
For your navy shall you mete in the viage,
At Portincragge,[1] shorte waye from Dunde,
With vitailes to refreshe your whole armye;

Beside the stuffe and vitaill of that lande,
Which ye shall fynde in the countre as ye go,
And market made alwayes to your hande,
Of all theyr vytayles, althoughe they bee your fo.
Now from S. Jhons towne, the soothe to say is so,
Xviii myles it is to the towne of Dundye,
The pryncypall burgh, by northe the Scotyshe see.

Than ryde Northeast all alongest the see,
Ryght from Dunde to Arbroith as I mene,
Than to Monrosse, and to Barvye,
And so through the Meernes to Cowy[2] as I wene,
Then xii myles of moore passe to Aberdyne,
Betwyxt Dee and Done a goodly cytee,
A marchaunt towne and universytee.

Of the whych waye xxx myles there is,
Of good corne lande, and xx large extente,
Full of catell and other goodes I wysse,
As to moore lande and heth dothe wele appente,[3]
From Brichan cytee to the orient,
Where doothe stande upon the see,
A goodly porte and haven for your navye.

Where that the same may easely you mete,
To vitayle your armye, whersoever ye go,
Over·all the mountaynes, drye mosses and wete,
Wher the wild Scottes do dwel, than passe unto,
That is in Mare and Garioth[4] also,
In Athill, Rosse, Sutherland, and Chatnesse,[5]
Mureffe (Moray), Lenox, and out ysles I gesse.

---

[1] Tayport, or Ferry Port on Craig. The name Portincray was once applied to Broughty and its adjacent lands on the opposite side of the Forth (Cosmo Innes, *Sketches of Early Scottish History*, p. 146). [2] Cowie, the district immediately to the north of Stonehaven. [3] Suit. [4] Garioch. [5] Caithness.

And when ye have that lande hole conquered,
Returne agayne unto Strivelyne,
And from thence to Glasco homewarde,
Twenty and foure myles to S. Mongos shrine.
Wherw^t your offeryng ye shall from thence decline,
And passe on forthwarde to Dumbertayne,
A castell stronge and harde for to obteine.

In whiche castell S. Patryke was borne,[1]
That afterwarde in Irelande dyd wynne,
About the whyche floweth, even and morne,
The westerne seas without noyse or dynne,
When forth of the same the streames dooe rynne,
Twyse in xxiiii houres, without any fayle,
That no man may that stronge castell assayle.

Upon a roçke so hye the same dothe stande,
That yf the walles were beaten to the rocke,
Yet were it full harde to clymbe with foot or hand,
And so to wynne, yf any to them approche,
So strong it is to get without reproche ;
That without honger and cruell famyshemente,
Yt cannot bee taken to my judgemente.

Than from Glasgo to the towne of Ayre,
Are twentie myles and foure wele accompted,
A good countree for your armye everywhere
And plenteous also, by many one recounted,
For there I was, and at the same I mounted,
Towarde Lamarke [2] towne xxiiii myles,
Homeward trudging for feare of Scottish giles,[3]

From the towne of Ayre in Kyle to Galloway,
Through Carryct (Carrick) passe unto Nithysdayle,
Where Dumfryse is a pretye towne alwaye,
And plentifull also of all good vytayle
For all your army, wythout any fayle ;
So that kepying this journey, by my instruccion,
That realme ye shall bring in subjeccion.

---

[1] Neither the place nor the date of St Patrick's birth is known. Kilpatrick (named from the Saint himself), near Dumbarton, is only one of many places that have been suggested. [2] Lanark. [3] Guiles.

Then from Domfrise to Carlill, ye shall ride
Xxiii miles of veray redy waye;
So maye ye wynne the lande on every syde,
Within a yere, withoute more delaye :
For castelles there is none, y^t withstande you may,
Nor abide your seage against your ordinaunce,
So simple and weake is their purveiaunce.

And yf ye like, good lorde,[1] at home to abide,
With litell cost your wardens ye may sende,
Charging theim all, with hostes for to ride,
In proper persone, through wynter to thende,
With morow forraies [2] they may them sore offend,
And burne Jedburgh, Hawike, Melrose, and Lāder,
Codingham,[3] Donglasse, and the toune of Dombarre.

Then send an hoste of footemen in
At Lammesse next, through all Lawdendayle,[4]
And Lammermore woddes and mossis over rynne,
And else therwith the Stowe of Weddale,[5]
Melrose lande, Etryke forrest, and Tyvydale,
Lyddis-dale, Ewys-dale,[6] and the Ryngwodfelde,[7]
To the Creke Crosse,[8] that ryden is full selde.

The wardens then of bothe the marches twoo,
To bee their stayle [9] and eke their castelles strong,
Them to reskewe from enemies wher ever thei go
With fleying stayles, to folowe theim ay emong,
Lest nor their foes theim suppresse and fong,[10]
And every night to releve to the hoste,
And lodge together all upon a coast.

And also than at the next Myghelmesse,[11]
The West warden to Domfryse ryde he maye,
Four and twentie myles from Carelyl as I gesse,
And than passe forthwarde through Galowaye

---

[1] Edward IV.   [2] Future forays.   [3] Coldingham.   [4] Lauderdale.   [5] Wedale, between the Leader and Gala, called the Vale of Woe by the interpolator of Nennius.   [6] Ewesdale.   [7] Within the lands of Rodonnald, Ettrickhead, or Esk-dalemoor.   [8] Appears as Craykcross in a commission to Sir William Scott of Branxholm by Queen Mary (*The Scotts of Buccleuch*, ii. p. 196).   [9] *Stell* is used in the sense of a *strong place* (Nare's *Glossary*, edited by Halliwell and Wright), and *stayle* is probably the same word.   The meaning of the two lines seems to be that the wardens were to give efficient support to the invading army.   The wardens would then be " flying stayles."   [10] Make captive.   [11] Michaelmas.

To Carricke after, into good araye,
And then from thence to the towne of Ayre
In Kile, that countree, plentifull, and fayre.

Next than from Ayre unto Glasgew go,
A goodly cytee and universitee,
Where plentifull is the countree also,
Replenished well with all commoditee ;
There maye the Warden of the East marche bee,
And mete the other twayne as I wene,
Within tenne dayes, or at the moost fyftene.

The thyrde army from Barwyke passe it shall,
Through Dumbarre, Edenburgh, and Lythko,[1]
And then to Sterlyng, with their power al,
And nexte from that unto Glasgo
Standyng upon Clyde, and where also
Of corne and cattell is aboundaunce,
Youre armye to vittayle at all suffysaunce.

Thus these thre armies at Glasgew shall mete,
Well arayed in theyr armour clene,
Which homward from thence thei shal returne complete,
Four and twentie myles to Lamarke so shene,[2]
To Pebles on Twede, is syxtene myles I wene,
To Soltray[3] as muche, then twentie miles w^t spede ;
From thence returne they shal to Wark on Twede.

Within a moneth this lande maye bee destroyed,
All asouth Forth, if wardens wyll assent,
So that our enemies shal bee sore annoied,
And wasted bee, and eke for ever shent ;[4]
If wardens thus woorke, after mine intent,
They maye well quenche the cruell enmitee,
This daye by South all the Scottishe see.[5]

Now of this matter I have sayed mine intent,
Like as I could espye and diligently inquire,
Whiche if it may your highnesse well content,
It is the thing that I hartely desire ;
And of your grace no more I dose require,
But that your grace will take in good parte,
Not only my peines, but also my true harte.

[1] Linlithgow.   [2] Beautiful.   [3] Soutra.   [4] Destroyed.   [5] The Firth of Forth.

ÆNEAS SYLVIUS

(Reign of James I.).

Æ NEAS SYLVIUS PICCOLOMINI (Pope Pius II.), born in 1405, is one of the most curious and interesting figures in the long line of the Papacy. "A Gil Blas of the Middle Ages"—such is the character his easy morals and equivocal career have gained for him. The child of poor but noble parents, he was sent at the age of eighteen to study law at Siena. At twenty-six he accompanied a certain cardinal to the Council of Basel in the capacity of secretary; and in the service of the various masters he successively served, he visited almost every country of Europe. Keen-witted, insinuating, the most agreeable of companions, devoid of all nice scruples, Æneas was an invaluable agent in the tortuous policy that followed the long schism in the popedom. At the age of forty he took orders with the sole purpose, as he himself frankly confesses, of bettering his worldly condition. He did not miscalculate, as he was in succession made Bishop of Trieste, Cardinal of Siena, and finally Pope under the title of Pius II. Æneas ranks as one of the most distinguished of the Italian humanists; and in the bulk, as likewise the grossness of his writings, he is surpassed by none of them.

Of his visit to Scotland, which took place in the reign of James I., there are two accounts in his works, which do not in every point agree. According to the one the object of his visit was to effect a reconciliation between the king and a certain bishop;[1] according to the other his object was to incite James to war against England.[2] By the one account he landed in England of his own accord, and was refused a passport to Scotland;[3] by the other he was driven on the English coast, and betrayed to the government by spies.[4]

---

[1] *Commentarii Rerum Memorabilium*, p. 4 (Frankfort, 1614). [2] *Opera Omnia*, Pii II. Pont. Max. per Joan. Antonium Camp. Episcopum Aretinum Vita (Basileæ). [3] *Commentarii Rerum Memorabilium*, p. 4. [4] *Opera Omnia*. See Life prefixed.

Both accounts agree, however, in stating that he reached
Scotland by sea after a succession of storms which deprived
him of all hope of reaching land. In his extremity Æneas
registered a vow that in the event of his life being spared he
would make a pilgrimage barefoot to the nearest shrine. No
one could well be less of an enthusiast or ascetic than Æneas,
and on this occasion he had good reason to regret his access
of pious feeling. "In fulfilment of his vow," says one of
his biographers, "he contracted the beginning of that disease,
which left its results in attacks of rheumatism that afflicted
him for the rest of his life. For, having gone all the way
to the shrine, a distance of 10 miles, barefooted on the frozen
ground, it was only by means of a litter that he could return
to the town." [1] His mission, whatever it may have been, was
not wholly successful, though the king treated him generously,
defraying his travelling expenses, and presenting him with two
horses, and a pearl, which Æneas destined for his mother.

Of the two extracts that follow the first is from the
De Europa, a geographical description of the various countries
of Europe; the second from the *Commentarii Rerum Memorabilium, quae temporibus suis contigerunt.*

SCOTLAND: ITS CLIMATE, ITS PEOPLE, AND THEIR HABITS— ÆNEAS'S EXPERIENCES IN THE COUNTRY (*De Europa*).

SCOTLAND is the remotest part of that island in which
England is situated. It stretches in a northerly direction, possesses no large rivers, and is separated from England
by a mountain (*quodam monte*). Here I once lived in the
season of winter, when the sun illuminates the earth little
more than three hours. At that time James (I.) was king,
robust of person, and oppressed by his excessive corpulence.
Formerly made a captive by the English, he had been kept
a prisoner for eleven years; [2] and on his return (with an
English wife) he was eventually slain by his own subjects.
After his death had been fully avenged, his son succeeded
him in the kingdom. I had previously heard that there was
a tree in Scotland, that growing on the banks of rivers
produced fruits in the form of geese, which, as they approached

---

[1] *Opera Omnia.* Æneas calls the church *Alba Ecclesia*, which has been identi-
fied with Whitekirk, near North Berwick. [2] James was eighteen years a captive.

ripeness dropped off of their own accord, some on the ground and some into the water; that those which fell on the ground rotted, but that those submerged in the water immediately assumed life, and swam about under the water, and flew into the air with feathers and wings. When I made enquiries regarding this story, I learned that the miracle was always referred to some place further off, and that this famous tree was to be found not in Scotland but in the Orkney Islands, though the miracle had been represented to me as taking place among the Scots.[1] In this country I saw the poor, who almost in a state of nakedness begged at the church doors, depart with joy in their faces on receiving stones as alms.[2] This stone, whether by reason of sulphurous or some fatter matter which it contains, is burned instead of wood, of which the country is destitute.[3]

(*Commentarii Rerum Memorabilium*, p. 4.)

Æneas found the following facts relating to Scotland worthy of mention. Scotland makes part of the same island as England,[4] stretching northwards 200 miles with a breadth of 50. Its climate being cold, it produces few crops, and is scantily supplied with wood. A sulphurous stone dug from the earth is used by the people for fuel. The towns have no walls, and the houses are for the most part constructed without lime. The roofs of the houses in the country are made of turf, and the doors of the humbler dwellings are made of

---

[1] As will be seen, this story of the barnacles and the geese appears in the succeeding narratives, down even to the end of the seventeenth century.
[2] The earliest mention of the working of coal in Scotland is said to be in a charter of date 1291 (Cosmo Innes, *Sketches of Early Scottish History*, p. 235). The frequent mention of coal by the various travellers who visited Scotland might suggest that it was widely in use in the Lowlands. The truth is, however, that peat was the common fuel, and that coal was confined to a narrow area. It will be seen that the descriptions of travellers, when they speak of coal, mainly refer to the Lothians, where it was wrought from very early times.
[3] From a misunderstanding of the term *forest* in ancient charters, Tytler and others were misled to believe that the Lowlands of Scotland abounded in timber. From Acts of Parliament of the reign of James I. (the period of Æneas's visit), we gather that wood must have been a scarce commodity in Scotland (2 James I. cap. 33, 34). All the travellers who visited Scotland were struck by the general absence of trees. Dr Johnson's remarks on the subject are well known. [4] It should be said that long after the time of Sylvius, it was believed on the Continent that England and Scotland were separate islands. This will appear in the sequel.

the hide of oxen.   The common people are poor, and destitute
of all refinement.   They eat flesh and fish to repletion, and
bread only as a dainty.   The men are small in stature, bold
and forward in temper ; the women, fair in complexion, comely
and pleasing, but not distinguished for their chastity, giving
their kisses more readily than Italian women their hands.[1]

There is no wine in the country unless what is imported.
All the horses are amblers, and are of small size.   A few are
kept for breeding, the rest being gelded.   They are never
touched either with an iron brush or a wooden comb, and
they are managed without bit.[2]   The oysters of the country
are larger than those found in England.   Hides, wool, salted
fish, and pearls [3] are exported to Flanders.   Nothing pleases
the Scots more than abuse of the English.   There are said
to be two distinct countries in Scotland—the one cultivated,
the other covered with forests and possessing no tilled land.
The Scots who live in the wooded region speak a language
of their own, and sometimes use the bark of trees for food.
There are no wolves in Scotland.[4]   The crow is unusual
in the country, and consequently the tree in which it builds
is the king's property.[5]   At the winter solstice in Scotland
(the season when Æneas was there) the day is not above four
hours long.[6]

His business in the country being finished, when he was on
the point of departure, the captain who had brought him to
Scotland came to him with the offer of the berth he had
previously occupied.   Æneas, thinking rather of his former
dangers than divining fresh ones, replied : " If he has no right

[1] Foreigners were struck by the same freedom of manners in English women
(see Rye, *England as seen by Foreigners*, pp. 90, 225, 261).   Erasmus has an
amusing letter on this custom of kissing among English women (*Epistolæ*, fol.,
Basil. 1558, p. 223).   [2] Compare what Major says of the Scotch horses (*Hist.
Maj. Brit.*, lib. i. cap. vi.).   [3] In the beginning of the twelfth century the
pearls of Alexander I. excited the envy of an English church dignitary (Cosmo
Innes, *Sketches of Early Scottish History*, p. 228).   [4] Æneas is here contradicted by an Act of Parliament (1427), which calls on the barons to extirpate
all wolves on their lands.   [5] Æneas misunderstood his informant.   From 1
James I. cap. 19, we learn that owing to the mischief done to the crops by
rooks, it was ordained that they should be prevented from building, and their
young destroyed.   If the young birds were allowed to escape, the trees in
which they had built were forfeited to the Crown.   [6] This statement, says
Major, "with all respect," must be regarded as a hyperbole.   The shortest
day at Edinburgh, he adds, is six hours (*Hist. Maj. Brit.*, lib. i. cap. iii.).

to accuse Neptune, who has twice risked his life, what shall
we say of him who should suffer shipwreck thrice ?   For my
part I prefer the tender mercies of man to those of the sea."
So saying he dismissed the sailor, and decided to make his
journey homewards through England.   As it happened, the
ship, which sailed immediately afterwards, had hardly left
the harbour when she foundered in a storm and went down
in sight of the shore.   The master (who was returning to
Flanders to celebrate his second marriage) was lost with all
his crew save four, who escaped to the shore by floating on
boards.   On hearing of this disaster Æneas at once concluded
that he owed his life to the special goodness of God.

Disguising himself as a merchant, he now made his way
through Scotland into England.   A river, which descends
from a lofty mountain, forms the boundary of the two
countries.   Crossing this river in a boat, he turned aside to
a large town, where he alighted at a farm-house.[1]   Here
with the priest of the place, and the host, he was entertained
to supper.   There was abundance of hens, geese, and various
relishes, but no wine or bread.   During supper the women
from the surrounding houses flocked to look on as if they
had never seen such a sight before, and stared at Æneas, as
in Italy the people stare at an Ethiopian or an Indian.[2]
" Of what religion is he," they ask ; " what has brought
him here ; is he acquainted with the Christian religion ? "
Having been cautioned beforehand, Æneas had provided
himself with a number of loaves and a measure of wine at
a certain monastery.   When these were laid on the board,
the wonder of the barbarians was greater than ever, since
wine and white bread were sights they had never seen before.
Pregnant women and their husbands approaching the table
handled the bread and smelt the wine, and prayed that a
portion might be given them.   As there was no avoiding it,
the whole had to be distributed amongst them.

[1] The " large town " must be Berwick.   At a very early period there were
bridges over the Tweed at Berwick ; but from 1294 till 1376 there was none.
At the time of Æneas's visit there appears to have been a wooden one (Scott,
History of Berwick, p. 411).   [2] The Indians or Ethiopians here referred to by
Æneas were in all probability gipsies, a band of whom had recently appeared
in Italy, and excited the astonishment of the people.   I am indebted for this
note to my friend Mr F. H. Groome, author of *In Gipsy Tents*.

At two o'clock in the morning (for the meal was protracted to that hour), the priest and the landlord, rising
hastily, quitted the house, leaving Æneas behind. "They
were going," they said, "to a distant keep[1] for fear of the
Scots, who for purposes of plunder were in the habit of
crossing the river at ebb-tide during the night." Æneas
besought eagerly to accompany them; but they gave no heed
to his entreaties. They were equally deaf to the prayers of
the women, though there were many handsome ones amongst
them, both married and unmarried. They give out that
strangers are safe at the hands of the Scots; and as for the
women, they do not regard outrage done to them as any
great misfortune.

Accordingly, with two male domestics and his guide,
Æneas was left among some hundred women, who, forming
a circle round the fire, spent the night in cleansing hemp,
and in lively conversation carried on through an interpreter.
A great part of the night had thus passed, when an uproar
arose from the barking of dogs and the cackling of geese.
The women at once fled in all directions and the guide along
with them. The confusion was as complete as if the enemy
were at the door. To Æneas the thought occurred that his
best course was to await the event in bed—that is to say,
in the stable; since, ignorant as he was of the country, any
attempt to escape would have placed him at the mercy of
the first marauder he met. In no long time, however, the
women returned, and announced through the interpreter that
there was no need for alarm, and that the newcomers were
friends and not enemies. At daybreak Æneas continued his
journey, and reached Newcastle, which is said to have been
built by Cæsar. Here for the first time it seemed to him
that he once more beheld civilisation, and a country with a
habitable aspect; for Scotland and that part of England
adjoining it bear no resemblance to Italy, but are nothing
but a rugged wilderness, unvisited by the genial sun.[2]

[1] Possibly Norham Castle, about 6 miles above Berwick on the banks of
the Tweed.   [2] In the Piccolomini Library there is a series of frescoes executed
by order of Pius III. in illustration of various incidents in the career of Æneas,
and among them is one by Pinturichhio representing his reception by James I.
It is a purely conventional production, and has no suggestion of reality.

JACQUES DE LALAIN

(1448).

A S a quaint picture of the manners of the time, the following account of the visit of a Burgundian knight to Scotland could not well be omitted from the present collection. Our extract is translated from a curious book entitled: "Histoire du bon chevalier Messire Jacques de Lalain frere et compagnon de l'ordre de la Toison d'Or: Ecrite par Messire George Chastellain Chevalier, Historiographe des Ducs de Bourgougne Philippe le Bon et Charles le Hardi."[1] As its author seems to have had his information from Lalain himself, or some one who accompanied him to Scotland,[2] his account may be regarded as virtually given at first hand.

Jacques de Lalain, whose exploits are here recorded, was the eldest son of a Burgundian noble of the court of Charles the Bold. If we may believe his partial biographer, Jacques had approved himself the doughtiest knight of his time in Christendom. He had visited in succession the courts of France, Spain, and Portugal, and matched himself against all comers; but had never once met his equal at any knightly weapon. It had come to his ears, however, that James Douglas, brother of William, Earl of Douglas,[3] was a champion with whom it was incumbent that he should break a lance. With the permission of his liege lord, the Duke of Burgundy, therefore, he dispatched a herald to Douglas with a challenge couched in all those

---

[1] The edition I have used is one published at Brussels in 1634, for which I am indebted to Sheriff Mackay. [2] pp. 2, 5 . [3] This was the Earl of Douglas afterwards slain by James II. at Stirling (Hume of Godscroft, *History of House and Race of Douglas*, vol. i. p. 360). The James Douglas challenged by De Lalain succeeded this William in the earldom (Godscroft, *ibid.*). Godscroft, it may be said, makes no mention of the combat at Stirling described by Chastellain.

terms of high-flown courtesy, which the usages of chivalry exacted.   Douglas, with the consent of his sovereign (James II.), wrote accepting the challenge in a letter as graciously circumlocutory as that of the redoubtable Burgundian himself.   Embarking in a vessel specially equipped by himself and his companions, Lalain sailed for Scotland in as gorgeous array as the court of Burgundy could supply. Of his achievements there we leave his biographer to tell the tale.   As a rendering in modern phrase would effectually have marred any interest the narrative may possess, the original is here reproduced with all its circumlocutions and endless iterations.

The end of Jacques de Lalain was not such as a hero of chivalry might have desired.   He was killed at the age of thirty-two by a musket ball, thus falling at the same age and in the same manner as the last and noblest of the knights, Sir Philip Sidney.   Lalain's biographer thus sums up his character : " As regards his virtues there is no human tongue, how eloquent soever, that were equal to the full roll of them.   He was a knight, pleasant, meek, amiable, and courteous, a bounteous giver and full of pity. Through all his life he was the help of widows and orphans. He had been endowed by God with five gifts.   And, in the first place, he was the flower of knighthood ; he was beautiful as Paris the Trojan, he was pious as Æneas, he was wise as Ulysses the Greek ; when he found himself in battle he had the wrath of Hector the Trojan ; but so soon as he felt or knew that he carried it over his enemies, never was man more *debonnair* or humble." [1]

---

[1] P. 308.   In Sir Walter Scott's *Diary* (vol. i. p. 129, David Douglas, Edinburgh, 1890), there is the following interesting reference to Chastellain's chronicle : " Being troubled with thick-coming fancies, and a slight palpitation of the heart, I have been reading the chronicle of the Good Knight Messire Jacques de Lalain.—Curious, but dull from the constant repetition of the same species of combats in the same style and phrase.   It is like washing bushels of sand for a grain of gold.   It passes the time, however, especially in that listless mood when your mind is half in your book and half in something else. . . . . . Still things occur to me.   Something might be made out of the Pass of the Fountain of Tears, a tale of chivalry, taken from the Passages of Arms, which Jacques de Lalain maintained for the first day of every month for a *twelve month*.   The first mention, perhaps, of red-hot balls appears in the siege of Oudenarde by the citizens of Ghent."

The combat of the Scots and Burgundian champions at Stirling is thus dryly related in the *Auchinleck Chronicle* (p. 40): "The yer of God MCCCCXLVIII, the XXV day of Februar, the master of Douglas, callit James, and twasom with him, that is to say, James of Douglas, brother to the larde of Lochlevyne, and the lard of Haukat, focht in the barres at Strivling aganis twa knychtis and ane squyar of Burgundy. And ther war thair names, Schir Jakkis de Lalane, Schir Symond de Lalane, and the larde of Mongavile, that was the squyar. And this was befoir King James the Secund."

Histoire du bon Chevalier Messire Jacques de Lalain.

WHEN Messire Jacques and his company had arrived in Scotland [1] the Scots who were with the same Maistre James de Duglas came before Messire Jacques; and when they had come, they expressed a desire to know why he of Lalain had sent his challenge to Maistre James de Duglas, and in such wise as to show that they were not well content. Nevertheless, he replied that it was neither for hatred nor envy nor any evil wish whatsoever, but to do the greatest honour in his power to one who came of such high descent, and was besides of such great renown and courage, that he desired his acquaintance more than that of any lord in the said kingdom of Scotland. So the friends of Maistre James de Duglas were satisfied. When Messire Jacques de Lalain and the said James de Duglas had spoken at length with each other, they agreed that they should each choose two companions, men of rank and known in arms; and so they did. And for his part, Messire Jacques took his uncle, Messire Simon de Lalain, lord of Montigny, and Hervé de Meriadet; and Maistre James de Duglas took as companions-in-arms two noble and powerful lords, one of whom was named the lord of Haguet, [2] and the other was also named

---

[1] According to the chronicle of d'Escouchy (*Société de l'Histoire de France*, i. p. 148), this visit of the Burgundian knights to Scotland was connected with the marriage of James II. and Mary of Gueldres. As the dates correspond, this was probably the case, though Chastellain gives no hint of it, making the visit turn entirely on De Lalain's challenge.   [2] The laird of Hacket.

James de Duglas—all of whom were renowned as valiant knights, powerful in body and limbs.

The affair being thus concluded, the king of Scotland agreed to be their judge, and appointed time and place, and had the lists made ready at Stirling. After these arrangements had been made and the day fixed, both parties prepared for the combat, and undertook to be in the lists on the day appointed ; and all six that they might with all honour achieve their deeds of arms, were entertained by the king. So after the festivities were over, the king ordered the said Messire Jacques, Messire Simon his uncle, and Hervé de Meriadet, two notable knights, to take counsel with themselves and act according to their wont.

When the appointed day came, the king mounted his throne : Messire Jacques de Lalain, and Messire Simon his uncle, and Hervé de Meriadet entered the lists unarmed, Messire Jacques and Messire Simon both being clothed in long robes of black velvet, furred with martens, and Meriadet in a short robe of black velvet, furred with martens, their arms being carried before them in two coffers, covered with the bearings of Messire Jacques de Lalain, and very richly broidered, and they were accompanied by noblemen who had come with them, and also by those whom the king had appointed to advise with them. And thus all three dismounted before their pavilion, which they entered. Then they went and did reverence to the King of Scotland. Afterwards they returned to their pavilion where they found their harness ready and fully adorned. So they armed themselves at their ease, and had abundant leisure, for they had come more than three hours before the others. The hour appointed having come, the said Maistre James de Duglas, the lord of Haguet, and James de Duglas arrived, and came to the entrance of the lists, attended by a great company, the Earl of Duglas and other great lords, knights, and other people, who, it was said, amounted to fully four or five thousand men.[1] Then the three champions, all armed, and clad in their coats of mail, dismounted at their pavilion, and afterwards all three went to do reverence to the King of

---

[1] This statement is interesting as showing the number of retainers the Douglas could bring into the field.

Scotland, and all three prayed that he would confer on them the order of knighthood, which he freely granted to them. So he descended from his throne, and made all three knights. Messire Jacques, his uncle Messire Simon, and Meriadet saw from their pavilion the three knights above named return from the presence of the King of Scotland, each clad in his coat of mail. So they recognised them by their arms, and they agreed among themselves that Messire Jacques should fight Messire James de Duglas, and Meriadet the lord of Haguet, who was renowned as the most powerful of body, and Messire Simon should give his care to the other James de Duglas; and their arms were of this kind—they were to fight with lances, axe, sword, and dagger *à outrance*, or till the king signified his will; but at the request of the above-named Scots, the throwing of the lance was forbidden, for they trusted greatly in their lances.

So the uncle, the nephew, and Meriadet agreed among themselves that they would neither fight with their lances nor throw them at their opponents, but that when they met them they would cast their lances behind them, and fight with their axes. Now, according to the rules of the combat, each one might carry assistance to his comrade. Wherefore Messire Jacques de Lalain said to Meriadet: "I believe that you will be the first to dispose of your man; nevertheless I pray you with all the zeal I can that you will neither aid me nor succour me in any way whatsoever, but permit me to meet such fortune, be it good or ill, as God may please to send me." Thus having spoken to each other, they resolved that so they would act.

When the six champions were apparelled and ready to issue from their tent, awaiting the proclamations, orders, and prohibitions that are wont to be made in the lists, straightway with sound of trumpet were thrice proclaimed at the four corners of the lists the conditions appointed by the King of Scotland. And at the close of this proclamation issued forth from their pavilion the said De Lalain and Meriadet armed and adorned with all their blazons, clad in their coats of mail, Messire Jacques de Lalain being between his uncle Simon and Meriadet. Then the Scots issued from their pavilion armed and emblazoned, each clad in his coat of mail; and

Messire James de Duglas was between his companions.
And so, very proudly and with rapid steps they marched
against each other, which was a very fair and pleasant sight
to behold.   And when they came near each other, because
the lord of Haguet was on the side of Messire Simon de
Lalain, the said Meriadet wished to cross before Messire
Jacques in order that he might have the lord of Haguet for
his foe, when Messire Simon said in a loud voice : " Let each
remain where he is ; " and in this order they went forward to
the combat.

Then the said Des Lalains and Meriadet threw their
lances behind them as they had agreed.   Then they seized
their axes, and with much vigour began to fight and strike
at the Scots who defended themselves with their lances.
Messire James de Duglas fought with his lance ; but it did
not remain long in his hand : so he took his axe and fought
for a little time with it, but not for long, for Messire
Jacques soon made him lose it as he had lost his lance.
And this Messire James being very wroth, and disturbed at
seeing himself thus disarmed of his lance and his axe, at once
with great fury seized his dagger and so tried to strike
Messire Jacques in the face as he fought without his vizor
and with his face uncovered.[1]   But Messire Jacques seeing
him approach, with great force struck him a blow with his
left hand and made him stagger backwards.   Notwithstanding this, Messire James sought with all his power to
strike him in the face.   Then Messire Jacques threw away
his axe, and with his left hand seized Messire James by the
head-piece, and held him so fast that he could not approach
him, and with the right hand he drew his sword (which was
a short blade), holding it near the point to use it as a dagger,
for he had lost his own and did not know how (some say
that he who armed him did not arm him with this).   And
thus he sought to make a dagger of the said sword, as has
been said, and sought to strike the said James with the
hand with which he held the beaver ; and in trying to
strike him, the said blade fell from his hand and he was

---

[1] From the descriptions of other combats in which De Lalain was engaged,
we gather that this was his habit.   It was considered a special proof of his
confidence in his skill and strength.

without a weapon.   And when he saw himself disweaponed,
very swiftly and furiously he seized the said James with
both hands by the hollow of his head-piece, and by the strength
of his arm made him move backwards to the throne of the
king, twice lifting him off his feet with the intention of
throwing him on the ground, and so putting him out of
breath ; and in so doing he did rightly, for Messire James
fought in his basinet with closed vizor, while the said De
Lalain was without his vizor and breathed freely, it being
quite the contrary with Messire James, and this soon
appeared, when his vizor was removed after the king had
thrown down his truncheon.—Now let us leave this combat
of these two champions and return to the others.

We have told how Messire Simon de Lalain bore himself
in his rencounter with the lord of Haguet, and how (as was
said before) this lord of Haguet began to fight with his lance,
in which he put great trust.   But it did not remain long
with him, for Messire Simon, who was an adroit, strong, and
hardy knight, and very expert in arms, quickly and furiously
made him lose his lance.   Then both betook themselves to
their axes, with which they struck great blows at each
other, for they were both very tall and well furnished in
body and limbs ; and to look at them they seemed knights
of high order, and well they showed it that day.   The lord
of Haguet was of great strength, and showed it by the great
blows that he rained on Messire de Lalain, which Messire
de Lalain knew well how to receive with his axe, and how
to strike great and terrible blows when he saw his chance
for his blow, and was lucky in delivering it.   For beyond
all men he had command of his temper, and knew well how
to chafe his man.   Very long, and over a great space of the
lists, and very valiantly they fought.   But from the great
haste and ardour of the lord of Haguet to strike and overcome
Messire Simon, the combat did not last so long as it might,
for he began to weary, and to lose strength and breath.
Messire Simon, who was ready of device [1] and cool tempered,
seeing that time and fortune were telling for him, recom-
menced with great liveliness and vigour to strike with thrust
and cut, and to wield with great force the axe which he

---

[1] *Imaginatif.*

held; and so overwhelmed the lord of Haguet with the
blows of his axe that he drove him back along the length
of the lists. And if the battle of these two had lasted
longer, the lord of Haguet, as all could see and know,
would have had the worst of it, and so it would have
happened, if they had not been parted by the king.

Now it is meet that we should speak of the valiant and
noble knight Breton Hervé de Meriadet, who this day met
and fought Messire James de Duglas, first cousin of the
count of Duglas, who was a very noble knight of good frame
and skilful in arms. They disposed themselves for the
combat and attacked each other. The Scottish knight
lowered his lance, and tried to strike the said Meriadet in
the face with its point; but he failed, and struck on the
sleeve of his coat of mail on the left arm; and as he sought to
steady himself after the blow, his lance slipt under Meriadet's
left arm, and Meriadet swiftly entered within his guard, and
with a blow of his axe struck him on the side of his basinet,
and bore him down quite stunned, laying bare his face.
Then the said Meriadet, seeing his adversary on the ground
(since by the conditions of the fight each could carry assistance to his comrades) looked towards them with the intention of bearing them help, if there was need. He perceived
that Messire James de Duglas, who was quick and agile, was
already on his knees and almost on his feet. Then he
returned upon him, took his axe in both his hands, and with
the shaft of the same at once levelled him with the ground
and stunned him with the blow, and made him fall extended
all his length; and it is the truth that if he had hastened
to slay him, he could easily have done so, and without blame
since the fight was à outrance. But neither of the two times
when he saw him on the ground did he wish to touch him,
which was nobly done, and ought to be set down to his
honour. Forthwith the said Meriadet turned his regard to
his comrades, and was making towards them to lend them
aid, which they did not need, when as swiftly as before the
Messire James de Duglas raised himself on his feet, axe in
hand, and the said Meriadet returned upon him, and they then
fought a long time, and like the others above named were laid
hold of (still fighting) by the guards, when the king threw

down his truncheon. But you should know that the noble Squire Meriadet was of as excellent and powerful frame as one could find. And all the remainder of the combat, after Messire James de Duglas had regained his feet, was to the great honour of the said Meriadet, who gave him very great blows, beating him back, and having him at his will.

After all the feats of arms above narrated had been accomplished, and when Messire James de Duglas and Messire Jacques de Lalain were in the position we have described, and when in the same manner Messire Simon de Lalain and the lord of Haguet fought valiantly and well with their axes, the King of Scotland, who was on the throne, without further delay threw down his truncheon. The guards, who had been appointed for this purpose, laid hands on the six champions as they had been ordered to do; and all were brought before the King of Scotland, who said that they had all fought valiantly and well, that he held the combat at an end, and that he wished that they should be good friends. The trial of arms over, each returned to his lodging. And some days after the king feasted them very grandly, and gave them honourable gifts for which they thanked him. After all the festivities, Messire Jacques de Lalain, and his uncle Messire Simon, and the said Meriadet, and those who had come with them to Scotland, took leave of the king and departed.[1]

[1] In the *Scotichronicon* (vol. ii. p. 515, Goodall's edit.) there is also a brief reference to this combat of the Burgundian and the Scottish knights. The chronicler assigns the palm to neither party; but had the Scots come off with greater honour, his words would have had a less uncertain sound. He thus sums up the result of the duel:—"Et hi sex milites in uno campo coram rege dimicaverunt apud Striveling; cujus belli triumphus pro omni parte stetit honore, regia disponente prudentia judicis."

DON PEDRO DE AYALA

(1498).

DON PEDRO DE AYALA, the writer of the following
letter, was the ambassador of Ferdinand and Isabella
at the court of James IV. He is described by Mr
Bergenroth (the editor of the *Simancas Papers* from which
the letter is taken) as "of agreeable manners, genial and
light-hearted," and as one who "made friends wherever he
went." He had, also, "a marked predilection for James,
who on his part was so attached to him that he called him
his father, and did not venture to decide on any great
question of state without asking his advice." The letter, it
should be said, was written by the express command of
Ferdinand and Isabella, who desired a full description of
Scotland and its king. It is dated 25th July 1498.

JAMES IV. AND HIS PEOPLE
(Bergenroth, *Simancas Papers*, vol. i. p. 169).

THE king is twenty-five years and some months old. He
is of noble stature, neither tall nor short, and as handsome in complexion and shape as a man can be. His address
is very agreeable. He speaks the following foreign languages:
Latin, very well; French, German, Flemish, Italian, and
Spanish; Spanish as well as the Marquis, but he pronounces
it more distinctly. He likes very much to receive Spanish
letters. His own Scotch language is as different from
English as Aragonese from Castilian. The king speaks,
besides, the language of the savages who live in some parts
of Scotland [1] and on the islands. It is as different from

---

[1] Professor Mackinnon informs me that this is the latest statement with
which he is acquainted regarding a Scottish king's knowledge of Gaelic. At
the same time he suggests that as James V. was in the habit of wandering in
the Highlands, it is not improbable that he also spoke that language.

Scotch as Biscayan is from Castilian. His knowledge of languages is wonderful.[1] He is well read in the Bible and in some other devout books. He is a good historian. He has read many Latin and French histories, and profited by them, as he has a very good memory. He never cuts his hair or his beard.[2] It becomes him very well.

He fears God, and observes all the precepts of the Church. He does not eat meat on Wednesdays and Fridays. He would not ride on Sundays for any consideration, not even to mass. He says all his prayers. Before transacting any business he hears two masses. After mass he has a cantata sung, during which he sometimes despatches very urgent business. He gives alms liberally, but is a severe judge, especially in the case of murderers. He has a great predilection for priests, and receives advice from them, especially from the Friars Observant,[3] with whom he confesses. Rarely, even in joking, a word escapes him that is not the truth. He prides himself much upon it, and says it does not seem to him well for kings to swear their treaties as they do now. The oath of a king should be his royal word, as was the case in bygone ages. He is neither prodigal nor avaricious, but liberal when occasion requires. He is courageous, even more so than a king should be. I am a good witness of it. I have seen him often undertake most dangerous things in the last wars. I sometimes clung to his skirts and succeeded in keeping him back. On such occasions he does not take the least care of himself. He is not a good captain, because he begins to fight before he has given his orders.[4] He said to me that his subjects serve him with their persons and goods, in just and unjust quarrels, exactly as he likes, and that, therefore, he does not think it right to begin any warlike undertaking without being him-

---

[1] Ayala's character of James, though coloured by the partiality of kindly feeling, is in the main fully borne out by the historians. Buchanan's portrait is as favourable as that of Ayala, though he denies to James any literary accomplishment—"vitio temporis ab literis incultus," he says of him. [2] In the account given by Young, the Somerset herald, of the first meeting of Margaret Tudor and James IV., the king is described as having "hys Beerde somthynge long" (Leland, *Collectanea*, vol. iv. p. 283). [3] A branch of the Franciscan Order—so-called on account of the stricter rule by which they bound themselves. Henry VII. also showed special favour to this body. [4] What Ayala here says was to be tragically proved on the field of Flodden.

self the first in danger. His deeds are as good as his words. For this reason, and because he is a very humane prince, he is much loved. He is active, and works hard. When he is not at war he hunts in the mountains. I tell your Highnesses the truth when I say that God has worked a miracle in him, for I have never seen a man so temperate in eating and drinking out of Spain. Indeed, such a thing seems to be superhuman in these countries. He lends a willing ear to his counsellors, and decides nothing without asking them ; but in great matters he acts according to his own judgment, and, in my opinion, he generally makes a right decision. I recognise him perfectly in the conclusion of the last peace, which was made against the wishes of the majority in his kingdom.[1]

When he was a minor he was instigated by those who held the government to do some dishonourable things. They favoured his love intrigues with their relatives, in order to keep him in their subjection. As soon as he came of age, and understood his duties, he gave up these intrigues. When I arrived, he was keeping a lady with great state in a castle.[2] He visited her from time to time. Afterwards he sent her to the house of her father, who is a knight, and married her. He did the same with another lady, by whom he had had a son. It may be about a year since he gave up, so at least it is believed, his lovemaking, as well from fear of God as from fear of scandal in this world, which is thought very much of here. I can say with truth that he esteems himself as much as though he were lord of the world. He loves war so much that I fear, judging by the provocation he receives, the peace will not last long. War is profitable to him and to the country.

I will give an account of his revenues. Although I do not know them to a certainty, I do not think that I shall be far wrong. I shall estimate them a little below their real amount.

He has a revenue from arable and pasture lands, which

---

[1] The seven years' truce with England concluded at Ayton in 1497. De Ayala acted as James's commissioner on the occasion. [2] About the date of Ayala's stay in Scotland, Joan or Janet Kennedy became James's mistress. After he had cast her off, she was married to Archibald Bell-the-Cat (Preface to *Exchequer Rolls*, vol. xii. p. xliii).

are let by leases of three years.[1]   The farmers pay a fine
upon entry.   This rent is said to amount to 50,000 pounds
Scotch, each pound Scotch being worth one Castiliano.   I
rather believe that it amounts to 40,000 ducats.

Another revenue is that from the customs.   The import
duties are insignificant, but the exports yield a considerable
sum of money, because there are three principal articles of
export, that is to say, wool, hides, and fish.   The customs
are worth about 25,000 ducats a year.[2]   They have much
increased, and still continue to increase.   Another revenue
is that derived from the administration of the law.   His
predecessors farmed it to certain persons called justices
(*justiciarios*), like our *corregidores*.   This king does not like
to farm the administration of the law, because justice is not
well administered in that way.   It is said that this revenue
amounts to more than 30,000 ducats, but I will put it down
at only 25,000 ducats.

He has another revenue from his wards, which is very
considerable, and which offers good opportunities for reward-
ing his servants.   If lords, or gentlemen of the middle class,
in whatever part of the kingdom they may be, die and
leave children under twenty-two years of age, the king is
the guardian of them.   He receives all their revenues till
they come of age.   He lets or sells such guardianships.
He even sells the marriages of his wards, male and female.
When the ward comes of age, and the king gives him the
title of his father, or brother, or testator, he pays the
amount of one or two year's rent, or any other sum that is
agreed upon, into the exchequer of the king.   I am told
that this is the richest source of revenue, but I will estimate
it at only 20,000 ducats.

He enjoys one year's revenue from the bishoprics and
abbacies for the presentation.   He likewise receives all the
revenues of them during the vacancy of the see.   The

---

[1] *Cf.* Major (*Hist. Maj. Brit.*, lib. i. cap. vi.):—"Præterea in Scotia rusti-
corum domus parvae tanquam casae sunt, et id rationis est, terras non habent
perpetuas, sed solum conductitias, seu ad firmans pro iv. vel v. annis,
secundum quod domino soli placet."   [2] "While the gross revenue from the
customs in the reign of James III. amounted on an average to £3000, their
yield during the five years now in question (1497–1501) was, as has been seen,
only £3106" (Preface to *Exchequer Rolls*, vol. xi. p. liii).

same is the case with respect to other livings, for they are all in his gift. I do not know to how much this amounts.

He has a rent from the fisheries, not in money, but in kind, for his kitchen, and likewise from meat and poultry, &c. This is his income, according to what I have been able to ascertain, and to what I have seen. He is in want of nothing, judging from the manner in which he lives, but he is not able to put money into his strong boxes. I shall speak hereafter of this.

The country is large. Your Highnesses know that these kingdoms form an island. Judging by what I have read in books and seen on maps, and also by my own experience, I should think that both kingdoms are of equal extent. In the same proportion that England is longer than Scotland, Scotland is wider than England; thus the quantity of land is the same. Neither is the quality very different in the two countries, but the Scotch are not industrious, and the people are poor. They spend all their time in wars, and when there is no war they fight with one another. It must, however, be observed, that since the present king succeeded to the throne they do not dare to quarrel so much with one another as formerly, especially since he came of age. They have learnt by experience that he executes the law without respect to rich or poor. I am told that Scotland has improved so much during his reign that it is worth three times more now than formerly, on account of foreigners having come to the country, and taught them how to live.[1] They have more meat, in great and small animals, than they want, and plenty of wool and hides.

Spaniards who live in Flanders tell me that the commerce of Scotland is much more considerable now than formerly, and that it is continually increasing.

[1] The foreigners here referred to must be the Flemings. " We can trace the settlement of these industrious citizens," says Tytler, " during the twelfth and thirteenth centuries, in almost every part of Scotland,—in Berwick, ... in St Andrews, Perth, Dumbarton, Ayr, Peebles, Lanark, Edinburgh; and in the districts of Renfrewshire, Clydesdale, and Annandale . . . . . , in Fife, in Angus, in Aberdeenshire, and as far north as Inverness and Urquhart (*History of Scotland*, vol. i., "Historical Inquiry into the Ancient State and Manners of Scotland "). Mr Burnett considered that Ayala exaggerated when he wrote that the land had trebled in value during the reign of James IV. (Preface to *Exchequer Rolls*, vol. xi. p. liii).

It is impossible to describe the immense quantity of fish.
The old proverb says already "piscinata Scotia." Great
quantities of salmon, herring, and a kind of dried fish, which
they call stock fish (*stoque fix*), are exported.[1]   The quantity
is so great that it suffices for Italy, France, Flanders, and
England.   They have so many wild fruits which they eat,
that they do not know what to do with them.[2]   There are
immense flocks of sheep, especially in the savage portions of
Scotland.[3]   Hides are employed for many purposes.   There
are all kinds of garden fruits to be found which a cold
country can produce.   They are very good.   Oranges, figs,
and other fruits of the same kind are not to be found there.
The corn is very good, but they do not produce as much as
they might, because they do not cultivate the land.   Their
method is the following : they plough the land only once
when it has grass on it, which is as high as a man, then they
sow the corn, and cover it by means of a harrow, which
makes the land even again.   Nothing more is done till they
cut the corn.   I have seen the straw stand so high after
harvest,[4] that it reached to my girdle.   Some kind of corn is
sown about the feast of St John,[5] and is cut in August.

The people are handsome.   They like foreigners so much
that they dispute with one another as to who shall have
and treat a foreigner in his house.   They are vain and
ostentatious by nature.   They spend all they have to keep
up appearances.   They are as well dressed as it is possible
to be in such a country as that in which they live.   They
are courageous, strong, quick, and agile.   They are envious
(jealous ?) to excess.

There are four duchies in the kingdom.[6]   Three of them

---

[1] The chartularies of the great abbeys of Melrose, Newbattle, Arbroath,
and Kelso, give us the most vivid idea of the extent of the fishing industry
in Scotland (see Cosmo Innes, *Sketches of Early Scottish History*).   [2] Camden
tells us that "in the low grounds the Scots have store of pease and beans,
which for the strength of their feeding are much used by the labouring
people" (*Britannia*, Gibson's translation, p. 1154).   What Ayala can mean by
"wild fruits" it is difficult to say.   [3] The chartularies above referred to fully
bear out what Ayala says of the number of sheep in Scotland (Innes, p. 99).
[4] This must refer to the practice of cutting the ears of corn, and leaving the
straw standing.   [5] 24th June, or according to old style the 13th.   [6] Ross,
Albany, Rothesay, and Montrose.   The dukedoms of Albany and Rothesay
were created in 1398, those of Ross and Montrose in 1488.

are in the possession of the king ; the fourth is held by the eldest brother of the king, who is Duke of Ross and Archbishop of St Andrews. There are fifteen earls, not counting the younger brother of the king, who holds two counties.

Nine other counties are in possession of the king.[1] Some of the fifteen earls are great men. I saw two of them come to serve the king in the last war with more than 30,000 men, all picked soldiers and well armed. And yet they did not bring more than one-half of their men. Many others came with five or six thousand followers ; some with more, and some with less. As I have already observed, this army does not cost the king a penny.[2]

There are two principalities ; one of them is the *principatus insularum*,[3] and the other the *principatus Gallovidiae*.[4] Both are held by the king. There are five and thirty great barons in the kingdom, without counting the smaller ones.

There are two archbishoprics and eleven bishoprics,[5] sixty-three monasteries, which they call abbeys, and many other religious houses, which are endowed with property and rents. The abbeys are very magnificent, the buildings fine, and the revenues great. All of them were founded by kings. There are seventy seaports. The harbours between the islands are not included in this number, though they are said to be very secure.

Sixty-four of the islands are inhabited. Some of them are 60 miles long, and as many miles in width. Besides,

[1] The counties or earldoms which, either by forfeiture or ward, were in the hands of James IV. were Fife, Strathearn, Monteith, Moray, Mar, Ross, Orkney, and Sutherland. In addition to these the shires of Stirling and Linlithgow were crown lands. It is not clear to what counties Ayala refers.   [2] But while this army was provided by the conditions of feudal tenure, the navy and artillery had to be maintained at the king's own expense (Preface to *Exchequer Rolls*, vol. xii. p. clxxxvi). [3] By the *principatus insularum*, we are probably to understand the lordship ʹof the Isles, which were not thoroughly subject to the Scottish crown till the battle of Harlaw in 1411—a victory more important for Scotland than Bannockburn. [4] The lordship of Galloway. Galloway seems to be loosely used here for all Scotland south of the Forth. The name formerly designated a much wider district than at present, and included at least part of Dumfriesshire and all the earldom of Carrick, which extended much further north than the modern boundary of that name. This may partly explain Ayala's use of the name.   [5] According to Keith (*Catalogue of Scottish Bishops*) there were twelve bishops.

there are the Orcades towards Norway. It is said they are very numerous.

On the islands there are many flocks, and great quantities of fish and of barley. The inhabitants are very warlike and agile. I saw them in the last war. They do not know what danger is. The present king keeps them in strict subjection. He is feared by the bad, and loved and revered by the good like a god. None of the former kings have succeeded in bringing the people into such subjection as the present king. He went last summer to many of the islands, and presided at the courts of law.[1]

The prelates are very much revered; they have the larger share in the government. Spiritual as well as secular lords, if they have a title or a dignity, belong to the General Council. It meets four times a year in order to administer justice.[2] It is a very good institution. All causes are decided after debating them. At the same time the king receives his revenues derived from the administration of the law. Both spiritual and secular lords have a certain number of followers, recorded in the books of the king, who are entitled to have their meals in the palace when they come to court. They have no other advantages. The king selects some of them for his Privy Council, and they always remain at court. They receive, nevertheless, no salary, except for other offices, which they may happen to hold. But they and their servants eat in the palace. The reason why they do so is, that the king may be always accompanied by them. It causes great expense.

The kings live little in cities and towns.[3] They pass their time generally in castles and abbeys, where they find lodgings for all their officers. They do not remain long in one place. The reason thereof is twofold. In the first place, they move often about, in order to visit their kingdom, to administer

---

[1] Yet an Act of Parliament of date 20th March 1503 begins as follows :— "Because there has baeen gret abuse of justice in the north parts and west parts of the realm, such as the North Isles and South Isles, for lack and fault of Justice Ayres, &c." [2] This refers to the ambulatory Sessions Court instituted by James I. (1457, cap. 61). Into the reign of James IV., however, the Court met only *thrice* in the year. A Daily Council fixed at Edinburgh by that king in 1503 seems to have superseded it (Sheriff Mackay, *Practice of the Court of Session*, vol. i. p. 13). [3] *Cf.* p. 9 (note).

justice, and to establish police where it is wanted. The second reason is, that they have rents in kind in every province, and they wish to consume them. While travelling, neither the king nor any of his officers have any expenses, nor do they carry provisions with them. They go from house to house, to lords, bishops, and abbots, where they receive all that is necessary. The greatest favour the king can do to his subjects is to go to their houses.

The women are courteous in the extreme. I mention this because they are really honest, though very bold. They are absolute mistresses of their houses, and even of their husbands, in all things concerning the administration of their property, income as well as expenditure. They are very graceful and handsome women. They dress much better than here (England), and especially as regards the head-dress, which is, I think, the handsomest in the world.[1]

The towns and villages are populous. The houses are good, all built of hewn stone, and provided with excellent doors, glass windows, and a great number of chimneys. All the furniture that is used in Italy, Spain, and France, is to be found in their dwellings. It has not been bought in modern times only, but inherited from preceding ages.

The queens possess, besides their baronies and castles, four country seats,[2] situated in the best portions of the kingdom, each of which is worth about fifteen thousand ducats. The king fitted them up anew only three years ago. There is not more than one fortified town in Scotland, because the kings do not allow their subjects to fortify them.[3] The town is a very considerable borough and well armed. The whole soil of Scotland belongs to the king, the landholders being his vassals, or his tenants for life, or for a term of years. They are obliged to serve him forty days, at their own expense, every time he calls them out. They are very good

---

[1] "The head-dress consisted of the kerchief or veil, which was at this period suspended from a lofty structure in the form of two horns, at first made by arranging the hair in this manner ; but as the fashion assumed exaggerated proportions, they were made of false hair, and of hemp and flax " (Dr Dickson, Preface to *Accounts of Lord High Treasurer of Scotland* (1473–1498), p. clxxxii).
[2] Linlithgow Palace was the jointure house of the Queens of Scotland, though, of course, they occasionally resided in other royal palaces.   [3] *Cf.* p. 19 (note).

soldiers.   The king can assemble, within thirty days, 120,000 horse.   The soldiers from the islands are not counted in this number.   The islands are half a league, one, two, three, or four leagues distant from the main land.   The inhabitants speak the language, and have the habits of the Irish.   But there is a good deal of French education in Scotland, and many speak the French language.   For all the young gentlemen who have no property go to France, and are well received there, and therefore the French are liked.   Two or three times I have seen, not the whole army, but one-third of it assembled, and counted more than twelve thousand great and small tents.   There is much emulation among them as to who shall be best equipped, and they are very ostentatious, and pride themselves very much in this respect.   They have old and heavy artillery of iron.   Besides this, they possess modern French guns of metal, which are very good.   King Louis gave them to the father of the present king in payment of what was due to him as co-heir of his sister, the Queen of Scotland.   This is all I am able to tell your Highnesses.   Now I shall describe where Scotland is situated, and by what countries she is surrounded.   She borders on England by land, and by sea on Brittany, France, Flanders, Germany, Denmark, Norway, and Ireland.   She is surrounded by these countries.[1]   Scotland is powerful enough to defend herself against her neighbours should any one of them attack her without fear of God.   No king can do her damage without suffering greater damages from her, that is to say, in a war on land; for they know that on the sea there are many kings more powerful than they are, although they possess many fine vessels.   On land they think themselves the most powerful kingdom that exists; for they say the King of Scots has always a hundred thousand men ready to fight, and they are always paid.   Towards the west there is no land between Scotland and Spain.   Scotland is nearer to Spain than London, and the voyage is not dangerous.   Scotland has succoured most of her neighbours.   With respect to France and Flanders this is notorious.   The Dukes of

---

[1] This is one indication among many of the vague notions even of educated men regarding the relative position of Scotland.   Other instances will appear in the sequel.

Burgundy wear the "tan of St Andrew,"[1] in memory of the succour which Scotland sent to Duke [*blank*]. Saint Andrew is the patron saint of Scotland. On the other hand, Scotland has never wanted foreign assistance. There is as great a difference between the Scotland of old time and the Scotland of to-day as there is between bad and good, as I have already written.

Ayala goes on to say that he is afraid his description of Scotland may appear partial; his intention, however, is to tell the truth. Feels himself the more obliged to do so when he considers what may happen. If the third daughter of Ferdinand and Isabella[2] be not yet engaged, it would be a service to God to marry her to the King of Scots. He would be always a faithful ally, near at hand, and ready to assist, without causing any inconvenience to Spain. The kingdom is very old, and very noble, and the king possesses great virtues, and no defects worth mentioning.[3]

---

[1] *Tan*, so printed in Bergenroth. It must, of course, be *tau*, a heraldic term for *cross*. As it happens, the cross of St Andrew is not shaped like a *tau ;* but it is a Spaniard who is writing. [2] Doña Maria, afterwards married to Don Manuel the Fortunate, King of Portugal (Note by Bergenroth). [3] The account of Scotland here presented by Ayala is doubtless somewhat highly coloured, yet in the main it is fully borne out by Dr Dickson, Sheriff Mackay, and the late Mr Burnett, in their prefaces to the various public records of the period. The same impression is also gained from the various lights thrown on the period by Mr Gregory Smith's excellent little book, *The Days of James IV.*

A Relation of Scotland about the Year 1500, from the Italian.

THE writer of the following account of Scotland was never actually in the country; but, as he himself tells us, speaks solely on the authority of direct information from Pedro de Ayala. What he says, therefore, may be regarded as a supplement to the foregoing description of Scotland by Ayala himself. It was first printed by the Camden Society in 1847 with the following title—" A Relation or rather a True Account of the Island of England with sundry particulars of the customs of these people and of the Royal Revenues under King Henry the Seventh. About the year 1500. Translated from the Italian with notes by Charlotte Augusta Sneyd." In the introductory notice by Mr Holmes of the British Museum, the following account is given of the manuscript edited and translated by Miss Sneyd:—" The MS. from which this is translated was formerly in the library of the Abbate Canonici at Venice, and is now in the possession of the Rev. Walter Sneyd. Neither the name of the writer of this history, nor that of the person to whom it was addressed, is known."

Since this was written, Mr Rawdon Brown has shown that the author of the " Relation " was Andrea Trevisano, the earliest Venetian ambassador at the English Court (Rawdon Brown, *Giustiniani's Four Years at the Court of Henry VII.*, 1854).

A Relation of the Island of England about 1500.

THE form of the island is triangular, as we have said before, and it is divided into three parts, thus: Scotland, Wales, and England.

Scotland lies to the north, and is separated from England by two arms of the sea, which penetrate very far inland, one to the east, and the other to the west. These do not, however, meet, for there is about 60 miles of mountainous country between them; and there are some who say that two rivers rise in these mountains, one of which falls into the eastern, and the other into the western sea. And as the tide rises and ebbs every six hours with great vehemence, and affects these rivers throughout their course, it is the common opinion that they themselves are the two arms of the sea. This is the modern opinion. For Bede does not positively say so.

Wales is in the western part of the island, and wherever it is not surrounded by the sea, it is bounded by England; from which it is separated to the north, by a river called by these inhabitants Da (the Dee), and to the south by another named Offa.

All the rest, which comprises the most beautiful, the best, and the most fertile part of the whole island, is called England.

I should not have ventured to speak of Scotland, had I not, during my stay in London, fallen in with my very particular friend, the most worshipful Don Peter de Ayala, who had lived there for above a year, as ambassador from the Catholic Majesties of Spain to that Crown, and had by his prudence and dexterity, during the time of the residence of your Magnificence, contracted a solid peace between the most sapient Henry the Seventh, King of England, and the magnanimous James the Fourth, King of Scotland; for which service, as he related to your Lordship, he received at the end of four or five days from that most serene English king, 300 nobles, neither seen nor counted by him; as, if I remember right, your Magnificence said. And here I must mention, that if I should state anything concerning Scotland, which your Lordship should not believe on *my* report, I appeal to the authority of the aforesaid most worshipful Don Peter, from whom, by means of the friendship I formed with his Secretary, M. Passamonte, in London, I collected many particulars: and amongst others, that the kingdom of Scotland is very rainy; and that the country, wherever there are no mountains (which are of the most rugged description, and almost uninhabitable), is the most fertile of the whole island; that the royal family is so ancient, that there is no mention in history of any but the present race; and that the people are very handsome, and are divided into two classes, one of which inhabits the towns, and the other the country.

The inhabitants of the country are called the wild or savage Scots, not however from the rudeness of their manners, which are extremely courteous. The nobility reside on their estates, where they have generally great forests for hunting game. They have excellent houses, built for the most part, in the Italian manner, of hewn stone or brick, with magnificent rooms, halls, doors, galleries, chimneys, and windows. These savages are great soldiers, and when they go to war, the privilege of guarding the king's royal person belongs to them.

The other class is composed of citizens and burgesses, who are devoted to mercantile pursuits, and to the other useful and mechanical arts.

Don Peter also says that all the Scotch nation are extremely partial to foreigners, and very hospitable, and that they all consider that there is no higher duty in the world than to love and defend their crown. And that whenever the king is pleased to go to war, he can raise, without any prejudice to the country, 50, or 60,000 men, who, being suddenly called together, with their rich and handsome equipments, serve at their own expense for the space of 30 days; and if the war should continue beyond that time, they are dismissed, having previously been replaced by another force of equal magnitude; that any who are not summoned to take part in the war, would consider themselves to be slighted, and under the displeasure of the king; and that the population is so great, that, should a larger army be required, it could at any time be obtained. Don Peter himself told me that he had seen them several times in the field, and that he never saw anything better appointed. This power, however, is never exercised but against the English, their natural enemies, as is commonly the case with near neighbours. Although I have found frequent mention in the histories of England, of sundry Kings of Scotland having paid homage to some of the Kings of England, and notwithstanding that the Scotch do possess a particle of land (in England), *i.e.*, they have passed the limits of the two arms of the sea, before named, yet at this present time they do not think of paying any homage to the King of England; and I imagine that when this was the case, it was not

because that ferocious Scotch nation was ever in subjection
to the English, but because, when all the Danes were
expelled from England in the year of grace 943, by King
Edward, son of King Edward the Elder, excepting from that
part which borders upon Scotland, he, accounting that those
Danes who were already become northern English, were
indomitable, made over the whole of that territory *in
commendam* to Malcolm, King of Scotland, as though he
would give them into the power of a people still fiercer than
themselves; and it is probable, that he or his descendants
may have done homage to the King of England for this
portion of land, which was then occupied by the said Danes.[1]
But however this may be, all the English chroniclers insist
that their king is the supreme Lord of Scotland, and that
they have changed the Kings of Scotland at their pleasure;
and the Scotch, on the other hand, pride themselves on having
always repulsed the English, and on having once more
regained possession of their country. But to counterbalance
this, the English possess beyond the eastern arm of the sea,
named Tivida (the Tweed) in the kingdom of Scotland, the
singular fortress of Berwick, which, after having belonged
for a considerable time to each kingdom alternately, and at
length had fallen into the hands of the Scotch, was made
over to King Edward the Fourth, by the Duke of Albany,
who was at war with his brother, James the Third, King of
Scotland.[2] And now King Henry the Seventh has built a
magnificent bridge across the aforesaid arm of the sea,[3] and
as he has the command of all the eastern coast, he can throw
as many troops as he pleases into the town, which is a very
strong place both by nature and art. And as this Berwick
has caused the death of many thousand men in former times,
so it might do so again, were it not for the peace consolidated

---

[1] In 924 Constantine II. commended himself and his kingdom to Edward
the Elder, and chose him as "father and lord." On this compact subsequent
English kings based their overlordship of the Scots.   [2] Berwick was acquired
by England in 1482. The chronicle of Lanercost describes Berwick (in the
middle of the thirteenth century) as "a city so populous and of such trade,
that it might justly be called another Alexandria, whose riches were the sea,
and the waters its walls."   [3] Scott in his History of Berwick makes no mention
of this bridge. He only says that in 1513 there was "a decayed wooden one,"
which must have been built about the end of the fifteenth century (p. 411).

by means of the wise Don Peter de Ayala.[1]   Although the
English historians assert that Man, one of the Menanian
isles, as it was before said, belongs to the kingdom of Scotland, it is nevertheless in the possession of the King of
England.   But the King of Scotland is lord of all the
Orcades, several of which have been conquered by the
present king, who derives a great, or rather an incalculable
profit from them ; howbeit, the kingdom of Scotland is very
poor in comparison with England.   It has 15 bishopricks,
two of which are arch-bishopricks.

The language of the Scotch is the same as that of the
Irish, and very different from the English ; but many of the
Scotch people speak English extremely well, in consequence
of the intercourse they have with each other on the
borders.

[1] See p. 41 (above).

PEDER SWAVE

(1535).

PEDER SWAVE visited Scotland in 1535. The object of his visit was to gain the support of James V. for Christain II. against the citizens of Lubeck, who had cast off his authority. The following passage is translated from the Diary kept by Swave during his stay in the country. The greater part of the Diary is taken up with the account of his endeavours to effect the object of his embassy. The relation of his dealings with James and his ministers is extremely interesting, but is beside our present purpose. The Diary is written in Latin, and is contained in the third volume of State Papers from the archives of Copenhagen, edited by C. F. Wegener (Copenhagen, 1861-1865).[1]

DIARY OF PEDER SWAVE (p. 232).

ON the fifth day after our departure we sighted England, and on the seventh we approached the coasts of Scotland. We saw a fortified place, called Basth,[2] situated on an immense rock. There are found birds which the Scots call *gannets,* of white colour, but mixed with black, and in such multitudes that they could not be easily estimated. From the feathers and fishes which these birds carry on to the rock the commander of the fort is said to be able to collect an annual sum amounting to 400 gold (pieces). During the night we lay at anchor under a rock[3] at no great distance from it (Basth). On the 3rd of May we came to the town of Dondie. There we were forced to wait for four days, because the captain meant one of his crew to accompany us with letters of the emperor to the king. In order that we might remain in company we were necessarily forced to await him, and he could not depart

---

[1] I have to thank Sheriff Mackay for drawing my attention to Swave's Diary.   [2] The Bass Rock in the Firth of Forth.   [3] Probably the Isle of May.

for four days on account of the unloading of the ship.   On
the 7th of May we departed and reached the arm of the sea
that divides Edinburgh from Dondii.   On Sabbath at midday
we arrived at Edinburgh ; there we hired horses for the following day, as the king was occupied on the English border.

On the 9th of May towards evening we came to Treborch.[1]
On the 10th at midday we came to Jeduart.[2]   There I met
Master John Campbell, I told him that I was sent by
Christian, duke of Holstein, and had business with the
king's majesty ; I requested that he would inform the
king of my presence, and said that wherever the king
might wish to give me audience I should be prepared to
place my instructions before him.——On the 11th of May I
met with a hermit, named John Scott, a person of noble
rank, who had quitted a beautiful wife, and children, and
all his household, and determined to live by himself in
solitude.[3]   He ate nothing but bread, and drank nothing
save water or milk.   He is believed to have endured a fast
of forty days and nights in Scotland, England, and Italy.
He also says that, when impelled by a higher power, he
could not perish by fasting, as by the kindness of the Holy
Virgin he has already been able to prove ; if he should wish
to do this by way of wager or bargain that he would fail.
He declares that he has no sensation of hunger when he
fasts, that he loses neither his strength nor his flesh, feels
neither heat nor cold, goes about with head and feet naked
equally in summer and winter, and that his manner of life
does not induce the approaches of age.   Asked by me why
he left such a beautiful wife, he replied that he wished to
be a soldier of Heaven, and that whether his wife determined
to serve God or the world was a matter of indifference to
him.   By chance there was among us a canon regular who
said that he had been asked by the hermit's wife to reconcile
them, but had taken the task upon him to no purpose.——
I enquired if there were any trees in Scotland from which
birds were produced.   All replied that no doubt was
possible on the matter, that it was a fact they were so

---

[1] Dryburgh.   [2] Jedburgh.   [3] This fasting-man appears in Buchanan,
Pitscottie, and other early Scottish historians.   Buchanan devotes nearly a
page to Scott, who seems to have been exploited by the church as a modern
miracle (*Rerum Scoticarum Historia* (Edin., 1715), p. 272).

produced, that those which fell into the water became alive,
and that those which fell on the land had no principle of life,
that in the sap of the wood and even in the root the shapes
of birds are found carved out, so that they can be perfectly
distinguished, that the hinder parts are produced first, that
the young adhere to the tree till they come to maturity,
that the birds themselves do not bring forth, and that when
full grown they are delicate eating. There is a certain
floating island in Scotland, which deflects from one shore to
the other with the ebb and flow of the tide.[1] There is a
district with an area of eight square miles in which cocks
do not crow, whether born in the place or brought thither;
when removed both crow in the ordinary fashion. The bird
called the gannet lays no more than one egg, and hatches it
under its foot in a standing position. The wild Scots live
in the manner of the Scythians, they are ignorant of the use
of bread; when they are hungry they outstrip a stag in swiftness
of foot, overtake it and kill it, and so sustain life : they eat the
flesh raw, only squeezing out the blood. Not far from Edinburgh there is a mountain that constantly smokes like Etna.[2]
I saw it myself. In a monastery close by there is a spot
where oil flows out of the ground.[3] In Irish Scotland there
is an island where in summer the sun is seen night and day.

On the 12th of May I was conducted to the king who
was then at a monastery, very richly endowed, by name
Jemoers.[4] Its abbot is said to have an annual income of
1500 crowns. When mass was over I paid my respects to
the king whom I found standing not far from the altar. I
presented my letters, and was ordered to defer my business
till the king should be able to summon his councillors. I
requested that he would do this as early as possible, as I
had reason for expedition. I was ordered to give up any
other document I might have besides letters. I replied
that such documents as I had could not be given up unless
at a formal audience. I was told that the council would
meet in a few days, when I should have an opportunity of

[1] The floating island in Lochlomond, as will be seen, regularly appears as one
of the marvels of Scotland. [2] Possibly Swave may have seen the heather on fire
on some neighbouring hill, and some mischievous Scot have suggested the volcano. [3] Swave is thinking of the Balm Well of St Katherine de Sienna, famous
for its miraculous virtues in cases of skin disease. [4] Melrose Abbey.

saying what I wished. I returned to John Campbell to
Jeduart. Near Dondie there is an abbey round which
to a radius of six miles there is found an innumerable multitude of serpents of a perfectly innocuous character. When
hurt or wounded, they do no harm ; they have no stings.

Master Campbell told me that in the Abbey of Jemoers,
in which I paid my respects to the king, on the approaching
death of a monk, a few days before his death, the brethren
hear the ringing of a bell in their cells, whereupon they
hasten to confession, uncertain which of their number
insatiate death now makes his prey.[1] He showed me three
columns hewn out of jasper taller than myself, and a cubit
or more in thickness. He told me that these columns are
hewn in Scotland, and that jasper is. found among the
mountains. He also told me that in England there is a
noble family of the name of Constable, who once received a
grant of land from the Danes. Every year at Christmas
the eldest of the family is still in the habit of going northwards to the sea shore, and thrice calling aloud that if there
is any one who bears the name of the king of the Danes,
and desires his dues, that he is prepared to give them ; and
at length fixing a coin on the tip of an arrow he shoots it
with all his force into the sea. Campbell informed me that
when he was in England in Marmaduke Constable's house
on Christmas day, he himself saw this done. Marmaduke
told him that the conditions of his tenure required this
ceremony, and that if his family ceased to observe it they
would be deprived of their land. He also showed him the
deed, which contained the instruction. Dr Marmaduke
Constable told me the same story four years before, with
the variation that a rose and not a coin was shot into the sea,
and it was on John Baptist's Day and not on Christmas.[2] In
England a coin is paid for every house from which smoke
issues ; hence the English call the coina " rycks pennynck." [3]

---

[1] Major mentions this tradition regarding Melrose Abbey, *Hist. Maj. Brit.*,
lib. ii. cap. xii. [2] This story of the Constables is not noticed in Blount's
Tenures. [3] Smoke-silver or smoke-penny. A tribute paid to the ministers of
various parishes in continuance of Peter's pence. In the churchwarden's
Accounts of Minchinhampton under 1575, there is the following entry :—" To
the sumner for peterpence or smoke farthinges sometyme due to the Antecriste
of roome, x^d " (*Archæologia*, vol. xxxv. p. 430).

NICANDER NUCIUS

(1545).

NICANDER NUCIUS was a native of Corfu, who, having been exiled for some reason unknown to us, had settled in Venice.[1] Here he attached himself to Gerard Veltwick, a minister of the Emperor Charles V., in whose train he visited Constantinople, and other courts of Europe. In 1545, still as an attendant of Veltwick, he visited England. It is not known whether he also came to Scotland, but from certain expressions in his narrative we are led to believe that he did. His stay must, at all events, have been short, as his knowledge of the country is evidently of the most superficial kind. His remarks are interesting, indeed, not so much from what he has to communicate, as from the tone in which, as a Greek, he makes them.

Our extract is from the translation of the *Second Book of the Travels of Nicander Nucius of Corcyra*, published by the Camden Society in 1841. The manuscript from which it is edited was found in the Bodleian Library, and appears to have originally belonged to Archbishop Laud.

TRAVELS OF NICANDER NUCIUS.

THE island itself is divided into two parts. And that portion verging towards the continent is named England, and the cities in it English cities. But the western portion[2] is called Scotland. And there is a considerable river named the Tweed, and it separates England from Scotland. And England possesses its own king; and Scotland itself likewise appoints a king from among its own people. And ever as it were these kings, being inimical, perpetually fighting about the limits of their country, cruelly

[1] Corfu at this time belonged to Venice. [2] In Ptolemy's map of Britain Scotland is made to trend in an *easterly* direction from England.

destroy each other in a kind of barbarous and savage warfare. And on the banks of the Tweed certain forts have been built, for protection of the boundaries. And that portion of Scotland is somewhat northern, hence also cold; yet fruitful in wheat, and abounding in animals common with us; they have also cities renowned and large, where is the royal residence and government, no way inferior to that of England. And here also commercial transactions take place, and ships arrive from the continent. And towards the French they are friendly disposed; but they are most hostilely bent against the English. And being tributary to the English, they have often stirred up war, to free themselves from the tribute; but they have been unsuccessful, since the English kept them down by superior skill in war and force. For the Scotch are a more barbarous people in their manner of living than the English. But they possess a soil as favourable to fruit and corn as that of the English; since, being continuous, it is only divided by the river Tweed.

And the whole island is diversified with fruitful hills and plains, and abounds with marshes and well-timbered oak forests; it has moreover woods and lakes near the sea. For the greatest portion of the country of the Britons, laved continuously by the ebb and flow of the ocean, is marshy; from the exhalation and denseness of which the atmosphere throughout that portion appears for the most part misty. Whence, as the waters flow and ebb, it accumulates a certain slimy deposit, in maritime places, from which the exhalations are drawn. There are also fountains and springs of sweet water in great abundance. And it breeds in the marshes, of wild and carnivorous animals, bears and hogs, besides the wolf and the fox; and of graminivorous animals, stags and hares, and others of the same sort, also of such as are tame and domesticated with us, there are almost too many to be enumerated; so many horses, and those of noble breed too, and so many oxen, and so many flocks of sheep, that wonder arises in the beholders, on account of the multitude of them. Nor in truth is there any shepherd placed over the sheep to tend them, neither indeed a herdsman over the oxen; but wherever the animals may be whilst feeding, on the second perhaps, or even the third day, they return to their owner's house. Yet no one dares to steal any of them; since the extreme punishment of death awaits the perpetrator.[1] But that each man may know his own, they smear some mark on the skin with some native pitch.[2] Generally, also, they abound in butter and cheese and milk. And the horses are naturally swift-footed and very fleet, and for the more part white. But they are deficient in the breeds of asses and mules; for this latter animal is not produced in colder regions. Hence indeed, also, rarely do horns grow upon oxen and sheep. And they have generous hunting and house dogs, so that they frequently send these against bears and wild boars. Both morasses and oak forests favourable for hunting, abound throughout the island. They lack, however, the vine, which produces wine; also the olive-tree, and the fig-tree, and other trees indigenous to warmer climates; but of other cultured and fruit-bearing trees they possess an abundant supply. And marble and smooth rocks, such as those very solid ones with us, they have not; but certain porous and terreous stones; wherefore also they are easily obtained, and easily polished. But the stone used for fire and black, is found in most places. They are rich in mines of metals, and of metallic substances of all kinds; they have not, however, much gold, but very much silver, and of tin, and of what is called white lead, called also *stagōn* (stanno); and of common lead; and of liquid and terreous pitch; and, moreover, of sulphur and nitre in vast quantities, and in some districts, other fossils of the hotter kinds are excavated.

The island being such, lacks nothing of the things that are necessary and profitable, and useful to men. Nay, even things apparently scarce, are easily to be procured, and at little cost. And the length of the day in the summer season, in England, extends to nineteen hours; and that of the night reaches to five. And in Scotland, that of the day extends to twenty hours, and that of the night to four.

---

[1] The penalties of theft in Scotland were not so severe as in England (Innes, *Sketches of Early Scottish History*, p. 190). By an ancient Scottish law a man was not to be hanged for less than the price of two sheep; in England he was hanged for stealing one. [2] This was the regular custom of the monks, who were extensive sheep-owners. This brand or mark was called the *buist*.

And not only so, but neither is the night itself so dark as with us; but the night is of such a kind, as the twilight produced in the interval betwixt day and night, so that one often sees even the minutest objects. Such, indeed, is the case with the regions which are situated towards the west. And the reason of this is, the privation of the sun's ray from the northern parts. On this account these regions are also cold, as the warmth of the sun is present in a very limited measure; and from its distance, congelations and snows almost perpetually succeed each other. But the rains are not apt to be very impetuous, as the west wind disperses the watery clouds of the south and opposes their further progress.

JEAN DE BEAUGUÉ

(1548–1549).

A FTER the battle of Pinkie, 10th September 1547, most
of the strongholds in the Lowlands of Scotland
remained in the hands of the English; and the invasion of
Lord Grey in the following year seemed likely to complete
the conquest. As it was always the interest of France to
save Scotland from the English, an armed force was despatched
to the help of the Scots by the French king (Henry II.) in
1548, under the command of André de Montalembert, Sieur
d'Essé. In this expedition d'Essé was accompanied by his
personal friend Jean de Beaugué, who afterwards published
an account of the war under the title, *Histoire de la Guerre
d'Écosse pendant les campagnes* 1548 *et* 1549. Besides its
special interest as a painful chapter of Scottish history,
Beaugué's book has considerable value as a picture of the
methods of warfare followed by the three different nations.
In the course of his narrative, also, he occasionally digresses
to describe the places in which he was interested as a member
of the expedition. Unfortunately, it is but seldom he makes
such digressions, and when he does make them, he forgets
his usual garrulity, and thus defrauds us of what would have
been by far the most interesting portions of his history.

Beaugué's book was printed at Paris in 1556; and in 1707
an English translation was published by Dr Abercromby,
author of the *Martial Achievements of the Scots Nation.*
Abercromby, however, takes such liberties with his original
that Beaugué's history becomes half his own. In the translation given here the original has been as closely followed as
clearness would permit.[1] The edition from which the translation is made is that published by the Maitland Club in

---

[1] It should be said that Beaugué's archaic words and involved turns render
his meaning at times somewhat obscure.

1830.   Of Beaugué himself it should be said that nothing is known except what we learn from his own book.

The Scottish Mode of Warfare (*Histoire de la Guerre d'Écosse, par* Jean de Beaugué).

THE Scots never take the field unless great and extreme necessity drive them to arms.   And, as far as I could see, this is because when at war they are wont to live at their own expense, and cannot protract the war as is the habit with almost all the other nations of Europe.   They bring with them as much as they will need for the time they wish to remain in camp or be on the march, which is only a few days.   And during this time they seek to meet the enemy face to face, fighting with invincible obstinacy,— especially the English, by reason of the natural hatred which comes of neighbourhood, arising in my judgment from their ambition to be masters and their jealousy of the greatness of the English.   As soon as they have consumed their provisions, they break up the camp, or gradually withdraw, even though their designs are unaccomplished.

The Low Estate of the Scots.

But before I proceed further in my account of the war, it is necessary that I should state to what extremity the Scots were reduced, when their enemies, after having burned their towns, plundered all the low country, and possessed themselves of the best places along the whole frontier, held them so closely besieged that they dared not venture abroad except in very large companies :[1] of which companies the English made so light (for that false heresy of theirs makes a people believe that there is no nation equal to themselves) that about 500 horse, which might be the number of English then in Scotland, had even the audacity to gallop day and night to the gates of Edinburgh, thundering along all that tract of country, and holding in subjection all the adjacent district. This does not imply that the Scots are less warlike than the English, or any whit inferior to them ; but by reason of those

[1] This is no exaggeration of the state of Scotland after the invasions of the Earl of Hertford and Lord Grey.

leagues and bonds (partialitez) which exist among them, and their mutual distrust, they allowed the English not only to gain authority over them, but suffered themselves to be afflicted with a thousand kinds of tyrannies and oppressions. For, in my judgment, they were abandoned by God, who sometimes creates as ministers of his justice tyrants, barbarians, and the Turks themselves; as he permitted Cam Zoroast[1] to afflict the Italians, Nemroth the Babylonians, Sardanapalus the Persians and Arabs, Pharaoh the posterity of Abraham, Attila the French, and in recent memory, Mahumet Otthoman[2] the Greeks and Eastern Christians. And not without reason I say was God irritated against the Scots, for if they had known how to appease his anger, very difficult would it have been for the English to reduce them to the point at which I saw them. We must believe, therefore, that the just judgment of God permits that a people should suffer these misfortunes to afford them an exercise of faith and to make them recognise their faults; since when it comes to the last extremity, He declares His will to favour and sustain His own. So has it happened to the Scots: for from the day when the army of France set foot in Scotland, the good fortune of the English, which had long been their companion, began to leave them more and more. Then all at once she declared herself their enemy and turned her back upon them, as I shall show in going through the details of my history.

St Andrews.—St Andrews is situated on the seashore, and used to be one of the best towns in Scotland. It has the disadvantage of two drawbacks, however; neither its harbour nor its roads are safe, and it cannot be fortified because it is nearly as large as Thurin.[3] Moreover, there is no commodious place for a citadel, which would not risk much damage to the abbey, the seat of the archbishop of all the province of Fife, and a very large and beautiful structure. So true is this, that the castle, which formerly stood there, and was in great

---

[1] By Cam Zoroast, Beaugué doubtless meant Odoacer, whose name underwent extraordinary transformations during the Middle Ages. [2] Mohammed II., who took Constantinople from the Greek Christians in 1451. [3] Turin.

part destroyed by the late Prior of Capua,[1] was commanded not only by the said abbey, but even by the whole town.

PERTH.—As to St Johnston, it is a very pretty place, pleasant and well fitted to be the site of a good town, which might be rendered secure for its inhabitants by building a citadel where is now the church of the Holy Cross.[2]

ABERDEEN.—Aberdeen is a rich and handsome town, inhabited by an excellent people, and is situated on the sea-shore. It has not a good roadstead, but its harbour is very safe and easy for ships to make were it not for the entrance, which is narrow. It is easy to fortify since it is shut in on two sides by the rivers Don and Dee, both of which are difficult to ford. On the other side it has an open and extensive plain, in which bulwarks and defences could be raised to prevent injury from any battery that might be built on a hill which rises on the side of the bridge. At very little expense a citadel could be raised which might command both the harbour and the whole town. Aberdeen has an episcopal see and a university sufficiently well ordered and equipped.

MONTROSE.—As to Monrosts, it is a beautiful town situated in the County of Marne,[3] where the river Hacs[4] enters the sea. Its roadstead is not safe; but it has a very good harbour, easy of entrance and exit in all states of the tide. The town could be very easily fortified; but to avoid greater expense, a fort could be conveniently built which would command all ships that might enter or leave the river. For, as regards the fort which at present exists, it has not the commodity of water, and is so small that it has no space for the stowage of provisions, or for lodging men-at-arms. And besides the disadvantage of being built on moving sand and being

---

[1] In 1547 Leo Strozzi, Prior of Capua, with a French fleet, took the Castle of St Andrews, in which a number of persons discontented with the regency of the Earl of Arran (among them being John Knox and Sir David Lyndsay) had sought refuge after the murder of Cardinal Beaton (Laing's *Knox*, vol. i. pp. 185–6). [2] This is the Church of St John which still stands on the west side of John Street. It was formerly known as the Kirk of the Holy Cross of St John the Baptist. Tradition has it that it was built by the Picts. There is, at all events, conclusive evidence that it was a building of high pretensions in the twelfth and thirteenth centuries. This was the church that was spoiled by the "rascall multitude" (1559), after a sermon preached by John Knox. [3] The Mearns, though Montrose is not in that county. [4] The Esk.

constructed of dry turf, it is flanked on none of its sides, nor indeed can be from the nature of its situation.

DUNDEE.—Dundee is one of the finest towns in Scotland, is situated on the river Tay, and capable of being easily fortified.

DUNBAR.—Dombarre is situated on the seashore ten leagues distant from Edinburgh on the side of Lothian (*du coste de Lodient*), and in such an excellent tract of country, and accommodated with so many of the good things which profit the life of man, that if the town were enclosed with walls (since a harbour could easily be made and at little cost) we might reckon it among the most beautiful towns in the isles of the ocean. And as for its castle, it is a very hand-some and strong place built on a lofty rock on the edge of the sea, very difficult of approach, and on which so much art has been displayed, that few places are to be found any-where at the present time, which are by nature more com-modious, less exposed to battery, and all other methods of storming, than this castle, which, besides, is sufficiently near Ladres,[1] Douglas,[2] Edimton,[3] Esmons,[4] Fauxcastel, and on the road of Berraic, and Roussebroa,[5] in Scotland.

THE BASS ROCK.—The place where they made their first attempt was the Isle des Magots,[6] so called on account of the large white birds like swans that make their nests there. The Scots receive it as a fact that the hundred or hundred and twenty soldiers who form the ordinary garrison of the Castle of Bass, which is built on the island, live for the most part on nothing else than the fish daily carried thither by these birds; and burn no other wood than what these wild geese bring in spring to build their nests with, this being sufficient to last them for a whole year.[7] The position

---

[1] Lauder. [2] Dunglass. [3] Haddington. [4] Eyemouth. [5] Roxburgh. [6] The Bass. [7] We find this statement of Beaugué in several old Scottish writers; and even into the present century the construction of the nests of the solan goose has been matter of controversy. Some maintain that the use of sticks is merely accidental and not habitual, and that the usual materials are sea-weed and grass. In either case, the decomposed materials furnish fuel, but not in such quantity as the early writers affirmed. In truth, the solan goose and its habits greatly exercised the imagination of the Scottish people. We shall find it constantly reappearing in subsequent narratives as one of the marvels of the country.

of the castle is as follows :—The island on which the castle
is situated is an impregnable rock, of small extent, fashioned
by nature of an oval shape, with but one approach, and that
on the side of the castle, so very difficult that it can only
be gained by very little boats, each following the other, the
island being surrounded by rocks covered by the sea, which
none except those acquainted with the place can avoid. The
island is so little inviting and so uneven that till you come
to the castle wall itself you cannot plant the foot on level
ground; and this is so much the case that (as I have often
myself seen) when the captain's servants wished to enter, it
was necessary to throw down a thick rope to help them in
the ascent, and when they have reached the foot of the wall
with the utmost difficulty, a basket is let down in which
they are drawn up, and this is the only means of entering
that castle. There used to be a postern, but it is now
banked up and built in in an incredible manner, and
the rest of the castle is so constructed that it seems
to rise sheer from the sea ("qu'il semble etre dressé à
plomb "[1]).

THE ISLE OF MAY.—The Isle de May is of much
greater extent than the Isle Dieu,[2] possessing beautiful
fountains, quarries of coal and stone, and very good pasture.
And since it is pertinent to my purpose, I think I ought
not to omit to say that this island has ever been the
retreat of all pirates, who have sought to injure the
fisheries, trade, and armies of the Scots and their friends ;
and that a secure retreat for the whole country could
be prepared here, as a harbour could be constructed
at very little expense, which would easily contain thirty
or forty ships. For the rest, possessing as it does all
the advantages of which I have spoken, and being suitable
besides for gardens and fields, it could be fortified and

---

[1] Hector Boece has a lively description of the Bass, which may be
compared with that of Beaugué. "It is," says he, "ane wounderful
crag, risand within the sea, with so narrow and strait hals (passage) that no
schip nor boit may arrive bot allanerlie at ane part of it. This crag is callit
the Bas ; unwinnable by ingine of man. In it are caves, als profitable for
defence of man, as (if) they were biggit by crafty industry. Everything that
is in that crag is full of admiratioun and wounder" (Bellenden's *Boece*, vol. i.
p. 37).   [2] Inchkeith.

inhabited.[1] By so doing, the Scots and the strangers
who trade with them could sail wherever and whenever
they wished, without being forced to wait for winds
necessary before they can sail from Petit lict,[2] Brutilan,[3]
or the river Fort, which would be a convenience so profitable that all Scotland would be the better for it.

INCHKEITH.—Isle Dieu was so named by the Queen
Dowager[4] on the day it was recovered from the English : for
the French formerly called it *Isle aux Chevaux ;*[5] for it had
never been inhabited, as being a place of no account. Nevertheless, it has great natural advantages, and is of sufficient size
to be occupied and fortified, seeing it is well provided with
fresh water, and with ground suitable for gardens and pas-
turage, and with spots for salt-pans and harbours.   And from
its convenient quarries of coal and stones, which are found in
abundance there, lime could be made and large buildings
erected at little expense, at once as fortifications and
dwelling-houses.[6]   It is situated in the middle of the river
Fort (*sic*), which is five leagues wide, and so advantageously,
that it opens or closes the entrance to those who wish to
sail from the best part of Scotland to France.   It is so
difficult of access and so strong by nature, that there are
only three places suitable for a descent—namely, where the
sea, which enters the river Fort, is only a foot or a foot
and a half deep.   And even these approaches are so difficult by reason of the rocks, which the sea never covers,
that no vessel whatever can reach the shore ; but one is

---

[1] The prevailing rock in the Isle of May is greenstone. Before the middle of
the twelfth century, David I. founded a monastery on the island, and granted
it to the Benedictine Abbey of Reading in Berkshire on condition that they
should maintain twelve priests therein to say mass for himself and his predecessors and successors.   In 1318 all the rights of the Priory of May were
transferred to the Canons of St Andrews.   In 1881 there were three houses
on the island, and twenty-two inhabitants (*Ordnance Gazetteer of Scotland*).
[2] Leith.   [3] Burntisland.   [4] The widow of James V. and mother of Mary
Queen of Scots.   [5] So called because the Scots placed their horses there to be
safe from the English.   [6] "The geology of Inchkeith is highly interesting. . . . . . Five-sixths or more of the island are great sheets of igneous
rocks, between which are thinner bands of sedimentary deposits ; including
shales, two thin seams of coal, some highly calcareous shales, and at least
one band of limestone" (*Ordnance Gazetteer*, edited by F. Hindes Groome, a
book of the highest value to the student of Scottish history and topography).

forced to descend on the rocks, and by leaping from one to
the other so gain the shore; unless, indeed, you prefer to
throw yourself into the water, in which case there is the
risk of falling into deep and narrow pools (which are
found among these rocks two or three fathoms' distance
from the island), if the foot should fail to choose these
usually covered by the sea.   On all other sides, the rock is
precipitous except on the west, where the rock is cut by
nature into steps of more than twenty fathoms high, by all
of which, descent is impossible.   Thus, the island is very
strong and well-situated.   For, besides those difficulties
which it offers to an enemy, the roads, which lead to the
shore of the island, are so narrow, tortuous, and painful,
that only with great difficulty could three men go abreast :
all of which roads, moreover, are commanded from the
summit, on which the English constructed a square fortalice,
rendering it capable of defence, in less than fifteen days.[1]

[1] Inchkeith has been noticed by more distinguished persons than Beaugué.
When Dr Johnson was in Scotland, he insisted on being taken to Inchkeith.
The place seems to have taken his fancy.   "I'd have this island," he
exclaimed ;   "I'd build a house, make a good landing-place, have a garden and
vines, and all sorts of trees.   A rich man of a hospitable turn here would
have many visitors from Edinburgh."   Carlyle and Edward Irving also visited
the island, of which the former has given a vivid account in his "Reminis-
cences."

ESTIENNE PERLIN.

(1551–1552).

ALL that we know of Estienne Perlin is that he was an ecclesiastic, that he wrote the book from which the following extract is taken, and also another in Latin, written he says, " d'un hault stille et d'un labeur non pareil, tractant du corps humain et de plusieurs sortes de maladies comme des fiebures tierces, quatres, quotidianes, continues, diares, hectiques, maramosdes, apoplepsies, peripelominies, letargies, spasmes, sincopes, ptisies, catharres, pestes, jaundices, et autres diverses maladies : et des situations des parties nobles du corps humain, avec plusieurs autres affaires dessus le faict de medecine." The book with which we are here concerned is more simply entitled, " Description des Royaulmes d'Angleterre et d'Escosse, composè par Estienne Perlin." It was published in Paris in 1558, and dedicated in a grandiloquent preface [1] to Marguerite, Duchesse de Berri, the sister of Henry II. A reprint of it was also published by W. Bower and J. Nichols at London in 1775, and a translation is given in the fourth volume of *The Antiquarian Repertory*. As this translation is in every respect a satisfactory one, it has been reproduced here.

From his own narrative we gather that Perlin's visit to Britain must have been made during the last two years of the reign of Edward VI. He resided chiefly in England, and of the thirty-seven pages which comprise his account of the two countries he has devoted only twelve to Scotland. In Perlin's narrative we have vivid illustration of that bitterness of feeling between England and France, which was the inheritance of the prolonged struggle between the two countries. As his translator says, " the author seems to

---

[1] It is in this dedication that the above portentous description of his Latin work appears.

have imbibed every national prejudice which ought to have been excluded from the mind of a traveller." A single sentence will show in what spirit he wrote of England. " One may say of the English," he writes, " that they are neither valiant in war nor faithful in peace ! " In view of the relations between Scotland and France, it was natural that he should speak more kindly of the Scots; and this, as will be seen, he actually does. At the same time, it is rather as the allies of France than from any merits of their own that they are honoured by his approval. Altogether, the narrative of this ecclesiastic, both in style and matter, compares ill with that of the soldier Jean de Beaugué.

DESCRIPTION DES ROYAULMES D'ANGLETERRE ET D'ESCOSSE
(*Antiquarian Repertory*, vol. iv.).

HAVING before spoken of England, my Sovereign Princess, with all possible truth and exactness, it at present remains to touch lightly on the kingdom of Scotland. Scotland is a kingdom beyond England, and is very cold and septentrional, that is to say, approaching the north, and still colder than England, for the farther one goes beyond the seas, tending towards the kingdom of d'Anemark [1] and Suest, otherwise barbarously called Sueden, the colder it is ; for in those kingdoms the cold would even split a stone. Scotland is one of the parts of the Greater Britain, which Britain is divided in two parts, that is, into England and Scotland, insomuch that these two kingdoms were formerly but one; but having been divided by war, which was done by two brothers,[2] England, which is the greater part, fell to one ; the lesser and worse part of Greater Britain, which is Scotland, fell to the other. To estimate the difference between these two, let us suppose that England is Paris, and Scotland the suburbs of Saint Marceau ; as that city is preferable to the suburbs, so in like manner is England preferable to Scotland, to which it bears no comparison. They are separated from each other only by a small river. It is

---

[1] See page 59 (above). [2] According to Geoffrey of Monmouth, King Brute divided his dominions among his three sons, assigning Loegria (England) to Locrine, Albania (Scotland) to Albanact, and Cambria (Wales) to Camber.

to be understood, that the kings of England and Scotland
are descended from the same house; but as the custom is, for
the great to endeavour to devour the small, so the rapacious
kings of England, not content with their own limits, have
endeavoured to invade and conquer the country of their
neighbours and allies, insomuch that they have exerted themselves to ravage, burn, and ruin the kings of Scotland and
this kingdom.

The Scots speak like the English, or at least there is
not a greater difference than between the speech of the
Normans and that of the Picards. The country is but poor
in gold and silver, but plentiful in provisions, which are as
cheap as in any part of the world; and truly the milors of
that country, and the *gentillemans* (that is to say, the gentry),
labourers, and tradesmen, who have any money, may live
very comfortably. The arable lands of that country are but
indifferent, and the greatest part of the country is a desert.
As to the size of the kingdom, you must understand it is of
a great compass; but with respect to habitable lands, it
may be styled small, that is to say, there is much bad and
wild uncultivated land; the country is likewise small with
respect to the size of its cities and villages.

The Scots have always been allied to the Crown of France,
and have always been faithful to the noble *fleur de lis*,
insomuch that they have been hitherto preserved from
their ancient enemy, who is worse than a dragon, serpent,
crocodile, or asp; and without the assistance of the kings of
France, their country would have been lost, and fallen into
the hands of the English. The kings of France never
abandoned their friends in distress, for once the English
took many of their places and burned much of their country,
but they had succour and assistance from the French, who
with great diligence drove the English out of Scotland like
mutineers and villains, where the said Scots showed themselves as bold and courageous as lions, at which time there
was a great defeat of the enemy.[1] On this point it is to be

---

[1] Perlin must here refer to the campaigns of the Sieur d'Essé, which are
recorded by the Sieur Beaugué in the historical sketch from which the preceding
extract is taken. By the aid of the French on that occasion the English were
forced to evacuate Scotland (April 1550).

observed, that if thirty thousand French should enter England through Scotland, they might soon conquer and overrun the whole country: this is certain; but the English always keep up an alliance with the emperor, otherwise both they and their country would soon be reduced to dust. Since that time, the noble and valiant King of France has caused several fortresses to be built in Scotland, and repaired others,[1] for the safeguard and defence of that country, which has cost an immense sum of money, but the said kingdom of Scotland serves him as a buckler against his enemies, and a means for conquering England.

It is to be understood, that within these fifty years it is nearly doubled, and is worth six times its former value;[2] and since Madame the Dowager of Scotland has been married to the King of Scotland, she has caused several estates to be tilled and cultivated, which before were of no great estimation, and has rendered the uncultivated part of the country much better than it was before, insomuch that throughout the kingdom the lands are rendered tolerable, as I leave the world to imagine. The style of the queen is thus proclaimed in Scotch, *Marie Stouart of grace lorde god the quinne Scottellement*, that is to say in French, Mary Stouart, by the grace of God, Queen of Scotland.

They are of person, bold and gallant enough, but are not so well armed as the French, for they have very little well-made, clean, and polished armour, but use jackets of mail in exercising daily with the French, and have the custom of using little ambling nags and small horses; their lances are small and narrow, and they have scarce any large horses, and few are brought to them, except from France. Their houses are badly built and proportioned, at least those of the common people. They have plenty of cows and calves, on which account their flesh is cheap; and in my time bread was tolerably cheap. In this place there are no vines, and wine is very dear; but the Scots drink beer, *godalles* and *alles*, with a quantity of milk.

---

[1] During the regency of Mary of Lorraine (1554–9).   [2] It is, perhaps, needless to say that this statement is in flat contradiction to all the historians, who tell us that from Flodden till the Union of the Crowns in 1603 Scotland retrograded rather than progressed.

In this kingdom there are twelve bishoprics, with an archbishopric called St Andrews, where there is a castle. Their capital city is called in Scotch, Ennebroc, in French, Lislebourg,[1] which is about the size of Pontoise, and not bigger, having been formerly burned by the English.[2] Here are some other seaports, as Dumbars, Domberterand,[3] and other little cities and towns. Their regent is named Madame de Longeville,[4] a lady of honour, born of an ancient house, that is to say, of the house of Gaudefroy de Baillon, King of Hierusalem and Cicile and Duke of Lorrain, one of the most valiant families in the world, without depreciating any other. This country, although it is in a bad neighbourhood, being near a haughty, treacherous, and proud enemy, has nevertheless sustained itself in a manly sort by the means and assistance of the most noble King of France, who has many times let the English know what were the consequences of the anger of so great a monarch and emperor. But, thanks to God, the affairs of this country have been regulated, and everything goes on well, and for their benefit and that of their kingdom.[5] How happy oughtest thou to esteem thyself, O kingdom of Scotland, to be favoured, fed, and maintained, like an infant, on the breast of the most puissant and magnanimous King of France, the greatest lord in the whole world, and future monarch of that round machine, for without him thou would'st have been laid in ashes, thy country wasted and ruined by the English, utterly accursed by God! Thou knowest well if I lie. He helpeth thee with gold, silver, and garrisons, and affords thee succour of every sort, and loves thee like his own.

In this country there is much broom, and the people do not warm themselves with wood, but with coals. A merchant in this country is well esteemed who has an annual

---

[1] Lislebourg is the name by which French writers of the sixteenth century designate Edinburgh. As having lakes both on its north and south sides, the town was almost literally an island. [2] Edinburgh had been burnt by the Earl of Hertford in 1544. The burning lasted three days. [3] Dumbarton. [4] When James V. married Mary of Guise, she was the widow of the Duc de Longueville. [5] Till the beginning of 1559 the government of the queen-regent was generally acceptable to the county. In that year, however, her policy began to be directly inspired by the interests of her relatives, the Guises, and eventually led to misunderstandings with the Protestant section of her subjects.

rent of four hundred livres, and is among the richest men
of the country, which is far from having twelve or fifteen
thousand livres per annum, as is often the case in France,
Flanders, Germany, Spain, Portugal, and England.   The
richest man in Scotland, at the time I was there, was the
Archbishop of St Andrews.[1]

The bishoprics of this country, as I understand, are but
small; one ought however to praise their fidelity and firm
attachment to the French, by the assistance of which all
England may be undermined and burned.   One thing I find
reprehensive among the Scotch, which is that it is difficult
to obtain a lodging from them.   If you say to an ordinary
sort of man in Scotch, *Guede guednit goud maistre praie qui
mi longini,* which is to say in our language, " Good night, my
master, I pray you to give me a lodging; " they will answer
you haughtily in their tongue, *est est no bet,* which is to say,
there is no bed; and will not vouchsafe to lodge you, unless
they expect a considerable recompense.   However, some are
more compassionate and humane, there being here, as in
other countries, both good and bad.   There is but one duchy
in this country, which is called the duchy of Hampton;[2] there
are many small counties.   They carry bucklers like the
English, and use the bow, and in other respects live like
them, except that they are not so great dealers and tradesmen, and have not, as every one knows, such weighty purses;
in other points they do not differ from the English, either in
dress, conditions, and stature.   The then Admiral of France
was called Milor Boduet,[3] and the King's Lieutenant,
Monsieur Dozay,[4] who was the Governor of the French, and
a man faithful even to death; and the Dowager of Scotland
has the government of the Scots.   They administer justice

---

[1] John Hamilton, natural son of James, first Earl of Arran.   He succeeded
Cardinal Beaton as Primate of Scotland.   [2] The Duke of Châtelherault must be
meant.   He was the head of the Hamilton family, and was made duke in 1544.
[3] *Boduct* is undoubtedly a misprint for *Boduel,* the French form of Bothwell.
The Bothwell meant is the notorious James, Earl of Bothwell, subsequently
husband of Queen Mary.   He was High Admiral of Scotland, the office having
been conferred on his ancester Patrick, Earl of Bothwell, by James IV.
[4] Dozay is probably d'Oysel, Oysel, or Dosell, as his name variously appears.
He was French ambassador in Scotland during the regency of Mary of Lorraine,
and was one of her chief advisers.   Knox describes him as " Lieutenant for
France " (*Works,* vol. i. p. 255, Laing's edit.).

very uprightly, according to their customs, and receive money from France.

In this country (as I have seen it practised) a man who is possessed of an hundred golden, or sun crowns, will lend them to a merchant, for which the merchant will maintain him a whole year in his house, and at his own table, and at the end of the year will return him his money.[1]　All the cities and places of this kingdom are small, except St Andrews, which is pretty large.　The Scotch who apply themselves to letters, become good philosophers and authors. I knew formerly at Paris two doctors of divinity who were the most learned that were to be met with, and principally in philosophy; they had all the books of Aristotle at their fingers' ends; one was called Master Simon Saneson,[2] living at the College of Sorbonne, and the other Monsieur Cranston,[3] who had been rector: they are both now bishops in Scotland, and in great reputation and honour, and augment and amplify the kingdom by their honour and virtue.　The arms of Scotland are a lion, sprinkled with *fleurs de lis.*　The kings of this country choose to be without guards, and their subjects are bound to go to the wars at their own charge and expense, whenever they are commanded.　On the death of the King Stouart,[4] the crown came to his noble daughter, who is at present married to Monsieur the Dauphin; and although there are many kings and queens richer than the Queen of Scotland, she is nevertheless well allied and related, being not only related to princes, but also to kings and queens, particularly to the Queen of England and the King of d'Annemarc,[5] insomuch that in default of heirs, she may lineally, and of right, succeed to the crowns of both kingdoms; and I do not know whether I might not venture to say that the kingdom of England belongs to her at present,

---

[1] *Cf.* what Fynes Moryson, our next traveller, says (p. 81).　[2] Simon Simson, a doctor of the Sorbonne, flourished *anno* 1585 ; he is mentioned by Dempster and Sir George Mackenzie.　[3] David Cranston, a notable Scotsman in the schools of Paris.　He was regent of Arts in Montaigu College, with which so many Scotsmen were associated, and afterwards Doctor of Theology. He died in 1526.　Neither Simson nor Cranston became bishops.　At least, their names do not appear in Keith's *Catalogue of the Scottish Bishops.* [4] James V.　[5] James III., Mary's great grandfather, married Margaret, Princess of Denmark, in 1409.

without speaking at random, as knowing a secret from those
who have much frequented England.   It is to be noted, that
the house of Scotland is a most noble house and lineage ;
and it ought likewise to be known, that the crown has for
three or four hundred years remained in the family of the
Queen of Scotland,[1] bearing her name, by which it may be
understood, that it is one of the most ancient royal houses
in the world.   And forasmuch as the kingdom of Scotland
ought to be extremely happy in its alliance with France, so
should we Frenchmen be glad to have the alliance, affinity,
and friendship of the said Scots, for from Scotland we may
repulse the English, and from thence enter easily into their
country, which gives no great odds against them, and thus
enables us to curb and check them.   Monsieur de Termes [2]
was formerly in Scotland, where he performed many great
acts of prowess and valour, and, with an army of some few
French and Germans, restored peace and tranquility to that
whole kingdom, and drove the English out of Scotland, where
they had taken seven or eight places from the Scots, and but
for this relief would have made themselves masters of all the
kingdom ; and this gallant Seigneur de Termes, for counsel
and judgment another Hannibal and Cato, retook Tinton,[3]
Quincornes,[4] and *Lisle aux Chevaux,*[5] and other towns and
fortresses, and gave battle to the English, and in a succession
of time quitted the whole kingdom.   It is to be remarked,
that in this kingdom of Scotland there are many towns, as
Dombarres, Dombertrant, Thinton, Quincornes, Lisle aux
Chevaux, Lislebourg, otherwise called Ennebroc, Sainct
Andrè, and many other little towns and castles.

It is to be noted, that nothing is scarce here but money.
Wine is brought them from Bordeaux and Rochelle ; and it
must be understood, that the Scots do not pay for the wine
they buy from the people of Bordeaux, but in lieu thereof

---

[1] Robert II. was the first of the Stewarts who sat on the throne.   His reign
began in 1371.   As will be seen from the accounts that follow, the royal
family of Scotland was regarded on the Continent as the oldest in Europe.
This belief is to be attributed to the ingenious audacity of the Scottish historians.   [2] De Thermes, with a reinforcement of 1000 foot and 300 horse from
France, effectually aided d'Essé in driving the English out of Scotland in the
campaigns 1548-50.   [3] Tantallon Castle ?   [4] Kinghorn.   [5] Inchkeith (see
p. 69).

give them other merchandise.   In their country they have barley, plenty of peas and beans.   In my time the poor people put their dough between two irons to make it into bread, and then made it what is esteemed good food in that country.   In this place there are many churches highly ornamented, and plenty of monasteries, in which there are plenty of religions; and it is to be noted, that the ecclesiastics are richer than the housekeepers or nobles.   Wherefore my most esteemed Princess, I shall put an end to this little tract of Scotland, which I have delineated as accurately as I could; and no one ought to be offended that I have said that money is scarce in this kingdom, nor need any one be scandalised thereat, as it behoves an historian to follow truth, and not to lie in anything, but to describe things as they are, without change or alteration: in like manner as if a man in describing France should say it was a bad country, would deserve to be put in a sack and thrown into the water, as was very properly done by Julius Cæsar, who himself described the wars, and when he could not take a town or castle, declared the resistance which he had met with, and that exactly, without addition.   This little country is useful and necessary to us, as much so as the richest.   And it is to be noted in concluding, that in this region the gentlemen take codfish and salmon in their moats.   Also it is to be noted, that there are some savages in some of the counties of Scotland, but that from day to day the country strengthens and amends, and is in a daily state of improvement.

FYNES MORYSON

(1598).

FYNES MORYSON gives the following account of himself:—" Being a student of *Peter-house* in *Cambridge*, and entered the eighteenth yeere of my age, I tooke the degree of Bachelor of Arts, and shortly after was chosen Fellow of the said Colledge by Queene *Elizabeths* Mandat. Three yeers expired from my first degree taken in the Universitie I commenced Master of Arts, and within a yeere after, by the favour of the Master and Fellowes, I was chosen to a vacant place of priviledge to studie the Civill Lawes. Then, as well for the ornament of this profession, as out of my innated desire to gaine experience by travelling into forraigne parts, (to which course my parents had given consent some few yeers past, upon my first declaring of my inclination to the said profession,) upon the priviledge of our Statutes permitting two of the Society to travell, I obtained licence to that purpose of the said Master and Fellowes, in the yeere 1589, being then full 23 yeeres old. And presently leaving the University, I went to *London*, there to follow some studies fit to inable me in this course; and there better taught, and these studies, the visiting of my friends in the country, my going to *Oxford* to take the same degree I had in Cambridge, and some oppositions upon new deliberation made by my father and friends against my journey, detained me longer in those parts than I purposed."

The title of Moryson's book of travels, published at London in 1617, will indicate the extent of his journeyings, and the weight that is due to his remarks on Scotland. It is as follows:—" An Itinerary written by Fynes Moryson, gent. First in the Latin tongue and then translated by him into English: containing his ten yeeres' travell through the twelve Dominions of Germany, Bohemerland, Sweitzerland, Netherland, Denmarke, Poland, Italy, France, England, Scotland and Ireland."

Moryson thus describes his own book:—"Touching the work in generall, I wil truly say, that I wrote it swiftly, and yet slowly. This may seeme a strange riddle, and not to racke your wit with the interpretation, myselfe will expound it: I wrote it swiftly, in that my pen was ready and nothing curious, as may appeare by the matter and style; and I wrote it slowly, in respect of the long time past since I viewed these dominions, and since I tooke this worke in hand. So as the worke may not unfitly be compared to a nose-gay of flowers, hastily snatched in many gardens, and with much leasure, yet carelessly and negligently bound together."

FYNES MORYSON'S ITINERARY (Part i. book iii. chap. 5).

MYSELF upon occasion of businesse in the month of Aprill, and the yeere 1598, tooke a journey to these said confines, namely, to *Barwick*, a Towne then very strongly fortified by the English, to restrain the sudden incursions of the Scots, and abounding with all things necessary for food, yea with many dainties, as salmons and all kinds of sheil-fish, so plentifully, as they were sold for very small prices. And here I found that for the lending of sixtie pound, there wanted not good citizens, who would give the lender a faire chamber and a good dyet, as long as he would lend them the mony.[1] Being to return from *Barwicke*, I had an earnest desire, first, to see the King of Scots Court. So from hence I rode in one day fortie[2] miles to *Edenborrow* the chiefe Citie of that kingdome. And in this said daies journey after foure miles riding I came to *Aton*,[3] a village where the Lord of *Humes* dwelles, whose family was powerfull in those parts. After sixteene miles more I came to *Dunbar*, which they said to have been of old, a Towne of some importance, but then it lay ruined, and seemed of little moment, as well for the povertie, as the small number of inhabitants.[4] After the

---

[1] *Cf.* Perlin, p. 77, above.   [2] We leave the reader to correct Moryson's measurements.   [3] Ayton.   [4] Macky, who travelled in Scotland rather more than a century after Moryson, gives a more favourable picture of Dunbar (see his *A Journey through Scotland* (London, 1723), p. 26).

riding of eight miles more, on the left hand towards the West, and something out of the highway, the pleasant Village *Hadirington* lay, which the English, in the raigne of Queene *Elizabeth*, tooke, and kept against the French,[1] who drawne over in the time of faction, kept the Towne of *Dunbar*, and fortified the same.   When I had ridden five miles further, I came to the ancient and (according to the building of that Kingdome) stately Pallace of the L. *Seton*[2] beautified with faire Orchards and Gardens, and for that clime pleasant.   Not farre thence lyes the Village *Prestongraung*, belonging to the Family of the *Cars* powerfull from these parts to the very borders of *England* within land.   After I had ridden three miles more, I came to the Village *Fisheruwe*, neere which beyond a Brooke lyes the Village *Musselborrow* in a stony soyle, famous for a great Victorie of the English against the Scots.[3]   On the left hand towards the West, and something out of the highway, the Queene of Scots[4] then kept her Court (in the absence of the King) at the Village *Dawkeith*, in a Pallace belonging to the Earle of *Murray*.[5]

From the said Village *Fishrawe*, I rode the rest of the way, being four miles, and so in one dayes journey (as I said) came to *Edenborrow*, seated in Lodoney[6] (of old called Pictland), the most civill Region of *Scotland*, being hilly and fruitfull of corne, but having little or no wood.   This City is the seat of the King of *Scotland*, and the Courts of Justice are held in the same.   Of old, according to the changeable fortune of warre, it was sometimes in the possession of the Scots, sometimes of the English inhabiting this Easterne part of *Scotland*, till the English Kingdome being shaken with the invasions of the Danes, at last about the yeere 960 it became wholly in the power of the Scots. This City is high seated, in a fruitfull soyle, and wholesome

---

[1] A full account of the siege of Haddington and the French expedition is given by the Sire de Beaugué, from whom extracts have been given above. Moryson should have told that the French forced the English to evacuate Haddington (1548–50).   [2] For a more detailed account of Seton Castle, see Macky, *A Journey through Scotland*, pp. 39–40. This palace or castle was built at different periods, and during the sixteenth and seventeenth centuries was regarded as the most magnificent structure of the kind in Scotland.   It was eventually pulled down in 1790 (*Ordnance Gazetteer of Scotland*).   [3] The battle of Pinkie (1547).   [4] Anne of Denmark.   [5] This should, of course, be the Earl of Morton.   [6] Lothian (Laudonia).

aire, and is adorned with many Noblemens Towers lying about it,[1] and aboundeth with many springs of sweet waters At the end towards the East, is the Kings Pallace joyning to the Monastery of the Holy Crosse, which King *David* the first built, over which, in a Parke of Hares, Conies, and Deare, an high mountaine hangs, called the chaire of *Arthur* (of *Arthur* the Prince of the Britanes, whose monuments, famous among all Ballad-makers, are for the most part to be found on these borders of *England* and *Scotland*). From the Kings Pallace at the East, the City still riseth higher and higher towards the West, and consists especially of one broad and very faire street[2] (which is the greatest part and sole ornament thereof), the rest of the side streetes and allies being of poore building and inhabited with very poore people, and this length from the East to the West is about a mile, whereas the bredth of the City from the North to the South is narrow, and cannot be halfe a mile. At the farthest end towards the West, is a very strong Castle, which the Scots hold unexpugnable. *Camden* saith this Castle was of old called by the Britaines, *Castle meyned agned*, by the Scots; the Castle of the Maids or Virgines (of certaine Virgines kept there for the Kings of the Picts), and by *Ptolemy the* winged Castle.[3] And from this Castle towards the West, is a most steepe Rocke pointed on the highest top, out of which this Castle is cut: But on the North and South sides without the wals, lie plaine and fruitfull fields of Corne. In the midst of the foresaid faire streete, the Cathedrall Church[4] is built, which is large and lightsome, but little stately for the building, and nothing at all for the beauty and ornament. In this Church the Kings seate is built some few staires high of wood, and leaning upon the pillar next to the Pulpit: And opposite to the same is another seat very like it, in which the incontinent use to stand and doe

---

[1] The number of noblemen's seats round Edinburgh seems to have struck other travellers besides Moryson (see p. 93, below). [2] High Street and Canongate. [3] "It is unnecessary," says Sir Daniel Wilson in his *Memorials of Edinburgh*, "to follow the fanciful disquisitions of zealous antiquaries respecting the origin and etymology of Edinburgh, it has been successively derived both in origin and name from Saxon, Pict, and Gael; and in each case, with sufficient ingenuity, only to leave the subject more deeply involved than at first" (p. 1, edit. 1872). [4] The church of St Giles.

pennance; and some few weekes past, a Gentleman, being a stranger, and taking it for a place whereir Men of better quality used to sit, boldly entred the same in Sermon time, till he was driven away with the profuse laughter of the common sort, to the disturbance of the whole Congregation. The houses are built of unpolished stone, and in the faire streete good part of them is of freestone, which in that broade streete would make a faire shew, but that the outsides of them are faced with wooden galleries, built upon the second story of the houses; yet these galleries give the owners a faire and pleasant prospect, into the said faire and broad street, when they sit or stand in the same. The wals of the City are built of little and unpolished stones, and seeme ancient, but are very narrow, and in some places exceeding low, in other, ruined.[1]

From *Edenborow* there is a ditch of waters (yet not running from the inland, but rising of springs) which is carried to *Lethe*, and so to the Sea. *Lethe* is seated upon a creek of the Sea, called the *Frith*, some mile from *Edenborow*, and hath a most commodious and large Haven. When *Monsieur Dessy* a *Frenchman*, did fortifie *Lethe* for the strength of *Edenborow*, it began of a bare Village to grow to a Towne.[2]   And when the French King *Francis* the second

---

[1] In 1450 Edinburgh was first enclosed by walls, remains of which still exist. After the battle of Flodden in 1513 the town, having overleapt the original wall, was enclosed by another of greater strength and extent. In 1591, seven years before Moryson's visit, the citizens were empowered by Parliament to collect money for the purpose of raising and strengthening the walls. It would seem from Moryson's account that this last intention was not carried out (Wilson, *Memorials of Edinburgh*).   [2] Knox in his *History of the Reformation* has the following passage relative to Leith at the period to which Moryson here refers :—" It is not unknowin to the maist pairt of this realme, that thair hes bene ane auld haitrent and contentioun betuix Edinburght and Leith ; Edinburgh seeking continewallie to possess that liberty, quhilk be donatioun of kyngis they have lang enjoyit ; and Leith, be the contrary, aspyring to ane libertie and fredome in prejudice of Edinburgh. The Queene Regent was nott ignorant how to compass hir owin matter, and thairfor secretlie sche gaif adverteisment to sum of Leith, that sche wald mak their Toun fre, gif that sche mycht do it with any cullour of justice." "Declaratioun of the Lordis " (Laing's *Knox*, vol. i. p. 426). The death of the queen-regent forestalled her erecting Leith into a royal burgh, and the citizens of Edinburgh afterwards obtained the superiority of the town for 10,000 marks. Leith never afterwards, however, lost the importance it had acquired during the siege of 1559–1560.

had married *Mary* Queene of the *Scots*: againe the *French*
(who now had in hope devoured the possession of that Kingdome, and in the yeere 1560, began to aime at the conquest
of *England*) more strongly fortified this Towne of *Lethe*:
but *Elizabeth* Queene of *England*, called to the succour of
the Lords of *Scotland* against these Frenchmen, called in by
the Queene, soone effected that the French returned into
their Country, and these fortifications were demolished.

From *Leth* I crossed over the *Frith* (which ebs and flows
as high as *Struelin*[1]) to the Village *King-horn*, being eight
miles distant, and seated in the Region or Country called
Fife, which is a Peninsule, that is, almost an Iland, lying
betweene two creekes of the Sea, called *Frith* and *Taye*, and
the Land yeelds corne and pasture and sea coales, as the
Seas no lesse plentifully yeeld (among other fish) store of
oysters and shel fishes, and this Countrey is populous, and
full of Noblemens and Gentlemens dwellings commonly
compassed with little groves, though trees are so rare in
those parts, as I remember not to have seene one wood.

From the said Village *King-horn*, I rode ten very long
miles to Falkeland then the Kings House for hunting, but
of old belonging to the Earles of *Fife*, where I did gladly see
James the sixth King of the Scots, at that time lying there
to follow the pastimes of hunting and hawking, for which
this ground is much commended; but the Pallace was of old
building and almost ready to fall, having nothing in it
remarkeable.[2] I thought to have ridden from hence to Saint
Andrewes a City, seated in *Fife*, and well known as an
University, and the seate of the Archbishop. But this
journey being hindered, I wil onely say, that the Bishop of
Saint *Andrewes*, at the intercession of the King of *Scotland*,
James the third, was by the Pope first made Primate of all
Scotland, the same Bishop and all other Bishops of that
Kingdome having formerly to that day beene consecrated
and confirmed by the Archbishop of *Yorke* in *England*.[3]
Likewise I purposed to take my journey as farre as *Strivelin*,[4]

---

[1] Stirling.   [2] It had been built by James V. who died there.   [3] St Andrews
was erected into an archbishopric by a bull of Sixtus IV., obtained by Patrick
Graham, the successor of Bishop Kennedy in the see of St Andrews. The superiority of York had always been contested by the Scottish church.   [4] Stirling.

where the King of the Scots hath a strong Castle, built upon the front of a steepe Rocke, which King *James* the sixth since adorned with many buildings, and the same hath for long time beene committed to the keeping of the Lords of *Eriskin*, who likewise use to have the keeping of the Prince of *Scotland*, being under yeeres.[1] And from thence I purposed to returne to *Edenborow*, but some occasions of unexpected businesse recalled me speedily into *England*, so as I returned presently to *Edenborow*, and thence to *Barwicke*, the same way I came. *Scotland* reaching so farre into the North, must needs be subject to excessive cold, yet the same is in some sort mitigated by the thicknesse of the cloudy aire and sea vapours. And as in the Northerne parts of *England*, they have small pleasantnes, goodnesse or abundance of Fruites and Flowers, so in *Scotland* they have much lesse, or none at all. And I remember, that coming to *Barwick* in the moneth of May, wee had great stormes, and felt great cold, when for two moneths before, the pleasant Spring had smiled on us at *London*.

On the West side of *Scotland* are many Woodes, Mountaines, and Lakes. On the East side towards the Sea, I passed *Fife*, a pleasant little Territory of open fields. Without inclosures, fruitfull in Corne (as bee all the partes neare *Barwick*, save that they yeeld little wheate, and much Barley and Oates), and all a plaine Country, but it had no Woodes at all, onely the Gentlemens dwellings were shaddowed with some little Groves, pleasant to the view. *Scotland* abounds with Fish, and hath plenty of all Cattell, yet not so bigge as ours, and their Horses are full of spirit, and patient of labour, but very little, so as the Scots then would give any price for one of our English Gueldings, which notwithstanding in Queene *Elizabethe* time might not upon great penalty be sold unto them.

The Navy or shipping of *Scotland*, was of small strength in the memory of our Age, neither were their Marriners of greet experience, but to make them more diligent Merchants,

---

[1] The family of Mar were the hereditary custodiars of the king. John, fourth Lord Erskine, who had the keeping of James V. during his minority, was the first who held the office, which carried with it the charge of Stirling Castle.

their Kings had formerly laid small or no impositions or customes on them : And whill the English had warre with the Spaniards, the Scots as neutrals by carrying of English commodities into *Spaine*, and by having their ships for more security laden by English Merchants, grew somewhat richer and more experienced in Navigation, and had better and stronger shippes then in former time. And surely since the Scots are very daring, I cannot see why their Marriners should not bee bold and courageous, howsoever they have not hitherto made any long voyages, rather for want of riches, then for slothfulnesse or want of courage. The inhabitants of the Westerne parts of *Scotland*, carry into Ireland and Neighbouring places, red and pickeled Herrings, Sea coales, and Aquavitæ, with like commodities, and bring out of Ireland Yarne and Cowes hides or Silver. The Easterne Scots carry into *France* course cloathes, both linnen and woollen, which be narrow and shrinkle in the wetting. They also carry thether Wooll, Skinnes of Goates, Weathers, and of Conies, and divers kindes of Fishes, taken in the Scottish Sea, and neere other Northerne Ilands, and after smoked, or otherwise dried and salted. And they bring from thence Salt and Wines: but the cheefe trafficke of the Scots is in foure places, namely, at *Camphire* in *Zetland*,[1] whether they carry Salt, the Skinnes of Weathers, Otters, Badgers, and Martens, and bring from thence Corne. And at *Burdeaux* in *France*, whether they carry cloathes, and the same skinnes, and bring from thence Wines, Prunes, Walnuts, and Chessenuts. Thirdly, within the Balticke Sea, whither they carry the said Clothes and Skinnes, and bring thence Flaxe, Hempe, Iron, Pitch, and Tarre. And, lastly, in *England*, whether they carry Linnen cloathes, Yarne, and Salt, and bring thence Wheate, Oates, Beanes, and like things.

[1] Campvere (now called Vere), in Zealand, the seat of a Scottish factory for three centuries and a half. This connection with Scotland originated in the marriage of Wolfaard van Borssele, Lord of Campvere, with a princess of the house of Stuart in 1444. A factory of merchants was formed, and by contract between the royal burghs of Scotland and the United Provinces, Campvere became the only staple port. The privileges thus gained by Scotland were not withdrawn till 1795. John Home, the author of *Douglas*, held the sinecure post of Conservator of Scots Privileges at Campvere.

The Scots have no staple in any forraigne City,[1] but trade in *France* upon the League of the Nations, and in *Denmarke* have priviledges by the affinity of the Kings, and flocke in great numbers into *Poland*,[2] abounding in all things for foode, and yeelding many commodities. And in these King-domes they lived at this time in great multitudes, rather for the poverty of their owne Kingdome, then for any great trafficke they exercised there, dealing rather for small fardels, then for great quantities of rich wares.

Touching their diet: They eate much red Colewort and Cabbage, but little fresh meate, using to salt their Mutton and Geese, which made me more wonder, that they used to eate Beefe without salting. The Gentlemen reckon their revenewes, not by rents of monie, but by chauldrons of victuals, and keepe many people in their Families, yet living most on Corne and Rootes, not spending any great quantity on flesh. My selfe was at a Knights House, who had many servants to attend him, that brought in his meate with their heads covered with blew caps, the Table being more then halfe furnished with great platters of porredge,[3] each having a little peece of sodden meate: And when the Table was served, the servants did sit downe with us, but the upper messe in steede of porredge, had a Pullet with some prunes in the broth. And I observed no Art of Cookery, or furniture of Houshold stuffe, but rather rude neglect of both, though my selfe and my companion, sent from the Governour of *Barwicke* about bordering affaires, were entertained after their best manner. The Scots, living then in factions, used

---

[1] Campvere was the staple port of Scotland.   [2] As Moryson had himself been in Poland, he states this fact from personal knowledge. In strong corrobora-tion of his statement may be quoted a passage from the *Travels* of William Lithgow, a Scot of the seventeenth century, who travelled through most of the countries of Europe, and visited Poland among the rest :—"The soil (of Poland) is wonderful fruitful of corns, so that this country is become the granary of Western Europe for all sorts of grain, besides honey, wax, flax, iron, and other commodities. And for auspiciousness, I may rather term it to be a mother and nurse for the youth and younglings of Scotland than a proper dame for her own birth, in clothing, feeding, and enriching them with the fatness of her best things, besides thirty thousand Scots families that live incorporate in her bowels. And certainly Poland may be termed in this kind the mother of her commons, and the first commencement of all our best merchants' wealth, or, at the least, most part of them " (Lithgow's *Travels*, p. 400, 11th edit.).   [3] That is, *pottage*, or *broth*.

to keepe many followers, and so consumed their revenew of victuals, living in some want of money. They vulgarly eate harth Cakes of Oates, but in Cities have also wheaten bread, which for the most part was bought by Courtiers, Gentlemen, and the best sort of Citizens. When I lived at *Barwicke*, the Scots, weekely upon the market day, obtained leave in writing of the Governour, to buy Pease and Beanes, whereof, as also of Wheate, their Merchants at this day send great quantity from *London* into *Scotland*.

They drinke pure Wines, not with sugar as the English, yet at Feasts they put Comfits in the Wine, after the French manner, but they had not our Vinteners fraud to mixe their Wines. I did never see nor heare that they have any publike Innes [1] with signs hanging out, but the better sort of citizens brew ale, their usuall drinke (which will distemper a stranger's bodie), and the same Citizens will entertaine passengers upon acquaintance or entreaty. Their bedsteads were then like Cubbards in the wall, with doores to be opened and shut at pleasure, so as we climbed up to our beds. They used but one sheete, open at the sides and top, but close at the feete, and so doubled. Passengers did seeke a stable for their Horses in some other place, and did there buy hors-meat, and if perhaps the same house yeelded a stable, yet the payment for the Horse did not make them have beds free as in *England*. I omit to speake of the Innes and expences therein, having delated the same in the Itinerary of the first Part, and a Chapter in this Part, expressely treating thereof. When passengers goe to bed,

[1] The Scottish monarchs did their best to establish comfortable inns throughout the country, as the following extracts from the General Index to the Acts of the Parliament of Scotland will show :—"All who sell bread and beer in burghs to receive travellers and supply their wants at current prices" (*anno* 1356). "The chamberlains ordered to see that sufficient inns are provided in the burgh" (1366). "In burghs and thoroughfares hostelries to be provided with accommodation for man and horse" (1424). "Inns to be established in all burghs for the reception of travellers and their horses" (1427). "Barons, magistrates, and others having the direction and rule of thoroughfares and hostelries to set prices on victuals, bread, ale, and other necessaries" (1496). "For eschewing exorbitant prices taken from travellers, the statutes of James I. and other sovereigns to be enforced ; burgh officers to cause hostelers to have sufficient accommodation and food at the usual rate of the neighbourhood ; the rate of charges to be fixed yearly" (1535) "The old acts anent hostelries to be augmented and put in execution" (1567).

their custome was to present them with a sleeping cappe of wine at parting. The Country people and Merchants used to drinke largely, the Gentlemen somewhat more sparingly —yet the very Courtiers, at Feasts, by night meetings, and entertaining any stranger, used to drinke healths not without excesse, and (to speake truth without offence), the excesse of drinking was then farre greater in generall among the Scots then the English.[1] My selfe being at the Court invited by some Gentlemen to supper, and being fore-warned to feare this excesse, would not promise to sup with them—but upon condition that my Inviter would be my protection from large drinking, which I was many times forced to invoke, being courteously entertained, and much provoked to garussing,[2] and so for that time avoided any great intemperance. Remembering this, and having since observed in my conversation at the English Court with the Scots of the better sort, that they spend great part of the night in drinking, not onely wine, but even beere, as my selfe will not accuse them of great intemperance, so I cannot altogether free them from the imputation of excesse, where-with the popular voice chargeth them.

---

[1] Foreigners, however, brought the same charge of intemperance against the English. Thus, Perlin, whose account of Scotland has been given, speaks of the English as "villanous, drunkards, and reprobates." [2] Carousing (German, *gar aus*).

HENRI, DUC DE ROHAN

(1600).

HENRI, DUC DE ROHAN, came to Scotland in 1600 in the course of a protracted tour through Italy, Germany, the Low Countries, and England. Born in 1579, of one of the most illustrious families of France, he had already distinguished himself in the wars of the League, and had gained the admiration and affection of Henry IV. By the Peace of Vervins (1598), he himself tells us, his career as a soldier was for the time closed ; and his youth precluded him from other employments in the state. Not to waste his time in inactivity, therefore, he set out on his travels, which appear to have been prolonged to twenty months. Of Huguenot birth and upbringing, he was received with the greatest cordiality both in England and Scotland. Elizabeth called him *son chevalier*, and James made him godfather to Prince Charles. By his subsequent conduct as champion of the Huguenots, Rohan achieved one of the most brilliant careers in the history of France. It should be said that in his *Travels* he does not shine as a writer, and that he often gives us reason to wish that he would forget himself, and tell us plainly what he saw and heard.[1]

VOYAGE DU DUC DE ROHAN, FAICT EN L'AN 1600 (p. 205).

IF the affection one naturally bears to a country, together with the obligations one has received not from one individual merely, but from the people in general, should induce one to say pleasant things, I ought to make Scotland excel not only all the other countries I have seen, but

[1] An elaborate biography of Rohan has lately been published—"Henri de Rohan ; son rôle politique et militaire sous Louis XIII. (1579–1638). Par Auguste Langel. Paris : Firmin Didot et Cie. 1891."

should make her the equal of France herself. . . . . . If we consider carefully the Scottish king's (James VI.) mode of life, both public and private, his manners, his actions, the excellence of his spirit, his learning and his eloquence, we shall judge him worthy to govern his own kingdom, and much more.   He seems to have been sent at a remarkable crisis; for God is wont to bring forth great men in a country, when He wishes to change a kingdom from one hand to another, or to ruin or elevate the nation.   At the present moment, England is in such a crisis, and what leads me to think that it is the Scottish king and no other whom God wishes to be the instrument of his purposes is the validity of that king's claim, his rare virtues, and the advantage he has by his residence in it of appropriating the whole island.   It is not to ruin the kingdom that God has sent so great a king; since in that case he would have sent a scourge of his church and not its restorer.[1]   Neither has he been sent to raise the state, for there is no need to raise that which is not fallen.   He must have been sent, therefore (and God grant I may be a true prophet!), that the whole of this kingdom might be placed under one head, that the whole of this beautiful island of Great Britain (which has never chanced before) might be brought under the same God, the same faith, the same law, the same king.

I shall not be at the trouble to give a particular description of the towns I saw in Scotland (which, indeed, are few in number), since they possess neither splendid buildings, nor remarkable antiquities, nor things worthy of special mention. Moreover, the origins of such things as it does possess are related in such conflicting fashion by the historians of the country, that no profit could be drawn from any account of them.   Accordingly, what I shall say will be prompted by my desire not to show myself ungrateful to places where I was so hospitably entertained, and to recall the memory of the courtesies I received at the hands of strangers.

To come to the town of Edinburgh, which is the capital of Scotland and the ordinary residence of the king, and was the first town I saw in the country.   It is situated on the river Forth, at rather less than half a league from the sea,

[1] As has been said, De Rohan was a Huguenot.

and is built upon two mountains. On one of these, and on
the western side, is a strong castle surnamed The Maidens
(Les Pucelles), and so inaccessible on every side, that its
natural position renders it more impregnable than if
strengthened by all the arts of modern engineers, from which
(be it said) it has profited nothing. As to the size of the
town, it may be a mile long and about half a mile wide. It
has no beauty except that of its great street, which stretches
from one end of the town to the other, and is both wide and
straight as well as of great length. As regards its buildings
they are by no means sumptuous, since almost all are constructed of wood.[1] In compensation, however, they are so
stocked with inmates that there can hardly be another town
so populous for its size. It is by far the busiest commercial
town in the country. Indeed, it would be against all reason,
were not this the case. For, in the first place, it is situated
in the most fertile district of Scotland, as is proved by the
fact that more than a hundred country-seats are to be found
within a radius of two leagues of the town [2]—it being the
ordinary residence of the court. The second and better
reason is that one of the best harbours in all Scotland is
within less than half a league. This harbour, with the village
beside it, is called Lits, or as we say in ordinary speech
Petit Lict.[3] In this village I may remark in conclusion that
the French sustained a siege, highly honourable to our nation,
and exceedingly profitable to the Scots, inasmuch as they not
only with unsurpassable courage restrained the fury of the
English before this unfortunate spot, but were also the means
of saving the whole kingdom.[4] This incident will serve to
testify how the two nations, the French and the Scots, have
stood by each other since the treaty made between Scotland
and Charlemagne—a period of eight hundred and seventy-

---

[1] De Rohan was a careless observer. The houses were built of stone, and
only faced with wood. As will be seen, other travellers, who visited Edinburgh,
used their eyes to better purpose. [2] Fynes Moryson was also struck by the
number of country-seats in the neighbourhood of Edinburgh (see p. 83, above).
[3] As we have seen, this was the name by which the Sire de Beaugué knew
Leith. [4] Rohan refers to the siege of Leith in 1560, when the Scots, assisted
by the English, beset the town. The issue was not so glorious for France as
Rohan thought, since by the Treaty of Leith (1560) the French were forced to
quit Scotland.

two years, during which it has ever held firm, never has been violated, and never even altered.[1]

Several reasons lead me to speak of certain places that did not commend themselves to me either by their beauty or antiquity, and I am induced to do so only by certain trifling considerations, which make me desirous of preserving some memory of them. Among these places I reckon three little towns, namely, Lescow,[2] Sterlin, and Domfarmelin (I name them in order of importance), and feel constrained to mention them here, if not on account of their history and their beauties, at least by reason of the notable sights I saw in each of them. In the first I saw the daughter[3] of the King of Scotland, who is being brought up there, and who is both well grown and pretty. In the second I saw his son,[4] who gives such promise of being the heir at once of the virtues and the kingdom of his father, that this spot where he has been reared will always have a place in men's memories. In the last I saw the Queen of Scotland,[5] a princess in whom beauty and virtue meet in such wise that for excellence the one cannot well yield to the other. This last place also deserves mention for the fact that the birth of the princes and princesses of Scotland have usually taken place there.[6] These, then, are the most remarkable spectacles I saw in the places above named, which certainly are as worthy of commemoration as the most beautiful palaces in the world. I shall conclude, therefore, not by describing the origins of these three towns and castles, but by praising with judgment what I saw in them, which, indeed, are things more rare and exquisite than the most beautiful antiquities, which men remark in other places—as much more worthy I say, as the reality transcends the copy. For the ancient statues we see are only esteemed for what they represent (which are usually kings, princes, or personages, who, by their

---

[1] This legendary alliance of the Scots and Charlemagne is recorded by Fordun, Boece, Major, and Buchanan. It even appears in the marriage-contract of Mary and the dauphin Francis, and is acknowledged by French as well as Scottish historians. [2] Linlithgow. [3] Elizabeth, afterwards Queen of Bohemia. [4] Prince Henry who died in 1612. [5] Anne of Denmark. [6] David II., James I. of Scotland, and Charles I. were born in Dunfermline. The town, however, is more noted as the burying-place than the birth-place of Scottish monarchs, since it contains the tombs of seven kings and three queens.

singular virtue, were equals of the greatest), or for the merit of the artists who made them. Now, finding in these children (if it be permitted to me to compare bodies with souls to bodies without them), the occasions which lead us to observe and prize these antiquities, equally for the lineage and beauty of themselves and the queen their mother, and for the rare virtue of the latter, I should deem it an unpardonable fault, if having curiously sought out such antiquities as are only representations and lifeless models, I were to pass over those originals which by the hope certain of them inspire me with of their future actions, and the knowledge I have of what the others are already accomplishing, will be, as I believe, among the most remarkable witnesses our century will bequeath to posterity.[1] This, then, is all I have remarked in the kingdom of Scotland, which if I found niggard in producing what is necessary to human life, I also found truly generous in the production of virtuous persons. For, besides the nobility whom I found full of civility and courtesy, the country possesses a multitude of learned men, and a people of such courage and fidelity, that our kings of France chose from among them the soldiers who formed the special guard of their persons.

---

[1] In the original this sentence is well-nigh hopeless.

SIR ANTHONY WELDON (?)

(1617).

THE authorship of the following pasquinade is uncertain. In some editions it is assigned to James Howell, the author of the *Familiar Letters*. As the tract itself proves, however, it must have been written by one who accompanied James VI. on his visit to Scotland in 1617, and Howell had then but left college to take charge of a glass-house in London. Moreover, the whole tone of this diatribe, so different from the genial spirit of the *Familiar Letters*, puts Howell's authorship out of the question. With more probability the tract has been assigned to Sir Anthony Weldon, who is known to have accompanied James on his northern visit. Anthony à Wood gives the following account of Weldon :—

"His (Weldon's) parents took rise from Queen Elizabeth's kitchen, and left it a legacy for preferment of this issue.[1] Sir Anthony went the same way, and by grace of the Court got up to the Green Cloth; in which place attending King James into Scotland, he practised there to libel that nation; which at his return home was found wrapt up in a record of that Board; and by the hand being known to be his, he was deservedly removed from his place as unworthy to eat his bread, whose birth-right he had so vilely defamed; yet by favour of the king, with a piece of money in his purse, and a pension to boot to preserve him loyal during his life, though as a bad creditor he took this course to repay him to the purpose. In his life-time he discovered part of this piece to his fellow courtier, who earnestly dissuaded him not to publish so defective and false a scandal. . . . . ."

The " piece " to which Wood refers is entitled *The Court*

---

[1] Wood is in error regarding Weldon's family, which belonged to Northumberland, and was of ancient standing (*The Antiquarian Repertory*, vol. ii. pp. 326, 327).

and Character of King James (London, 1650)—a description
which cannot apply to the following tract. The text produced here is that of a small volume with the title, " A
Perfect Description of the People and Country of Scotland ;
reprinted from a very scarce pamphlet, written by James
Howel, gent." (printed at London for J. S. 1649).[1]

A PERFECT DESCRIPTION OF THE PEOPLE AND COUNTRY
OF SCOTLAND.

FIRST, for the country, I must confess it is good for those
that possess it, and too bad for others, to be at the
charge to conquer it.   The air might be wholesome but for the
stinking people that inhabit it ; the ground might be fruitful
had they wit to manure it.

Their beasts be generally small, women only excepted, of
which sort there are none greater in the whole world.   There
is great store of fowl too, as foul houses, foul sheets, foul
linen, foul dishes and pots, foul trenchers and napkins, with
which sort we have been forced to say as the children
did with their fowl in the wilderness.   They have good
store of fish too, and good for those that can eat it raw ;
but if it come once into their hands, it is worse than if it
were three days old : for their butter and cheese, I will not
meddle withal at this time, nor no man else at any time that
loves his life.

They have great store of deer, but they are so far from
the place where I have been, that I rather believe than go to
disprove it : I confess, all the deer I met withal, was dear
lodgings, dear horse-meat, and dear tobacco, and English
beer.[2]

As for fruit, for their grandsire Adam's sake they never
planted any ; and for other trees, had Christ been betrayed

---

[1] I found in the Bodleian Library what appears to be the original manuscript
of this pamphlet (Tanner's MSS., No. 237).   It is in the form of a letter dated
from Leith, near Edinburgh, in Scotland, 1617, and signed J. S.   The initials,
which are doubtless a pseudepigraph, throw no light on the authorship of the
letter.   [2] The crowd that accompanied James to Edinburgh would, of course,
raise prices ; but at ordinary times, as other testimonies in this collection prove,
English travellers found most commodities cheaper in Scotland than in their
own country.

in this country (as doubtless he should, had he come as a stranger), Judas had sooner found the grace of repentance, than a tree to hang himself on.

They have many hills, wherein they say is much treasure, but they shew none of it; nature hath only discovered to them some mines of coal, to shew to what end he created them.

I saw little grass but in their pottage: the thistle is not given of nought, for it is the fairest flower in their garden. The word hay is Heathen-Greek unto them;[1] neither man nor beast knows what it means.

Corn is reasonable plenty at this time; for since they heard of the king's coming, it hath been as unlawful for the common people to eat wheat,[2] as it was in the old time for any but the priests to eat shew-bread. They prayed much for his coming, and long fasted for his welfare;[3] but in the more plain sense, that he might fare the better. All his followers were welcome but his guard; for those, they say, are like Pharaoh's lean kine, and threaten death wheresoever they come: they could persuade the footmen that oaten cakes would make them long-winded, and the children of the chapel[4] they have brought to eat of them for the maintenance of their voices.

They say our cooks are too saucy, and for grooms and coachmen they wish them to give to their horses no worse than they eat themselves. They commend the brave minds of the pensioners and the gentlemen of the bed-chamber, which chuse rather to go to taverns, than to be always eating of the king's provision; they likewise do commend the yeomen of the buttery and cellar, for their readiness and silence,.in that they will hear twenty knocks before they will

---

[1] The Scots had expressed a desire that James should defer his visit till the grass had grown for cattle (*State Papers of Reign of James VI.*, 22nd Feb. 1617). *Cf.* what Morer, a later traveller, says regarding hay in Scotland (p. 266). [2] All the early travellers in Scotland, we have seen, agree in stating that oatmeal was the chief fare of the lowland Scots. Subsequent travellers bear the same testimony. There was, therefore, no need for any prohibition such as Weldon mentions. [3] The *State Papers* say distinctly that James's journey was "disliked by both nations as too costly" (15th March 1617). [4] James had lately sent choristers and an organ down from England to the Royal Chapel at Holyrood. It was the first time such music had been heard there since the dethronement of Mary (Calderwood, vii. 264).

answer one.   They persuade the trumpeters that fasting is
good for men of that quality ; for emptiness, they say, causes
wind, and wind causes a trumpet to sound well.

The bringing of heralds they say was a needless charge;
they all know their pedigrees well enough, and the harbingers
might have been spared, seeing they brought so many beds
with them ; and of two evils the least should be chosen.
They wish the beds might remain with them, and the poor
harbingers keep their places and do their office as they return.
His hangings[1] they desire might likewise be left as reliques
to put them in mind of his majesty : and they promise to
dispense with the wooden images;[2] but for those graven images
in his new beautified chapel, they threaten to pull down soon
after his departure, and to make of them a burnt offering, to
appease the indignation they imagine conceived against them
in the breast of the Almighty, for suffering such idolatry to
enter into their kingdom : the organ I think will find mercy,
because (as they say) there is some affinity between them
and bag-pipes.

The skipper that brought the singing men with their
papistical vestments, complains that he hath been much
troubled with a strange singing in his head ever since they
came aboard his ship, for remedy whereof, the parson of the
parish hath persuaded him to sell that profane vessel, and to
distribute the money among the faithful brethren.

For his majesty's entertainment, I must needs ingenuously
confess, he was received in the parish of Edinburgh (for a
city I cannot call it), with great shouts of joy, but no shews
of charge for pageants ;[3] they hold them idolatrous things,
and not fit to be used in so reformed a place : from the castle
they gave him some pieces of ordnance, which surely he gave
them since he was king of England ; and at the entrance of

---

[1] It was reported that the German tapestry makers were entreated by the Scots
to make hangings that should look old in order that Scotland might not seem
to have wanted such things (*State Papers*, 9th May 1617).   [2] Following the
organ and choristers, images of the patriarchs and apostles were sent by James
for the adornment of his chapel.   So alarming was the tumult on their arrival,
however, that he was forced to forgo his purpose of introducing them.   In a
characteristic letter to the bishops, James gave his reason for abandoning his
intention (*Original Letters*, Bannatyne Club, 466).   [3] According to the *State
Papers* his court was magnificently entertained in Edinburgh, and the king
and his nobles were much content with their reception (6th May and 9th June).

the town they presented him with a golden bason, which was carried before him on mens shoulders to his palace, I think, from whence it came. His majesty was conveyed by the younkers of the town, which were about an hundred halberds (dearly shall they rue it, in regard of the charge) to the Cross, and so to the high church, where the only bell they had stood on tip-toe to behold his sweet face, where I must intreat you to spare him; for an hour I lost him.[1]

In the mean time, to report the speeches of the people concerning his never-exampled entertainment, were to make this discourse too tedious unto you, as the sermon was to those that were constrained to endure it. After the preachment he was conducted by the same halberds unto his palace, of which I forbear to speak, because it was a place sanctified by his divine majesty; only I wish it had been better walled for my friends sake that waited on him.

Now I will begin briefly to speak of the people according to their degrees and qualities: For the lords spiritual, they may well be termed so indeed, for they are neither fish nor flesh, but what it shall please their earthly God, the king, to make them. Obedience is better than sacrifice, and therefore they make a mock at martyrdom, saying, That Christ was to die for them, and not they for him. They will rather subscribe than surrender, and rather dispense with small things than trouble themselves with great disputation; they will rather acknowledge the king to be their head than want wherewith to pamper their bodies.

They have taken great pains and trouble to compass their bishopricks, and they will not leave them for a trifle; for the deacons, whose defects will not lift them up to dignities, all their study is to disgrace them that have gotten the least degree above them; and because they cannot bishop, they proclaim they never heard of any. The scriptures, say they, speak of deacons and elders, but not a word of bishops. Their discourses are full of detraction, their sermons nothing but railing, and their conclusions nothing but heresies and

---

[1] An interesting memorial of James's visit to Edinburgh is a collection of congratulatory Latin poems presented to him by the college, contained in a volume entitled "ΝΟΣΤΩΔΙΑ. In serenissimi, potentissimi, et invictissimi monarchæ, Jacobi Magnæ Britanniæ, Franciæ, et Hiberniæ Regis, fidei defensoris, &c., felicem in Scotiam reditum, Academiæ Edinburgensis congratulatio."

treasons.   For the religion they have, I confess they hold it above reach, and, God willing, I will never reach for it.

They christen without the cross, marry without the ring, receive the sacrament without reverence, die without repentance, and bury without divine service : they keep no holydays, nor acknowledge any saint but St Andrew, who they said got that honour by presenting Christ with an oaten cake after his forty days fast.   They say likewise, that he that translated the Bible was the son of a maltster, because it speaks of a miracle done by barley-loaves ; whereas they swear they were oaten cakes, and that no other bread of that quantity could have sufficed so many thousands.

They use no prayer at all,[1] for they say it is needless ; God knows their minds without pratling, and what he doth, he loves to do it freely.   Their Sabbath exercise is a preaching in the forenoon, and a persecuting in the afternoon ;[2] they go to church in the forenoon to hear the law, and to the crags and mountains in the afternoon to louse themselves.

They hold their noses if you talk of bear-baiting, and stop their ears if you speak of play ; fornication they hold but a pastime, wherein man's ability is approved, and a woman's fertility is discovered ; at adultery they shake their heads ; theft they rail at ; murder they wink at, and blasphemy they laugh at ; they think it impossible to lose the way to heaven, if they can but leave Rome behind them.

To be opposite to the pope, is to be presently with God : To conclude, I am persuaded, that if God and his angels, at the last day, should come down in their whitest garments they would run away and cry, " The children of the chapel are come again to torment us, let us fly from the abomination of these boys, and hide ourselves in the mountains."

For the lords temporal and spiritual, temporising gentlemen ! if I were apt to speak of any, I could not speak much of them ; only I must let you know they are not Scottishmen ;

[1] It would, of course, be absurd to take Weldon seriously ; but it is worth mentioning that we have Alexander Henderson's testimony that a set of form of prayer was in use in the Presbyterian churches at this time (*The Order and Government of the Church of Scotland*, " Address to the Reader ").   [2] Persons were appointed by the church to see that there were no loiterers in the streets during time of service (see below, p. 144).

for as soon as they fall from the breast of the beast their mother, their careful father posts them away for France,[1] which as they pass, the sea sucks from them that which they have sucked from their rude dams ; there they gather new flesh, new blood, new manners ; and there they learn to put on their cloaths, and then return into their country to wear them out : there they learn to stand, speak, discourse and congee, to court women, and to compliment with men.

They spared for no cost to honour the king, nor for no complimental curtesy to welcome their countrymen ; their followers are their fellows, their wives their slaves, their horses their masters, and their swords their judges ; by reason whereof, they have but few labourers, and those not very rich : their parliaments hold but three days, their statutes are three lines, and their suits are determined in a manner in three words, or very few more.

The wonders of their kingdom are these ; the Lord Chancellor, he is believed,[2] the Master of the Rolls well spoken of,[3] and the whole council, who are the judges for all causes, are free from suspicion of corruption. The country, although it be mountainous, affords no monsters but women, of which the greatest sort (as countesses and ladies) are kept like lions in iron gates ; the merchants wives also prisoners, but not in so strong a hold ; they have wooden cages,[4] like our Boar-franks, through which sometimes peeping to catch the air, we are almost choaked with the sight of them. The greatest madness amongst the men, is jealousie ; in that they fear what no man that hath but two of his senses will take from them.

The ladies are of opinion, that Susanna could not be chaste, because she bathed so often. Pride is a thing bred in their bones, and their flesh naturally abhors cleanliness ; their body smells of sweat, and their splay feet never offend in socks.

---

[1] There were still many Scotsmen to be found in France at the beginning of the seventeenth century ; but their numbers had, of course, decreased since Scotland had become Protestant. [2] The Lord Chancellor of Scotland at this date was Alexander, Earl of Dunfermline, who died in 1622. [3] By Master of the Rolls must be meant the Lord Clerk Register, who was, in fact, known as "clericus rotulorum." The office was at this time held by Sir George Hay, afterwards Earl of Kinnoul. [4] Weldon is probably thinking of the small windows and the wooden facings of the houses. See below, p. 232.

To be chained in marriage with one of them, were to be tied to a dead carcass, and cast into a stinking ditch; formosity and a dainty face are things they dream not of.

The ointments they most frequently use amongst them are brimstone and butter for the scab, and oil of bays, and stavesacre.[1] I protest I had rather be the meanest servant of my two pupils chamber-maids, than to be the master-minion to the fairest countess I have yet discovered. The sin of curiosity of ointments is but newly crept into the kingdom, and I do not think it will long continue.

And therefore, to conclude, the men of old did no more wonder that the great Messias should be born in so poor a town as Bethlem in Judea, than I do wonder that so brave a prince as king James, should be borne in so stinking a town as Edinburgh in lousy Scotland.[2]

---

[1] *Stavesacre*, or larkspur.   [2] A contemporary reply by an indignant Scot to his above pasquinade will be found reprinted in the *Abbotsford Miscellany*.

TAYLOR, THE WATER-POET
(1618).

O F the early travellers who visited Scotland, none is better known than Taylor, the Water-Poet; and his account of his travels, if not the most instructive we possess, is certainly not the least entertaining. In his rollicking spirits and good-humoured acceptance of everybody and everything, we have an agreeable contrast to the cankered spite of Weldon. There were many reasons that disposed him to speak kindly of the Scots and their country. Its inferiority to England in the conveniences and refinements of social life would not thrust itself on a man of Taylor's birth and upbringing. His narrative proves that he was everywhere entertained by nobles and gentry in a manner that would have made it gross ingratitude for him to speak of their country in any but the most flattering terms. He knew, also, that King James himself· would read his book, and would not be slow to resent any slight on the country of his birth.[1] But above all there can be no doubt that Taylor was one of those easy souls, who are not disposed to haggle with fortune, but take in good part whatever fare she may please to set before them.

In spite of his own protestations, it seems probable that Taylor's visit was prompted by the rumoured intention of a similar visit on the part of Ben Jonson. For some time, it had been the talk of the town that Jonson purposed making a pedestrian tour to Scotland.[2] As he was now in his forty-fifth year, and, according to his own description of himself, was "of mountain belly" and "prodigious waist,"[3] the wits

---

[1] It would seem that James had a high opinion of Taylor's poetical powers. One of Drummond's notes of Ben Jonson's conversation with him is—" Neither did he (James) see ever any verses in England [equal] to the Sculler's."
[2] Jonson's intended visit to Scotland is referred to in the *State Papers of Reign of James VI.* as early as the 4th of June 1617.   [3] The first of these expressions occurs in a poem entitled, " My Picture left in Scotland."

had made merry at his projected expedition. It was Jonson's belief, therefore, that certain mischievous persons had given the cue to Taylor by way of caricaturing the absurdity of his own intention. Jonson, however, was not the man to be laughed out of any scheme on which he had set his mind; and, accordingly, towards the end of June or the beginning of July, 1618, he set out on his travels. A week or two later, on July 14, Taylor followed in his steps; and to outdo Ben, undertook not only to achieve the journey on foot, but without a coin in his pocket, and under a pledge neither to beg or borrow—a pledge, as will be seen, which he certainly did not keep to the letter.

It would seem that such whimsical wagers were not uncommon at the time. A certain "loving friend" of Taylor's own, Samuel Rowlands, refers to some of these in the following lines :—

> Ferris gave cause of vulgar wonderment,
> When unto Bristom in a boat he went :
> Another with his sculler ventured more,
> That rowed to Flushing from our English shore :
> Another did devise a wooden whale
> Which unto Calais did from Dover sail :
> Another with his oars and slender ferry
> From London unto Antwerp o'er did ferry :
> Another, maugre fickle fortunes' teeth,
> Rowed hence to Scotland and arrived at Leith.[1]

According to Southey, Taylor " came into the world at the right time, and lived in an age when kings and queens condescended to notice him, nobles and archbishops admitted him to their table, and mayors and corporations received him with civic honours." [2] Taylor's experiences in Scotland fully bear out what Southey says. From his own narrative, written in no spirit of vain self-laudation, it is clear that

---

[1] Another preposterous undertaking of Taylor's own was to sail from London to Queenborough in a brown paper boat with two stock-fish tied to two canes for oars. Before he and his companion had been half an hour in the water the paper went to pieces. Fortunately, the skeleton of the boat was supported by four large bladders on either side, and after being on the water from Saturday evening till Monday morning, they reached their destination in safety.
[2] Southey, *Lives of Uneducated Poets*, p. 86.

the leading Scottish nobles and gentry gave him a friendly hand, and did their best to make him think well of their country.   Doubtless, their hospitality was the more readily given that they would have their own laugh at the sculler-poet's expense.   Taylor himself, however, evidently saw nothing of this, and he was not the man to be made a butt of with impunity.   On the 15th October, after an absence of precisely three months, he returned to London equally pleased with himself and with all that he had seen.   His friends met him at Islington at the sign of the Maidenhead, where after an excellent supper they had a play of the "Life and Death of Guy of Warwick" performed by the Earl of Derby's men.

As it had been part of Taylor's object to make capital out of his adventures, he lost no time in putting together his account of them.   By the introduction of hackney-coaches his business as a waterman had become somewhat precarious, so that he had been driven to various shifts to add to his earnings.   His method of publication was to print his books at his own expense, and hawk them about among such patrons of literature as he found in London or elsewhere in the course of his travels.   This was the method he followed in the present case, and he seems to have had no reason to grumble at the result.   To set himself right with Ben Jonson he accompanied his book with the following dedication :—

"To all my loving adventurers, by what title soever, my general salutation—Reader, these Travels of mine into Scotland were not undertaken neither in imitation, nor emulation of any man, but only devised by myself on purpose to make trial of my friends both in this Kingdom of England, and that of Scotland, and because I would be an eye-witness of divers things which I had heard of that country, and whereas many shallow-brained critics do lay an aspersion on me that I was set on by others, or that I did undergo this project, either in malice or mockage of Master Benjamin Jonson, I vow by the faith of a Christian that their imaginations are all wide, for he is a gentleman to whom I am obliged for so many undeserved courtesies that I have received from him, and from others by his favour that I durst never be so impudent or ungrateful as either to suffer

any man's persuasions, or mine own instigation, to incite me
to make so bad a requital for so much goodness formerly
received."

THE PENNYLESS PILGRIMAGE, OR THE MONEYLESSE PERAMBULA-
   TION OF JOHN TAYLOR, ALIAS, THE KING'S MAJESTIES
   WATER-POET: HOW HE TRAVAILED ON FOOT FROM
   LONDON TO EDENBOROUGH IN SCOTLAND, NOT CARRYING
   ANY MONEY TO OR FRO, NEITHER BEGGING, BORROWING,
   OR ASKING MEATE, DRINKE, OR LODGING.

MY first night's lodging in Scotland was at a place called
      Mophot, which, they say, is thirty miles from Carlile,
but I suppose them to be longer than forty of such miles as
are betwixt London and Saint Albanes (but indeed the Scots
doe allow almost as large measure of their miles, as they
doe of their drinke, for an English gallon, either of ale or
wine, is but their quart, and one Scottish mile, now and
then, may well stand for a mile and a halfe, or two English);
but howsoever short or long, I found that dayes journey the
weariest that ever I footed; and at night being come to the
towne, I found good ordinary countrey entertainment; my
fare and my lodging was sweet and good, and might have
served a farre better man then my selfe, although my selfe
have had many times better [1]: but this is to be noted, that
though it rained not all the day, yet it was my fortune to be
well wet twise, for I waded over a great river called Eske
in the morning, somewhat more then foure miles distance
from Carlile in England, and at night, within two miles of
my lodging, I was faine to wade over the river of Annan in
Scotland, from which river the county of Annandale hath
its name. And whilst I waded on foot, my man was
mounted on horse-backe, like the George without the dragon.
But the next morning, I arose and left Mophot behind me,

[1] The traveller of 1704, already quoted, was not so well pleased with
Moffat, though after the lapse of nearly a century the village should have
been a more creditable place than in the time of the Water-Poet. "This
(Moffat)," he says, "is a small stragling town, among high hills, and is the
town of their wells, in sumer time people comeing here to drink waters; but
what sort of people they are, or where they get lodgings, I can't tell, for I did
not like their lodgings well enough to go to bedd, but got such as I could to
refresh me, and so came away" (p. 60).

and that day I traveled twenty-one miles to a sory village called Blithe,[1] but I was blithe my selfe to come to any place of harbour or succour, for since I was borne, I never was so weary, or so neere being dead with extreme travell; I was founderd and refounderd of all foure, and for my better comfort, I came so late, that I must lodge without doores all night, or else in a poore house where the good-wife lay in child-bed, her husband being from home, her owne servant mayde being her nurse. A creature naturally compacted, and artificially adorned with an incomparable homelines; but as things were I must either take or leave, and necessity made mee enter, where we gat egges and ale by measure and by tale. At last to bed I went, my man lying on the floore by mee, where in the night there were pidgeons did very bountifully mute in his face: the day being no sooner come, and having but fifteene miles to Edenborough, mounted upon my ten toes, and began first to hobble, and after to amble, and so being warme, I fell to pace by degrees; all the way passing thorow a fertill countrey for corne and cattle: and about two of the clocke in the afternoone that Wednesday, being the thirteenth of August, and the day of Clare the Virgin (the signe being in Virgo), the moone foure dayes old, the wind at west, I came to take rest, at the wished, long expected, ancient, famous city of Edenborough, which I entred like Pierce, pennilesse,[2] altogether monyles, but I thanke God, not friendlesse; for being there, for the time of my stay, I might borrow (if any man would lend), spend if I could get, begge if I had the impudence, and steal if I durst adventure the price of a hanging, but my purpose was to house my horse, and to suffer him and my apparell to lye in durance, or lavender[3] in stead of litter, till such time as I could meete with some valiant friend, that would desperately disburse.

Walking thus downe the street (my body being tyred with travell, and my minde attyred with moody, muddy, Moore-

---

[1] Now Blythe Bridge in the south of Linton parish, Peebleshire. [2] *Pierce Pennilesse*, by Thomas Nash (London, 1592). [3] "To lay in lavender" is to lay by carefully, as clothes with sprigs of lavender among them. "Good faith, waiter, rather than that thou should'st pawn a rag more I'll lay my ladyship in lavender, if I know where" ("Eastward Hoe," 1605, Ogilvie's *Imperial Dictionary*).

ditch melancholy), my contemplation did devoutly pray, that I might meete one or other to prey upon, being willing to take any slender acquaintance of any map whatsoever; viewing and circumviewing every mans face I met, as if I meant to draw his picture, but all my acquaintance was *Non est inventus* (pardon me, reader, that Latine is none of mine owne, I swear by *priscians paricranion*,[1] an oath which I have ignorantly broken many times). At last I resolv'd, that the next gentleman that I met withall, should be acquaintance whether hee would or no: and presently fixing mine eyes upon a gentleman-like object, I looked on him, as if I would survay something through him, and make him my perspective: and hee, much musing at my gazing, and I much gazing at his musing, at last he crost the way and made toward me, and then I made downe the street from him, leaving to encounter with my man, who came after me leading my horse, whom he thus accosted, My friend (quoth he), doth yonder gentleman (meaning me) know me, that he lookes so wistly on me? Truly Sir, said my man, I thinke not, but my master is a stranger come from London, and would gladly meete some acquaintance to direct him where he may have lodging and horse meate. Presently the gentleman (being of a generous disposition) over-tooke me with unexpected and undeserved courtesie, brought me to a lodging, and caused my horse to bee put into his owne stable, whilest we discoursing over a pinte of Spanish, I related as much English to him, as made him lend him tenne shillings (his name was Master John Maxwell), which money I am sure was the first that I handled after I came from out the walls of London: but having rested two houres and refreshed myselfe, the gentleman and I walked to see the city and the castle, which as my poore unable and unworthy pen can, I will truly describe.

The castle on a loftie rocke is so strongly grounded, bounded, and founded, that by force of man it can never be confounded; the foundation and walls are unpenetrable, the rampiers impregnable, the bulwarkes invincible, no way but

---

[1] *Cf.* the phrase "to break the head of Priscian," that is, to violate grossly the rules of grammar.

one to it is or can be possible to be made passable.   In a
word, I have seene many straights and fortresses in Germany,
the Netherlands, Spaine, and England, but they must all
give place to this unconquered castle, both for strength and
scituation.

Amongst the many memorable things which I was shewed
there, I noted especially a great peece of ordnance of iron ;
it is not for batterie, but it will serve to defend a breach,
or to tosse balles of wilde-fire against any that should assaile
or assault the castle ; it lyes now dismounted ; and it is so
great within, that it was told me that a childe was once
gotten there : but I, to make tryall crept into it, lying on
my backe, and I am sure there was roome enough and spare
for a greater than my selfe.[1]

So leaving the castle, as it is both defensive against any
opposition, and magnificke for lodging and receite, I descended
lower to the city, wherein I observed the fairest and
goodliest streete that ever mine eyes beheld, for I did never
see or heare of a street of that length (which is halfe an
English mile from the castle to a faire port which they call
the Nether-bow), and from that port, the streete which they
call the Kenny-hate[2] is one quarter of a mile more, downe to
the kings palace, called Holy-rood-house, the buildings on
each side of the way being all of squared stone, five, six, and
seven stories high, and many by-lanes and closes on each
side of the way, wherein are gentlemens houses, much fairer
then the buildings in the high-street, for in the high-street
marchants and tradesmen do dwell, but the gentlemens
mansions and goodliest houses are obscurely founded in the
aforesaid lanes : the walles are eight or tenne foote thicke,
exceeding strong, not built for a day, a weeke, or a moneth,
or a yeere ;[3] but from antiquitie to posteritie, for many
ages ; there I found entertainment beyond my expectation
or merit, and there is fish, flesh, bread and fruit, in such

---

[1] The "piece of ordnance" is, of course, Mons Meg, which was regarded by
the Scots themselves as a national possession, and which, as will be seen,
excited the astonishment of all their visitors.   It seems now to be settled that
it was of foreign manufacture (Preface to *Exchequer Rolls*, vol. xiii. p. clxxi).
[2] Canongate.   [3] Taylor seems to have been more impressed by the city walls
than Fynes Moryson.   As far as we know, they were in the same condition
when both travellers saw them.

variety, that I thinke I may offencelesse call it superfluity,
or saciety.   The worst was, that wine and ale was so scarce,
and the people were such mizers of it, that every night
before I went to bed, if any man had asked me a civill
question, all the wit in my head could not have made him a
sober answer.

I was at his Majesties palace, a stately and princely seate,
wherein I saw a sumptuous chappell, most richly adorned
with all appurtenances belonging to so sacred a place, or so
royall an owner.   In the inner court, I saw the kings armes
cunningly carved in stone, and fixed over a doore aloft on
the wall, the red lyon being the crest, over which was written
this inscription in Latine,

Nobis hæc invicta miserunt 106 *proavi.*

I enquired what the English of it was ?   It was told me as
followeth, which I thought worthy to be recorded :

106 fore-fathers have left this to us unconquered.

This is a worthy and memorable motto, and I thinke few
kingdomes or none in the world can truly write the like,
that notwithstanding so many inroades, incursions, attempts,
assaults, civill warres, and forraigne hostilities, bloody
battles, and mighty foughten fields, that maugre the strength
and policy of enemies, that royall crowne and scepter hath
from one hundred and seven descents, kept still unconquered,
and by the power of the King of Kings (through the grace
of the Prince of peace), is now left peacefully to our peacefull
king, whom long in blessed peace, the God of peace defend
and governe.[1]

But once more, a word or two of Edenborough, although
I have scarcely given it that due which belongs unto it,
for their lofty and stately buildings, and for their faire and
spacious streete, yet my minde perswades me that they in
former ages that first founded that citie did not so well, in
that they built it in so discommodious a place ; for the sea,
and all navigable rivers, being the chiefe meanes for the

---

[1] This is the latest description we possess of the Old Palace of Holyrood,
which was destroyed by fire during its occupation by Cromwell's soldiery in
1650 (Wilson, *Memorials of Edinburgh*, p. 407, ed. 1886).

enriching of townes and cities, by the reason of traffique with forraine nations, with exportation, transportation, and receite of variety of marchandizing; so this citie had it beene built but one mile lower on the seaside, I doubt not but it had long before this beene comparable to many a one of our greatest townes and cities in Europe, both for spaciousness of bounds, port, state, and riches. It is said, that King James the fifth (of famous memory) did graciously offer to purchase for them, and to bestow upon them freely, certaine low and pleasant grounds a mile from them on the sea-shore, with these conditions, that they should pull downe their citie, and build it in that more commodious place, but the citizens refused it;[1] and so now it is like (for me) to stand where it doth, for I doubt such another profer of removall will not be presented to them till two dayes after the faire.

Now have with you for Leeth, whereto I no sooner came, but I was well entertained by Master Barnard Lindsay, one of the groomes of his Majesties bed-chamber, hee knew my estate was not guilty, because I brought guilt with me (more then my sins, and they would not passe for current there), hee therefore did replenish the vaustity of my empty purse, and discharged a piece at mee with two bullets of gold, each being in value worth eleven shillings white money: and I was credibly informed, that within the compass of one yeere, there was shipped away from that onely port in Leeth, foure score thousand boles of wheat, oates, and barley into Spaine, France, and other forraine parts, and every bole containes the measure of foure English bushels, so that from Leeth onely hath beene transported three hundred and twenty thousand bushels of corne; besides, some hath beene shipped away from Saint Andrewes, from Dundee, Aberdeene, Disert, Kirkady, Kinghorne, Burnt-iland, Dunbar, and other portable townes, which makes mee to wonder that a kingdome so populous as it is, should neverthelesse sell so much bread-corne beyond the seas, and yet to have more then sufficient for themselves.

So I having viewed the haven and towne of Leeth, tooke

---

[1] I have been unable to discover Taylor's authority for this offer of James V.

a passage boate to see the new wondrous well,[1] to which
many a one that is not well, comes farre and neere in hope
to be made well: indeed I did heare that it had done much
good, and that it hath a rare operation to expell or kill
divers maladies; as to provoke appetite, to helpe much for
the avoyding of the gravell in the bladder, to cure sore eyes,
and old ulcers, with many other vertues which it hath, but
I (through the mercy of God, having no need of it) did make
no great inquisition what it had done, but for novelty I
dranke of it, and I found the taste to be more pleasant than
any other water, sweet almost as milke, yet as cleare as
cristall; and I did observe, that though a man did drinke
a quarte, a pottle, or as much as his belly could containe,
yet it never offended or lay heavy upon the stomacke, no
more then if one had dranke but a pint, or a small quantity.

I went two miles from it to a towne called Burnt-iland,
where I found many of my especiall good friends, as Master
Robert Hay, one of the groomes of his Majesties bed-
chamber, Master David Drummond, one of his gentlemen
pentioners, Master James Acmooty [Auchmuchty], one of
the groomes of the privie chamber, Captaine Murray, Sir
Henry Witherington, knight, Captaine Tyrie, and divers
others: and there Master Hay, Master Drummond, and the
good olde Captaine Murray did very bountifully furnish mee
with gold for my expenses, but I being at dinner with those
aforesaid gentlemen, as we were discoursing, there befell a
strange accident, which I thinke worth the relating.

I know not upon what occasion they began to talke of
being at sea in former times, and I (amongst the rest) said,
I was at the taking of Cales:[2] whereto an English gentleman replyed, that hee was the next good voyage after at the
Ilands:[3] I answered him that I was there also. He demanded,
in what ship I was? I tolde him in the Rainebowe of the
Queenes: why (quoth he), doe you not know me? I was
in the same ship, and my name is Witherington.

Sir, said I, I do remember the name well, but by reason

---

[1] The medicinal spring at Kinghorn was first brought into repute by Dr
Patrick Anderson in his "Colde Spring of Kinghorne Craig, his admirable
and newe tryed properties." (1618.) The spring no longer attracts attention.
[2] Cales, *i.e.*, Cadiz, which was taken by the Earl of Essex in 1596.   [3] The
West Indies.

that it is neere two and twenty yeers since I saw you, I may
well forget the knowledge of you. Well, said he, if you
were in that ship, I pray you tell me some remarkable token
that happened in the voyage, whereupon I told him two or
three tokens; which he did know to be true. Nay then, said
I, I will tell you another, which (perhaps) you have not
forgotten; as our ship and the rest of the fleet did ride at
anchor at the ile of Flores (one of the iles of the Azores),
there were some fourteene men and boyes of our ship, that
for novelty would goe ashore, and see what fruit the iland
did beare, and what entertainment it would yeeld us: so
being landed, we went up and downe and could finde nothing
but stones, heath and mosse, and wee expected oranges,
limonds, figges, muske-millions,[1] and potatoes: in the meane
space, the wind did blow so stiff, and the sea was so extreme
rough, that our ship-boate could not come to the land to fetch
us, for feare she should bee beaten in pieces against the
rockes: this continued five dayes, so that we were almost
famished for want of food; but at last (I squandring up and
downe) by the providence of God, I hapned into a cave, or
poore habitation, where I found fifteene loaves of bread, each
of the quantity of a penny loafe in England, I having a
valiant stomacke, of the age of almost a hundred and twenty
houres breeding, fell to, and ate two loaves and never said
grace: and as I was about to make a horse-loafe[2] of the
third loafe, I did put twelve of them into my breeches,[3] and
my sleeves, and so went mumbling out of the cave, leaning
my backe against a tree, when upon the sudden a gentleman
came to me, and said, Friend, what are you eating? Bread
(quoth I). For Gods sake, said he, give me some. With
that, I put my hand into my breech (being my best pantrey),
and I gave him a loafe, which he received with many
thankes, and said, that if ever he could requite it, he would.

I had no sooner told this tale, but Sir Henry Witherington did acknowledge himself to be the man that I had given
the loafe unto two and twenty yeeres before; here I found

---

[1] Musk-melon.   [2] A large loaf composed of beans and wheat ground
together, used for feeding horses.

"O! that I were in my oat-tub with a horse loaf—
Something to hearten me."—*Beaumont and Fletcher.*

[3] This was the period of trunk-hose, so that this is no exaggeration.

the proverbe true, that men have more priviledge then mountaines in meeting.

In what great measure hee did requite so small a courtesie, I will relate in this following discourse in my returne through Northumberland: So leaving my man at the towne of Burnt-ilande, I tolde him, I would goe to Sterling, and see the castle there, and withall to see my honourable friends the Earle of Marr, and Sir William Murray, knight, Lord of Abercarny, and that I would returne within two dayes at the most: But it fell out quite contrary; for it was five and thirtie dayes before I could get backe againe out of these noblemen's company. The whole progres of my travell with them, and the cause of my stay, I cannot with gratefulness omit; and thus it was.

A worthy gentleman, named Master John Fenton, did bring me on my way sixe miles to Dumfermling, where I was well entertained, and lodged at Master John Gibb his house, one of the groomes of his majesties bed-chamber, and I thinke the oldest servant the King hath: withall I was well entertained there by Master Crighton at his owne house, who went with me, and shewed me the Queenes palace, (a delicate and princely mansion), withall I saw the ruines of an ancient and stately built abbey, with faire gardens, orchards, medows belonging to the palace: all which, with faire and goodly revenues, by the suppression of the abbey, were annexed to the crowne. There also I saw a very faire church, which though it bee now very large and spacious, yet it hath in former times beene much larger. But I taking my leave of Dumfermling, would needs goe and see the truely noble knight Sir George Bruce, at a towne called Cooras:[1] there hee made mee right welcome, both with

---

[1] Cooras, *i.e.*, Culross, locally pronounced as Taylor wrote it. The pit of which he speaks was near Culross Abbey Church. It ran out under the Forth for nearly a mile, and had a sea-shaft that communicated with an insulated wharf. This mine, reckoned one of the wonders of Scotland, was drowned in the great storm of March 1625, six years after Taylor's visit. Tradition has it that James VI. during his visit to Scotland in 1617 was, at his own request, taken through the pit by Sir George Bruce to the above-mentioned wharf. Finding himself in the midst of the waves he raised his usual cry of "Treason," when Sir George pointed to a pinnace at the wharf, and offered him the choice of going ashore in it, or returning by the way they had come. His majesty chose the shorter way.

varietie of fare, and after all, hee commanded three of his
men to direct me to see his most admirable cole-mines,
which (if man can or could worke wonders) is a wonder :
for my selfe neither in any travells that I have beene in,
nor any history that I have read, or any discourse that I
have heard, did never see, read, or heare of any worke of
man that might parallell or bee equivalent with this unfellowed and unmatchable worke : and though all I can say
of it cannot describe it according to the worthines of his
vigilant industry, that was both the occasion, inventor, and
maintainer of it ; yet rather then the memory of so rare an
enterprise, and so accomplisht a profit to the common-wealth
shall bee raked and smothered in the dust of oblivion, I will
give a little touch at the description of it, although I, amongst
writers, am like he that worst may hold the candle.

The mine hath two wayes into it, the one by sea and the
other by land ; but a man may goe into it by land, and
returne the same way if he please, and so he may enter into
it by sea, and by sea he may come forth of it : but I for
varieties sake went in by sea, and out by land.   Now men
may object, how can a man goe into a mine, the entrance of
it being into the sea, but that the sea will follow him and
so drown the mine ?   To which objection thus I answer,
That at low water, the sea being ebd away, and a great part
of the sand bare ; upon this same sand (being mixed with
rockes and cragges) did the master of this great worke build
a round circular frame of stone, very thicke, strong, and
joined together with glutinous and bitumous matter, so high
withall, that the sea at the highest flood, or the greatest
rage of storme or tempest, can neither dissolve the stones so
well compacted in the building, or yet overflowe the height of
it.   Within this round frame (at all adventures) hee did
set workemen to digge with mattockes, pick-axes, and other
instruments fit for such purposes.   They did dig forty foot
downe right, into and through a rocke.   At last they found
that which they expected, which was sea-cole, they following
the veine of the mine, did dig forward still : so that in the
space of eight and twenty, or nine and twenty yeeres, they
have digged more then an English mile under the sea, that
when men are at worke belowe, an hundred of the greatest

shippes in Britaine may saile over their heads. Besides, the mine is most artificially cut like an arch or a vault, all that great length, with many nookes and by-wayes; and it is so made, that a man may walke upright in the most places, both in and out. Many poore people are there set on work, which otherwise through the want of employment would perish. But when I had seene the mine, and was come forth of it again, after my thankes given to Sir George Bruce, I told him, that if the plotters of the Powder Treason in England had seene this mine, that they (perhaps) would have attempted to have left the Parliament House, and have undermined the Thames, and so have blown up the barges and wherries, wherein the King, and all the estates of our kingdome were. Moreover, I said, that I could affoord to turne tapster at London, so that I had but one quarter of a mile of his mine to make mee a Cellar, to keep Beere and Bottle-ale in.

The sea at certaine places doth leake, or soake into the mine, which, by the industry of Sir George Bruce, is all conveyed to one well neere the land, where he hath a device like a horse-mill, that with three horses and a great chaine of iron, going downeward many fadomes, with thirty-six buckets fastened to the chaine; of the which eighteene goe downe still to be filled; and eighteene ascend up to be emptied, which doe emptie themselves (without any man's labour) into a trough that conveyes the water into the sea againe; by which means he saves his mine, which otherwise would be destroyed with the sea; besides he doth make every weeke ninety or a hundred tunnes of salt, which doth serve most part of Scotland; some he sends into England, and very much into Germany: all which shewes the painfull industry with Gods blessing to such worthy endeavours: I must with many thankes re-member his courtesie to me, and lastly how he sent his man to guide mee tenne miles on the way to Sterling, where by the way I saw the outside of a faire and stately house called Allaway,[1] belonging to the Earle of Marr, which by reason that his Honour was not there, I past by and went to

[1] Alloa Tower built about 1223. In 1800 a fire destroyed all later additions to the original building.

Sterling, where I was entertained and lodged at one Master John Archibalds, where all my want was that I wanted roome to containe halfe the good cheere that I might have had there ; hee had me into the castle, which in few words I doe compare to Windsor for situation, much more then Windsor in strength, and somewhat lesse in greatnesse ; yet I dare affirme, that his Majestie hath not such another hall to any house that he hath neither in England or Scotland, except Westminster Hall which is now no dwelling hall for a prince, being long since metamorphosed into a house for the law and the profits.[1]

This goodly hall was built by King James the fourth, that marryed King Henry the eights sister, and after was slaine at Flodden field ; but it surpasses all the halls for dwelling houses that ever I saw, for length, breadth, height and strength of building ; the castle is built upon a rocke very lofty, and much beyond Edenborough castle in state and magnificence, and not much inferiour to it in strength, the roomes of it are lofty, with carved workes on the seelings, the doores of each roome being so high, that a man may ride upright on horseback into any chamber or lodging. There is also a goodly faire chappell, with cellers, stables, and all other necessary offices, all very stately and befitting the majesty of a King.

From Sterling I rode to Saint Johnston, a fine towne it is, but it is much decayed, by reason of the want of his Majesties yeerely comming to lodge there. There I lodged one night at an inne, the goodman of the house his name being Petricke Pettcarne, where my entertainement was with good cheere, good lodging, all too good to a bad weary guest. Mine host told me that the Earle of Marr, and Sir William Murray of Abercarny were gone to the great hunting to the Brea of Marr ; but if I made haste I might perhaps finde them at a towne called Breekin, or Breechin, two and thirty miles from Saint Johnstone whereupon I tooke a guide to

---

[1] Stirling Palace was begun by James V. and completed by Mary. Defoe, who visited Scotland about a century later than the Water-Poet, is even more eloquent in his praise of Stirling. The hall of which Taylor speaks, Defoe describes as " the noblest I ever saw in Europe, both Height, Length, and Breadth."

Breekin the next day, but before I came, my Lord was gone
from thence foure dayes.

Then I tooke another guide, which brought me such
strange wayes over mountaines and rockes, that I thinke my
horse never went the like; and I am sure I never saw any
wayes that might fellow them. I did go through a countrey
called Glaneske,[1] where passing by the side of a hill, so
steepe as the ridge of a house, where the way was rocky, and
not above a yard broad in some places, so fearfull and horrid
it was to looke downe into the bottome, for if either horse
or man had slipt, he had fallen (without recovery) a good
mile downeright; but I thanke God, at night I came to a
lodging in the Laird of Eggels land,[2] where I lay at an Irish[3]
house, the folkes not being able to speake scarce any English,
but I supped and went to bed, where I had not laine long,
but I was enforced to rise; I was so stung with Irish
musketaes, a creature that hath sixe legs, and lives like a
monster altogether upon mans flesh; they doe inhabite and
breed most upon sluttish houses, and this house was none of
the cleanest: the beast is much like a louse in England,
both in shape and nature; in a word, they were to me the
A and the Z, the prologue and the epilogue, the first and
the last that I had in all my travels from Edenborough;
and had not this Highland Irish house helped me at a pinch,
I should have sworn that all Scotland had not been so kind
as to have bestowed a louse upon me; but with a shift that
I had, I shifted off my canibals, and was never more troubled
with them.

The next day I travelled over an exceeding high mountaine, called mount Skeene,[4] where I found the valley very
warme before I went up it; but when I came to the top of
it, my teeth beganne to dance in my head with cold, like
virginals jacks;[5] and withall, a most familiar mist embraced
me round, that I could not see thrice my length any way:
withall, it yeelded so friendly a deaw, that it did moysten
thorow all my clothes; where the old proverbe of a Scottish

---

[1] Glenesk, the basin of the upper reaches of the North Esk, in the parish of
Lochlee, Forfarshire. [2] The Castle of Lochlee, which belonged to Lindsay of
Edzell. Edzell is locally pronounced *Aigle*. [3] Irish, *i.e.*, Highland. [4] Mount
Keene, in the parish of Lochlee. Its height is 3079 feet. [5] The Virginal was
a kind of small pianoforte, having a quill and jack like those of the spinet.

miste was verified, in wetting me to the skinne. Up and downe, I thinke this hill is six miles, the way so uneven, stony, and full of bogges, quagmires, and long heath, that a dogge with three legs will out-runne a horse with foure : for doe what wee could wee were foure hours before we could passe it.

Thus with extreme travell, ascending and descending, mounting and alighting, I came at night to the place where I would be, in the Brea of Marr, which is a large country, all composed of such mountaines, that Shooter's hill, Gads hill, Highgate hill, Hampsted hill, Birdlip hill, or Malvernes hill, are but mole-hills in comparison, or like a liver, or a gizard under a capons wing, in respect of the altitude of their tops, or perpendicularitie of their bottomes. There I saw mount Benawne,[1] with a furr'd mist upon his snowie head instead of a nightcap : for you must understand, that the oldest man alive never saw but the snow was on the top of divers of those hills, both in summer, as well as in winter. There did I finde the truely noble and right honourable Lords John Erskin Earle of Marr, James Stuart Earle of Murray, George Gordon Earle of Engye,[2] sonne and heire to the Marquesse of Huntly, James Erskin Earle of Bughan, and John Lord Erskin, sonne and heire to the Earle of Marr, and their Countesses, with my much honoured, and my best assured and approved friend, Sir William Murray knight, of Abercarny, and hundred of others knights, esquires, and their followers ; all and every man in generall in one habit, as if Licurgus had beene there, and made lawes of equality. For once in the yeere, which is the whole moneth of August, and sometimes part of September, many of the nobility and gentry of the kingdome (for their pleasure) doe come into these high-land countries to hunt, where they doe conforme themselves to the habite of the High-land-men, who for the most part, speake nothing but Irish ; and in former time were those people which were called the Red-shankes.[3] Their

---

[1] Benavon in Braemar, Aberdeenshire. Height, 3843 feet. [2] Engye, i.e., Enzie, in Banffshire. Earl of Enzie is, since 1836, a second title of the Marquis of Huntly. [3] Redshanks was the name applied to the Highlanders and Irish from their legs being bare to the knee. In his speech from the scaffold, Raleigh spoke of the Irish as Redshanks.

habite is shooes with but one sole apiece ; stockings (which
they call short hose) made of a warm stuffe of divers colours,
which they call Tartane : as for breeches, many of them, nor
their forefathers, never wore any, but a jerkin of the same
stuffe that their hose is of, their garters being bands or
wreathes of hay or straw, with a plead about their shoulders,
which is a mantle of divers colours, much finer and lighter
stuffe then their hose, with blue flat caps on their heads, a
handkerchiefe knit with two knots about their necke; and
thus are they attyred.   Now their weapons are long bowes
and forked arrowes, swords and targets, harquebusses,
muskets, durks, and Loquhabor-axes.   With these armes I
found many of them armed for the hunting.   As for their
attire, any man of what degree soever that comes amongst
them, must not disdaine to weare it : for if they doe, then
they will disdaine to hunt, or willingly to bring in their
dogges : but if men be kind unto them, and be in their
habit ; then are they conquered with kindnesse, and the
sport will be plentifull.   This was the reason that I found
so many noblemen and gentlemen in those shapes.   But to
proceed to the hunting.

My good Lord of Marr having put me into that shape, I
rode with him from his house, where I saw the ruines of an
old castle, called the castle of Kindroghit.[1]   It was built by
King Malcolm Canmore (for a hunting-house) who raigned
in Scotland when Edward the Confessor, Harold, and Norman
William raigned in England : I speake of it, because it was
the last house that I saw in those parts ; for I was the space
of twelve days after, before I saw either house, corne-field, or
habitation for any creature, but deere, wilde horses, wolves,
and suche like creatures, which made mee doubt that I
should never have seene a house againe.

Thus the first day wee traveled eight miles, where there
were small cottages built on purpose to lodge in, which they
call Lonquhards.[2]   I thanke my good Lord Erskin, he commanded that I should alwayes bee lodged in his lodging, the
kitchin being alwayes on the side of a banke, many kettles and

---

[1] In the *New Statistical Account of Scotland* it is stated that this castle
was built by Malcolm Canmore ; but its name is not given.   [2] Forest huts
built of turf.

pots boyling, and many spits turning and winding, with great variety of cheere; as venison bak't, sodden, rost, and steu'de beefe, mutton, goates, kid, hares, fresh salmon, pidgeons, hens, capons, chickens, partridge, moorecoots, heathcocks, caperkellies, and termagants; good ale, sacke, white, and claret, tent, or allegant,[1] with most potent *Aquavitœ*.

All these, and more then these wee had continually, in superfluous aboundance, caught by faulconers, fowlers, fishers, and brought by my Lords tenants and purveyors to victuall our campe, which consisteth of foureteen or fifteene hundred men and horses; the manner of the hunting is this: Five or sixe hundred men doe rise early in the morning, and they doe disperse themselves divers wayes, and seven, eight or tenne miles compasse, they doe bring or chase in the deere in many heards (two, three, or foure hundred in a heard) to such or such a place, as the noblemen shall appoint them; then when day is come, the Lords and gentlemen of their companies, doe ride or goe to the said places, sometimes wading up to the middles through bournes and rivers: and then they being come to the place, doe lye downe on the ground, till those foresaid scouts which are called the Tinckhell,[2] doe bring downe the deere: but as the proverbe sayes of a bad cooke, so these tinckhell men doe like [lick] their owne fingers; for besides their bowes and arrowes which they carry with them, wee can heare now and then a harquebusse or a musket goe off, which they doe seldome discharge in vaine: Then after we had stayed there three houres or thereabouts, we might perceive the deere appeare on the hills round about us (their heads making a shew like a wood), which being followed close by the tinckhell, are chased downe into the valley where we lay; then all the valley on each side being way-laid with a hundred couple of strong Irish grey-hounds, they are let loose as occasion serves upon the heard of deere, that with dogges, gunnes, arrowes, durkes, and daggers, in the space of two houres, fourescore fat deere were slaine, which after are disposed of

[1] The wine of Alicante in Spain is known as *vino tinto* from its dark colour.
[2] "A circle of sportsmen, who by surrounding a great space, and gradually narrowing, brought immense quantities of deer together, which usually made desperate efforts to break through the *Tinchel*" (Scott, note to *Lady of the Lake*, Canto v.).

some one way, and some another, twenty and thirty miles,
and more than enough left for us to make merry withall at
our rendezvous.

Being come to our lodgings, there was such baking,
boyling, roasting, and stewing, as if Cooke Ruffian[1] had
beene there to have scalded the Devill in his feathers : and
after supper, a fire of firre-wood as high as an indifferent
may-pole : for I assure you, that the Earle of Marr will
give any man that is his friend, for thankes, as many firre
trees (that are as good as any shippes masts in England) as
are worth (if they were in any place neere the Thames,
or any other portable river) the best Earledome in England
or Scotland either :   For I dare affirme, hee hath as many
growing there, as would serve for masts (from this time to
the end of the worlde) for all the shippes, carackes,[2] hoyes,
galleyes, boates, drumlers,[3] barkes, and water-crafts, that are
now, or can be in the worlde these fourty yeeres.

This sounds like a lye to an unbeleever ; but I and many
thousands doe knowe that I speake within the compasse of
truth : for indeed (the more is the pitty) they doe grow so
farre from any passage of water, and withall in such rockie
mountaines, that no way to convey them is possible to be
passable, either with boate, horse, or cart.

Thus having spent certaine dayes, in hunting in the Brea
of Marr, wee went to the next county called Bagenoch,[4]
belonging to the Earle of Engie, where having such sport
and entertainement as wee formerly had after foure or five
dayes pastime, wee tooke leave of hunting for that yeere ; and
tooke our journey toward a strong house of the Earles,
called Ruthven in Bagenoch, where my Lord of Engie and
his noble Countesse (being daughter to the Earle of Argile)
did give us most noble welcome three dayes.

From thence we went to a place called Ballo Castle,[5] a
faire and stately house, a worthie gentleman being the owner
of it, called the Lard of Grant ; his wife being a gentlewoman honourably descended, being sister to the right

---

[1] "Cook Ruffian who roasted the devil in his feathers. A bad cook."
(Dictionary of Buckish Slang, University Wit, and Pickpocket Eloquence. By
Captain Grose. Lond., 1811.)   [2] A large ship of burden. Spanish *carraca*.
[3] "She was immediately assaulted by divers English pinasses, hoys, and
drumblers" (Hakluyt).   [4] Badenoch.   [5] Now Castle Grant.

honourable Earle of Atholl, and to Sir Patricke Murray,
knight; she being both inwardly and outwardly plentifully
adorned with the gifts of grace and nature: so that our
cheere was more then sufficient; and yet much lesse then
they could affoord us.   There stayed there foure dayes, foure
Earles, one Lord, divers knights and gentlemen, and their
servants, footmen and horses; and every meale foure longe
tables furnished with all varieties: Our first and second
course being threescore dishes at one boord; and after that
alwayes a banquet: and there, if I had not forsworne wine
till I came to Edenborough, I thinke I had there dranke my
last.

The fifth day with much adoe we gate from thence to
Tarnaway,[1] a goodly house of the Earle of Murrayes, where
that right honourable Lord and his Lady did welcome us
foure dayes more.   There was good cheere in all variety,
with somewhat more then plenty for advantage: for indeed
the countie of Murray is the most pleasant, and plentifull
countrey in all Scotland; being plaine land, that a coach
may be driven more then foure and thirtie miles one way in
it, alongst by the sea-coast.

From thence I went to Elgen in Murray, an ancient citie,
where there stood a faire and beautifull church with three
steeples, the walls of it and the steeples all yet standing;
but the roofes, windowes, and many marble monuments and
toombes of honourable and worthie personages all broken
and defaced:[2] this was done in the time when ruine bare
rule, and Knox knock'd downe churches.

From Elgen we went to the Bishop of Murray his house
which is called Spinye, or Spinaye:[3] a reverend gentleman

[1] Darnaway Castle, in parish of Dyke and Moy, Elgin.   [2] The original
cathedral of Elgin was founded in 1224, but was subsequently destroyed by
fire.   The cathedral erected in its place, of which the ruins are still so
impressive, must have been one of the finest Gothic structures in Europe.
The early Scottish historians vie with each other in sounding its praises.
Thus Bowar calls it "the glory of the whole land," and Buchanan "the
most beautiful of all that had been erected in Scotland."   An elaborate,
though somewhat fanciful, description is also given by the Scottish humanist,
Florentius Volusenus, a native of Elgin, in his De Animi Tranquillitate.
Taylor's reference to the cathedral is interesting as an indication of the state
of the ruins at the time of his visit.   It should be said that the Wolf of
Badenoch is mainly responsible for the ruin of Elgin Cathedral.   [3] Spynie.

he is, of the noble name of Dowglasse, where wee were very well wel-comed, as befitted the honour of himselfe and his guests.

From thence wee departed to the Lord Marquesse of Huntleyes, to a sumptuous house of his, named the Bogg of Geethe,[1] where our entertainement was like himselfe, free, bountifull and honourable.   There (after two dayes stay), with much entreatie and earnest suite, I gate leave of the Lords to depart towards Edenborough : the noble Marquesse, the Earle of Marr, Murray, Engie, Bughan, and the Lord Erskin ; all these, I thanke them, gave me gold to defray my charges in my journey.

So after five and thirty dayes hunting and travell, I returning, passed by another stately mansion of the Lord Marquesses, called Straboggi,[2] and so over Carny Mount [3] to Breekin, where a wench that was borne deafe and dumb came into my chamber at midnight (I being asleepe), and shee opening the bed, would faine have lodged with mee : but had I beene a Sardanapalus, or a Heliogabalus, I thinke that either the great travell over the mountaines had tamed me : or if not, her beautie could never have moved me. The best parts of her were, that her breath was as sweet as sugar-carrion, being very well shouldered beneath the waest ; and as my hostesse tolde me the next morning, that shee had changed her maiden-head for the price of a bastard not long before.   But howsoever, shee made such a hideous noyse, that I started out of my sleepe, and thought that the Devill had beene there : but I no sooner knew who it was, but I arose, and thrust my dumb beast out of my chamber ; and for want of a locke or a latch, I staked up my doore with a great chaire.

Thus having escaped one of the seven deadly sinnes as at Breekin, I departed from thence to a towne called Forfard ; and from thence to Dundee, and so to Kinghorne, Burnt-iland, and so to Edenborough, where I stayed eight days, to recover myself of falls and bruises·which I received in

---

[1] Bog-of-Gight Castle, now Gordon Castle, the Scottish seat of the Duke of Richmond and Gordon.   [2] Strathbogie.   [3] Carnymount = Cairn-o'-Mount, commonly called the "Cairn," in the parish of Fettercairn.   It was the road over the Mounth or Grampians from Braemar to the Mearns or Low Country.

my travell in the High-land mountainous hunting. Great
welcome I had shewed me all my stay at Edenborough, by
many worthy gentlemen, namely, old Master George Todrigg,
Master Henry Levingston, Master James Henderson, Master
John Maxwell, and a number of others, who suffered mee to
want no wine or good cheere, as may be imagined.

Now, the day before I came from Edenborough, I went to
Leeth, where I found my long approved and assured good
friend Master Benjamin Johnson, at one Master John
Stuarts house : I thanke him for his great kindnesse towards
me : for, at my taking leave of him, he gave me a piece of
gold of two and twenty shillings to drink his health in
England. And withall, willed me to remember his kind
commendations to all his friends : So, with a friendly farewell,
I left him as well, as I hope never to see him in a worse
estate : for he is amongst noblemen and gentlemen that
knowe his true worth, where, with much respective love he
is worthily entertained.

So leaving Leeth I return'd to Edenborough, and within the
port or gate, called the Netherbowe, I discharged my pockets
of all the money I had : and as I came pennilesse within in
the walls of that citie at my first comming thither; so now
at my departing from thence, I came monneylesse out of it
againe;[1] having in company to convey me out, certaine
gentlemen, amongst the which was Master James Acherson,
laird of Gasford,[2] a gentleman that brought mee to his house,
where with great entertainement he and his good wife did
welcome me.

On the morrow he sent one of his men to bring me to a
place called Adam,[3] to Master John Acmootye his house, one
of the Groomes of his Majesties Bed-chamber; where with
him and his two brethren, Master Alexander and Master
James Acmootye, I found both cheere and welcome, not
inferiour to any that I had had in any former place.

Amongst our viands that wee had there, I must not forget
the soleand goose, a most delicate fowle, which breeds in
great aboundance in a little rocke called the Basse, which
stands two miles into the sea. It is very good flesh, but it

---

[1] See introductory account of Taylor. [2] Gosford, near Aberlady. [3] Adam,
i.e., Aldham, or Auldhame, a decayed village on the coast of Haddingtonshire.

is eaten in the forme as wee eate oysters, standing at a side-boord, a little before dinner, unsanctified without grace; and after it is eaten, it must be well liquored with two or three good rowses of sherrie or Canarie sacke. The lord or owner of the Basse doth profit at the least two hundred pound yeerely by those geese; the Basse it selfe being of a great height, and neere three quarters of a mile in compasse, all fully replenished with wildfowle, having but one small entrance into it, with a house, a garden, and a chappell in it;[1] and on the toppe of it a well of pure fresh water.

From Adam, Master John and Master James Acmootye went to the towne of Dunbarr with me, where ten Scottish pints of wine were consumed, and brought to nothing for a farewell: there at Master James Baylies house I tooke leave, and Master James Acmootye comming for England, said, that if I would ride with him, that neither I nor my horse should want betwixt that place and London. Now I having no money or meanes for travell, begin at once to examine my manners and my want; at last my want persuaded my manners to accept of this worthy gentlemans undeserved courtesie. So that night he brought me to a place called Cober-spath, where we lodged at an inne, the like of which, I dare say, is not in any of his Majesties dominions. And for to shewe my thankfulnesse to Master William Arnet and his wife, the owners thereof, I must explaine their bountifull entertainement of guests, which is this:

Suppose ten, fifteene, or twenty men and horses come to lodge at their house, the men shall have flesh, tame and wild-fowle, fish, with all varietie of good cheere, good lodging, and welcome; and the horses shall want neither hay or provender; and at the morning at their departure, the reckoning is just nothing. This is this worthy gentlemans use, his chiefe delight being only to give strangers entertainement *gratis:* And I am sure, that in Scotland, beyond Edenborough, I have beene at houses like castles for building; the master of the house his beaver being his blue bonnet, one that will weare no other shirts but of the flaxe that growes on his owne ground, and of his wives, daughters,

---

[1] This chapel was supposed to be built on the site of the cell of St Baldred on the island.

or servants spinning; that hath his stockings, hose, and jerkin of the wooll of his owne sheepes backes; that never (by his pride of apparell) caused mercer, draper, silkeman, embroyderer, or haberdasher to breake and turne bankerupt: and yet this plaine home-spunne fellow keepes and maintaines thirty, forty, fifty servants, or perhaps more, every day releeving three or foure score poore peeple at his gate : and besides all this, can give noble entertainement for foure or five dayes together, to five or sixe Earles and Lords, besides Knights, Gentlemen, and their followers, if they bee three or foure hundred men and horse of them; where they shall not onely feede but feast, and not feast but banket.   This is a man that desires to know nothing so much, as his duty to God and his King, whose greatest cares are to practise the workes of piety, charity, and hospitality : he never studies the consuming art of fashionlesse fashions ; he never tries his strength to beare foure or five hundred acres on his backe at once, his legs are alwayes at liberty, not being fettered with golden garters, and manacled with artificial roses, whose weight (sometime) is the reliques of some decayed lordship.   Many of these worthy housekeepers there are in Scotland, amongst some of them I was entertained ; from whence I did truely gather these aforesaid observations.

So leaving Coberspath, we rode to Barwicke, where the worthy old soldier and ancient knight, Sir William Bowyer, made me welcome, but contrary to his will, we lodged at an inne, where Mr James Acmooty paid all charges : but at Barwicke there was a grievous chance hapned, which I thinke not fit the relation to be omitted.

In the river of Tweed, which runnes by Barwicke, are taken by fishermen that dwell there, infinite numbers of fresh salmons, so that many housholds and families are relieved by the profit of that fishing; but (how long since I know not) there was an order that no man or boy whatso-ever should fish upon a Sunday :   This order continued long amongst them, till some eight or nine weekes before Michael-mas last, on a Sunday, the salmons plaid in such great aboundance in the river, that some of the fishermen (con-trary to Gods law and their owne order) tooke boates and nettes, and fished three hundred salmon ; but from that time untill Michaelmas-day, that I was there, which was nine weekes, and heard the report of it, and saw the poore people's lamentations, they had not seene one salmon in the river ; and some of them were in despaire that they should never see any more there ; affirming it to be Gods judgement upon them for the prophanation of the Sabbath.

The thirtieth of September we rode from Barwicke to Belford, from Belford to Anwicke, and next day from Anwicke to Newcastle, where I found the noble knight, Sir Henry Witherington ; who, because I would have no gold nor silver, gave mee a bay mare, in requitall of a loafe of bread that I had given him two and twenty yeeres before, at the iland of Flores, of the which I have spoken before. I overtooke at Newcastle a great many of my worthy friends, which were all comming for London, namely, Master Robert Hay, and Master David Drummond, where I was welcom'd at Master Nicholas Tempests house. From Newcastle I rode with those gentlemen to Durham, to Darlington, to Northalerton, and to Topcliffe in Yorkeshire, where I tooke my leave of them, and would needs try my pennilesse fortunes by my selfe, and see the city of Yorke, where I was lodged at my right worshipfull good friend, Master Doctor Hudson, one of his Majesties Chaplaines, who went with me, and shewed me the goodly Minster Church there, and the most admirable, rare-wrought, unfellowed Chapter-house.

From Yorke I rode to Doncaster, where my horses were well fed at the Beare, but myselfe found out the honourable knight, Sir Robert Anstruther, at his father in lawes, the truely noble Sir Robert Swifts house, he being then high Sheriffe of Yorkeshire, where with their good ladies, and the Right Honourable the Lord Sanquhar, I was stayed two nights and one day, Sir Robert Anstruther (I thanke him), not only paying for my two horses meat, but at my departure, he gave me a letter to Newarke upon Trent, twenty eight miles in my way, where Master George Atkinson mine host made me as welcome as if I had beene a French Lord, and what was to be paid, as I call'd for nothing, I paid as much ; and left the reckoning with many thankes to Sir Robert Anstruther.

So leaving Newarke, with another gentleman that over-

tooke me, we came at night to Stamford, to the signe of the
Virginitie (or the Maydenhead) where I delivered a letter
from the Lord Sanquhar; which caused Mr Bates and his
wife, being the master and mistresse of the house, to make
me and the gentleman that was with me great cheere for
nothing.

From Stamford the next day we rode to Huntington,
where we lodged at the post-masters house, at the signe of
the Crowne; his name is Riggs. He was informed who I
was, and wherefore I undertooke this my pennilesse pro-
gresse: wherefore he came up to our chamber, and supp'd
with us, and very bountifully called for three quarts of wine
and sugar, and foure jugges of beere. He did drinke and
beginne healths like a horse-leech, and swallowed downe his
cuppes without feeling, as if he had had the dropsie, or nine
pound of spunge in his maw. In a worde, as he is a poste,
he dranke poste, striving and calling by all meanes to make
the reckoning great, or to make us men of great reckoning.
But in his payment he was tyred like a jade, leaving the
gentleman that was with me to discharge the terrible shott,
or else one of my horses must have laine in pawne for his
superfluous calling, and unmannerly intrusion.

But leaving him, I left Huntington, and rode on the
Sunday to Puckeridge, where Master Holland, at the Faulkon
(mine old acquaintance), and my loving and ancient host,
gave mee, my friend, my man, and our horses, excellent
cheere, and welcome, and I paid him with not a penny of
money.

The next day I came to London, and obscurely comming
within Moregate, I went to a house and borrowed money:
and so I stole backe againe to Islington, to the signe of the
Maydenhead, staying till Wednesday, that my friends came
to meete me, who knew no other but that Wednesday was
my first comming: where with all love I was entertained
with much goode cheere: and after supper we had a play of
the Life and Death of Guy of Warwicke, played by the
Right Honourable the Earle of Darbie his men. And so on
the Thursday morning, being the fifteenth of October, I came
home to my house in London.

The Epilogue, to all my Adventurers, and Others.

Thus did I neither spend, or begge, or aske,
  By any course, direct or indirectly :
But in each tittle I perform'd my taske,
  According to my bill most circumspectly.

I vow to God, I have done Scotland wrong,
  And, justly, 'gainst me it may bring an action,
I have not given't that right which doth belong,
  For which I am halfe guilty of detraction :

Yet had I wrote all things that there I saw,
  Misjudging censures would suppose I flatter,
And so my name I would in question draw,
  Where asses bray, and prattling pies doe chatter :

Yet (arm'd with truth) I publish with my pen,
  That there th' Almighty doth his blessings heape,
In such aboundant food for beasts and men,
  That I ne'er saw more plenty or more cheape.

Thus what mine eyes did see, I doe beleeve,
  And what I doe beleeve, I know is true :
And what is true unto your hand I give,
  That what I give, may be beleev'd of you.

But as for him that sayes I lye or dote,
  I doe returne, and turne the lye in 's throate,
Thus Gentlemen, amongst you take my ware,
  You share my thankes, and I your moneyes share.

Your's in all observance and gratefulnesse,
  ever to be commanded,

JO. TAYLOR.

SIR WILLIAM BRERETON
(1636).

SIR WILLIAM BRERETON'S account of his travels was published by the Chetham Society in 1844. With the exception of certain portions relating to Ireland, it had lain in manuscript till that date. The manuscript had been previously placed in the hands of Sir Walter Scott, who offered to edit it with notes; but through some objection to Scott's publisher, his offer was rejected. Though the original manuscript bears no signature, the handwriting proves it to have been the work of Sir William Brereton, a gentleman of Cheshire, who subsequently distinguished himself as a general in the Parliamentary army. It is the record of his travels in Holland, the United Provinces, England, Scotland, and Ireland during the years 1634 and 1635. "This volume," says Mr Hawkins, who edited it for the Chetham Society, "was not the companion of his travels, neither was this journal exactly what he wrote down from day to day. It was, however, probably made up, and in a great degree transcribed, from notes actually made at the time; for there are abrupt changes of construction which give the appearance to a passage of having been put together from two separate memoranda." It should be added that Brereton had strong Puritan leanings, and that Clarendon describes him as " most considerable for a known aversion to the government of the Church."

TRAVELS OF SIR WILLIAM BRERETON (p. 94, Chetham Society).

JUNE 25.—We arrived about five o'clock at Barwicke, where we passed a very fair, stately bridge over Tweede, consisting of fifteen arches, which was built by King James, and, as it is said, cost £17,000.[1] This river most infinitely

---

[1] This bridge, begun in 1611 and opened about 1624, still exists (Scott, *History of Berwick*, p. 415).

stored with salmon, one hundred or two hundred salmons at one draught; but much more was reported by our host, which is almost incredible, that there were two thousand salmons taken since Sunday last. This town seated upon the main sea, the Northern Ocean, and seems to be almost environed with the sea.

The haven is a most narrow, shallow, barred haven, the worst that I have seen; it might be made good, a brave and secure haven, whereas now only one little pink of about forty ton belongs unto it, and some few fishing-boats. There being, therefore, no trade in this town, it is a very poor town, many indigent persons and beggars therein. Here were the strongest fortifications I have met with in England, double-walled and out-works of earth, and the outer walls like unto Chester walls, and without the inner walls a deep and broad moat well watered; the inner walls of invincible strength, stone wall within, and without lined with earth about twenty yards thick, with bulwarks conveniently placed to guard one another, like unto the Buss [Bois le Duc], Bergen, Antwerpe, or Gravelin: these were begun by Queen Mary, finished by Queen Elizabeth, but something in decay; these walls environ the town.[1]

A stately, sumptuous, and well-seated house or castle was here begun by the last Earl of Dunbar[2] where the old castle stood: but his death put an end to that work. Here was a most stately platform propounded and begun: a fair long gallery joiced, not boarded, wherein is the largest mantle-tree[3] I have seen, near five yards long of one piece; this leaded over, which gives the daintiest prospect to the sea, to the town, to the land, and the river. This, with much lands hereabout, was bestowed upon him by King James, who left all to his daughter and heir, who married the now Earl of Suffolk. This town is seated on the north side of the Twede, and is placed upon the sloping of a steep hill.

---

[1] A more favourable account of Berwick and its trade is given by a later traveller, Monsieur Jorevin de Rochefort, who visited the town some twenty or thirty years after Brereton. See below, p. 229.   [2] George Hume attended King James from Scotland; he was created Lord Hume of Berwick in England, and Earl of Dunbar in Scotland. He died in 1611, leaving only one child, who married Theophilus, Earl of Suffolk.   [3] The lintel of a fire-place when made of wood.

They speak of three hundred and sixty salmons taken at one draught, and ordinarily about eighty, and one hundred, or one hundred and twenty, at one draught. We lodged at the Crown, were well used ; 8*d.* ordinary, and 6*d.* our servants, and great entertainment and good lodging, a respective host and honest reckoning.

Junii 26.—Upon Friday we departed from Berwicke, which, though it be seated in Scotland, yet it is England, and is annexed to the crown of England by acts of Parliament, and sends two burgesses to the Parliament-house, and here the country is not reputed Scottish, until you come to a town, four miles distant from Barwick, called Aten, which belongs to Lord Aten, who hath there a pretty castle[1] placed on the side of an hill ; hence you pass (after you leave a few corn-fields near the town) over the largest and vastest moors that I have ever seen, which are now dry, and whereupon (in most parts) is neither sheep, beast, nor horse.[2] Here is a mighty want of fire in these moors ; neither coal, nor wood, nor turf ; only they cut and flea top-turves with linge [3] upon them. These moors you travel upon about eight miles, and then come to a village called Apthomas,[4] and not far hence you leave the castle and town of Dunglass[5] on left hand, which is pleasantly seated, and seemeth to be in good repair, and not far hence is there an high-built house or castle, called Anderwick,[6] belonging to Mr Maxwell of the bedchamber.

Enquiring the way before, how far to Dunbar, it was

[1] Berwick bounds extend only two miles from the town. Ayton is nine miles distant. The castle of which Brereton speaks has long since disappeared. [2] This same route is thus described by a traveller who visited Scotland in 1704 :—" I passed over severall champaign open grounds, and down severall steep rocky hills, but commonly over a hard way, except on some moors and heaths, that are so strangely rotten and barren that they bear only a sort of moss, and some gorse, ling, or furze, and some places of these even on hills will swallow up a horse." Nothing is known of the traveller here quoted. His manuscript, which fell into the hands of Johnes the translator of Froissart, was published by Blackwood in 1818 under the title of *North of England and Scotland in* 1704. Coming after 1700 he is excluded from the present collection. As he is little known, however, we shall quote him where he seems to illustrate some earlier traveller. [3] To *flay* is to pare turf. *Ling* or *linge* is heather. [4] Old Cambus ? [5] The Castle of Dunglass was a stronghold of the Earls of Home and afterwards of the Douglases. It was destroyed by the Protector Somerset in 1548, but was afterwards rebuilt and enlarged. [6] Innerwick.

answered, it was three miles. I demanded whether so far; he said, "Yes, it was three bonnie mile." About a mile from Dunbar, we observed this husbandry; the grass, weeds and wreck, brought by the sea and with the tide, and left upon the sands, was carried and laid thick upon the ground. This used for corn.

Here is my Lord Rocksburne's[1] house or castle,[2] seated with[in] six score of the main sea, where groweth and prospereth many kinds of wood; the highest thorns that I ever saw; this I admired, because I have observed all the sea-coasts whereby we passed, almost an hundred miles, and could not find any manner of wood prospering near the sea-coast. Here, in the village, we observed the sluttish women washing their clothes in a great tub with their feet, their coats, smocks and all, tucked up to their breech.

We came from Barwicke about seven o'clock, and came to Dunbarr about twelve, which is twenty English miles: it is not improperly called Dunbarr,[3] because it is so environed with shelfs, bars and sands, as there is no manner of haven, though the main sea beat upon the town, which indeed is not seated upon any river, which might furnish it with an haven or a navigable channel; only here is an haven made of great stones piled up, whereinto at a spring-tide a ship of one hundred ton may enter, but not without much hazard. Six miles hence in the sea (though it be a far shorter cut by land) is the island of Bass, which is here very conspicuous; a mighty high rock placed in the sea, whereinto there is only one passage, and that for a single person. This is now fortified, and inhabited by the lord of the Bass. It is about one English mile about. Herein are kept sheep, and some kine and coneys; abundance of fowl breed here, solem-geese, storts,[4] scoutes,[5] and twenty several sorts of fowl, which make such a noise as that you may hear them and nothing else a mile before you come to them. These solem-geese (as it is reported of them), when their eggs are sufficiently sitten,

---

[1] Roxburgh's.　[2] Broxmouth House. The present building is comparatively modern. It was in the park adjoining this house that Cromwell stood during the Battle of Dunbar. The mound on which he stood still bears his name. [3] *Dunbar* is *dun barr* (Gael.), "fort on the point." [4] Probably the cormorant, which is known in Scotland as the *scart*. [5] Guillemots.

they stamp upon them with their feet, and break them; they breed in the sides of the rocks, and there is fowl (said to be) sold here, taken in this island, worth £200 per annum. Here is excellent fresh water in this isle, a dainty pure spring which is to be the more admired. The isle of May is not hence above three leagues, and it is easy to be discerned, wherein also abundance of fowl breed.

From Dunbarr to Edenburgh we came this day in the afternoon; it is called but twenty miles, but it is twenty-five or twenty-six miles at least; and by the way we observed very many stately seats of the nobles. One we passed near unto, which is the Earl of Winton's, a dainty seat placed upon the sea.[1] Here also are apple-trees, walnut-trees, sycamore, and other fruit-trees, and other kinds of wood which prosper well, though it be very near unto, and within the air of, the sea. In this house the king lodged three nights; and in this earl's chamber at Edenborough, in Mr William Callis his house in the High-street near the Cross, I lodged, and paid one shilling and sixpence per noctem for my lodging.

About six or seven miles from this city I saw and took notice of divers salt-works in poor houses erected upon the sea coast.[2] I went into one of them, and observed iron pans eighteen foot long and nine foot broad; these larger pans and houses than those at the Sheildes. An infinite, innumerable number of salt-works here are erected upon this shore; all make salt of sea-water. About four miles hence stands Mussleborrow, touching which they have this proverb: Mussleborrow was a borrow when Edenborough was none, and shall be a burrough when Edenborough shall be none.

About nine o'clock at night we came into Edenborough, where, by reason of the foot-boy's negligences, we were put upon great straights, and had our lodging to seek at ten o'clock, and in conclusion, were constrained to accept of mean and nasty lodging, for which we paid one shilling and eight-pence; and the next morning, *Saturday, 27 Junii,* we

---

[1] Seaton House, already referred to by Fynes Moryson. George, third Earl of Winton, entertained both James I. and Charles I. in this house. [2] Prestonpans, formerly known as Salt Preston on account of its salt pans.

went to the Towle-boothe, where are the courts of justice,
which are six : 1. The Court wherein meet the Lords of
the Privy Council, whereof are most of the eminent nobles of
the land.   2. That Court wherein there are fifteen judges sit
attired in purple gowns, turned up with velvet of the same
colour; hereof the President is Sir Robert [Spottiswoode].[1]
As it is here reported, if any of those fifteen be absent
hence any day, they incur the forfeiture of, and pay, one
pound a day for absence.[2]   The Archbishop of St Andrewe's,
Lord Chancellor of Scotland, is the prime man in this
kingdom.   3. There is another inferior Court near adjoining
hereunto, wherein sits weekly and successively every one
of these fifteen judges alone ; this court takes only cognizance of inferior causes, and of less importance : and, as it
seems unto me, is erected in favour and ease of the rest
fifteen judges; and if any intricate cause or of greater consequence occur, the present judge then propounds unto and
consults with the rest of the fifteen judges.   In this court
I observed the greatest rudeness, disorder, and confusion,
that ever I saw in any court of justice ; no, not the like
disorder in any of our sessions, for here two or three plead
and speak together, and that with such a forced, strained
voice as the strongest voice only carries it ; yea, sometimes
they speak about two or three several causes at one and
the same time, which makes an extraordinary disorder and
confusion, so as no man breathing can hear distinctly or
understand anything so promiscuously spoken.   4. There is
an Exchequer, or court of the king's revenue.   5. There is
a court below, under the before-named courts, wherein sit
the judges touching criminal matters and misdemeanours.
6. The Consistory, which takes only cognizance of ecclesiastical affairs.

In this kingdom the clergy of late extend their authority
and revenues.   Archbishoprick of St Andrewes is Lord

[1] Sir Robert Spottiswoode, President of the Court of Session, was the second
son of Archbishop Spottiswoode, the historian, who is mentioned below.   [2] In
an Act for regulating the sederunts of the Lords, the Lords resolve " that such
(Lords) as come in after the Lords are sett and entered upon business, shall
lose the sum of five merks, and such as are altogether absent . . . . . shall
lose the sum of twenty merks for each sederunt " (Acts of Sederunt, 16th July
1701).

Chancellor of Scotland and Regent here. And, as I was informed by some intelligent gentleman, it is here thought and conceived that they will recover so much of that land and revenues belonging formerly to the Abbeys, as that they will in a short time possess themselves of the third part of the kingdom. The Duke of Lennox and Marquis Hamilton are possessed of the largest proportion of Church-land : it is expected that they should resign and deliver up their interests and rights therein to the Church, whose example it is thought will induce the rest of the nobility to do the like.[1]   And to the end that they may carry some sway in Parliament, it is now endeavoured (as some here informed me, Mr Calderwood [2] and Dr Sharpe [3]) to restore abbots, and to invest them in the revenues and seats of abbeys : hereof they say there are forty-eight which are intended to be established, who are all to sit and carry voices in Parliament ; which, if it can be effected, then there will be always in the parliament-house so strong a party for the king, considering those officers that have an immediate dependance upon him and the bishops and abbots, as that they will be able to sway the whole house.   Divers of the clergy incline this way, and many also are mighty opposite and averse hereunto.[4]

This *Saturday*, after dinner, I took a view of the castle here, which is seated very high and sufficiently commanding, and being able to batter the town ; this is also seated upon the top of a most hard rock, and the passage whereunto was (as they there report) made through that hard and impregnable rock, which cannot be touched or hewed, and it is indeed a stately passage, wherein was used more industry, pains, art, and endeavour, than in any place I have found amongst the Scotts.   It is but a very little castle, of no great

---

[1] In 1629 a compromise was made between Charles I. and the Scottish nobles regarding these church lands. By this arrangement "the church lands were to remain in the hands of those who held them, upon the payment of certain rents to the king" (Gardiner, *The Personal Government of Charles I.,* vol. i. p. 350).   [2] David Calderwood, author of the *History of the Kirk of Scotland.*   [3] Not the notorious archbishop of that name, who was at this date only eighteen years of age.   [4] About the period of Brereton's visit, Charles I. was feeling his way towards the establishment of Episcopacy in Scotland. The memorable attempt to introduce the English liturgy in St Giles was made about two years later.

receipt, but mighty strength; it is called Castrun Puel-
larum, because the kings of the Picts kept their virgins
therein; upon the wall of the castle, towards the top, is
this insculpsion, part thereof gilt,—a crown and sceptre,
and dagger placed under it cross-wise, with this super-
scription : " Nobis hæc invicta miserunt, 106 proavi ; " the
same arms and inscription is placed upon the front of the
abbey, which is the king's house.   Out of the court of this
high-seated castle, there was one that watched (a soldier in
his turn) in a little wooden house or cabin, which by a
whirlwind was taken and thrown down both together over
the castle wall and to the bottom of this high and steep
rock, and the man not hurt or bruised, save only his finger
put of joint.   Hence you may take a full view of the
situation of the whole city, which is built upon a hill
nothing oversteep, but sufficiently sloping and ascending to
give a graceful ascent to the great street, which I do take
to be an English mile long, and is the best paved street
with bowther[1] stones (which are very great ones) that I
have seen : the channels are very conveniently contrived on
both sides the streets, so as there is none in the middle ;
but it is the broadest, largest, and fairest pavement, and
that entire, to go, ride, or drive upon.

Here they usually walk in the middle of the street, which
is a fair, spacious, and capacious walk.   This street is the
glory and beauty of this city : it is the broadest street
(except in the Low Countries, where there is a navigable
channel in middle of the street) and the longest street I have
seen, which begins at the palace, the gate whereof enters
straight into the suburbs, and is placed at the lower end of
the same.   The suburbs make an handsome street ; and
indeed the street, if the houses, which are very high, and
substantially built of stone (some five, some six stories high),
were not lined to the outside and faced with boards, it were
the most stately and graceful street that ever I saw in my
life ; but this face of boards, which is towards the street,
doth much blemish it, and derogate from glory and beauty ;
as also the want of fair glass windows, whereof few or none
are to be discerned towards the street, which is the more

_____
[1] Boulder.

complete, because it is as straight as may be. This lining with boards (wherein are round holes shaped to the proportion of men's heads), and this encroachment into the street about two yards, is a mighty disgrace unto it, for the walls (which were the outside) are stone; so, as if this outside facing of boards were removed, and the houses built uniform all of the same height, it were the most complete street in Christendom.

This city is placed in a dainty, healthful pure air, and doubtless were a most healthful place to live in, were not the inhabitants most sluttish, nasty, and slothful people. I could never pass through the hall, but I was constrained to hold my nose; their chambers, vessel, linen and meat, nothing neat, but very slovenly; only the nobler and better sort of them brave, well-bred men, and much reformed. This street, which may indeed deserve to denominate the whole city, is always full thronged with people, it being the marketplace, and the only place where the gentlemen and merchants meet and walk, wherein they may walk dry under foot though there hath been abundance of rain. Some few coaches are here to be found for some of the great lords and ladies, and bishops.

Touching the fashion of the citizens, the women here wear and use upon festival days six or seven several habits and fashions; some for distinction of widows, wives and maids, others apparalled according to their own humour and phantasy. Many wear (especially of the meaner sort) plaids, which is a garment of the same woollen stuff whereof saddle cloths in England are made, which is cast over their heads, and covers their faces on both sides, and would reach almost to the ground, but that they pluck them up, and wear them cast under their arms. Some ancient women and citizens wear satin straight-bodied gowns, short little cloaks with great capes, and a broad boun-grace[1] coming over their brows, and going out with a corner behind their heads; and this boun-grace is, as it were, lined with a white stracht cambric suitable unto it. Young maids not married all are bareheaded; some with broad thin shag ruffs, which lie flat to

[1] *Bongrace* or *boungrace*, a shade in front of the bonnet to protect from the sun.

their shoulders, and others with half bands with wide necks, either much stiffened or set in wire, which comes only behind; and these shag ruffs some are more broad and thick than others.

The city of Edenborough is governed by a lord provost (which is equivalent to a lord mayor) and two or three bailiffs, who execute the office of sheriffs, who, as they assume no extraordinary state, only some few officers attending them, so they do not maintain any great houses and hospitalities: and when any occasion of greater consequence and importance occurs, they then call unto them and consult with, as assistants, some of those that have been formerly lords provosts. The people here are slothful, that they fetch not fresh water every day, but only every other day, which makes their water much worse (especially to drink), which when it is at best is bad enough. Their houses of office are tubs or firkins placed upon the end, which they never empty until they be full, so as the scent thereof annoyeth and offendeth the whole house.

I was this day with an intelligent, understanding man, who told me there were about sixty back lanes or streets, which were placed in the side of this street, and went out of it [1] narrow and inconvenient straight lanes, some wider, some narrower, some built on both sides, others only on one side; and enquiring what number of persons might be in this city, I found that it was generally computed that they were no more than sixty thousand persons, because there are only four parish churches in this city, and it is observed that there are no more than about four thousand communicants in every parish. Here is a dainty hospital [2] erecting, not yet finished. I took notice here of that common brew-house which supplieth the whole city with beer and ale, and observed there the greatest, vastest leads, boiling keeves, cisterns and combs, that ever I saw: [3] the leads to cool the liquor in

---

[1] "This made an English gentleman, that was here with the Duke of York, merrily compare it (High Street) to a double wooden comb, the great street the wood in the middle, and the teeth of each side the lanes" (Macky, *A Journey through Scotland*, p. 67). [2] Heriot's Hospital, which was not completed till 1648. [3] *Keeve*, a large vessel, in which the liquor is placed to ferment. *Comb*, a large wooden vessel or tub.

were as large as the whole house, which was as long as my court.

Junii 27.—We went this morning to behold and take a view of Leith, where is the haven belonging to this city; which is a pretty little haven, neither furnished with near so many ships as it is capable of, nor indeed is it a large haven capable of many ships.   There are two neat wooden piers here erected, which run up into the river, but not one ship saw I betwixt them.   There are two churches in this town, which belongs unto and is subordinate to the city of Edenborough.   This towne of Leith is built all of stone, but it seemeth to be but a poor place, though seated upon a dainty haven : the country 'twixt this and Edenborough, and all hereabout this city, is corn, is situate betwixt the hills and the sea.   Upon the top of the Toole-bowthe stands the head of Gawrie.[1]   Here are pies (whereof I have had some this day to dinner) which are sold twelve for a penny English.   Here upon the Toole-boothe stands the head of Earl Gawrie.   Many Highlanders we observed in this town in their plaids, many without doublets, and those who have doublets have a kind of loose flap garment hanging loose about their breech, their knees bare ; they inure themselves to cold, hardship, and will not diswont themselves ; proper, personable, well-complectioned men, and able men ; the very gentlemen in their blue caps and plaids.

The sluttishness and nastiness of this people is such, that I cannot omit the particularizing thereof, though I have more than sufficiently often touched upon the same : their houses, and halls, and kitchens, have such a noisome taste, a savour, and that so strong, as it doth offend you so soon as you come within their wall ; yea, sometimes when I have light from my horse, I have felt the distaste of it before I have come into the house ; yea, I never came to my own lodging in Edenborough, or went out, but I was constrained to hold my nose, or to use wormwood, or some such scented plant.

Their pewter, I am confident, is never scoured ; they are

---

[1] The Earl Gowrie meant is probably the son of the Earl of the Raid of Ruthven.   The son also (in 1600) was engaged in a plot for the assassination of James.

afraid it should too much wear and consume thereby; only sometimes, and that but seldom, they do slightly rub them over with a filthy dish-clout, dipped in most sluttish greasy water. Their pewter pots, wherein they bring wine and water, are furred within, that it would loathe you to touch anything which comes out of them. Their linen is as sluttishly and slothfully washed by women's feet, who, after their linen is put into a great, broad, low tub of water, then (their clothes being tucked up above their knees) they step into the tub and tread it, and trample it with their feet (never vouchsafing a hand to nett[1] or wash it withal) until it be sufficiently cleansed in their apprehensions, and then it looks as nastily as ours doth when it is put unto and designed to the washing, as also it doth so strongly taste and smell of lant and other noisome savours, as that when I came to bed I was constrained to hold my nose and mouth together. To come into their kitchen, and to see them dress their meat, and to behold the sink (which is more offensive than any jakes) will be a sufficient supper, and will take off the edge of your stomach.

Junii 28.—*Lord's Day.*—Touching the government and orders of the church here established. It is governed by pastors, elders, and deacons; there are about twelve elders, eight deacons, and two pastors in every parish, (as Mr Wallis, a judicious merchant informed me:) these deacons, their employment and office is to provide for the poor; the elders take notice and cognizance of all misdemeanors and offences committed in their parish, unto every of which elders there is proportioned and alloted a part of the parish, which is under their care and charge, who take notice of all fornications, adulteries, thefts, drunkards, swearers, blasphemers, slanderers, extortioners, and all other scandalous offences committed in their parishes: these (by virtue of their offices and strict vows, and protestations) are to present all these offenders unto the minister and church-officers, who proceed to ecclesiastical censure; it is the duty of these to provide bread and wine for the parishioners at the communion, and this upon the parish charge; these also are assistants to the pastors in the administration of the sacra-

---

[1] To clean. Fr. *nettoyer.*

ment.   All these officers are yearly changed, and chosen by
the parishioners, and are proclaimed in the church, to be
designed for those places a year before they are invested
with those places, that so if any just exception can be made
against them, they may be put by that office and others
elected.

Once every week, the pastors and elders, and sometimes
the deacons, assemble and meet together, to consult upon and
consider of the affairs of the parish; they are most strict in
their censures against fornicators and adulterers; those that
commit fornication under colour of intended marriage, and
after promise of marriage, are enjoyned to sit upon the stool
of repentance one day.   This stool is a public and eminent
seat, erected towards the lower end of the church about two
yards from the ground, either about some pillar, or in some
such conspicuous place, where the whole congregation may
take notice of them; this seat is capable of about six or
eight persons.   Here this day, 28 *Junii*, I was at sermon in
the Gray Friors, where there stood three women upon the
stool of repentance, who are admitted to sit during the sermon.
Those other fornicators are enjoined three days penance on
this stool; adulterers are censured to stand every Lord's
day upon this stool during twelve months in a sheet of hair,
and this enjoined them in divers churches.   This day, after
sermon, the preacher admonished some who had persevered in
a course of impenitence and uncleanness, and had often been
admonished and enjoined to give testimony of their repentance,
and to make satisfaction to the congregation; this hath been
delayed, and is not performed.   He said, he wondered that
people were not ashamed to sin against God and against their
brethren, and against their own souls, and yet they were
ashamed to make satisfaction unto the church, which had
conceived just matter of offence against them, for so great
scandal thereby given.   He added, that they had proceeded
with much remissness against them, and forborne them not
one year but two, but if at the next meeting they did not
make their appearance, the next Lord's day they would
publish their names to the congregation.   They proceed in
their ecclesiastical censures with all meekness, endeavouring
a reformation first by those means, and very rarely, not once

in many years, do they denounce any excommunicate. There are some officers made choice of to take notice of, and to apprehend all those that loiter in the streets upon the Lord's day, during service and sermon-time, these are punished by being committed to the Toll-bowth; and if any are found in any house tippling, or gaming in church-time, they are committed to prison. Those also called to account that are met walking fromwards the church, and are detained in durance until they be brought before the bailiffs of the town, who punisheth them severely.

Good provision is here made by the deacons, the church-officers, for the poor, a collection and contribution every Lord's day before sermon, every well-affected parishioner doth receive the alms and bounty of those who come to church (all which give something), in box; hereunto they are chosen and designed by the church-officers; this they receive at the church door, and there is also a monthly taxation and assessment laid upon all the inhabitants of the parish, towards the relief of the poor, so as none beg, nor are suffered to wander upon and down the parish; but though many poor people swarm and abound here, and more than I have met with in any part of the world, yet these most abound here, and the most miserable creatures in the world.[1]

Bought in Edenburgh; Thanksgiving Sermon upon birth of Prince,[2] and the Itinerary of Scotland and Ireland:[3] two pair of pistols, which cost eight rixdollars, which is £1, 18s. 4d., a dudgeon-hafted dagger and knives, gilt, 3s. 8d.

Divers earls' and lords' houses here in Edenburgh, as mean buildings as gentlemen's and knights' in London and England. Here I saw the Earl of Trequhere's [4] house, who is deputy treasurer under my Lord Morton; he was made earl when the king was last here. I paid here for my horses two rixdollars, and for our lodging for six persons, three beds

---

[1] As has been said in the Introduction to Brereton's *Travels*, he left his notes in a somewhat fragmentary condition. This must explain such sentences as the above. [2] Probably James, afterwards James II. [3] Possibly that of Fynes Moryson. [4] The Earl of Traquair was made Lord High Treasurer of Scotland in 1636. His house was "a lofty stone tenement on the south side of the main street (the Canongate) to the east of Gillon's Close" (Wilson, *Memorials of Edinburgh*, p. 285, ed. 1872).

every night, 1s. 6d.; for victuals, Saturday, 7s. 2d.; Sunday, Monday, Tuesday, breakfast about £1, 5s.; washing, 1s. 8d.; rewards to the maid and cook, 2s.

The College of Edinburgh, called King James his college, was founded by the citizens about seventy years ago, by the direction of Mr Rollock, the first principal thereof, and minister of the college church. The order that is observed in the worship of God is this; upon the Lord's day, they do assemble 'twixt eight and nine hour in the morning, and spend the time in singing psalms and reading chapters in the Old Testament, until about ten hour; then the preacher comes into the pulpit, and the psalm being ended, he reads a printed and prescribed prayer, which is an excellent prayer; this being ended, another psalm is sung, and then he prays before sermon, and concludes his sermon betwixt eleven and twelve hour; and during the intermission, many continue in the church until the afternoon's exercise, which begins soon after one, is performed in the same manner as in the morning, save the chapters then read out of the New Testament, and they conclude about four hour. I was in the morning at the Gray Friors, where I heard a very worthy man, Mr James Sherley; in the wall of the yard of this church, I observed very fair tombs and monuments, erected in memory and honour of divers merchants and others interred in this church-yard; which custom, if they continue, in the revolution of a short time the whole wall will be most gracefully adorned with tombs, which are most stately ornaments round about the same. In the afternoon I went to the College Kirk, where I heard a blind man preach, much to be admired. Here I saw the sacrament of Baptism administered in this manner:—The preacher standing in the pulpit, and there being placed and fastened into the same a frame of iron, shaped and proportioned to a basin, wherein there stands a silver basin and ewer; here the minister useth an exhortation of gratitude for God's great goodness, in admitting them to this privilage, &c., and demanding from the witnesses (which are many, sometimes twelve, sometimes twenty), according to a printed form of Baptism; the parent receives the child from the midwife, presents the same unto the preacher, who doth baptize it without any manner of ceremony, giving a strict care of Christian and religious education, first unto the parent, then to the witnesses.

When the sacrament of the Lord's Supper is administered, a narrow table is placed in the middle aisle, the whole length of the aisle, about which the most of the receivers sit, as in the Dutch and French churches, but now the ceremonies of the Church of England are introduced, and conformity is much pressed, and the gesture of kneeling is also much pressed.

About twenty years last past, by virtue of an Act of Parliament made in this kingdom, there was every year once assembled a national council, consisting of one burgess for every burough, one baron or elder in every presbytery, and two or three ministers or pastors for a presbytery; but these meetings were dissolved and taken away about twenty years last past, and now that Act of Parliament is made void and abrogated.[1]

The discipline of the Church of England is much pressed and much opposed by many pastors and many of the people. (Quære touching aire 77.) The greatest part of the Scotts are very honest and zealously religious. I observed few given to drink or swearing; but if any oath, the most ordinary oath was, " Upon my soul." The most of my hosts I met withal, and others with whom I conversed, I found very sound and orthodox, and zealously religious. In their demands they do not so much exceed as with us in England, but insist upon and adhere unto their first demand for any commodity. I observed few bells rung in any of their churches in Edenborough, and, as I was informed, there are but few bells in any steeple, save in the Abbey Church steeple, which is the king's palace. Herein is a ring of bells erected by King Charles immediately before his coming into Scotland, anno Dom. 1635, but none here knew how to ring or make any use of them, until some came out of England for that purpose, who hath now instructed some Scotts in this art. In most of the eminent churches in this city, the king hath a stately seat placed on high, almost round about some pillar opposite to the pulpit.

Junii 30.—About twelve hour we left Edenborough, and

[1] Brereton, of course, refers here to the General Assembly of the Church of Scotland.

came to Light-Goaw,[1] twelve miles from thence.[2] This seems to be a fair, ancient town, and well built, some part of it of stone. Here is a fair church, and a dainty conduit in the middle of the street.[3] Here the king hath a very fair palace, built castle-wise, well seated, so as it may command the whole town, which is governed by a provost and bailiffs, who have power to punish with death offences committed within their liberties. By the way, I observed gentlemen's (here called lairds) houses built all castle-wise. We lodged this night at Failkirk, whence about seven miles distant (which we discerned as we came) is seated the best house or castle of his Majesty in this kingdom, called Sterlin, which is placed upon an high commanding rock and hill, and not far from the fair navigable river Frithe,[4] near adjoining whereunto this is situate. Here is another of his Majesty's houses, an abbey called Drum-farmalin,[5] which is not above ten miles distant hence; and his Majesty's most pleasant and gallant houses are Falkeland, and Sterlin, and Luthgow; and there is also another palace in the abbey of Scune, where the kings formerly were crowned.

All along the shore of Frithe are placed, even almost to Sterlin, from beyond Mussleborough, salt-pans, wherein a mighty proportion of salt is boiled, which cannot be estimated and guessed, because the works are not easily to [be] numbered, which are placed all along the shore, at least thirty English mile. The conveniency of coals gives greatest encouragement to the erection and pursuit of these works; coals abound all along the shore, yea, it is conceived that the vein lies all under the river, seeing it is found on both sides as it were reaching towards the other. Here the chief charge is the getting, which is not easy, seeing the vein lies sometimes sixteen or twenty fathom deep. The greatest part of salt here made is transported into Holland. Here now are some of their ships, which are also supplied with coals hence, now the rather, because the custom of 4s. upon a chaldron being increased, they decline the trade there, and none or few of them are there to be now found. Coals are sold for 3s. or 3s. 6d. chaldron, and carriage 2s. 8d. Here

[1] Linlithgow is locally known as Lithgow. [2] Linlithgow is seventeen miles from Edinburgh. [3] This is the ancient Cross Well, which was erected in 1620. The present fountain is of recent date (1805). [4] Forth. [5] Dunfermline.

was (about seventeen hundred years since) a great stone and earth wall, called Grahames Wall,[1] leading from Forth, six mile below Leith, over the main land to Dumbarton, which is upon the West Sea ; which wall was thirty-two [2] miles long, and gave bounds to the kingdoms of Scots on the south and Picts on the north ; at every mile's end was there erected a tower for the watchmen, and a castle at every two miles' end, wherein was a strong garrison.

About half a mile hence was there a cruel battle fought betwixt the English and Scotts, in anno 1298, in Julii 22.[3] Then was there slain, which here are buried in the church-yard, and whose monuments are still extant, Stewart of Butts [4] (out of which house it is said his majesty that now is hath descended) and Sir John. Grahames,[5] both brave men. About fourteen miles hence is a meare or lake called Loe-mund, in Perth, wherein are the flitting islands which move (my host, Mr Fleemeing, affirmed he hath seen it) : it is most rough in calm weather ; the fish are without fins.[6]   There is in Caricke a rock three yards long and one broad, upon which if you tingle with your knife, it will ring like brass pan : this is called the Ringing Rock, and is near the high-way, about sixteen miles from Port Patrick.   Strange foot-steps in the cave of Caricke,[7] wherein (as my host here affirmed that he had often seen it) are always to be seen and found the prints and footsteps of men, women, and children, of dogs, cats, sheep, kine, horses, deer, and all manner of beasts ; yea, he further protested that he had seen it, that though the sand were overnight sifted, yet these impressions were to be found next morning.   And whereas some write and some report of a deaf rock, it is but a fable, so I was informed by very judicious men.   Here we paid 6s. English supper for seven persons, and lodged in Mr

---

[1] The wall of Antonine.   The appellation *Graham's Dyke* is applied to several ancient ditches and ramparts in England.   [2] It is about thirty-six miles long.   [3] Battle of Falkirk, in which Wallace was defeated by Edward I.
[4] Bute.   [5] Sir John Grahame, the bosom friend of Wallace.   [6] Loch Lomond was famous for three wonders—" Waves without wind, fish without fins, and a floating island."   But according to Geoffrey of Monmouth and the inter-polator of *Nennius*, Loch Lomond boasted still greater wonders than these. It had 300 islands peopled with human beings, 340 rocks peopled with eagles, and 340 rivers flowing out of it while it received only one (*Nennius*, chap. 74).   [7] See p. 156.

Fleemeing's house, who is a very intelligent, proper, complete, and well-bred man. There is a great Earl of this country; his name is Fleemeing, and his title Weghkton,[1] whose house or palace[2] we saw; but there was so much wood encompassed the same, as we could not discern the same. Here we were shewed by Mr Guordon a meadow of his, reputed the fairest meadow in Scotland. I would not give in exchange for it the Broad Meadow, though it be much larger; one acre of the Broad Meadow, worth two of this. I paid for hay here 6d. per noctem, and 12d. peck per oats.

Julii 1.—Hence I departed, and about twelve miles hence there is a town called Cuntellen.[3]

. . . . . .

Here, by the way, we were showed the relics of a stately wood cut down, which belonged to this Earl of Weghkton. There is very little or no timber in any of the south or west parts of this kingdom, much less than in England. I have diligently observed, but cannot find any timber in riding near one hundred miles; all the country poor and barren, save where it is helped by lime or sea-weeds. Limestone here is very plentiful, and coals; and where there are no coals, they have abundance of turves. Poorest houses and people that I have seen inhabit here; the houses accommodated with no more light than the light of the door, no window; the houses covered with clods; the women only neat and handsome about the feet, which comes to pass by their often washing with their feet.

About one hour we came to the city of Glasgoaw, which is thirty-six miles from Edenburgh, eighteen from Failkirke. This is an archbishop's seat, an ancient university, one only college consisting of about one hundred and twenty students, wherein are four schools, one principal, four regents. There are about six or seven thousand communicants, and about twenty thousand persons in the town, which is famous for the church, which is fairest and stateliest in Scotland, for the Toll-boothe and Bridge.

This church I viewed this day, and found it a brave and

[1] Wigton. [2] Cumbernauld House. [3] Kirkintilloch, locally known as *Kintilloch.*

ancient piece. It was said, in this church this day, that
there was a contribution throughout Europe (even Rome
itself contributed), towards the building hereof.[1] There is a
great partition or wall 'twixt the body of the church and
the chancel ; there is no use of the body of the church,
only divine service and sermon is used and performed in
the quire or chancel, which is built and framed church-
wise ; and under this quire there is also another church,
which carries the same proportion under this, wherein also
there is two sermons every Lord's day. Three places or
rooms one above another, round and uniformed, like unto
chapter-houses, which are complete buildings and rooms.

The Tole-boothe, which is placed in the middle of the
town, and near unto the cross and market-place, is a very
fair and high-built house, from the top whereof, being leaded,
you may take a full view and prospect of the whole city.
In one of these rooms or chambers sits the council of this
city ; in other of the rooms or chambers preparation is
made for the lords of the council to meet in : these stately
rooms. Herein is a closet lined with iron ; walls, top, bottom,
floor, and door, iron ; wherein are kept the evidences and
records of the city : this made, to prevent the danger of fire.
This Tole-booth said to be the fairest in this kingdom : the
revenues belonging to this city are about £1000 per annum.
This town is built : two streets, which are built like a cross,
in the middle of both which the cross is placed, which looks
four ways into four streets, though indeed they be but two
straight streets ; the one reaching from the church to the
bridge, a mile long,—the other which crosseth, that is much
shorter.

Two archbishops ; of St Andrewes, Spotswood, Chancellor,
Regent : the other, of Glasgoaw, Dr Lindsey, Bishops, above
twenty.[2]

The prime cities in Scotland : Edenborough, St Andrewes,
Dondye, Aberden, Glasgoaw, Perth or St Johnstone, Light-
gow ; Aire, Sterling, Dumbarton, Erwing,[3] Don Frise,[4]

[1] I have found no authority for this statement of Brereton. According to
the latest historian of Glasgow, the building of the cathedral was probably
begun by Bishop Bondington, who was consecrated in 1233 (Macgeorge, *Old
Glasgow : the Place and its People*). [2] As has been already said, there were
only twelve bishops in Scotland. [3] Irvine. [4] Dumfries.

Haddington, Dunbarr, Erwin,[1] Elgin, Murray, Banffe, Enverness, Boughan.[2]

Fairest bridges in Scottland : Done,[3] which is in the north, under which, as Mr Guordon informed me, that a ship of fifty or sixty ton may pass with her sails full spread.   This is but one arch, placed on a high rock, upon either side much above the water.   A very fair bridge at Glasgoaw,[4] over Cleyd the river ; St Johnstones is a gallant bridge, stands upon Tay ; Aberdeen.   Glasgoaw is a fair bridge, consisting of seven or eight fair arches, which are supported and strengthened with strong buttresses : this river is now navigable within six miles of this city ; it ebbs and flows above the bridge, though now the water is so shallow, as you may ride under the horse belly.   Beyond this river there is seated pleasantly a house, which was Sir George Elvinstones,[5] and is to be sold to pay his debts : the revenue thereunto belonging is above £300 per annum.   The price offered by this city, who are about to buy it, is £6000, the suburbs and privileged places belonging unto it induce them to buy it.[6]

We lodged at Glasgoaw, in Mr David Weyme's house ; his wife's name is Margrett Cambell (the wives in Scotland never change, but always retain, their own names), no stabling hereunto belonging ; in the town we were constrained to provide stabling, I paid 5d. for pease straw, for my straw ; no hay would be gotten.   We paid for victuals, dinner, and breakfast, seven persons, two rix-dollars.

There is a good handsome foundation propounded and set out, to add a good fair and college-like structure to be built quadrangular ; one side is already built, and there hath been collections throughout Scotland towards the building of this

---

[1] This is probably an unconscious repetition.   [2] By Buchan Brereton may have meant Brechin, which is mentioned below (p. 219) as one of the principal towns of Scotland.   He must have been misled about Murray.   [3] Built in the reign of Robert Bruce by Bishop Cheyne.   This is the " Brig o' Balgownie," the prophecy regarding which is well known from " Don Juan : "—

> " Brig' o' Balgownie, though wight be your wa',
>   Wi' a wife's ae son, and a meare's ae foal, down ye shall fa'."

[4] Built in 1350 in place of the wooden bridge by which Wallace crossed the river to attack the bishop's palace.   [5] Elphinstone was Provost of Glasgow. [6] The Gorbals, in early times the compulsory retreat of persons affected with leprosy.

college, and much more money is collected than is needful to the building hereof.[1]   Here the library is a very little room, not twice so large as my old closet; that part of it which is now standing is old, strong, plain building.   This college is governed by one principal, four regents, and about one hundred and twenty students.   Here the scholars may be distinguished from others by gowns (in Edenborough they use coloured cloaks), though coloured, some red, some gray, and of other colours, as please themselves.

Here I visited the Archbishop of Glasgoaw's palace, which seems a stately structure, and promises much when you look upon the outside.   It is said to be the inheritance of the Duke of Lennox, but the archbishops successively made use of it.[2]   Here I went to see the hall and palace, and going into the hall, which is a poor and mean place, the archbishop's daughter, an handsome and well-bred proper gentlewoman, entertained me with much civil respect, and would not suffer me to depart until I had drunk Scotch ale, which was the best I had tasted in Scotland, and drunk only a draught of this ale in this kingdom.   One fair house is here lately built, he that built it died before he finished it. Upon the way hence to Erwin, we discerned many islands, and, amongst the rest, the great isle of Arran, belonging to the Marquess Hamilton.   Many more islands hence appear, and indeed the isles, belonging and annexed unto this kingdom, are said to be more land than half the main land of this kingdom.   Mr Guordon informed me that they were above three hundred in number.

One more remarkable isle, hence shows itself at forty miles' distance; this is placed in the sea about sixteen miles from shore.   It is a mighty high rock, seeming very steep and high, round at the top; the name of it is Ellsey,[3] and

---

[1] The building of which Brereton speaks was the new pedagogium or college of the Faculty of Arts acquired by gift from the Hamilton family in 1460. It was the desire of the college authorities to extend this building; but so low were their funds that it was not completed before the Reformation overtook them.   In 1631 a new attempt was made to extend and restore the original building; but the work was not completed till 1656 (*Munimenta Alme Universitatis Glasguensis*, Preface to Index, pp. xxxix, xl).   [2] Its site is now occupied by the infirmary, near the western entrance of the cathedral.   It is mentioned in an old charter as early as 1290 (Macgeorge, *Old Glasgow: the Place and its People*).   [3] Ailsa Craig.

it belongs to my Lord Castle : [1] not inhabited, but with abundance of fowl, and two eareis [eyries] of goose-hawks, this year
stolen by some Highlanders. This rock or island was in our
view three days, whilst we travelled betwixt sixty and seventy
mile, and when you are at a great distance, it presents itself
in shape like a sugar-loaf, and when you approach nearer, it
seems lower and flatter at the top, but it is a much-to-be-
admired piece of the Lord's workmanship. In this isle of
Ellsey, which is my Lord Castle's, there breed abundance of
solemne (solan) geese, which are longer necked and bodied
than ours, and so extreme fat are the young, as that when
they eat them, they are placed in the middle of the room, so
as all may have access about it ; their arms stripped up and
linen cloaths placed before their clothes, to secure them from
being defiled with the fat thereof, which doth besprinkle and
besmear all that near unto it.

Julii 1.—I came from Glasgoaw about eight hour, and came
to Erwin about twelve hour, which is sixteen mile. We
passed through a barren and poor country, the most of it
yielding neither corn nor grass, and that which yields corn
is very poor, much punished with drought. We came to
Mr James Blare's in Erwin, a well-affected man, who
informed me of that which is much to be admired : above
ten thousand persons have within two years last past left
the country wherein they lived, which was betwixt Aberdeen
and Ennerness,[2] and are gone for Ireland ; they have come
by one hundred in company through this town, and three
hundred have gone hence together shipped for Ireland at one
tide : none of them can give a reason why they leave the
country, only some of them who make a better use of God's
hand upon [them], have acknowledged to mine host in these
words, " that it was a just judgment of God to spew them
out of the land for their unthankfulness."

This country was so fruitful formerly, as that it supplied
an overplus of corn, which was carried by water to Leith,
and now of late for two years, is so sterill of corn as they
are constrained to forsake it. Some say that, these hard
years, the servants were not able to live and subsist under
their masters, and therefore, generally leaving them, the

---

[1] Cassillis.   [2] Inverness.

masters being not accustomed, nor knowing how to frame,[1]
to till, and order their land, the ground hath been untilled;
so as that of the prophet David is made good in this their
punishment: "a fruitful land makes He barren, for the
wickedness of them that dwell therein;" for it is observed
of these, that they were a most unthankful people: one of
them I met withal and discoursed with at large, who could
[give] no good reason, but pretended the landlords increasing
their rents: but their swarming in Ireland is so much
taken notice of and disliked,[2] as that the Deputy [3] hath sent
out a warrant to stay the landing of any of these Scotch
that came without a certificate. Threescore of them were
numbered returning towards the place whence they came, as
they passed this town. Some of them complain of hard
years (the better to colour and justify this their departure),
but do withal acknowledge that corn is as cheap with them
as in this town; but in the distraction and different relation
of themselves, there may be observed much matter of admiration; and, doubtless, *digitus Dei* is to be discerned in it.

Here we were well used, and paid about 4s. 4d. for our
dinners. Here I exchanged Mr Hobbye's nag with Mr
James Blare, for the white nag, and paid £1, 6s. 8d. to
boot.

This town of Erwin is daintily situate, both upon a
navigable arm of the sea, and in a dainty, pleasant, level,
champaign country; excellent good corn there is near unto
it, where the ground is enriched and made fruitful with the
sea-weeds or lime: the other ground which lies at too
great distance to be thus helped, either very poor corn, if
it be sown; or if it lie, no grass at all. The minister of
this town is Mr David Dike,[4] a worthy man; and upon
further conference with my host, I found him a right
honest man of approved integrity, who is also part owner of
the best ship belonging to this town, wherein I spoke with

[1] That is, "to arrange the course of cultivation in a methodical manner."
[2] This emigration had been encouraged by James I. and Charles I., and
specially by Charles's minister Thomas Wentworth, Earl of Strafford. [3] Wentworth, who was made Deputy of Ireland in 1631, and Lord-Lieutenant in 1639.
[4] This must be the well-known Rev. David Dickson, minister of Irvine, who
took a prominent part in the ecclesiastical affairs of his day, was Moderator of
the General Assembly in 1639, and was appointed Professor of Divinity in the
University of Glasgow in 1640.—Scott, *Fasti Ecclesiæ Scoticanæ.*

a merchant, who came lately from West Chester, and performed the journey in five or six miles (days), being about one hundred and eighty miles :—from hence to Don Frise forty-four miles ; thence to Carlile twenty-four, and so to Pereth,[1] &c. Hence to Dublin by sea is about forty hours' sail with a good wind. Hence they trade much into Bourdeaux in France, and are now furnished with good wine. Not far hence, about two miles, lives the Earl of Egglington, at Killwinning, he hath a dozen or sixteen halls or houses hereabouts, and sways much in these parts.

Hence we came to Aire, which is eight miles upon the sea coast, a most dainty, pleasant way as I have ridden, wherein you leave the sea on your right hand ; here we taught our horses to drink salt-water, and much refreshed their limbs therein. Coming late to Aire, we lodged in one Patrick Mackellen's house, where is a cleanly neat hostess, victuals handsomely cooked, and good lodging, eight (sic) ordinary, good entertainment. No stable belonging to this inn ; we were constrained to seek for a stable in the town, where we paid 8d. a night for hay and grass for an horse, and 1s. a peck for base oats. This also is a dainty, pleasant-seated town ; much plain rich corn land about it ; and better haven, there being a river, whereon it is placed, which flows much higher than the bridge, which is a great and fair neat bridge, yet nevertheless it is but a bare naked haven, no pier, nor defence against the storms and weather. Better store of shipping than at Erwin. Most inhabiting in the town are merchants trading unto and bred in France.

Enquiring of my hostess touching the minister of the town, she complained much against him, because he doth so violently press the ceremonies, especially she instanced in kneeling at the communion ; whereupon, upon Easter day last, so soon as he went to the communion-table, the people all left the church and departed, and not one of them stayed, only the pastor alone.

Julii 2.—Hence we went to the cave of Carick, which is about eight miles from Aire, where there dwells a laird, Sir Alexander Kendrick of Cullen,[2] who hath a pretty pleasant seated house or castle, which looks full upon the main sea ; hereinto we went, and there found no hall, only

---

[1] Penrith.   [2] Kennedy of Colzean.

a dining-room or hall, a fair room, and almost as large as
the whole pile, but very sluttishly kept, unswept, dishes,
trenchers and wooden cups thrown up and down, and the
room very nasty and unsavoury.   Here we were not entertained with a cup of beer or ale ; only one of his sons,
servants and others, took a candle, and conducted us to the
cave, where there is either a notable imposture, or most
strange and much to be admired footsteps and impressions
which are here to be seen of men, children, dogs, coneys, and
divers other creatures.   These here conceived to be Spirits,
and if there be no such thing, but an elaborate practice
to deceive, they do most impudently betray the truth ; for
one of this knight's sons and another Galloway gentleman
affirmed unto me that all the footsteps have been put out
and buried in sand over night, and have been observed to be
renewed next morning.[1]   This cave hath many narrow
passages and doors, galleries also, and a closet and divers
rooms hewed with mighty labour out of an hard limestone
rock.   Herein are two dainty spring wells, whereof I tasted ;
a foul, slippery, dark passage is thereinto, and it was first
framed and intended for a stronghold or place of defence, no
way to be offended or annoyed by any assault, if the port be
made good ; though one door looks towards and conveys light
from the seaward, yet these seas are so guarded with rocks
all along the shore of Caricke (such terrible rocks and stones
I never saw) as no ships dare nor do frequent those seas.

This day we were exceedingly punished for want of drink
and meat for ourselves and our horses, and could not meet
with any good accommodation in riding forty long miles ;
the entertainment we accepted, in a poorer house than any
upon Handforth Green, was Tharck-cakes,[2] two eggs, and
some dried fish buttered ; this day, as many days before, I
drunk nothing but water ; and divers of our horses, and
Will. Baylye almost fainted for lack of relief.   This day we
passed up and down many high and steep hills, which you
cannot ride, and very much hard and stony beaten way,
exceeding much moorish barren land.

We came into Galloway about six miles from the chapel,
and therein observed one of the widest, broadest, plainest
moors that I have seen ; it is much moss, but now so dry, as

---

[1] *Cf*. Burns's "Hallowe'en."   [2] Oat cakes.

it is good hanking.   Coming off this moor, we observed an
eminent stone, and tried it with our knives, and it did ring
and sound like metal.   About eight hour we came to this
long desired chapel,[1] the town is thence denominated and so
called.   This is situate upon a long loch,[2] four miles long,
wherein the sea ebbs and flows.   Here we found good accommodation (only wanted wheat bread) in Hughe Boyde's house ;
ordinary 6d., good victuals, well-ordered, good wine and beer,
lodging, and horse meat.   This house is seated four miles
from the Port Patrick, whence it is to Carlingworke[3] 32
miles ; best lodging there is Tho. Hutton ; thence to Don-Frise
28 miles ; best lodging is John Harstein ; thence to Carleil 24.

Julii 4.—We went from hence to the Port Patrick, which
is foul winter way over the mossy moors, and there we
found only one boat, though yesternight there were fifteen
boats here.   We hired a boat of about ten ton for five horses
of ours, and for five Yorkshiremen and horses ; for this we
paid £1 and conditioned that no more horses should come
aboard, save only two or three of an Irish laird's, who then
stayed for a passage, and carried his wife and three horses.
His name is Levinston, laird Dun Draide.[4]   Here we shipped
our horses two hours before we went aboard.   It is a most
craggy, filthy passage, and very dangerous for horses to go in
and out ; a horse may easily be lamed, spoiled, and thrust
into the sea ; and when any horses land here, they are
thrown into the sea, and swim out.   Here was demanded
from us by our host, Thos. Marsh-banke, a custom of 2s. an
horse, which I stumbled at, and answered that if he had
authority to demand and receive it, I was bound to pay
it, otherwise not ; and therefore I demanded to see his
authority, otherwise I was free to pay or refuse ; herewith
he was satisfied, and declined his further demand.   Here is a
pretty chapel lately built by Sir Hugh Montgomeries, laird of
Dunskie on this side,[5] where he hath a castle, and of Newton
de Clanyboyes on the Irish side, where he hath a market-town.

---

[1] A chapel dedicated to St John stood in that part of the parish of Inch,
which was detached to form the parish of Stranraer (*New Statistical Account
of Scotland*).   This explains the old name *The Chapel* by which Stranraer was
known.   [2] Loch Ryan.   [3] Castle-Douglas sprang from a hamlet of the name
of Carlinwark.   Its present name dates from 1792.   [4] Sir William Livingston
of Kilsyth, who also owned the lands of Duntreath.   [5] The family of Mont-
gomery possessed extensive lands both in Scotland and Ireland.   Dunskey
Castle is about half a mile from Portpatrick.

JAMES HOWELL

(1639).

THE following is one of the *Familiar Letters* of James Howell. We have cause to regret that it is one of his briefest, and that it has no companion, as a more detailed account of Scotland by so experienced a traveller and so accomplished a writer as Howell, would have been among the most valuable in the present collection.

LETTER XXVI.—TO MY LORD CLIFFORD, FROM EDINBURGH.

MY LORD,—I have seen now all the King of Great Britain's dominions; and he is a good traveller that hath seen all his dominions. I was born in Wales, I have been in all the four corners of England: I have traversed the diameter of France more than once, and now I am come through Ireland into this kingdom of Scotland. This town of Edinburgh is one of the fairest streets that ever I saw (excepting that of Palermo in Sicily), it is about a mile long, coming sloping down from the castle (called of old the Castle of Virgins, and by Pliny,[1] Castrum Alatum) to Holyroodhouse, now the royal palace; and these two begin and terminate the town. I am come hither in a very convenient time, for here is a national assembly, and a parliament, my Lord Traquair being his Majesty's Commissioner. The bishops are all gone to wreck, and they have had but a sorry funeral: the very name is grown so contemptible that a black dog if he hath any white marks about him, is called Bishop.[2] Our

---

[1] This should, of course, be Ptolemy. [2] By the date of Howell's visit the Scottish nation had made it clear that they would have none of the religious innovation which Charles I. wished to thrust upon them. In 1638 the Covenant had been renewed amid the enthusiasm of all classes in the country; and in the same year the General Assembly, held at Glasgow deposed all

Lord of Canterbury[1] is grown here so odious, that they call him commonly in the pulpit, the Priest of Baal, and the son of Belial.

I will tell your Lordship of a passage which happened lately in my lodging, which is a tavern. I had sent for a shoemaker to make me a pair of boots, and my landlord, who is a pert smart man, brought up a chopin of white wine; and for this particular, there are better French wines here than in England and cheaper,[2] for they are but a groat a quart, and it is a crime of a high nature to mingle or sophisticate any wine here. Over this chopin of white wine, my vintner and shoemaker fell into a hot dispute about bishops. The shoemaker grew very furious, and called them the firebrands of hell, the panders of the whore of Babylon, and the instruments of the devil; and that they were of his institution, not of God's. My vintner took him up smartly and said, " Hold neighbour there, do you not know as well as I, that Titus and Timothy were bishops? that our Saviour is entitled the Bishop of our Souls? That the word Bishop is as frequently mentioned in Scripture as the name Pastor, Elder, or Deacon? Then, why do you inveigh so bitterly against them?" The shoemaker answered, "I know the name and office to be good, but they have abused it." My vintner replies, "Well then, you are a shoemaker by your profession, imagine that you, or a hundred, or a thousand, or a hundred thousand of your trade should play the knaves, and sell calf-skin leather boots for neats-leather, or do other cheats, must we therefore go barefoot? Must the gentle craft of shoemakers fall therefore to the ground? It is the fault of the men not of the calling." The shoemaker was so gravelled at this, that he was put to his last; for he had not a word more to say, so my vintner got the day.

There is a fair parliament house built here lately,[3] and it was hoped his Majesty would have taken the maiden head of it, and come hither to sit in person; and, they did ill who advised him otherwise.

the bishops, excommunicated eight of them, and annulled all Acts of Assemblies held since 1606.   [1] This is, of course, Archbishop Laud.   [2] Other English travellers in Scotland besides Howell noted this.   [3] The Parliament House had been built in 1632.

I am to go hence shortly back to Dublin, and so to London, where I hope to find your Lordship, that according to my accustomed boldness I may attend you.   In the interim, I rest

       Your Lordship's most humble servitor,

                       J. H.

EDINBURGH, 1639.

THOMAS TUCKER

(1655).

O N the 18th March 1652, the English Parliament, under the Protectorate of Cromwell, resolved "that an Act should be brought in for incorporating Scotland into one Commonwealth with England;" and in 1655 commissioners were appointed to proceed to Scotland, and "by all possible waies and meanes to inform themselves of the state of that countrie, and consider of the readiest and best way for settling and continuing the peace and good government of the same, and how the union may be preserved, and the interest of the Commonwealth promoted and maintayned." It was in connection with this object that Thomas Tucker was sent to Scotland. As Register to the Commissioners for the Excise in England, he received orders on the 17th August 1655 to proceed "unto Scotland to give his assistance in settling the excise and customs there;" and it is from the report he prepared that the following extracts have been taken. The entire report is valuable and interesting; but the only portions that require to be reproduced here are Tucker's descriptions of the various seaports of Scotland. As a careful official report, these descriptions will serve to check the irresponsible accounts of other strangers in Scotland. At the same time it should be said that Tucker's report is to this extent misleading, that he evidently measures Scotland by the standard of England, whereas such a country as Denmark would have been a fairer measure to go by.

REPORT BY THOMAS TUCKER UPON THE SETTLEMENT OF THE
     REVENUES OF EXCISE AND CUSTOMS IN SCOTLAND (*Ban.
     Club*, 1825).

A LTHOUGH Scotland is almost encompassed with the sea, (which hath very many inletts into the mayne land,) and hath a very greate number of islands adjoyneing

out-ports remayne constantly here for the lookeing after this port, and the districts thereof, with the citty of Edinburgh.

The members, or creekes rather, of this port, though lye-ing all along the coast, are not many in respect the height and rockinesse thereof, in many places, will not give way for landing goods in every place. The most materiall ones are Eyemouth, not farre from South Barwick, where the Scots and English both did usually shippe out skyns, hides, wooll, and other prohibited comodityes, and againe bring in such, which were there landed, and afterward carryed away for the consumption and expence of the northerne parts of England. The distance of it from the first head-port of Scotland, and the vicinity of it to the east of England, whose officers had noe power there, gave occasion of much deceipt, which hath beene remedyed of late by placeing an officer there constantly to attend at that place, but to have an eye to all the creeks between that and Dunbarre, when any goods passe up by him into the Firth.

The towne of Dunbarre, or village rather, (for all the townes of Scotland, unless the burgh townes deserve noe other appellation, did not use and custome of speech give them a bigger title,) is a fisher towne, famous for the herring fishing, who are caught thereabout, and brought thither and afterward made, cured, and barrelled up either for merchan-dize, or sold and vended to the countrey people, who come thither farre and neere at that season, which is from about the middle of August to the latter end of September, and buy greate quantityes of fish, which they carry away, and either spend them presently or els salt and lay up for the winter provision of theyr familyes. The trade here is little else except salt, which is brought hither and layd up, and after sold for the fishing; the people of these parts which are not fishermen, employing themselves in tillage and in affaires of husbandry. But yett the conveniency of an indifferent good harbour[1] and landing-place hath occasioned the place-ing of a wayter here, not only for preventing any goods from being brought privately on shoare, but alsoe to looke

---

[1] As has been already mentioned, the old harbour at Dunbar began with a grant of £300 from Cromwell.

backward as farre as Eyemouth, and forward as Prestonpans and Newhaven,[1] two small places adjoyneing one to
another, and both lyeing on a flatt shoare where there are
many salt-pans, which is the trade of the place and employment of the people.   Hither many small vessells come to
fetch salt, and oftentimes bringe goods with them, which
would bee stolne ashoare were there not a wayter at these
places who takes care of them, and upon all occasions looks
backe as farre as Dunbarre and forward to Musselburgh ; a
small, or rather three or foure small townes joyneing together,
the inhabitants fishermen and husbandmen, haveing an
open harbor on the outside theyr towne for small boats or
vessells, and a very opportune place for carryeing out and
bringing in of goods, unto or from any shippe that shal be
lyeing in the roade if not looked after.   From this to Leith
the shoare being open upon a flatt sand with some rockes
before it, nothing can either safely or comodiously be landed ;
besides that it lyes all in sight.   As for the tract of ground
beyond Leith, and yett in the district thereof, there are onely
a few fishermen with some two or three empty houses, the
ruins of some salt-workes, and the little country village of
Cramond, not worth the placeing any officer there, and for
that cause left to the care of all the officers in generall, who
may easily in the day-time from the towne of Leith discover
any vessells (or boates from them) goeing to the shoare,
and bee as soone as themselves at theyr place of landing.
And yett, if any thing doe, or should happen to slippe in at
night, the same being for account of the Leith or Edinburgh merchants, must afterwards bee brought to some of
those two places, and if soe, or to any other burgh towne
where there are officers attendng, they can hardly escape
the being seized upon.   There are belonging to the port of
Leith and members, some twelve or fourteene vessells, two or
three whereof are of some two or three hundred tons apiece,
the rest small vessells for ladeing and carryeing out salt,
and to and from the coast of England, the cheife part of the
trade of these parts being driven thence, the rest being

[1] Now called Morrison's Haven, the harbour of Prestonpans.   It was built
by the monks of Newbattle Abbey for the exportation of coal from Prestongrange, and was originally known as Newhaven.

from Norway, the East-land,[1] Low countryes, or France, immediately from the places themselves.

The next port is Burrostonesse, lyeing on an even lowe shoare on the south side of the Firth, about the midway betwixt Leith and Sterling. The towne is a mercat towne, but subservient and belonging (as the port) to the towne of Lynlithquo, two miles distant thence. The district of this port reacheth from Cramond exclusive, on the south side of the Firth to Sterling inclusive, and thence all along the north side of the same Firth as farre as a little towne called Lyme-Kills.[2] This port, next to Leith, hath of late beene the chiefe port one of them in Scotland, as well because it is not farre from Edinburgh, as because of the greatt quantity of coale and salt that is made and digged here, and afterwards carryed thence by the Dutch and others, and the comodityes some time brought in by those Dutch who, avoyding and passing by Leith, doe runne up the Firth, and did usually obtayne opportunity of landing theyr goods on either side in theyr passage, the Firth a little above Brunt-Island contracting and running along in a more narrowe channell. There are constantly resident at this porte a collector, a checque, and some foure wayters to attend to the coast and Inchgarvy.

The member ports on this side of the head port, and on the south side, are Queenesferrye, a small towne, where formerly goods have beene landed, but not of late, because of Inchgarvy lyeing over against it in the middle of the river, and that being furnished with soldiers and an officer or two, to examine and search all shipps in theyr passage, have kept them from that practice thereabout.

Blacknesse, Cuffe-abowt,[3] and Grange,[4] the former of them sometimes reported to have beene a towne,[5] and at that time the port of Lythquo, but now nothing more than three or foure pittifull houses, and a peice of an old castle. The other two are likewise some few houses standing on two places of the shoare nigh some salt-pans and coale-hughs.[6]

On the other side of the port (but of the same side of the

---

[1] Denmark. [2] A pan-house, started for the manufacture of salt, gave a temporary impulse to Limekilns ; but it has long ceased to be a place of any commercial importance. [3] Cuffabouts, a hamlet in Carriden parish, Linlithgowshire. [4] Grangemouth. [5] Borrowstounness became the recognised port of Linlithgow in 1680, and since then Blackness has steadily declined. [6] The shaft of a pit.

Firth) is Elphiston,[1] a small towne, where there is pretty store of greate coale shipped for beyond the seas. And although there bee never a vessell belong to this place, yett the Dutch mostly, and some others, choose to lade there because of the goodnesse of the coale and its measure. The river here being narrowe, the waiter on the opposite side takes care as well as accompt of what is shipped here.

The next place beyond and furthest of the district this way, is Sterling, a pretty burgh, famous for the strength of the castle and bridge, which is layd over the Firth at that place, this being the head of it, and the tyde floweing not a mile above it. Here live some merchants, but the shallownesse of the river, with the windeings thereof, makeing the way long, and not permitting a boat of burthen to passe up soe high, all goods are entred first and cleered belowe at Burrostonesse, and thence afterward carryed up in small boates, as the merchant hath occasion for them.

On the north side of the Firth, there is a pretty fine burgh called Alloway,[2] haveing a fine harbour, and an excellent coale, which is for the most part shipped out and carryed away by the Dutch, there being noe vessell belonging to the place. Nevertheless, there hath usually beene a pretty trade for that comodity, but interrupted of late by some difference happened amongst some of the proprietors of the coalhughes.[3] Here is a wayter constantly resident, to take care of this and the towne of Kennett,[4] where likewise is a very good greate coale, but cheifly sent from port to port, and never or seldome outwards.

The next are Kincarne[5] and Culrosse, the first a small, and the other a burgh towne. From these two places salt onely goes out. There is indeede a coale at Vallefeild[6] adjoyneing to Culrosse, and at Kincarne alsoe, but bought up and spent by the countrey, and not sent out. There were lately some fine vessells belonging to Culrosse, but lost and taken all except two of the best, which still remayne. These two places have a wayter constantly to attend them, with the adjoyneing towne of Torriburne,[7] the cheife place for

---

[1] Elphinstone, in parish of Airth, in Stirlingshire. [2] Alloa. [3] Scotticé, coalheughs. [4] A collier village in Clackmannanshire. [5] Kincardine-on-Forth. [6] Valleyfield in the parish of Culross. [7] Torryburn.

shipping out small coales, where he is mostly resident. There are three vessells belonging to this towne, one of some an hundred and twenty, another of an hundred, and the third of sixty tons.

The last place of this district is Lyme-kills, a towne whence some small coale hath some time beene sent out, but very little of late; and, for this reason, it hath beene comended to the wayter of the next place, to have an eye and take accompt when any coale shal be shipped out, but not esteemed worth the placeing of an officer purposely.

The next head port is Brunt Island, lyeing opposite to Leith, on the north side of the Firth, whose districts reach from Innerkeithen all along the shoare of the county of Fife, unto the bankes of the river Tay. The trade of these parts inwards, is from Norway, the East countrey, and sometimes from France with wines, and outwards with coale and salt, at all times very small, and worth little. For, although this bee the bounds of one of the best and richest countyes of Scotland, yett the goodnesse and riches of the countrey, ariseing more from the goodnesse and fertility of the soyle and lands than any trafficque, hath made it the residence and seate of many of the gentry of that nation, who have wholly driven out all but theyr tenants and peasants even to the shoare side. There is one collector and five officers constantly attending in this port, and members thereof, which are on the west of Brunt Island, Innerkeithen; on the east Abirdore, Kinghorne, Kircaldy, Disert, Wems,[1] Leven, Ely,[2] St Minas,[3] Petten-Weym, Ainster,[4] Craill, St Androes, and South-ferry;[5] all pittifull small townes on the coast, inhabited by seamen, colliers, salt makers, and such like people, except St Androes, which (if I mistake not) is a burgh towne, but if not a pretty neate thing;—which hath formerly beene bigger, and although sufficiently humbled in the time of intestine troubles, continues still proud in the ruines of her former magnificence, and in being yett a seate for the Muses.

To this port and members thereof, there are very many vessels belonging, which are imployed for the carryeing coale and salt outwards and to the coast, and generally every-

---

[1] Wemyss.   [2] Elie.   [3] St Monance.   [4] Anstruther (locally pronounced *Anster*).   [5] Newport.

where in Scotland rather than the ports to which they doe belong, but have received theyr names and denominations from the places of abode and habitation of theyr respective masters, owners, or marriners, who live plentifully hereabouts, because of the roade lyeing before them, and are in number, and of the tunnage each, as followith, viz. :—

		Tonnes.
To Brunt Isle, seaven, whereof	1	40
	2	30
	1	24
	3	20
„ Kinghorne, one of		50
„ Kircaldy, twelve,	2	100
	1	70
	3	40
	3	36
	1	24
	2	30
„ Disert foure,	1	50
	2	20
	1	14
„ Wems, sixe, viz.,	3	20
	1	18
	1	14
	1	12
„ Leven, two, viz.,	1	20
	1	18
„ Ely, two, viz.,	1	50
	1	40
„ St Minas, one,		36
„ Petten Wems, two,	1	100
	1	80
„ Ainster, ten, viz.,	1	50
	1	40
	1	30
	1	25
	1	20
	2	15
	1	14
	2	13

					Tonnes.
To Craill, one of	.	.	.	.	90
„ St Androes, one of	.	.	.	20
„ Southferry, one of	.	.	.	18

The port of Dundee comes next in view, which is a pretty considerable place, lyeing by the mouth of the river Tay, which, springing out of the mountaynes of Albany,[1] and running through the feilds, at length spreads itself into a lough full of islands, and afterward contracting itself, taketh in Amund,[2] (a river of Athol,) passeth on to Dunkell, and thence by Scoone maketh its way into the German Ocean. The towne of Dundee was sometime a towne of riches and trade, but the many rencontres it hath mett with all in the time of domestick comotions, and her obstinacy and pride of late yeares rendring her a prey to the soldier,[3] have much shaken and abated her former grandeur; and notwithstanding all, shee remaynes still, though not glorious, yett not contemptible. The trade of this place inwards is, from Norway, the East countrey, Holland, and France; and outwards, with salmon and pladding. Here is a collector, a checque, and five wayters established, three of which wayters constantly reside here, and the rest are bestowed in the member ports, which are :—

1. St Johnstons,[4] an handsome walled towne, with a cittadell added thereunto of late yeares,[5] lyeing a good way up the river Tay, where there is a wayter always attending, not soe much because of any greate tradeing there, as to prevent the carryeing out wools, skyns, and hide, of which comodityes greate plenty is brought thither out of the

[1] Albany, or Albainn, a name applied to the Highlands of Scotland. [2] The Almond. [3] Dundee was besieged by the Marquis of Montrose in 1645, and stormed by General Monk in 1651. On the latter occasion, in retribution for the stubborn resistance of the inhabitants, 1200 of the garrison were put to the sword, and the town was so thoroughly sacked that each of Monk's men received nearly £60 sterling. [4] Perth. Hector Boece says that Perth began to be called St Johnstone in his day (*Episcoporum Murthlacen. et Aberdonen. Vitæ*, p. 23, Bannatyne Club). But we have seen that more than a half a century before the time of Boece, Hardyng speaks of Perth under the name of St Johnston, and that still earlier it is so called in the narrative of Edward I.'s expedition into Scotland. [5] This citadel, built by Cromwell's army in 1652 on the South Inch of Perth, was one of the four raised to overawe Scotland after the Battle of Dunbar. The very gravestones and walls of Greyfriars' Churchyard were used in its construction.

Highlands, and there bought up and engrossed by the Lowlandmen.

2. Arbroth, a small towne without any trade, but for theyr owne expence, which is but little.

3. Montrosse, seated betwixt the North and South Eskes. A pretty towne, with a safe harbour, risen by the fall and ruine of another towne of the same name, not farre offe.[1] Here, likewise, is a wayter, because there hath usually beene salt brought in; and salmon, pladding, and corne, usually sent forth. The vessells belonging to this port and members are :—

		Tons.
To Dundee, ten, viz.,	2	1
	1	90
	1	60
	1	55
	1	50
	1	40
	1	30
	2	25

		Lasts.
„ Montrose, twelve, viz.,	1	26
	2	18
	2	16
	2	12
	1	7
	3	6
	1	5

The port of Aberdeene lyes next northward, being a very handsome burgh, seated at the mouth of the river Donne, and is commonly called the New towne, for distinguishing it from another towne hard by, of the same name, but more antiquity, lyeing at the mouth of the river Dee, some a mile distant from the New towne, and is the cheife academie of Scotland.[2] This being now a place more for study then trade, hath

---

[1] Old Montrose two miles distant, in the parish of Maryton, where the great Marquis of Montrose was born. [2] Tucker is in error here. New Aberdeen is at the mouth of the Dee, Old Aberdeen at the mouth of the Don. The fame of the "Aberdeen Doctors" had given Aberdeen its first place among the Universities of Scotland at this period. See p. 204 (below).

willingly resigned her interest that way, unto the New towne, which is noe despicable burgh, either for building or largenesse, haveing a very stately mercat place, sundry houses well built, with a safe harbour before it for vessells to ride in. But the widenesse of the place, from the inlett of the sea comeing in with a narrowe winding gut, and beateing in store of sand with its waves, hath rendred it somewhat shallowe in a greate part of it, and soe lesse usefull of late than formerly. But the inhabitants are remedyeing this inconveniencye, by lengthning theyr key, and bringing it up close to a necke of land, which, jetting out eastward, towards an headland lyeing before it, makes the comeing in soe streight. At the end of which formost neck of land there is a little village called Footie, and on the other headland, another called Torye,[1] and both nigh the harbour's mouth, and lyeing very neere unto the place where the ships usually ride, (being forced to keep some distance from the key, because of the shallownesse of the water,) have given opportunity of much fraude, in landing goods privatly, but prevented of late, by appointeing the wayters by turnes, to watch those two places narrowly, when there are any shipping in harbour. The trade of this place, (as generally all over Scotland,) is, inwards, from Norway, Eastland, Holland, and France; and outwards, with salmon and pladding, comodityes caught and made hereabout in a greater plenty then any other place of the nation whatsoever.

In this port there is a collector, a checque, and three wayters, some of which are still sent into the member ports as often (which is but seldome) as any opportunity is offered, or occasion requires. Those are in number five: Stonehive,[2] a little fisher towne, where formerly goods have beene brought in, but not of late, because hindred from doeing soe by the neighbourhood and priviledges of the burgh of Montrose; Newburgh,[3] where sometimes a few deales and timber are brought; Peterhead, a small towne, with a convenient harbour, but spoyled of late by stresse of weather; Friselburgh[4] and Bamffe, where, in like manner, something

---

[1] Futtie and Torrie were fishing hamlets at the mouth of the Dee. Futtie is *Footdee*. [2] Stonehaven, locally pronounced *Stanchive*. [3] Newburgh at the mouth of the Ythan. [4] Fraserburgh.

now and then is brought in from Norway, but theyr onely
trade is coasting, except that from the latter of them some
salmon may happen to be shipped out.   The vessels to this
district belonging are, viz. :—

	Tons.

		Tons.
To Aberdeene, nine, viz., . .	1	80
	1	70
	1	60
	3	50
	2	30
	1	20
„ Frazerburgh, four, . . .		20
„ Peterhead, one of . . .		20

The last port northerly, is Invernesse, lyeing at the head
of the Firth of Murray, not farre from Loquh Nesse, where
the towne is a small one, though the cheife of the whole
north, and would bee yett worse, were it not for the large
cittadell built there of late yeares.[1]   This port hath for its
district all the harbours and creekes of the shires of Murray,
Rosse, Southerland, and Caithnes, with the Isles of Orkney ;
in which, although there bee many large rivers which,
riseing in the hills, runne downe into the sea, and the
oceane hath indented many more creeks and inletts, with
its stormy waves still beateing on the shoare, yett few of
them are serviceable, and those few much too bigge for any
trade that is or may be expected in these parts.   For as the
roughnesse of the sea and weather lye constantly on the
east of them, soe on the west they have the hills for theyr
portion.   The inhabitants beyond Murray land[2] (except in
the Orkneys) speake generally Ober garlickh,[3] or Highlands,
and the mixture of both in the towne of Invernesse is such
that one halfe of the people understand not one another.
The trade of this port is onely a coast trade, there being noe
more than one single merchant in all the towne, who brings
home sometimes a little timber, salt, or wine.   Here is a
collector, a checque, and one wayter, who attends here, and
lookes (as occasion serves) to Garmouth[4] and Findorne in
Murray-land, two small places, from whence some 60 lasts[5]

---

[1] Built in 1652 by the army of Cromwell.   [2] Morayshire.   [3] *i.e.*, Highland
Gaelic.   [4] At the mouth of the Spey.   [5] Loads, generally estimated at 4000 lbs.

f salmon in a yeare are sent out, for which salt is brought
n from France, and sometimes a small vessell comes in from
Holland or Norway.

In the shire of Rosse there are onely two ports, the one
called Cromarty, a little towne in a bottome, with one of
he delicatest harbours reputed in all Europe,[1] the tide come-
ng in a greate depth betwixt two stately rockes, (called the
Sooters,[2]) through which the water passes into a large bay,
where the greatest shipps of burden may ride in safety; and
he other Tayne, a small towne lyeing neere the mouth of a
river of that name. To the former of these nothing comes
nore than a little salt to serve the countrey, and to the
other it may bee a small barke once in a yeere from Leith, to
fetch deales, which are brought downe thither from the hills.

In Southerland there is onely Dun Robin, and some two
small creekes more, where some barkes used to come for
carryeing the Earle of Southerland's corne for some other
parts of Scotland, according as hee findes his best markett.
In these two shires it was never thought worth the charge
of appointing an officer; but the collector keeps a correspondence with some on the place for giveing him intelligence
when any barkes come in or goe out.

In Caithness there is a wayter constantly resident for
lookeing after Thursoe and Weeke, two small ports, from
whence good store of beefe, hides, and tallowe, are usually
sent to the coast; his worke is rather preventive, for
hindering those comodities from being sent into forraigne
parts, than profitable by any thing hee is likely to receive
there. The like alsoe is practised at Kirkewaile, in the Isles of
Orkney, where there is another officer for lookeing after those
Isles, whence they send corne, fish, butter, tallowe, hides, and
sometimes some timber is brought in from Norway, or els a
Dutch vessell may happen to touch there in her passing about.

As for Shetland, (thought to be the Ultima Thule, soe
much spoken of and reputed by the ancients to bee the
furthest part of the world,) it lyes over against Bergen in
Norway, and very difficult to get thither but in some
certaine moneths of the summer. There was never yett

---

[1] In Mercator's map, reproduced in this volume, Cromarty is styled "portus
salutis." [2] "The Sutors" well known to readers of Hugh Miller.

officer either sent or that would adventure thither till of late, when the farmer of the inland comodityes of those parts haveing prevailed with one to undertake his affaires there, the comissioners did comission the same party likewise as to custome and foraigne excise alsoe; but what successe this enterprise may have, must be left to the discovery of some further time. Report speakes the place to bee frequented about May with some Dutch, who come to fish there, bringing beere, strong waters, and tobaccoes with them. The vessels or barkes of this district belonging are, viz. :—

					Tonnes.
To Invernesse, one of	.	.	.		10
„ Garmouth, one of	.	.	.		12
„ Cromarty, one of .	.	.	.		16
„ Thirsoe, one of	.	.	.		30

			Chaldrons.
		1	15
„ Orkney, three, viz.,	.	.	1	13
		1	12

There were lately some nine barkes more belonging to those isles, which have beene taken or lost by storme, this and the last yeare.

Being advanced as farre as the furthest coast of all Brittaine, I shall passe over Stranaverne,[1] Assinshire,[2] and the Western Isles, (places mangled with many armes of the Westerne Sea, imbosomeing it selfe within many parts thereof, and destitute of all trade, being a countrey stored with cattell, craggie hills, and rockes, and planted with the ancient Scotts or wilde Irish, whose garbe and language they doe still retayne amongst them,) and returne southerly as farre as Glasgowe, a very neate burgh towne lyeing upon the bankes of the river Cluyde, which, riseing in Anandale, runnes by Glasgowe and Kirkpatrick, disburthening it self into the Firth of Dunbarton. This towne, seated in a pleasant and fruitfull soyle, and consisting of foure streets, handsomely built in forme of a crosse, is one of the most considerablest burghs of Scotland, as well for the structure as trade of it. The

---

[1] In Mercator's map, Strathnaverna occupies the northern half of Sutherland-shire.   [2] District of Assynt in same shire.

inhabitants (all but the students of the colledge which is here) are traders and dealers: some for Ireland with small smiddy coales, in open boates, from foure to ten tonnes, from whence they bring hoopes, ronges, barrell staves, meale, oates, and butter; some from France with pladding, coales, and herring, (of which there is a greate fishing yearly in the Westerne Sea,) for which they return salt, paper, rosin, and prunes; some to Norway for timber; and every one with theyr neighbours the Highlanders, who come hither from the isles and westerne parts; in summer by the Mul of Cantyre, and in winter by the Torban[1] to the head of the Loquh Fyn, (which is a small neck of sandy land, over which they usually drawe theyr small boates into the Firth of Dunbarton,) and soe passe up in the Cluyde with pladding, dry hides, goate, kid, and deere skyns, which they sell, and purchase with theyr price such comodityes and provisions as they stand in neede of, from time to time. Here hath like-wise beene some who have adventured as farre as the Barbadoes; but the losse they have sustayned by reason of theyr goeing out and comeing home late every yeare, have made them discontinue goeing thither any more. The scitua-tion of this towne in a plentifull land, and the mercantile genius of the people, are strong signes of her increase and groweth, were she not checqued and kept under by the shallownesse of her river, every day more and more increas-ing and filling up, soe that noe vessells of any burden can come neerer up then within fourteene miles, where they must unlade, and send up theyr timber, and Norway trade in rafts on floates, and all other comodotyes, by three or foure tonnes of goods at a time, in small cobbles or boates of three, foure, five, and none of above six tonnes, a boate. There is in this port a collector, a checque, and foure wayters, who looke to this place, Renfrew, Arskin[2] on the south, and Kirkepatrick[3] on the north side of Cluyde, with Dunbarton, a small and very poore burgh at the head of the Firth. The former of these are inhabited with fishermen, that make herring and trade for Ireland with open boates, and the latter gives shelter some time to a vessell of sixteen tons, or thereabouts, comeing from England or Ireland with corne.

[1] Tarbert. In Blaeu's Map, Torbaet. [2] Erskine Ferry. [3] Kilpatrick.

The member ports of this district are :—

1. Newarke, a small place where there are (besides the laird's house of the place) some foure or five houses, but before them a pretty good roade, where all vessells doe ride, unlade, and send theyr goods up the river to Glasgowe in small boates; and at this place there is a wayter constantly attending.

2. Greenocke, such another, onely the inhabitants are more; but all seamen or fishermen tradeing for Irelande or the isles in open boates; at which place there is a mole or peere, where vessells in stresse of weather may ride, and shelter themselves before they passe up to Newarke, and here likewise is another wayter.

3. Fairly, Culburgh,[1] Salcoates, shoares onely of the roade with a few houses, the inhabitants fishermen, who carry fish and cattell for Ireland; bringing home corne and butter for theyr owne use and expense. A wayter in extraordinary here takes care of these places, and advertises the head port when any thing comes in thither.

4. Bute, a small island lyeing in the mouth of the Firth, under which some vessels in stormy weather shelter themselves, but passe afterward up the river. The inhabitants are all countreymen and cowheards, who feede cattell, and spinne, and make some woollen clothe, which carryed to bee dyed and dressed at Glasgowe, where they buy still whatever they have occasion of for theyr expence and provision.

And lastly, Irwyn, a small burgh towne, lyeing at the mouth of a river of the same name, which hath some time beene a pretty small port, but at present clogged and almost choaked up with sand, which the Western Sea beats into it, soe as it wrestles for life to maintaine a small trade to France, Norway, and Ireland, with herring and other goods, brought on horsebacke from Glasgowe, for the purchasing timber, wine, and other comodityes, to supply theyr occasions with. Here alsoe is another wayter in extraordinary. The vessells belonging to this district are, viz. :—

---

[1] Kelburn.

		Tonnes.
To Glasgowe, twelve, viz., . .	3	150
	1	140
	2	100
	1	50
	3	30
	1	15
	1	12

  „ Renfrew, 3 or 4 boates of 5 or 6 tonnes a-piece.
  „ Irwin, 3 or 4, the biggest not exceeding 16 tonnes.

  The next and last head port of Scotland is Ayre, a small towne in Kyle, lyeing over against the Isle of Arren, where formerly the inhabitants, before the troubles of Ireland, report themselves to have had a pretty trade thither. How flourishing soever theyr former condition hath beene, it is now certainely to bee deplored, the place groweing every day worse and worse, by reason of theyr harbours being clogged and filled up with sand, which the Westerne Sea and the winds from the neighhouring islands beate up into it, in soe much that it is very difficult for any vessell to come in or goe out. That which will most conduce to the preserveing the towne either in trade, name, or memory, wil be the strong cittadell built there of late yeares by the English.[1]

  The lymitts or district of this port are of a very large extent and circuit, being all the shoare that bounds and terminates the shires of Kyle, Carrick, and Galloway, places fuller of moores and mosses then good townes or people, the same being in many places not planted, and all of it voyde of tradeing except the towne of Ayre, Kircowbright, and Dunfreeze ; nor in any likelihood of obtayneing any when there is not a shippe or barke belonging to any port in these parts except to Ayre, where there is one shippe of one hundred, another of forty, and a third of some thirty tonnes, and two barques, one of three and the other of some foure tons onely, which are employed most comonly in a coasting trade to Glasgowe, and sometimes with coales for Ireland.

  The creekes along the coast from this place to Port-

---

[1] Built by the soldiers of Cromwell in 1652, on the site of the ancient church of St. John and out of its materials, and at such cost that he declared it might have been built of gold.

patricke, are Dundufmull,[1] Dunneure,[2] Maidenhead,[3] Turne-
berry, Drumgarloch,[4] Girven, Armillian,[5] Ballantry,[6] Garran,[7]
and Glenfoote,[8] at which places there are some five or sixe
fisher-boates, and not many more houses, except Ballantry,
which is a mercate towne, as poore as little.

From the Glenfoote there is noe creeke up the lough,
untill one come as farre as Stranrawer, otherwise called the
Chappell,[9] being a small mercate towne the side of the lough,
which would prove a pretty harbour for shelter of vessells,
in time of storme to putt in there, which is certainely very
seldome and rare, in respect there is not now nor ever was
any trade to bee heard of here.

Next to Stranrawer is Girvellen,[10] a creeke, whether boates
come and goe to and from Ireland, and next to those two
is Port-patrick, a place much frequented by those who
have any trade or affaires towards Ireland, because of its
nearnesse to that countrey, and conveniency of transporting
horse, cattell, and other materialls for planting thither, which
is the sole trade of these parts : as there is noe harbour
soe noe vessell of any burden can possibly come in.

The next to these are Whithorne and Wigton, to the
latter of which there comes sometimes a small boate from
England, with salt or coales.

Betwixt these and Kircowbright there is noe creeke
nor port, but one creeke at the foot of the water of Fleete,
not worth the nameing.[11]   As for Kircowbright, it is a
pretty and one of the best ports on this side of Scotland,
where there are a few, and those very poore, merchants, or
pedlars rather, tradeing for Ireland.   Beyond this, there are
the small creekes of Balcarie,[12] the Water of Ore,[13] and
Satternis,[14] whither some small boates come from England
with salt and coales.   And last of all Dunfreeze, a pretty
mercat towne, but of little trade, that they have being
most part by land, either for Leith or Newcastle.   The

---

[1] Dunduff in parish of Maybole, where, acccording to the *New Statistical
Account*, smuggling was once actively practised.   [2] Dunure.   [3] The Maidens.
[4] Dungyrdloch, a little to the south of Turnberry (see Blaeu's *Atlas*).
[5] Ardmillan.   [6] Ballantrae.   [7] Garran ?   [8] Lendalfoot ?   [9] See above, p. 157.
[10] Port Garvilland, 1½ miles south-west of Corsewall Point.   [11] Gatehouse of
Fleet, which in the middle of last century promised to be a possible rival of
Glasgow.   [12] Balcary.   [13] Urr.   [14] Southerness.

badnesse of comeing into the river upon which it lyes, hindering theyr comerce by sea, soe as whatever they have come that way is comonly and usually landed at Kircowbright. This towne of Dumfreeze was formerly the head port of these parts, the towne of Ayre being then within the district of Glasgowe; but there being nothing to doe, the, comissioners thought fitt to remove the collector to Ayre, (which is much the better towne of the two,) where there is a checque and three officers; one of which officers attends constantly at that towne, one other of them resides at Port-patrick, and lookes to that and the adjacent creekes of Stranrawer, Garvellen, Whitehorne, and Wigton, and the last of them at Kircowbright, for lookeing after that place, with Dunfreeze and the Water of Fleete, Balcarie, the Water of Ore, and Satternis; the rest of the ports and places of this district haveing beene never esteemed worth either the care or charge of a wayter, and indeede the whole will not doe much more then defray the charge which is necessarily expended on them.

RICHARD FRANCK
(1656).

OF Richard Franck we know little more than he has himself casually told us in the book from which the following extracts have been made. It has been conjectured that he was born in 1642, and that he died in the year 1708. From himself we learn that he was a native of Cambridge, that he received "a slender education" at its university, and that the impending civil wars drove him for a time to make his residence in London. We have it also from himself that he at one time resided in Nottingham, though in what capacity, or whether before or after his visit to Scotland, he does not specify. His first acquaintance with Scotland was made as a trooper in the army of Cromwell in 1650. It was probably in 1656 or 1657, however, that he made the northern tour of which his *Memoirs* is the record. He seems to imply that the unsettled state of affairs under the Commonwealth led him to quit England for a time; but a perusal of his book suggests another and a sufficient reason. Franck was an enthusiastic angler, and in his own fantastic manner a lover of nature as keen as Izaak Walton himself. From his occasional references to Walton, indeed, we gather that he had the ambition of improving on the *Compleat Angler;* and certainly there could hardly be a greater contrast than between the simplicity of Walton and the grandiloquence of Franck. When on service in Scotland, Franck had noted the riches of her lochs and rivers, and when the opportunity came he simply gratified what seems to have been the ruling passion of his life. From another work of Franck's, a strange rhapsodical book, entitled "A Philosophical Treatise of the Original and Production of Things Writ in America in a Time of Solitude, by R. Franck, London, 1687," we learn that he subsequently visited America. Besides this fact nothing more is known of his later life.

Franck's book on Scotland was edited by Sir Walter Scott in 1821 with a few notes and a short preface. Its title sufficiently indicates its quality. It runs as follows :— "Northern Memoirs, calculated for the Meridian of Scotland, wherein most of all the Cities, Citadels, Sea-ports, Castles, Forts, Fortresses, Rivers, and Rivulets, are compendiously described. Together with choice Collections of various Discoveries, Remarkable Observations, Theological Notions, Political Axioms, National Intrigues, Polemick Inferences, Contemplations, Speculations, and several curious and industrious Inspections, lineally drawn from Antiquaries, and other noted and intelligible Persons of Honour and Eminency. To which is added the Contemplative Angler by way of Diversion. With a Narrative of that dextrous and mysterious Art experimented in England, and perfected in more remote and solitary Parts of Scotland. By way of Dialogue. Writ in the year 1658, but not till now made publick, by Richard Franck, Philanthropus." The book is in the form of a dialogue between Arnoldus (Franck himself) and Theophilus,[1] which is resolutely maintained without a break throughout their tour. Beginning with a discourse on the glories of creation, on man's place in the general order, and the effects of Adam's first sin, the interlocutors (at the fifteenth page) at length propose the northern journey ; and the remainder of their dialogue is made up of rambling talk on angling, Scottish scenery, and of theosophic disquisition, which proves Franck to have been a kind of compound of Quaker and Fifth Monarchy man. As will be seen, Franck's style is as absurd as anything in English literature. To his perverse grandiloquence Scott could find a parallel only in Sir Thomas Urquhart, with whose name at least Franck was acquainted.[2] Moreover, that this was sheer coxcombry is proved by the fact that on occasion Franck could write as plainly as might be

---

[1] There is a third interlocutor, but he drops off at an early stage of the dialogue.   [2] Franck refers to Urquhart when he has occasion to speak of Cromarty (pp. 216–217).

expected of the quondam trooper of Cromwell. While the
value of his book is seriously marred by his foolish
affectations, it nevertheless, as Scott has said, " contains a
deal of interesting matter concerning the state of Scotland
during the civil wars." Franck had one merit of an
intelligent traveller—he was good-natured. In an age
of acrimonious tempers he speaks with fairness of both
parties in politics and religion—of Montrose as kindly as of
David Leslie. He has unfavourable remarks on the habits
and poverty-stricken condition of the Scottish people, yet on
the whole he is not an unfriendly observer. Of the natural
beauties of the country he shows an appreciation which is
usually supposed to be the privilege of our own century.
Scott was struck by this feeling in Franck, and quotes
with approval his description of Scotland as "a legible
fair draught of the beautiful creation, dressed up with
polished rocks, pleasant savannas, flourishing dales, deep
and torpid lakes, with shady woods, immerged with rivers
and gliding rivulets, where every fountain overflows a
valley, and every ford superabounds with fish." It remains
to be said that the highest modern authorities on angling
speak with respect of Franck's proficiency in what he
characteristically calls "the solitary and piscatorial art."

FRANCK'S MEMOIRS.   (Scott's Edit., 1821.)

DUMFRIES.—*Theophilus.* However, in the mean while
reflect on yourself, and give us a description of the town of
Dumfreez.

Arnoldus. I fancy e're long you will change your note, when
you traverse these pleasant northern tracts. In the mean
time I'll gratify you with a breviate of Dumfreez, where a
provost, as superintendent, supplies the place of a mayor, a
magistrate almost as venerable as an English constable.

Theoph. That's wittily applied ; what comes next ?

Arn. Nay, hold a little, I have not done yet with the
eminencies and the remarks of the town of Dumfreez; for
you are to consider it was anciently a town girt about with
a strong stone wall ; but the late irruptions, or perhaps some
state-disagreement, has in a manner defaced that regular

ornament, otherwise the cankrous teeth of time have gnawn
out the impressions, as evidently appears by those ruinous
heaps.   Nor is the Arnotus[1] in all parts portable, notwithstanding her shores are so delightful.

Theoph. What, is there more yet ? pray, go on.

Arn. In the midst of the town is their market-place, and
in the centre of that stands their tolbooth, round about which
the rabble sit, that nauseate the very air with their tainted
breath, so perfumed with onions, that to an Englishman it is
almost infectious.

But the kirk is comely,[2] and situated southward, furnished
once a week with moveable spectrums, (you know what that
means,) yet the outside than the inside is more eminently
imbellished, if sepulchres and tombstones can be said to be
ornaments ; and where death and time stand to guard the
steeple, whose rings of bells seldom or rarely exceed the
critical number of three.

Here also you may observe a large and spacious bridg,[3]
that directly leads into the country of Galloway, where thrice
in a week you shall rarely fail to see their maid-maukins
dance corantos in tubs.   So on every Sunday some as seldom
miss to make their appearance on the stool of repentance.

Theoph. Then it seems by your relation they keep time
with their Comers, that hazard their reputation for a country-
custom (or the love of liquor) rather than omit a four-hours
drinking.

Arn. That's true enough; and it's an antient practice
among the female sex, to covee together (about that time) as
naturally as geese flock'd to the Capitol.   Now the very
name of *Comer*[4] they mightily honour ; but that of *Gossip*
they utterly abominate, as they hate the plague, or some
mortal contagion.   So that whether to conclude it a vulgar
error, and an abomination among the Scots to lick up
an English proverb, it matters not ; or, whether to fancy a
more laudable emphasis in the word *Comer*, then there

[1] The Nith.   *Portable* is Franck's usual word for *navigable*.   [2] The ancient
church of St Michael.   The present church dates from 1744.   Burns is
buried in the graveyard of this church.   [3] This bridge, originally consisting
of nine arches, is said to have been built by Devorgilla, mother of John
Baliol.   [4] Cummer.

is in *Go-sip*. I leave you to judg of that, and those other abominable customs, that drink till they sigh to do penance for their sins.

Franck's Experience as a Trooper in Scotland.

Arn. Near the English promontories stands the town of Jedard[1] whose skirts are wash'd by the famous Tweed. But westward from thence (and inclining yet more norward) are the remarkable antiquities and ruins of Bog-hall;[2] and not far from thence is the admirable Tintaw,[3] a prodigious mountain over-looking the Marshes. From whence, or from Erricsteen[4] (that's not far from it) there issue forth three eminent and considerable rivers; as that of the Tweed, Loyd, and the river Annon: But of these three rivers we shall discourse more at large, as opportunity presents in its proper place.

And now let's advance to our country cottage, since compelled by the extremity of rain, and encreasing waters. To which place when we arrived, like men in amaze, we stood gazing at one another, because to see the sheep grazing on the tops of those houses, where there was hardly grass enough to graze a goose in. By this you may conclude their buildings but low, and I'm sure their doors and entrances were so strait, that they exercised our strength beyond our art. Archimedes' engines signified but little, till the souldiers set their shoulders to support the eves, by which means the horse got an entrance in; and that horseman that was not throughly wet, was doom'd that night to go supperless to bed.

Thus in a storm we stormed the town, and 'twould make a man storm to be treated only with oatmeal, of which we made cakes; for every souldier became a baker; and the flesh-meat they procured us was drest without slaughter; for none we had except my duck (you formerly discours'd), so that most of us roosted with an empty appetite; and every man that went that night to bed, was sufficiently alarum'd

---

[1] Jedburgh, locally called Jeddart. [2] Boghall, a castle of the Earls of Wigton, is about a mile from the town of Biggar, the town where Franck's comrades were quartered. [3] Tinto Hill. [4] Erickstanebrae, in which the Tweed, Clyde, and Annan have their sources.

before it was day. Oat-straw was our sheets, and portmantles our pillows. It's true, some had cloaks, and 'twas well they had them, otherwise they had been constrained to use plads; and he that used one but to cover his carcass, mustred (I uphold him) more gray coats than black coats, that claw'd him more perniciously than a Middlesex bailiff.

The next day we recruited with some country ale, but so thick and roapy it was, that you might eat it with spoons. Besides, some small quantity of mutton was brought us, enough to discover the cookery of the country: and the linen they supplied us with, were it not to boast of, was little or nothing different from those female complexions that never washed their faces, to retain their christendom. But among the rest I had almost forgot to remind you that the souldiers and people were jointly agreed to part without the loss of one tear in the morning.

SANQUHAR.—*Theoph.* Zanker [1] stands situate on a flat or level, surrounded, as you see, with excellent corn-fields: but more remote it's besieged with mountains that are rich in leadmines.[2] The planets I fancy them very benevolent to influence this swompy rocky earth, and shine metallick blessings into them, to commode the indigent and almost uncultivated native. Heaven, it's true, is always propitious, because never to impose the law of sterility, when to supply the whole world with the bounty of increase. And tho the people hereabouts are destitute of ingenuity, and their fields for the most part impoverish'd for want of cultivation; yet are their rivers and rivulets replenished with trout, because undisturb'd with the noosy net, which augments the angler's, if not the artizan's entertainment.

Arn. Here's no character of Zanker all this while.

Theoph. I am just coming to tell you, that Zanker is a town and a corporation too; tho not bulky in buildings, yet there is a bailiff, master sometimes of a brew-house, whose entertainments (in my opinion) may easily be guest at, provided you reflect on our late accommodation.

---

[1] Sanquhar.   [2] The lead-mines of Wanlockhead, in the parish of Sanquhar, are said to have been discovered by a German, named Cornelius Hardskins, during the minority of James VI. With the permission of James, Sir Bevis Bulmer, Master of the English Mint, employed 300 men in working these mines (*New Statistical Account*).

There is also a market-place, such an one as it is, and a
kind of a thing they call a tolbooth, which at first sight
might be suspected a prison, because it's so like one; whose
decays, by the law of antiquity, are such, that every prisoner
is threatned with death before his trial; and every casement,
because bound about with iron bars, discovers the entertainments destined only to felons.   Now the market-place is less
worthy of a description than the tolbooth; for no man
would know it to be such, were he not told so.

There is also a kirk, or something like it; but I might as
reverently call it a barn; because so little to distinguish
betwixt them, and the whole town reads daily lectures of
decays; so do her ports, her avenues, and entrances.   Where
note, I call her the child of antiquity, by reason of her ruins
and irreparable decays.   It's true, I was not murdered, nor
was I kill'd outright, yet I narrowly escaped as eminent a
danger, when almost worried to death with lice.

KILMARNOCK.—*Arn.* Yes, that is Kilmarnock, an antient
corporation, heap'd up and crowded with men and mechanicks;
through the midst of whose crazy tottering ports, there runs a
river eplenished with trout, where we may treat our appetites,
as already our apprehensions, with the entertainments of
Dumbarton, whose rapid streams, when we come to examine
them, are enough, one would think, to surfeit the angler.
To which place it is now but one day's journy, nor need we
hackney it at more than an ordinary rate, before we discover
those beautiful ascents, and the hostile habitation of our
friend Aquilla, that dwells in those western florid fields, who
will bid us welcome, and rejoice to see us.   Nor will
Glasgow be any impediment in our way, whilst we only
survey her beautiful palaces, so direct to the lofty turrets of
Dumbarton.

Theoph. Let the sun, or his star the beautiful Aurora,
arrest me, if otherwise I arise not before break of day, and
be in readiness for a march to the famous Glasgow, where
you purpose to refresh, and briefly examine the city curiosities; as also the customs of their magnificent situations;
whose academick breasts are a nursery for education, as the
city for hospitality.   And let this be your task as we travel
to Dumbarton, to give us a narrative of the antiquities of

Cloyd, as also of the town of Kilmarnock, where we slept this night, that so bravely refresh'd us.

Arn. That I can do as we ride along.

Theoph. Do so, it will be very acceptable.

Arn. Then to expostulate the antiquities of Kilmarnock; as it would puzzle the pen of an ingenious historiographer, so I, for that end, was thinking to evade it, and refer it to some other of more mature judgment; since you yourself, and consequently others that read my relation, will probably reduce me to the probate of a censure. On the other hand, the native who lives under an expectation, would equally condemn me for my taciturnity, should I silently pass by and imprint no remarks on their silty sands, and silver streams. To this dilemma I am driven by the censures of some, nor can I escape the clamours of others; so that I sail betwixt Sylla and Charibdis. However, I shall use my best endeavours to gratify both as near as I can, and consult the mean and mediums of veracity, so far as experience and discovery can inform me: So that I shall say but little more than to tell the world that Kilmarnock is an antient corporation, crowded with mechanicks and brew-houses.

Theoph. But that's not all.

Arn. If not enough, then you must have more, it seems; and not only for yourself, but for those that are more inquisitous. And what will they say? Why you and they both will tell me, it's only rifling into ruins. Nor, indeed, is it other, when in our progress we proceed to prove little more, save only a discovery of ruins and decays.

Theoph. Be it what it will, however, let us have it.

Arn. Well, then, if to go one step further, surely it won't cripple me; let me tell you, then, it's an antient manufactory.

Theoph. And what of all that? Is this more than what we formerly knew?

Arn. It's more than I knew, that you knew so much. But this discourse, Theophilus, better becomes an antiquary, than one that queries; for, should I but step into her dirty streets, that are seldom clean but on a sun-shiny day, or at other times, when great rains melt all the muck, and forcibly drive it down their cadaverous channels into the river

Marr,[1] whose streams are so sullied then, that the river loses its natural brightness, till the stains are wash'd out, so become invisible. All which to examine, is enough to convince you, that the influence of planets are their best scavenger: for the natives in this northern latitude, are naturally so addicted to idleness and nastiness, that should not the heavens contribute the blessings of rain, they would inevitably surfeit with their own uncleanliness.

Theoph. All this we will grant you; the footsteps are evident.

Arn. Where, note, these inhabitants dwell in such ugly houses, as, in my opinion, are but little better than huts; and generally of a size, all built so low, that their eves hang dangling to touch the earth; nor are they uniform, nor hold they correspondency one with another; and that which is worse than all the rest, is their unproportionate ill contrivance; because, when to consider a dwarf of a house so covered over with a gigantick roof. By which, you may imagine, our former projectors had but little project for curious contrivances; and, to speak plain English, as little costly.

The next thing in course that falls under our consideration, will be their artificers. But the Moors (more than all the rest) have gain'd the reputation for the temper of dirks, razors, and knives, whose temper is so exact, that it super-excels all the mechanicks in Scotland. Where, note, you may observe there are artists amongst them, though not one good structure to be found in Kilmarnock; nor do I remember any wall it has, but a river there is, as I formerly told you of, that runs through the town; over which there stood a bridg so wretchedly ancient,[2] that it's unworthy our commendations any otherwise, than as travellers commend the bridg they go over.

Another part of their manufacture is knitting of bonnets, and spinning of Scotish cloth; which turns to very good account. Then, for their temper of metals, they are without compeer; Scotland has not better. And, as they are artizans in dirks, so are they artists in fudling, as if there were some rule in drinking. So that, to me, it represents as

---

[1] The Marnock.   [2] This bridge existed till 1762.

if art and ale were inseparable companions. Moreover, their wives are sociable comers too; yet, not to compare with those of Dumblain, who pawn their petticotes to pay their reckoning.

Theoph. Here's a jolly crew of alemen (but very few anglers) crowded together in the small compass of a little corporation, curiously compacted. For the houses, you may observe, besiege the river; and that river, to divide the ruinous ports, left only as reliques that remain discoverable; however, it's my opinion, that a stone wall has incircled the town, since hitherto, as to observation, there's rarely a town of any eminency in Scotland, but is, or has been, beleagured with a strong stone wall;[1] but as to that I'le silence my self.

GLASGOW.—*Arn.* [Glasgow] is a city girded about with a strong stone wall, within whose flourishing arms the industrious inhabitant cultivates art to the utmost. There is also a cathedral (but it's very ancient) that stands in the east angle, supervising the bulk of the city, and her ornamental ports. Moreover, there are two parish churches;[2] but no more, to the best of my observation. Then, there is a college, which they call an university; but I'm at a stand what to call it, where one single college compleats a university.

Now, let us descend to describe the splendor and gaity of this city of Glasgow, which surpasseth most, if not all the corporations in Scotland. Here it is you may observe four large fair streets, modell'd, as it were, into a spacious quadrant; in the centre whereof their market-place is fix'd; near unto which stands a stately tolbooth, a very sumptuous, regulated, uniform fabrick, large and lofty, most industriously and artificially carved from the very foundation to the superstructure, to the great admiration of strangers and travellers. But this state-house, or tolbooth, is their western prodigy, infinitely excelling the model and usual built of town-halls; and is, without exception, the paragon of beauty in the west; whose compeer is no where to be found in the north, should you rally the rarities of all the corporations in Scotland.

---

[1] See pp. 19, 47 (above).   [2] The Cathedral and the Church of St Mary. The latter continued in use till 1793, when it was destroyed by fire.

Here the reader (it's possible) may think I hyperbolize; but let him not mistake himself, for I write no ambiguities : Truth stands naked in plain simplicity; and partiality I abhor as a base imposture.   He that reads my relation, and the morals of this famous Glasgow, will vindicate my description, and place the fault to him that invents the fable; for it's opposite to my genius, as also to my principles, either to deface a beautiful fabrick, or contract a guilt by magnifying it beyond its due merit.   I have, and therefore shall, as near as I can, in an equal poize ballance things aright.   Permit me, therefore, as a licentiat, to read you but a short, yet pertinent lecture, and I'le tell you what entertainments we met with in Glasgow, as also what hopes we have to meet with the like in the circuit of our intended northern progress.   But this I offer to the dubious only; if, peradventure, there be any such as scruple, I'le refer them to the natives to evidence for me, which I am satisfied they will with ten thousand manifesto's.

In the next place, we are to consider the merchants and traders in this eminent Glasgow, whose store-houses and ware-houses are stuft with merchandize, as their shops swell big with foreign commodities, and returns from France, and other remote parts, where they have agents and factors to correspond, and inrich their maritime ports, whose charter exceeds all the charters in Scotland; which is a considerable advantage to the city-inhabitants, because blest with privileges as large, nay, larger than any other corporation. Moreover, they dwell in the face of France, and a free trade, as I formerly told you.   Nor is this all, for the staple of their country consists of linens, friezes, furs, tartans, pelts, hides, tallow, skins, and various other small manufactures and commodities, not comprehended in this breviat.   Besides, I should remind you, that they generally exceed in good French wines, as they naturally superabound with fish and fowl; some meat does well with their drink.   And so give me leave to finish my discourse of this famous Glasgow, whose ports we relinquish to distinguish those entertainments of Dumbarton, always provided we scatter no corn.

Theoph. What to think, or what to say of this eminent Glasgow, I know not, except to fancy a smell of my native

country.　The very prospect of this flourishing city reminds
me of the beautiful fabricks and the florid fields in England,
so that now I begin to expect a pleasant journey.　Pray,
tell me, Arnoldus, how many such cities shall we meet with
in our travels, where the streets and the channels are so
cleanly swept, and the meat in every house so artificially
drest ?　The linen, I also observed, was very neatly lap'd up,
and, to their praise be it spoke, was lavender proof ; besides,
the people were decently drest, and such an exact decorum
in every society, represents it, to my apprehension, an
emblem of England, though, in some measure, under a deeper
die.　However, I'le superscribe it the nonsuch of Scotland,
where an English florist may pick up a posie ; so that should
the residue of their cities, in our northern progress, seem as
barren as uncultivated fields, and every field so replenished
with thistles that a flower could scarcely flourish amongst
them, yet would I celebrate thy praise, O, Glasgow ! because
of those pleasant and fragrant flowers that so sweetly
refresh'd me, and, to admiration, sweetned our present
enterments.

STIRLING AND DUNBLANE.—*Arn.* So let us pass on with our
travelling design (by the house of Cardrus [1]) to the ports of
Sterling ; where stands a beautiful and imbellished Castle,
elevated on the precipice of an impregnable rock, that commands the vallies (as well as the town) and all those habitable
parts about it : those are the turrets that present before us,
let us enter her ports, both strong and spacious ; whose
incircling arms surround a city (but not a great one) that's
built all with stone ; so is her castle ; and situated close by
the river Firth, as above explain'd, upon lofty, craggy, and
mountanous rocks, almost inaccessable.　More southward yet
the city spreads itself into many sweet situations, that
invigorate the inhabitants, and accommodate the Low-land
merchant rather than the mariner with profitable returns from
the hills, by the Highlander.　The Firth [2] runs here that
washeth and melts the foundations of the city, but relieves
the country with her plenty of salmon ; where the burgo-
masters (as in many other parts of Scotland) are compell'd

---

[1] Cardross Castle, built by Robert Bruce, and where he died in 1329.
Nothing of it now remains.　[2] The Forth.

to reinforce an ancient statute, that commands all masters and others, not to force or compel any servant, or an apprentice, to feed upon salmon more than thrice a week.[1]

Theoph. Is there such a law in force now ?

Arn. Yes sure, for ought I know it remains to this day: and the reason of it is, as I conceive, from the plenty of salmon in these northern parts, that should the inhabitants daily feed upon them, they would inevitably endanger their health, if not their lives, by surfeiting ; for the abundance of salmon hereabouts in these parts, is hardly to be credited. And the reader I fancy will be of my perswasion, when he comes to consider that the price of a salmon formerly exceeded the value of sixpence sterling, which I suppose no English man will grudg, nor think it unreasonable to give at any time ; so that the danger, in my opinion, lies most in the diet : for as salmon is a fish very apt to surfeit, more especially fresh salmon, when only boiled ; which if too frequently fed on, relaxes the belly, and makes the passages so slippery, that the retentive faculties become debilitated ; so suffers the body to be hurried into a flux, and sometimes into a fever, as pernicious as death. Which is much better prevented by abstinency, than to stand the test of uncorrected physick.

This famous Firth is the most portable river in Scotland, whose streams, because meandring, make it deep and torpid ; so fit it for navigation ; for below Bridg there are neither streams nor sharps ;[2] but above Bridg there's enough, more especially towards the flourishing fields of Montieth, which I rather prefer, than Alan[3] and Althrwery,[4] for the angler's diversion, except Frith and Koak ;[5] the one for pearl, but the other for trout.

Theoph. What town is this ?

Arn. Dirty Dumblain ; let us pass by it, and not cumber our discourse with so inconsiderable a corporation : our itch after Mockeny[6] puts a spur to quicken our expectation ; for who knows but the various alteration of weather may in

---

[1] There was no such statute as Franck refers to ; but servants did stipulate with their employers that they should not have to eat salmon more than thrice a week. [2] *Sharps* are the parts of the stream where the current is swiftest. [3] Allan Water. [4] Athrwery ? [5] Koak ? I have been unable to identify these two streams. [6] Machany in the parishes of Muthil and Blackford.

some measure frustrate those expectations we may have of those admirable streams to answer our designs ?

Theoph. Do what you please.

Arn. Truly I think it but time lost, to survey the reliques of a ruinous heap of stones, that lean o're the verge of a river, facing the mountains. The houses, it's true, are built with stone, but then to consider them low and little, it plainly demonstrates there's nothing eminent but narrow streets, and dirty houses; a convincing argument there's no scavengers amongst them. And for their houswifery, let that alone; for if you touch it, you sully your fingers. There is a market-place, such an one as it is; but as for merchants, there's no such thing in nature. But a palace there is, and a cathedral too, otherwise Dumblain had nothing to boast of.

But there is one thing remarkable, and that's the house of Domine Caudwel (a formal pedagogue) that absolv'd the thief, and conceal'd the theft, so lost his breeches; for you must know, the good woman his wife was a notable comer, one of the first magnitude; who, with two more of her consorts, (as I was told, at a four hours' drinking,) guzled down as much ale and brandy, wine and strong waters, as amounted to the sum of forty pound Scots. But wanting money to pay her reckoning, she liberally pawned her husband's breeches; and he, like a fop, to redeem his wife's reputation, would never redeem his breeches, lest suspecting they should smell of the tears of the tankerd. And here, as reported, was celebrated that famous union of *Doh* and *Doris*,[1] stark love and kindness, a custom inviolable. Here also resided jovial Bille Sincleer.

Now, you are to consider, that this pittiful pedling corporation of Dumblain, has little or no trade amongst them, except now and then a truck with a brandy-man, a tobacco-merchant, or a brewster-wife; for ale, tobacco, and strong waters, are the staple of the town : And so let us leave them, to pursue our intended design for Minever,[2] and Dromon-Castle,[3] that stands distant about some three miles

---

[1] The reference is to the well-known story of *Doch an Dorough*, which Franck afterwards tells in his most tedious manner in connection with Cupar-Angus.
[2] Methven (?). [3] Founded by the first Lord Drummond in 1491. It was almost levelled with the ground by the Jacobite Duchess of Perth in 1745.

from the Bridg of Ardoch; where there runs a small rivulet
of a rapid motion, paved with a slaty bottom, but the access
difficult.

And here we cross the moor to Mockeny, whose limpid
streams are pleasant beyond report, and her fords generally
furnished with trout, as if nature had there designed to
entertain the contemplative angler, in those liberal streams,
where the artist in a storm may shelter himself under shady
trees, elevated upon lofty mountains, over the melting
amorous smiling banks; as if the boughs were barnicles, and
ready to drop into the silent glittering streams, that glide
softly along a delightful meadow; excepting here and there
some small cataracts of water that tumble down a precipice
of rocks, that encircles and surrounds great stones in the
sandy foundation of this mystical Mockeny, whose glittering
sholes are gently moved by the soft breathings of Zephyrus,
that dash the smaller waves ashore, and discover to the
angler the intricate angles of Mockeny, so that here we
assume a poetick liberty, in some sort, to call Scotland
Arcadia.

Loch Ness, Inverness.—*Theoph*. What new inviting object
have we now discovered?

Arn. The famous Lough-Ness,[1] so much discours'd for the
supposed floating island; for here it is, if any where in
Scotland. Nor is it any other than a natural plantation of
segs and bull-rushes, matted and knit so close together by
natural industry, and navigated by winds that blow every
way, floats from one part of the Lough to another, upon the
surface of the solid deeps of this small Mediterrane: and
here it is, in these slippery streams, that an English ship,
by curious invention, was haled over the mountains to this
solitary Lough; brought hither on purpose to reclaim the
Highlander.

Theoph. Do you romance, or not, to tell me that an
island swims in the midst of the ocean, and a ship fluctuates
in the midst of the Highlands; where every rock represents
a Charibdis, and every wave threatens an inundation; where

---

[1] Franck seems to have thought that the phenomenon of the floating island
had been erroneously assigned to Loch Lomond. When he speaks of Loch
Lomond he expressly assigns it to Loch Ness, as he also does here.

there's no harbour without hazard of life, nor sea enough to promise security to the mariner, when the winds mingle themselves with the waves, that wash the pallid cheeks of the polish'd rocks? Now tell me that can, where the mariner must have birth (and the passinger supplies) in this fluctuating ocean, when a storm arises to ecclipse his eye from a land discovery?

Arn. If eye-sight be good evidence, there's enough to convince you; behold the ship.

Theoph. How came she here? Was she not built in some creek hereabouts?

Arn. No.

Theoph. By what means then was she moved into this small Mediterrane? I solicite advice, and you can solve the doubt.

Arn. Art was both engin and engineer to invite this ship into this solitary Lough.

Theoph. If so, it's strange that a vessel of her force should leap out of the ocean, and over the hills, to float in a gutter surrounded with rocks.

Arn. Not so strange as true, for here she is.

Theoph. Was there a possibility of her sailing from the citadel, to this eminent Lough Ness, when a boat of ten tun can't force her passage half way up the river? This looks romantick beyond the ingenuity of art, or possibility of invention.

Arn. Let it look as it will look, I am sure it was so.

Theoph. You are sure it was so; then, pray, resolve the point.

Arn. Why thus it was: In the time of war betwixt the King and Parliament, this navigate invention was consulted by Maj. General Dean; who to compleat a conquest over the Highlanders (in regard hitherto the law of a foreign power had never bridled them) he accomplished this new navigation of sailing by land: who contrived the transportation of this fair ship (that you now see) into these torpid and slippery streams.

Theoph. What, without sails?

Arn. Yes, without sail, pilot, card or compass; by dividing only the ambient air, as formerly she plowed the pondrous ocean. Nor was she compell'd to encounter sea or land in all her passage; which, by some, may be thought a ridiculous report. On the other hand, for a ship of this burden to transport her self, or suffer her self to be transported without ordinary, nay, extraordinary means, looks like an impossibility; however, here you find her, nor is it to be denied that she had a passage to this solitary Lough.

Theoph. But how?

Arn. First, you must conclude no vessel, without a miracle, could remove her self so far from sea; and I'le assure you in this here's nothing miraculous. Then you are to consider that so eminent a ship could never shove her self to reach this limit, as extends from the Orchean seas to this obscure Lough Ness, without probable endeavours, and very considerable assistance. Lastly, to admit of a violent motion, were a kind of madness; because to impose a contradiction upon the design.

Theoph. Pray explicate the ænigma.

Arn. A motion must be had (that you'l grant) and means considerable to move by, (this you must allow,) which to accomplish, the sailers and the souldiers equally contributed. For a regiment (or it may be two) about that time quartered in Inverness; who, by artifice, had fastned thick cables to her fore-castle, and then they got levers and rollers of timber, which they spread at a distance, one before another; whilst some are of opinion these robust engineers framed a more artificial and politick contrivance: but thus it was, and no otherwise, I'le assure you; save only they fastned some cheeks and planks to the solid sides and ribs of the ship, the better to secure her from crushing upon transportation.

Theoph. And did she pass in this manner as you tell me, to this famous Ness?

Arn. Yes, she relinquished the brinish ocean, to float in the slippery arms of Ness. But to keep her steddy in her passage, and preserve her from rocking and rolling by the way, they consulted no other project than what I tell you: save only some additional supplies from Inverness, that with ropes and tackle haled her along to this very place where you now observe her. For you are to consider, she no sooner got motion, but by industry and art she was steer'd without a compass, to this remarkable Ness; where now she floats obvious enough to every curious observer.

For let me tell you, that strength, artifice, and resolution, are indisputable arguments to reach the possibility of any thing possible; a threefold cord is not easily broken. Motion therefore was no sooner begot, but the whole mystery was almost accomplished; the plover, you observe, never breaks the shell, before the lapwing is ready to run; nor will the sailer spread the sails, until he observe a wind presents. Nor got our ship the mediums of motion, but by argument of force (not of artillery) which forced her by graduate means, till arriving in this Ness, obvious to all men.[1]

And this is that famous and renowned Lough Ness (Loemon excepted)[2] inferiour to none in the kingdom of Scotland; whose streams are strewed with eel and trout, whilst her deeps are saluted with the race of salmon; whose fertil banks and shining sands are hourly moistned by this small Mediterrane: which I fancy is besieged with rocks and mountains; whilst her polite shores are frozen in the winter, by the frigid lungs of blustring Boreas, that perplexes her banks, and masquerades her rocks with a cristalline hue of polished ice. Where the Tritons and Sea-nymphs sport themselves on the slippery waves, sounding an invasion to her moveable inmate; supposed by some, the floating island.

Theoph. Do these fair mountains that interdict the dales, survey the forcible streams of Inverness?

Arn. Yes surely, these torrents, which you now discover, frequently wash the walls of Inverness, (a derivative from Lough Ness,) at the west end whereof stands a diminutive castle, about a mile distant from that magnificent citadel, that subjects those precarious Northern Highlanders. This Inverness, or model of antiquity, (which we now discourse.) stands commodiously situated for a Highland trade; defended with a weather-beaten tottering wall, that's defaced with age and the corruptions of time, where yet there remains two

---

[1] This "curious account," says Scott in a note on this passage, "was an instance among many of the determined perseverance, as well as the ingenuity, of the republican commanders."   [2] Loch Lomond.

parish-churches : But I remember a third, that was a kind of a cathedral or collegiat-church, that now, like old Troy, sleeps in dust and ashes, as part of the walls do, charging time and neglect with their tottering decays.

North and by east, near the forcible streams of the Ness, stands the fortress,[1] or pentagon, drawn out by regular lines, built all with stone, and girt about with a graff, that commodes it with a convenient harbour.   The houses in this fair fortress are built very low, but uniform; and the streets broad and spacious, with avenues and intervales for drilling of foot, or drawing up horse.   I must confess, such and so many are the advantages and conveniencies that belong to this citadel, it would be thought fabulous, if but to numerate them: for that end I refer my self to those that have inspected her magazines, providores, harbours, vaults, graffs, bridges, sally-ports, cellars, bastions, horn-works, redoubts, counterscarps, &c.   Ocular evidence is the best judg, and gives the plainest demonstration; which, without dispute, will interpret this formidable fortress a strength impregnable; and the situation, as much as any, promises security, by reason it's surrounded with boggy morasses; standing in swamps, on an isthmus of land, that divides the Ness from the Orchean Seas.

Yet here is one thing more among our northern novelties very remarkable; for here you shall meet with a wooden bridg to convoy you over the rapid Ness; but certainly the weakest, in my opinion, that ever stradled over so strong a stream.   However, it serves to accommodate the native, to those pleasant and fragrant meadows, north and north-west, that direct to the demolishments of the Castle of Lovet,[2] near to which stand the antiquities of Brawn,[3] planted upon the brow of a considerable bank, that hangs, one would think, o're a spacious river, above all in Scotland, replenished with salmon; whose numbers are numberless, if not improper to say so; and careless of their lives, they cast them away.

Ross and Sutherland.—*Theoph.* Here's another Hellespont; must we cross this also ?

[1] One of the four built by Cromwell.   [2] Beaufort Castle, which existed as early as the reign of Alexander I.   [3] Brahan Castle, in the Parish of Urray in Ross-shire.

Arn. Yes surely, we must cross this rugged ferry, especially if intending the bounds of Innerbrachy,[1] in the cultivated fields in the country of Ross; where the rocks are undermin'd by the sea quellem, that serves for a filtre to riddle the ocean, and separate her saline brinish taste, from those more sweet and luscious fountains; where the inhabitants will flatter you with an absurd opinion (an old tradition received from their ancestors) that the earth in Ross hath an antipathy against rats,[2] as the Irish oak has against the spider: And this curiosity, if you please to examine, you may, for the natives do; but had they asserted there were no mice in Ross, every tongue had contradicted them. Now, mice and rats are cousin-german, every body knows that knows any thing, and for the most part keep house together: But what difference has hapned amongst them here, as to make such a feud in this country of Ross, that the rats in Ross should relinquish their country, and give possession wholly to the mice; this is a mystery that I understand not.

Besides this fond opinion of the natives hereabouts, some others more remote (as ignorant as themselves) transport the earth of Ross into most parts of Scotland; perswading themselves, that if they do but sprinkle it in the fields, fens, moors, mountains, morish or boggy grounds (all is one as to that), for it alters not the property, nor does it diminish the quality, nor impair the virtue, but that still it retains a certain antipathy against that enormous vermin the rat, nay, the very scent on't shall force him to become an exile. This odd kind of creed they had when I was resident amongst them; yet to the best of my observation, I never saw a rat; nor do I remember of any one that was with me ever did; but for mice, I declare, so great is their plenty, that were they a commodity, Scotland might boast on't. And that they have owls with horns, some favour the report; yet are they not horns, but as like horns as any thing that are no horns; nor is it any other than a sort of feathers, that's clung and twisted so naturally together, that represents the

---

[1] Inverbreakie. [2] The same was anciently believed of various districts. The earth of Liddesdale, for example, in Roxburghshire, was formerly sent for from a considerable distance to lay the floors of barns withal (Scott's Note).

idiom or form of a horn, if when to observe them at a reasonable distance, which seemingly beautifies the ivy-bush, as horns adorn the head of a buffulo.

The next curiosity to entertain you with, is the country of Southerland; which we enter by crossing a small arm of the ocean from Tain to Dornoch. So from thence we travel into Cathness, and the country of Stranavar; where a rude sort of inhabitants dwell (almost as barbarous as Canibals) who when they kill a beast, boil him in his hide, make a caldron of his skin, browis of his bowels, drink of his blood, and bread and meat of his carcase. Since few or none amongst them hitherto have as yet understood any better rules or methods of eating. More north in an angle of Cathness, lives John a Groat, upon an isthmus of land that faceth the pleasant Isles of Orkney; where the inhabitants are blessed with the plenty of grass and grain; besides fish, flesh, and fowl in abundance. Now that barnicles (which are a certain sort of wooden geese) breed hereabouts, it's past dispute; and that they fall off from the limbs and members of the fir-tree, is questionless; and those so fortunate to espouse the ocean (or any other river, or humitactive soil) by virtue of solar heat are destinated to live; but to all others so unfortunate to fall upon dry land, are denied their nativity.

Theoph. Can you credit your own report; or do you impose these hyperboles ironically upon the world, designedly to make Scotland appear a kingdom of prodigies?

Arn. No certainly! and that there is such a fowl I suppose none doubts it; but if any do, let him resort to Cambden, Speed, or Gerhard's herbal, and there he shall find that in Lancashire, thousands were gathered up, adhering to the broken ribs of a ship wreck'd upon that coast; but these are not like the barnicle geese that I speak of: the like accident hapned in Kent sometime past, and in many other parts of England, &c. So that few ingenious and intelligible travellers doubt a truth in this matter; and the rather, because if sedulously examined, it discovers a want of faith to doubt what's confirmed by such credible authority. But if eye-sight be evidence against contradiction, and the sense of feeling argument good enough to refute fiction, then let me bring these two convincing arguments to maintain my assertion; for I have held a barnicle in my own hand, when as yet unfledg'd, and hanging by the beak, which as I then supposed of the fir-tree; for it grew from thence, as an excrescence grows on the members of an animal: and as all things have periods, and in time drop off, so does the barnicle by a natural progress separate it self from the member it's conjoin'd to.

But further, to explicate the method and manner of this wooden goose more plainly: The first appearing parts are her rump and legs; next to them, her callous and unploom'd body; and last of all her beak, by which she hangs immature, and altogether insensible; because not as yet having any spark of life hitherto discovered to shine about her. Then, like the leaves in October that leisurely drop off (since predestinated to fall) even so the barnicle drops off from the twig of the tree to which Nature had fastned her, and gave her a growth, and an inanimate being. Where note, to so many as providentially fall into water, protection is immediately sent them to live; but to all others as accidentally encounter dry land, such I presume are doom'd to die without redemption. And though some of them are commissioned to live, yet how difficult is it to preserve life, when hourly sought after by the luxurious devourer?

ABERDEEN, STONEHAVEN, DUNNOTTAR, &c.—*Arn.* And this is that famous Aberdeen, whose western suburbs are guarded by the hills; as are those levels more easternly saluted by the ocean.

Theoph. Is this that Aberdeen so generally discours'd by the Scots for civility?[1]

Arn. Yes, and humanity too; for it's the paragon of Scotland.

Theoph. Why do not you call it by the name of a city?

Arn. It matters not much for that, since the general vogue of a town serves as well: however it's a corporation, and that's enough; and I'm convinc'd it stands in a cultivated country, that never knew the force of sterility;

[1] As has been already said, the fame of the "Aberdeen Doctors," distinguished alike by their learning and their opposition to the principles of the Solemn League and Covenant, had given great lustre to Aberdeen during the first half of the seventeenth century. Among these doctors were Robert Barron, William Leslie, James Sibbald, Alexander Scroggy, William and John Forbes.

whose banks are bathed with the glittering streams of Dee, and her walls shaded with fertil corn fields, promulgates plenty; for heaven, by the law of generosity, certainly has bless'd her: for here the sun so moderates the cold in winter, that it seldom or rarely freezes her sands; whose increase is multiplied from the generous breasts of the ocean. And from whence both mariner and merchant accumulate treasure, because to drag it forth from the solid deeps of the sea; when at other times they import their goods into the Highlands, as they export commodities into remote countries.

Theoph. But the harbour, I fancy, that's somewhat too strait; and the entrance, as I conceive, much too narrow; however it's examined secure enough.

Arn. Peradventure it is; yet these rocks at the entrance terrify the pilot, as her harbour, when entred, exhilarates the passenger. Now the buildings of this city are framed with stone and timber; facing the sun, and fronting this pleasant harbour: the streets also are large and spacious, and the walls strengthned with towers and buttresses of stone. So that nothing, in my opinion, remains defective to compleat them happy; for if not to waste by an overpluss, they can never pine away by a want.

Theoph. I fancy this place situate in a pleasant part of a country; and so was that relique of antiquity we but newly past by, when approaching the suburbs of this flourishing city.

Arn. You do well to remind me, for I had almost forgot it; that was Old Aberdeen: things that grow ancient, grow out of fashion; however, it's the mother city of New Aberdeen, and a university to boot, wherein stands an old weather-beaten cathedral, that looks like the times, somewhat irregular: but of that I have little to say, since others before me thought requisite to erect such public places for private devotion, when this present generation conform themselves, by contracting their congregations to lesser now.

Theoph. Is this Old Aberdeen an old university? why then a sophister may pick up as much ethicks and politicks as will serve him to stuff out a pair of lawn sleeves. Cathedrals in some countries influence the inhabitants, as planets, you know, have government over the vital parts.

Arn. You must have a slash at the gown, I perceive; but what think you of the church in New Aberdeen (that's no cathedral) where the magistrates sit under the soveraignty of the mace, and every merchant in his peculiar pew; where every society of mechanicks have their particular seats, distinguished by escutcheons, sutable to their profession; so that confusion seldom or rarely happens amongst them, in quarrelling for places; where strangers are unsuspected for informers and intruders, and the civillity of the people such, that no man is left destitute of a seat to sit on, but every one entertained answerable to his quality?

Theoph. This is something like; for it far exceeds the custom of England, where a man may stand in some churches till his feet are surbeat, yet nobody proffer him a remove, or a stool to sit on.

Arn. But this is not all neither; for here you shall have such method in their musick, and such order and decorum of song-devotion in the church, as you will admire to hear, though not regulated by a cantor or quirister, but only by an insipid parochial clerk, that never attempts further in the mathematicks of musick, than to compleat the parishioners to sing a psalm in tune.

Theoph. You have concisely characterized Aberdeen, with her inhabitants; but what have we here? Cawses uncartable, and pavements unpracticable, pointed with rocky stumpy stones, and dawb'd all over with dingy dirt, that makes it unpassible; and the fields, as I conceive, are ten times worse, because o'erspread with miry clay, and incumbred with bogs that will bury a horse.

Arn. For better for worse, we must through it, if intending to climb the southern elevations. Now at the foot of this pavement there's a small little harbour which they call Steenhive,[1] but I take the liberty to call it *stinking hive*, because it's so unsavory; which serves only for pirates and pickeroons;[2] but it bravely accommodates the Highlander for depredations.

Theoph. What fabrick is this that peeps out of the ocean?

---

[1] The local name for Stonehaven.   [2] Picaroon, a rogue or cheat (Spanish, *picaron*).

Arn. Donnotter-Castle surrounded with sea, and waves for recreation dance about it; it's a house so inoculated and cemented into rocks, that a man would fancy it to swim in the ocean; and the natural strength so impregnable, supposeth the artificial but inconsiderable, whose rocky foundations, like Atlas's pillars, support the bulk of this gaudy fortress. For art and artist are but nature's substitutes; where-ever therefore nature ceaseth to operate, then is the time for artist to begin his progress. But nature has finished what she had to do, and has left nothing for the artist to practise, save only to adorn the natural excellency. After this manner is that artificial imbellishment, for the rock it self is the natural strength, then the castle can be but the artificial. From when we conclude, that nature and art have form'd such a fabrick for strength and beauty, that amuzes and amazes every beholder.

Theoph. I behold and consider this invincible castle, lifted up like a cloud into the ambient air. I have also considered the gaity of her galleries, and those ornaments that adorn her gaudy frontiers. I have also considered those opposite mountains, whose formidable aspect are no pleasing prospect to those imbellish'd battlements, that seemingly float in the arms of the ocean.

Arn. You have hit the key, and now let me tune up the instrument; those mountains mar all: yet in this fair fortress they conceal the Regalia's of Scotland,[1] from such sacrilegious hands that would steal diadems to adorn their ambitions; so rob their prince to inrich themselves; for here it is, in this solitary rock besieged with sea, that Scotland has conceal'd both ornament and treasure; and what greater ornament to a prince than a crown?

Theoph. That I can believe as an article of my creed, yet all is not gold that glisters; for should all reports pass muster for realities, truth it self might be brought into the scandal of suspicion. That the crown has been lodg'd in

---

[1] During the civil wars the Regalia of Scotland were deposited for safety in Dunnottar Castle. The castle having been besieged, and being at the point of surrender, they were secretly conveyed thence, and buried in the Kirk of Kineff, where they remained till the Restoration. At the time of Franck's visit, it was generally received that they were hidden somewhere about the castle.

Donnotter, I dispute not, yet Dumbarton I should think in all respects as secure, and Edinburgh-Castle as secure as either, to conceal that treasure from degenerate mercenaries, that would violate their trust though they venture to hang for it.

Arn. You are in the right on't, but the road I fancy runs not so rough as it did; nor are my apprehensions of England so remote as they were : both the way and the weather favour our designs in this southern expedition : for England's our prospect, now propound you the object : and as we ride along to the town of Montrose, signify your opinion of the flourishing Aberdeen.

Theoph. You impose a little too hard upon me; I can scarcely express my opinion of a place, but I must be sentenced too much to commend it. On the other hand, should I lessen or impair their civilities, then you challenge me to reflect on our civil entertainments. This dilemma I am driven to. However you cannot deny, but acknowledg, that Aberdeen is sweetly situated, and under the government of well-regulated magistrates : No complaint of poverty, nor luxurious superfluities; where the houses are fill'd with hospitality, not with prophaneness; their streets and allies cleanly swept and paved, and their church and state-house very curiously kept, after the best methods of the Scotish mode. But how Montrose will represent unto us, that I suspend to determine till farther examination.

Arn. Trouble not your self with that affair, for Montrose will murder all your suspicions. Her generous entertainments in every angle, like radiated beams of the sun that invigorate the earth, so naturally do the inhabitants influence their civilities amongst strangers; which remonstrates Montrose a beauty that lies conceal'd, as it were, in the bosom of Scotland; most delicately drest up, and adorn'd with excellent buildings, whose foundations are laid with polish'd stone, and her ports all wash'd with the silver streams that trickle down from the famous Ask.[1] This is Montrose in the county of Angus, antiently known by the name of Cælurcha. Tell me how you like it, whose gaity and gallantry springs from the nobility and gentry ; but the wealth of the city, from her merchants and manufacture :

---

[1] The South Esk.

and though you see not her harbours deck'd with delicate
shipping, yet she contents herself with a pleasant river, that
commodes the inhabitant with the blessings of plenty, and
that's enough.   So to sum up all in a compendious narrative,
we intitle Montrose the Mount of Roses.[1]

Theoph. What encomium more elegant, or what character
more eminent for these sweet situations, than the Rosy
Mount of our northern latitude ?   Nay, what expressions
could be added more compendiously significant to characterize
the beautiful elevations and imbellishments of Montrose, I
know not : then let this short derivation answer all objec-
tions ; whilst we enter her ports, and use arguments of
refreshment to our hostile appetites, in regard so famous a
river as the famous Ask salutes her banks and flourishing
shores with daily supplies, to relieve her inhabitants, and
accommodate strangers.

Arn. Now our next advance is to the town of Dundee :
but give me leave to call it deplorable Dundee, and not
to be exprest without a deluge of tears ; because storm'd
and spoil'd by the rash precipitancy of mercenaries, whose
rapinous hands put a fatal period to her stately imbellishments, with the loss of many innocent lives, altogether
unconcern'd in that unnatural controversy.

Ah, poor Dundee ! torn up by the roots ; and thy natives
and inhabitants pick'd out at the port-holes.   Can honour
shine in such bloody sacrifices, to lick up the lives of inhabitants, as if by a studied revenge ?   Can nothing sweeten
the conquerour's sword, but the reeking blood of orphans and
innocents ?   Blush, O heavens, what an age is this !   There
was wealth enough to answer their ambitions, and probably
that as soon as any thing betrayed her.   Could nothing
satisfy the unsatiable sword, but the life of Dundee to atone
as a sacrifice ?   English men without mercy, are like
Christians without Christianity ; no moderation nor pity
left, but parcelling out the lives of poor penitents in cold
blood ?   Who must answer for this at the bar of heaven,
before the judg of all the world ?   But he that doom'd
Dundee to die, is dead himself, and doom'd e're this ; and
Dundee yet living to survive his cruelty.

---

[1] In Gaelic, Montrose is *Alt-moinc-ros,* " the burn of the mossy point."

Theoph. Is this Dundee! Disconsolate Dundee,[1] where
the merciless conquerour stuck down his standard in streams
of blood ?

Arn. Yes, this is that unfortunate and deplorable Dundee,
whose laurels were stript from the brow of her senators, to
adorn the conquering tyrant's head.　Here it was that every
arbour flourished with a fruitful vine ; and here every border
was beautified with fragrant flowers.　Yet her situation
seems to me none of the best ; for if bordering too near
the brinks of the ocean proves insalubrious, or stooping too
low to salute the earth, incommodes health by unwholsom
vapours ; then to stand elevated a pitch too high, suffocates
with fumes that equally offend and infect the air, by blotting
out sanity with the soveraignty of life.

Theoph. This somewhat answers my former opinion, that
neither honour nor riches, nor the ambitions of men, stand
in competition with the mediocrity of health ; nor is there
any blessing under the sun adequate to the soveraign
sanctions of sanity on this side eternity, but the radies of
sanctification from the sun of righteousness.　The world's a
fool, and none but fools admire it : Yet not that I prophane
the beautiful creation ; when only censuring that fictitious
and imaginary world in man.　Go on with Dundee ; I over-
flow with pity, and could wish my reluctancy penitency
enough to weep her into a religious repentance, but not with
Rachel never to be comforted.　Hark, Arnoldus ! Don't
you hear the bells ?

Arn. Yes, I hear them, and what of that ?　Bells and
bonfires are two catholick drumsticks, with which the church
beats up for volunteers only to debauch them.　For what
end were bells hung up, if not to jangle ; and bonfires
kindled, if not to blaze like an *ignis fatuus ?*　Thus people
uncultivated are like land untill'd and arts unimprov'd print
the footsteps of penury.　But arts are improv'd by industrious
ingenuity ; when through want of ingenious industry they
slide into a non-entity.　As no man can be truly religious

---

[1] Monk's merciless treatment of Dundee has already been referred to.　In
his lament over the misfortunes of Dundee, as in many other passages, Franck
shows that he was not a blind sectary, but could see two sides of a question,
which so few of his contemporaries, either in England or Scotland, could do.

without good morals, so no man without good morals can be in any measure religious. Not that I assert religion is morality; but morality is the porch that lets into the temple.

Theoph. You paraphrase upon bells; I wonder how you miss'd bag-pipes, since the one has as much the root of the matter in't as the other. By these mystical metaphors, if I hit the mark, you present England an emblem of Canaan, and Scotland but a piece of English imitation.

Arn. You don't hit the key right, but I perceive England lies close siege in your bosom; however there ought to be some charity for Scotland, that so generously entertained you with all sorts of varieties.

Theoph. Scotland 'tis true has variety enough to confuse and confound all the cooks in England.

Arn. All this I'll grant.

Theoph. Then you must grant their butter but little better than grease we usually grease cart-wheels withal; which nauseates my palat if but to think on't, or remember the hand that made it up. I know there are men that have maws like muck-hills, that can feed as freely upon tainted flesh, as you and I upon pheasant and partridge.

Arn. What then ?

Theoph. Why then you argue as if you had lost your English appetite, and I would not for all the varieties in Scotland, ʋhat the resentments of England should expire in my palat.

Arn. Does hunger make any distinction in dainties ? if not, then why should Scotish kale blot out the character of English colliflowers ?

Theoph. I shan't dispute the point, but the very thoughts of England sweetens my apprehensions, that possibly e're long I may taste of a southern sallad : However, this I'll say in the honour of Scotland, that cold and hunger are inseparable companions, but their linens are fresh ; and were not their beds so short, they would serve well enough for weary travellers.

Arn. Then I fancy they will serve well enough for us, whilst we trace the fragrant levels of Fife. For now we relinquish the beautiful ports of Dundee, to transport in boats that are steer'd with a compass of straw, by reason of the embodied mists, to which Dundee is as incident as any part, because standing in a bottom that's besieged with mucky miry earth; from whence there insurrect such pernicious vapours, as nauseate the air; whereby it becomes almost infectious.

Theoph. Why so?

Arn. Because it debilitates both the native and inhabitant, and would certainly incapacitate them of health and long life, did not custom and a country-habit plead a prescription, both as to physick and diet: Insomuch, that neither gass nor blass,[1] nor any nauseating suffocating fumes, nor hardly death it self can snatch them from Scotland; where some natives have lived to a prodigious age.

Theoph. But to the country of Fife, I fear you'l forget it.

Arn. No, no, doubt it not, nor would I have you startle the mariner, who, because destitute of a card to pilot us over by, is compell'd to make use of a compass of straw.

Theoph. A very ingenious invention; pray tell us the manner on't.

Arn. Don't push too hard upon me; and I'll tell you this new way of navigation. When cloudy mists arise that darken the face of the firmament, and threaten danger without any disturbance, you shall then see the seamen stuff the stern with straw, as now they do with little trusses, which they successively expose one at a time; and so supply it time after time from the stern of the vessel, till at length they arrive at the desired shoar, as now we do: And thus have I past and repast from Dundee. Nor is there any difficulty nor danger to any man more than hazarding his carcase in timber. Now welcome ashore to the fields in Fife; where we must exchange our navigable horses for hackneys.

Theoph. What must we call the name of this town?

Arn. Cooper in Fife;[2] it's a corporation.

Theoph. And what other town is that yet more eastward, that seems to lean on the skirts of the ocean?

Arn. That's antient Saint Andrews, their metropolitan

---

[1] The Belgian chemist Van Helmont invented two corresponding terms, *gas* and *blas*, of which the former passed into use, the latter has been forgotten (Skeat, *Etymological Dictionary*).   [2] Cupar-Fife.

university.   Upon the same coast lie Creel and Petenweems.
More southerly yet lies cockly Carcawdy[1] facing the ocean.
and the frontiers of Leith : we shall only take a view of the
palace of Faulkland, though her fair imbellishments outlustre
Dumfermling.

Theoph. What's our next stage ?

Arn. Brunt-Island : but I must remind you of the
magnificent Palace of Scoon, forgot as we past by the ports
of Saint Johnstons, near whose elevated turrets there stands
a kirk, that stands upon all the land in Scotland ; which
kirk is immur'd with a fair stone wall ; and in that kirk
they crown their kings, and perform the formalities of all
other royal duties ; which regalia are the sword, spurs, purse,
crown, globe, scepter, and Bible.   Now he's a dunce that
knows not this duty, because it's incumbent on all the
kingdom of Scotland.

Theoph. But how stands the kirk upon all the kingdom ?

Arn. There's not a royalty in the kingdom of Scotland,
but has sent some part of earth (from every angle) to this
place called Scoon ;[2] which earth was dispersed by laborious
industry ; upon which the foundations of the kirk were
laid.   So that now you are to consider this variety of mould
represents but one uniform and compact body of earth :
which earth represents the great volume of Scotland in a
breviat, or as I may term it, a little compendium.

Thus our discourse of the kirk of Scoon has accompanied
us to a view of pleasant Carcawdy, a little pretty maritime
town (built all with stone) that stands in the face of the
ocean, and the frontiers of Fife.   But the time and our
occasion constrains us to pass by Carcawdy, where the
inhabitants live more upon fish than flesh ; from whose
slender ports we must hasten to Brunt-Island, otherwise we
endanger losing our tide, which will much incommode us ;
nor can we stay there to examine their curiosities.

Theoph. What's this that so naturally represents the
ocean ?   And what are those ships, under sail ? or must I
fancy them a landskip of moveable mountains ?

---

[1] Crail, Pittenweem, Kirkcaldy.   [2] According to the tradition of the
neighbourhood, it was the *mote-hill* and not the foundations of the church that
was formed as Franck relates.

Arn. If you fancy them ships fluctuating to and fro on those solid deeps to attempt that harbour, you are not much mistaken.

Theoph. Is there any town on those rocky foundations ?

Arn. Yes surely there is; for we now discover the pleasant shores of beautiful Brunt-Island, guarded with rocks that front the harbour and pier of Leith; over whose rubified sands we must plough the ocean, to those delectable flourishing ports; provided the vessel be tite and unleaky, as questionless this is, design'd for our passage.

Theoph. However, I'll remind you of our hazardous passage from Innerbrachy to the famous Ness, as at another time our personal hazard, when fording over Forres, and the rapid Trespey;[1] besides other great rivers and rivulets in our march, of very swift and violent motion; which we often discharg'd without the artifice of boats : and yet I cannot help that natural antipathy and aversion, that I find against timber fortifications; nor can I think them such soveraign security, but that sometimes they are accompani'd with difficulties and danger. It's true, I grant, that no man has an infallible protection for life; nor a pre-knowledg of sickness nor sudden solution.

Arn. Well then, if so, transplant those fears into foreign parts; for we must certainly, and that suddenly, expose ourselves to the mercy of the sea, by the providence of God. Nor is the danger more than imagination; for the fear of death to some men is more dreadful and terrible than death it self; which great sea we must all sail through, before we cast anchor in the port of eternity.

Theoph. You have sodred the breach, and salv'd the wound, that now I itch to be floating on the ocean. However, before we embark for Leith, let us give nature a Philip in the arms of Brunt-Island.

Arn. All this we may do, and view the situations too, which stands on a flat and flourishing level, back'd by Fife, and the mountains of Mirt,[2] whose foundations are laid in rocky stone, and beautified with the regularities of art, where there's a small but secure harbour, to rescue the retreats

---

[1] Spey.   [2] Evidently a hopeless corruption of some other name.

of the terrified passenger, when pursued with the furious hostility of Neptune, whose waves storm the shores, insinuating themselves into every creek. But the beauty of Brunt-Island lies most in her market-place, which serves for an exchange, fronting the harbour, and facing the ocean; where all or most of her merchant's houses stand gazing on the beautiful Pier of Leith.

LEITH AND EDINBURGH.—*Arn.* Leith stands, as you see, situated on a level surrounded by sea on the north-east; and guarded on the south with Neal's Craigs,[1] and Arthur's Seat, that hangs over Edinburgh. But the fabricks of Leith are built with stone, hovering over the pier, and fronting the ocean, almost drown'd under water; and that which is worse, if worse can be, those nauseating scents suckt greedily from the sea, bring arguments of disease, and sometimes summons for death. On the other hand, Scotland cannot present you with a more pleasant port; for here the houses and structures are large and lofty, and the pier like a gnomen directs to the tolbooth. Here also stands a substantial cawsey that leads to the bridg, that brings you to a citadel that was, but now is not, because hudled in dust, and ruinous heaps; yet not ruin'd by age, nor torn with the scars and impressions of war; but policy, and not piety, laid her surface in the sand.

Theoph. What merchandize doth she trade in?

Arn. For the most part she trades in foreign commodities, except some manufactures of their own, as ticking, bedding, tartan, pladding, Scots-cloth, &c. So that Leith for trade, with her merchandize for treasure, excels most, if not all the maritime ports in Scotland.

Theoph. Pray, what other accommodation hath she?

Arn. She has fish and flesh in abundance, viz., oysters, cockles, muscles, crabs, craw-fish, lobsters, soles, plaice, turbet, thornback, cod, keeling, haddock, mackrel, herring, &c. Then there's salmon, trout, pike, perch, eel, &c., but their flesh are beeves, veals, porks, veneson, kid, mutton, lamb, &c. And their fowl are eagles, signets, hawks, geese, gossander, duck and mallard, teal, widgeon, cock, pidgeon, heath-game, moorfowl, curlue, partridg, pheasant, plover, grey and green,

---

[1] I have been unable to identify these " Craigs."

and many more that I cannot remember.   So great is their
plenty and variety, that did not the popularity in Edinburgh
render things more chargeable than other parts more remote
up the country, a man might live almost without expence.
And now we relinquish the flourishing ports of Leith, whose
foundations are daily saluted by the ocean.   O, how sweetly
the weather smiles, the horizon looks clear, the sky is serene,
and the birds you may see them beat the ambient air with
their tunable notes !   Come, Theophilus, let us mount our
horses, and lift up your eyes to behold those lofty imbellishments of Edinburgh.

Theoph. They are obvious enough, half an eye may
see them.

Arn. Welcome to these elevated ports, the princely court
of famous Edinburgh.   This city stands upon a mighty
scopulous[1] mountain, whose foundations are cemented with
mortar and stone ; where the bulk of her lofty buildings
represent it a rock at a reasonable distance, fronting the
approaching sun ; whose elevations are seven or eight stories
high, mounted aloft in the ambient air.   But the length, as
I take it, exceeds not one mile, and the breadth on't
measures little more than half a mile ; nor is there more
than one fair street, to my best remembrance.   But then it's
large and long, and very spacious, whose ports are splendid,
so are her well-built houses and palaces, corresponding very
much to compleat it their metropolis.

Theoph. What fabrick is that on the east of Edinburgh ?

Arn. Hallirood-House, the regal court of Scotland.

Theoph. But there's yet another great fabrick, that presents westward.

Arn. That's Edinburgh-Castle, elevated in the air, on an
impregnable precipice of rocky earth, perpendicular in some
parts, rampir'd and barrocadoed with thick walls of stone,
and graffs proportionable, to contribute an additional strength.
So that you are to consider this inaccessible castle shines
from a natural as well as an artificial product, because part
of it you see contiguous with the rock ; but the other part,
because affixed by cemented stone, which inoculates and

---

[1] It is due to Franck to say that his *scopulous* appears in Dr Johnson's
Dictionary as the equivalent of the Latin *scopulosus*, full of rocks.

incorporates them so firmly together, that the whole mass of building is of such incredible strength, that it's almost fabulous for any man to report it, or sum up the impregnable lustre and beauty of this fair fortress, that defies all attempts, except famine, disease, or treachery be conduct; so that culverins and cannons signify but little, without bombs and carcasses.[1]   On the other hand, the defendants must not be too liberal, lest their water forsake them sooner than their ammunition; so inevitably draw upon them the foregoing consequence, and incommode them with a thousand inconveniences.   True it is, many arguments of art and artillery have been sent to examine this impregnable castle, but none were ever found more successful than hunger and disease, or the golden apples of the Hesperides.   Such kind of magnets muzzle mercenaries, and make them a golden bridg to pass over.

Theoph. Is this fair fabrick the Parliament-House where the grandees sit on national affairs ?

Arn. Yes, this is their palace where the parliament sits to accommodate the kingdom; whose famous ports we now relinquish to take a review of the bars of Musselburg.   But that on our right hand is delicate Dalkeith, surrounded with a park; and that on our left hand is Preston-pans, where the natives make salt from the brine of the ocean.   That other town before us is the corporation of Haddington; and this is the Brill;[2] but the Bass you may see is a prodigious rock, that makes an island on the skirts of the ocean.

---

[1] A special kind of bomb.   [2] I cannot discover what Franck meant by the Brill.

JOREVIN DE ROCHEFORD

(1661 ?).

THE following narrative is taken from the fourth volume of the *Antiquarian Repertory* (1809). It is a translation from a very scarce book of travels published at Paris in 1672. The name of its author does not appear in the French biographical collections; and nothing seems to be known of him except what is implied in his own narrative of his travels, which extended over England and Ireland as well as Scotland. From certain of his remarks we gather that his visit to Scotland took place shortly after the Restoration.

ANTIQUARIAN REPERTORY, vol. iv., p. 599.

THE kingdom of Scotland is ordinarily divided into two parts, which are on this side and beyond the river Tay; each part is subdivided into provinces, called Chirifdomes. This kingdom is bounded on the north side by the Orcade Islands, Schetland and Farro, inhabited only by fishermen, and persons who subsist almost entirely on fish, and a little game they take by hunting in the mountains, with which these islands are generally covered. It is bordered on the west by the Ebudes[1] Islands, and divers other small islets, which are at the entrance of an almost infinite number of great gulfs advanced into the kingdom, which they furnish with fish, in abundance. But the country is so mountainous and so ingrateful in some places, that it is not worth cultivation; and the cold so intense as scarcely to permit grain to ripen. On the south is the kingdom of England; and on the east the German Sea, otherwise the fishy sea, or *Haringzee*, because there are caught by the Flemish and Dutch the salmoncod, but principally herrings,

---

[1] Hebrides.

with which, after salting, they serve France and other kingdoms; this fishery making the best part of their riches.

I know very well that the northern part of this kingdom,
beyond the river Tay, is almost uninhabited, on account of
the high mountains, which are only rocks, where there is
no want of game in great quantities; but there grows but
very little corn; which obliges the inhabitants of the interior
parts of the country to subsist on fish, which they dry by
means of the great cold, after having caught them in the
lakes, which are to be found all over the kingdom; and
some of the villages by the sea-side export as much fish
as furnishes them with corn and other necessaries of life. It
is said, that there are certain provinces on that side of the
country, where the men are truly savage, and have neither
law nor religion, and support a miserable existence by what
they can catch. But I likewise know, that the southern
part of the kingdom on this side the Tay contains many fine
towns, good sea-ports, great tracts of fertile land, and
beautiful meadows filled with herds of all sorts of cattle; but
the extreme cold prevents their growing to the common size,
as is the case all over Europe. The principal towns are,
Edinbourg, Lyth, Sterling, Glasgo, Saint Andreau, Abernethy,
Dunkeld, Brechin, the old and new Aberdeen, the port of
Cromary, Dornok, the town of St Johnstone, where are the
four fine castles of Scotland.

After having passed through Nieuwark [1] that is on the
side of the gulf of Dunbriton,[2] which lay on my left hand,
to enter into a country surrounded almost on all sides
by mountains, I descended into some very agreeable valleys,
as Kemakoom,[3] &c. From thence I followed a small river,
where the country grew a little better, to go to Paslet,[4] on a
river forded by a large bridge abutting to the castle, where
there is a very spacious garden enclosed by thick walls of
hewn stone. It was once a rich abbey, as I discovered by a
mitre and cross, that appeared half demolished, upon one of
the gates of the castle, which was the abbey house. Those

[1] Newark. [2] Dumbarton, *i.e.*, fort of the Britons. Like most of the
intelligent travellers who visited Scotland, Rocheford was evidently acquainted
with the early historians of the country. [3] Kilmalcolm. [4] Paisley, which is
situated on the White Cart. Its abbey was founded by Walter Stewart, who
married Marjory, the daughter of Robert the Bruce.

who go from Krinock[1] to Glasgo pass from Kemakoom by
Reinfreu; but the way is full of marshes, difficult to pass
over, and where there is a boat which does not work on
Sundays, according to the custom of England, as it happened
when I was travelling that road; which caused me, in order
to avoid these difficulties, to change my route, which was
after Paislet, to enter into a fine country upon the banks of
the river Clyd, which I followed to the suburbs of Glasgo,
joined to the town by a large bridge. This I passed before
I could enter Glasgo.

GLASGO.—Glasgo is the second town in the kingdom of
Scotland,[2] situated upon a hill that extends gently to the brink
of the river of Clyd, which is capable of bearing vessels,
since the tide rises here a little from the gulf of Dunbritton,
into which it empties itself; so that vessels can come from
Ireland to Glasgo. The streets of Glasgo are large and
handsome, as if belonging to a new town; but the houses
are only of wood, ornamented with carving. Here live
several rich shopkeepers. As soon as I had passed the
bridge, I came to the entry of two broad streets. In the
first is a large building, being the hospital of the merchants,[3]
and farther on the market-place, and town-hall,[4] built with
large stones, with a square tower being the town clock-
house; under which is the guard-house, as in all the towns
of consequence in England. Although Glasgo has no other
fortification, that does not prevent it from being very strong,
for towards the east side it is elevated upon a scarped rock,
the foot whereof is washed by a little river,[5] very convenient
to that part of the town through which it passes. I lodged
in this fine large street. The son of the owner of the house,
being then studying philosophy at the university, conducted
me everywhere, in order to point out to me what was most
remarkable in the town. He began by the college,[6] of which
he showed me the library, which is nothing equal to that I

[1] Greenock. [2] In the middle of the sixteenth century Glasgow held only the
eleventh place amongst the towns of Scotland (Denholm, *History of Glasgow*,
p. 110). [3] Hutcheson's Hospital. [4] This was the New Tolbooth erected in
1626. It served as a prison and a place for county meetings till early in the
present century. The tower still stands, and is known as the Cross Steeple
(Macgeorge, *Old Glasgow*). [5] The Molendinar Burn. [6] As the college was
completed in 1656, Rocheford would see it in its completed state.

saw at Oxford. From hence I came into a large and very fine garden, filled with all kinds of fruit-trees, deemed scarce in that country. At length we entered into the great court, the façade whereof is the great body of the house, newly built, under which are the classes sustaining the galleries, and lodgings for the scholars and students. He introduced me to the regent in philosophy, who asked me many things respecting the colleges and universities of France, principally of that of the Sorbonne;[1] upon which he told me, he was astonished that throughout all Europe there was not one uniform faith, since we all sought the same end to go to Paradise, the road to which we Catholics had made so difficult, although God by his sufferings and mercy had rendered it very easy, and was desirous all the world should enter. To whom I answered that God was at once both merciful and just, and that we could not arrive at heaven but by the difficulties and labours that he himself had suffered, in order to point out the way to us. I was unwilling to continue this discourse, whereby I could learn nothing useful in my voyage, wherefore I took leave of him, in order to visit the metropolitan church of the archbishopric. It is perhaps the longest and best built in the kingdom, and ornamented round about with many figures of saints, some of which were thrown down and broken at the time the Protestants made themselves masters of it, after having driven out the Catholics. The chapel behind the choir contains some very remarkable tombs. There are two high towers over the principal doors of this handsome church. The archbishop's palace[2] is large, and very near it. We went and walked in the market-place, where a market is held twice a week; it is a cross-way, formed by the handsomest streets in the town; on that towards the left hand is the butchery, and the great general hospital.[3]

In the environs of Glasgo are several pits, from whence they dig very good coal, which is used for fires instead of wood in winter time, here severe, and of long duration. One had only need to look at the sphere to know this, and at the

---

[1] The original college of the Sorbonne had been founded in 1253 by Robert de Sorbon ; but a new building (that which still stands) was begun by Cardinal Richelieu in 1627. [2] See page 153 (above). [3] The Bishops' Alms-houses are probably meant. The other hospitals were St Nicholas and that of the Lepers.

time too, when the days in summer are more than twenty-two hours long, since the sun sets only three or four hours at night ; so that as the days are long in summer, they are proportionately short in winter.

I left Glasgo to go to Edinbourg, and passed over a great plain, where stands Cader,[1] and afterwards Cartelok,[2] where there is a castle on a river. And shortly after, towards my left hand, I left a great castle[3] in the bottom of a little valley, at the foot of the mountains, from whence issues a little river that I passed at Falkirk. Here great quantities of stuffs and cloths of all sorts are made. Leaving it, on the left hand one sees the extremity of the gulf of Edinbourg, where the river of Forthna empties itself near the town of Stirling, situated at the foot of a range of the highest mountains in Scotland, to go to Lithquo.

LITHQUO.—Lithquo is situated in a very good country, although it is environed by high mountains. It stands on the banks of a large lake, with a castle on the highest part of the town, being on a rock commanding its whole extent. It is flanked by several large towers, which render it one of the strongest places in the kingdom. There is a very handsome church[4] at one end of the market-place, in the center of which is a fountain,[5] in a bason which receives its waters. The chief street crosses the market-place and the whole town. Here is a manufactory of cloth and fine linen. I left this place, and passed through Kalkester[6] to go to Edenburgh.

EDENBURGH.—Edenburgh is the capital town, and the handsomest of the kingdom of Scotland, distant only a mile from the sea, where Lith is its sea-port. It stands on a hill, which it entirely occupies. This hill, on the side whereon the castle is built, is scarped down as steep as a wall, which adds to its strength, as it is accessible only on one side, which is therefore doubly fortified with bastions, and a large ditch cut sloping into the rock. I arrived

---

[1] Cadder.   [2] This is the Cuntellon of Brereton, *i.e.*, Kirkintilloch. The odd spelling was suggested by the local name *Kintilloch.*   [3] Castlecary (?)
[4] This church, probably founded by David I., is considered one of the finest, as it is one of the best-preserved, specimens of Gothic architecture in Scotland. It was here that James IV. saw the apparition so vividly described by Pitscottie.   [5] The Cross Well (see above, p. 48).   [6] Kirkliston.

by the suburbs, at the foot of the castle where at the entry is the market-place, which forms the beginning of a great street in the lower town, called Couguet.[1] On coming into this place, one is first struck with the appearance of a handsome fountain,[2] and, a little higher up, with the grand hospital [3] or alms-house for the poor : there is no one but would at first sight take it for a palace. You ascend to it by a long staircase, which ends before a platform facing the entry at the great gate. The portico is supported by several columns, and the arms and statue of the founder, with a tablet of black marble, on which there is an inscription, signifying, that he was a very rich merchant, who died without children. There are four large pavilions, ornamented with little turrets, connected by four large wings, forming a square court in the middle, with galleries sustained by columns, serving for communications to the apartments of this great edifice. One might pass much time in considering the pieces of sculpture and engraving in these galleries, the magnitude of its chambers and halls, and the good order observed in this great hospital. Its garden is the walk and place of recreation for the citizens, but a stranger cannot be admitted without the introduction of some inhabitant. You will there see a bowling-green, as in many other places in England : it is a smooth even meadow, resembling a green carpet, a quantity of fruit-trees, and a well-kept kitchen-garden. From thence I proceeded along this great street, to see some ancient tombs in a large burial-ground,[4] and, farther on, the college of the university.[5] I was shown a pretty good library, but the building is not remarkable; it has a court, and the schools are round about it. This lower town is inhabited by many workmen and mechanics, who, though they do not ennoble the quarter, render it the most populous. Here are a number of little narrow streets mounting into the great one, that forms the middle of the

[1] Cowgate. [2] Hence Fountainbridge. [3] George Heriot's Hospital, which seemed to have arrested the attention of all visitors to Edinburgh. [4] Greyfriars, which had been made a burying-ground about 1580. [5] The original College of Edinburgh, which Rocheford saw, was simply the house of the Duke of Chatelherault, adjusted to the necessities of a college, together with a wing containing fourteen chambers, added by the town council (Grant, *Hist. of the Univ. of Edin.*, i. p. 129).

town, and which from the castle extends gently to the
bottom of the hill, that seems on two sides enclosed by a
valley, which serves for a ditch; in one is what we have
called the lower town, and in the other are the gardens,
separated from the town by a great wall. I lodged at
Edenburgh in the house of a French cook,[1] who directed me
to the merchant on whom I had taken a bill of exchange at
London. He took me into the castle, which one may call
impregnable, on account of its situation, since it is elevated
on a rock scarped on every side, except that which looks
to the town, by which we entered after having passed the
drawbridge, defended by a strong half-moon, where there
is no want of cannon. This brings to my mind one seen in
entering the court, which is of so great a length and
breadth,[2] that two persons have laid in it as much at their
ease as in a bed. The people of the castle tell a story of it
more pleasant than true: they say it was made in order
to carry to the port of Lyth against such enemies as might
arrive by sea; we saw several of its bullets, of an almost
immeasurable size. This court is large, with many buildings
without symmetry. There are some lodgings, pretty well
built, which formerly served for the residence of the kings
of Scotland, and at present for the viceroys, when the
King of England sends any; for at the time I was there,
there was only the Grand Chancellor,[3] who had almost the
same authority and power as a viceroy.

Descending from this castle by the great street, one may
see its palace, and, a little before the great market-place, the
custom-house,[4] where are the king's weights. This street is
so wide that it seems a market-place throughout its whole
extent. The cathedral church is in the middle; its only
ornament is a high square tower.[5] Beside it is the parliament-
house, where the chancellor resides. There are several large
halls, well covered with tapestry, where the pleadings are

[1] The traveller of 1704 already quoted says: " In all the best houses here
(Edinburgh) they dress their victuals after the French method " (p. 46).
[2] Mons Meg, which excited the admiration of every visitor to Edinburgh.
[3] The Lord Chancellor at the date of Jorevin's visit was George, Earl of
Aberdeen.   [4] The old weigh-house had been destroyed by Cromwell in 1650.
That which Jorevin saw had been built in 1660.   [5] The Crown Tower of St
Giles's had been only recently built (1648) when Jorevin visited Edinburgh.

held, and a fine court. In the great hall are several shopkeepers, who sell a thousand little curiosities. There is
besides a large pavilion, having a little garden behind it,
where there is a terrace commanding a view over all that
part of the town called the Couguet,[1] at the foot of the palace
and pavilion where the chancellor resides. This fine large
street serves for the ordinary walk of the citizens, who
otherwise repair to the suburbs of Kanignet,[2] in the ancient
palace of the kings of Scotland.

This suburb is at the end of the great street, where there
is another of the same size, and almost as handsome, which
adjoins to the palace called the king's house, said to have
been formerly an abbey, great appearances thereof being
still remaining. In entering, you pass the first great court
surrounded with lodgings for the officers; and from thence
into a second, where appears the palace, composed of several
small pavilions, intermixed with galleries and turrets, forming
a wonderful symmetry; but it has been much damaged by
fire.[3] There is likewise the church, the cloisters, and the
gardens of this ancient abbey. This suburb is separated from
the town by a gate with a bell tower, wherein is a clock;
and on one side appears the little suburb of Leyth-oye, the
way leading to the port of Leyth. In the middle of the
street is a very fine hospital,[4] which carries some marks of
having formerly been a convent, and close to it a handsome
church, once belonging to a priory, when the Catholic religion
was prevalent in the kingdom of Scotland,

It is difficult to hear mass at Edinburgh, for it is strictly
forbidden to be celebrated, although there are some Catholics,
Flemings and Frenchmen, who dwell there, with whom I
made an acquaintance, and who visited me sometimes in my
inn. They one day begged me to go a shooting with them,
assuring me that we should not return without each of us
filling his bag with game; nevertheless, it was not this
consideration that caused me to go, but rather the hope of

---

[1] Cowgate.   [2] Canongate.   [3] The greater part of Holyrood was burned by
the troops of Cromwell after the Battle of Dunbar (1650). It was rebuilt
between 1671 and 1679, subsequently to Jorevin's visit.   [4] Trinity Hospital,
swept away by the North British Railway Company in 1845. It is described
by Sir Daniel Wilson (*Memorials of Edinburgh*, p. 50, edit. 1886) as "the most
ancient and interesting building that Edinburgh possessed."

learning some curiosity of the country and the city of Edinburgh, where these gentlemen had resided a long time.   We
set out at four o'clock in the morning, being four in company,
with three good dogs.   We came to the sea-side on a great
beach,[1] from whence the tide had retired, where we found
some water-fowl, of which we killed three, and six large
wood-cocks, and near this place were some little hills covered
with heath and bushes, where we went to beat for hares and
rabbits, which frequently stroll near the sea-side.   Our dogs
put out a large leveret, which was soon knocked down.   We
then went to get some of our game cooked for breakfast, at a
village[2] not far off, and afterwards returned to hunt along that
gulf which we coasted in going to Edenburgh, whither we
carried, of our shooting, six young wild ducks, four wood-
cocks, and two rabbits.   I was very much fatigued, yet
nevertheless lent my hand as heartily to the business as any
present in getting the supper ready, in order to have it the
sooner done; when in the combat that ensued, every one did
wonders, where the glasses served for muskets, the wine for
powder, and the bottles for bandileers; whence we returned
from the field all conquerors and unwounded.

These gentlemen invited me several other times to go
sporting with them, but I always refused, on account of the
great fatigue I had undergone.   I chose rather to visit Leyth,
a mile distant from Edinburgh, from whence coaches set out
every moment to go by a paved road over a large and very
fertile plain.   Seeing a gibbet in my way, I could not refrain
from laughing, as it brought to my mind the many tricks
played at Rome with the hangman's servant, who is obliged
to carry a ladder from his house to the place of punishment,
where his master is to execute the criminal.   He, carrying
this ladder, is mounted on a horse, led by a man with a
drawn sword in his hand, to defend him.   But let him do
what he will, every one will have a stroke at him; some
refresh him with pails of water, which they throw out of
the windows; others embroider his clothes with handfuls of
mud; some greet him with rotten melons, and others over-
whelm him with stones, accompanied with this reproach,
Boya, so odious among the Italians; they also pull his feet

Probably the Figgate Whins.   [2] Restalrig.

and ladder, to make him fall; insomuch that it is pleasant to see in what a pickle he arrives on the gallows. But in England it is not so, for the executions are performed only every six months; and it signifies nothing at what time the criminal is condemned to death, he being always kept till that day, and is taken from the gibbet to be interred on Good Friday.

LYTH.—Lyth is a little trading town, and a good sea-port, situated at the mouth of the little river Lyth in the gulf of Edenburgh, which is above forty miles in length, and twelve broad at its entry, and before Lyth about eight.[1] In the middle there is a small island,[2] on which is an impregnable fort. There are many good harbours and large towns along this gulf, with mines yielding tin, lead, and sea-coal, in such quantities that the Flemish, the Dutch, the Danes and the Swedes, and even the French, are served from hence. Moreover in this same gulf they prepare salt, which the Dutch purchase to cure the fish catched in the Scotch seas; although many persons say this salt will not preserve them long, and that the things pickled with it are apt to spoil. But without straying from Lyth, I can say it is the most famous sea-port in Scotland, frequented, on account of its traffic, by all the nations in Europe; and it is at the mouth of this little river,[3] which is so deep that the largest vessels can come up into the center of the town, and lie loaded along the quay, sometimes to the number of more than fifty. The river forms the separation of a large village,[4] which lies on the other side, to which you must pass over a stone bridge that joins it to the town. This village is the residence of fishermen and sailors, and here sometimes large vessels are built. On the same side is a citadel, close to the sea, which has almost ruined it by its waves, having undermined the bastions in such a manner, that it is as it were abandoned, for there is no garrison to guard it. Adjoining to the quay is a mole, fashioned like a wooden bridge, advancing more than two hundred paces into the sea, to prevent the sand brought by the tide from choking up the entrance of the port, which is extremely necessary for the town

---

[1] Our traveller's measurements are here far astray.   [2] Inchkeith.   [3] The Water of Leith.   [4] Newhaven.

of Edenburgh, for the merchandizes that arrive by sea, or are shipped for foreign countries, principally for the north.

I returned to Edinburgh, and, after taking my leave of some French people of my acquaintance, departed for Barwick, by the following route. Leaving the town, I had the gulf on my left hand, and on my right the great road to Newcastle, near a small river at Nedrik,[1] where there is a castle.   At Molsburg[2] there is also a castle on a river, still within the agreeable view of this gulf; which one is obliged continually to follow, on account that the road is bordered by high mountains, which are impassable.   Come to Trenat,[3] where there are mines of very good coal, with which I saw several vessels loaded.   The country where they are commonly found, is somewhat mountainous, and covered with bad soil, as hereabouts at Arington[4] on a river.   Here is a large market-place, and a fine street adjoining to the principal church,[5] which it is said the French held a long time,[6] when they made themselves masters of a good part of this kingdom, and from whence they were at length driven out, as I was informed by my landlord's son, in conducting me out of the town.   I followed the river,[7] full of good fish, particularly trout of a delicious taste; on it I saw a large castle,[8] on the right hand, going to Linton,[9] where I passed this river, which runs among the rocks.   Shortly after, one has a view of the same gulf, passing over a country covered with sandhills to Dunbart.

The village is famous for its great fishery of herrings and salmon, which are carried into France and other parts of Europe.   The port would be good for nothing, if the road,

---

[1] Niddrie. [2] Musselburgh. The castle referred to is probably Pinkie House, which dates from the reign of James VI. The river is, of course, the Esk. [3] Tranent. He could not have seen the vessels loaded at that village, however, as it is fully two miles from the sea. [4] Haddington. A name we have seen mutilated in so many different ways. [5] The present parish church, by some supposed to be the "Lamp of Lothian" celebrated by Fordoun and other early historians. [6] Rocheford has but a hazy notion of the real achievements of his nation on the occasion he refers to. It would seem, however, that the French preserved the memory of the Sieur d'Essé's expedition. We have seen that both Perlin and De Rohan make special reference to it. [7] Tyne. [8] Hailes Castle, a seat of the Bothwell family, and associated with Queen Mary. [9] East Linton.

which is before it, was not covered by high rocks, which border these coasts. At the foot of these is a part of the village, the habitation of fishermen; and another above it, where there is a fine large street. I lodged in the house of one who spoke French, and had served Louis the Thirteenth in the Scots Guards. He related to me many things that had happened in his time. He had been at the siege of Rochelle,[1] the history of which he gave me, with many particulars. He treated me with fish of all sorts, among others, with a piece of salmon dressed in the French manner, and a pair of soles of prodigious size. The beer usually drank in Scotland is made without hops, they call it ale; it is cheaper than the English beer, which is the best in Europe.

From Dunbarton, through a champaign country, I next came to Cobrspech,[2] whence, having passed some little mountains, I still followed the sea, and went through five or six small hamlets, in a plain near a river. The country hereabouts is but badly cultivated, and full of heaths, till I descended into a bottom to Aiton,[3] where there is a castle on a river, which I crossed, and afterwards passed a high mountain, adjoining to some meadows near the sea-side,[4] and along the banks of a river, following which, I arrived at Berwick.

BARRWICK.—Barrwick is the first town by which I re-entered England, and, being a frontier to Scotland, has been fortified in different manners. There is in it at present a large garrison, as in a place of importance to this kingdom. It is bounded by the river Tweed, which empties itself into the sea, and has a great reflux, capable, but for sands at the entrance into its port, of bringing up large vessels. I arrived here about ten of the clock on a Sunday; the gates were then shut, it being church time, but were opened at eleven, as is the custom in all fortified places. Here is an upper and a lower town, which are both on the side of a hill, that slopes towards the river. On its top there is a ruined and abandoned castle, although its situation makes it appear impregnable; it is environed on one side by the ditch of the

---

[1] La Rochelle was taken by Richelieu in 1628.   [2] Cockburnspath.   [3] Ayton.
[4] Marshall Meadows and Homildon Hill.

town, and on the other side by one of the same breadth,
flanked by many round towers and thick walls, which
enclose a large palace, in the middle of which rises a lofty
keep, capable of a long resistance, and commanding all the
environs of the town.

The high town encloses within its walls and ditches those
of the lower, from which it is only separated by a ditch filled
with water. In the upper town the streets are straight and
handsome; but here are not many rich inhabitants, they
rather preferring the lower town, in which there are many
great palaces, similar to that which has been rebuilt near the
great church. In all the open areas are great fountains, and
in one of them the guard-house and public parade, before the
town-hall or sessions house, over which is the clock-tower of
the town; so that by walking over Barwick, I discovered it
to be one of the greatest and most beautiful towns in
England.

The greatest parts of the streets in the lower town are
either up or down hill; but they are filled with many rich
merchants, on account of the convenience and vicinity of its
port, bordered by a large quay, along which the ships are
ranged. There is not a stone bridge, in all England, longer
or better built than that of Berwick, with sixteen [1] large and
wonderfully well-wrought arches; it is considered as one of
the most remarkable curiosities of the kingdom.

---

[1] There are only fifteen arches.

JOHN RAY

(1662 ?).

JOHN RAY (1627–1705), known as " Ray the Naturalist,"
was one of the most widely-travelled Englishmen of
his time, and his contributions to botany and zoology have
given him a distinguished place in the history of these
sciences. The son of a blacksmith, he received a learned
education at Trinity College, Cambridge, of which he became
a Fellow. Deprived of his Fellowship in 1662 by the Act
of Uniformity, Ray, accompanied by his friend Francis
Willoughby, set out on a course of travel through the United
Kingdom in the interests of the science to which he had
already devoted his life. From the " Itinerary," in which he
records his observations made on these travels, the following
extracts relating to Scotland have been taken.

SELECT REMAINS OF THE LEARNED JOHN RAY
(Lond. 1760), p. 187.

THIS night we lodged at Berwick; our journey was of
about 25 miles. The river Tweed is here joined
with a stone bridge of 15 arches. Here hath been a very
goodly castle, which is now demolished. The upper town is
encompassed with a wall which is not very strong; within
this wall is a large void ground or green, whereunto the
inhabitants bring their cattle, and let them stay all night,
and in the morning drive them out again to pasture. The
lower town is very strongly fortified with a broad and deep
ditch of water, and against it an impenetrable bulwark or
bank of earth, faced with free stone against the ditch.
There are also for defence, four tall platforms or ports,
besides external fortifications. This town is still kept with
a strong garrison. There is in it a fair church,[1] built by

---

[1] Trinity Church, begun in 1650 but not completed till 1657. Cromwell
does not appear to have had any hand in its construction (Scott, *History of
Berwick*, p. 361 *et seq.*).

Oliver Protector.   Here we saw in the cliff by the shore, a
cave called the Burgesses Cave, not worth the remembering,
and an hole in a rock, through which a boat may pass at
full sea, called the Needle's Eye.

August the 17*th*.—We travelled to Dunbar, a town noted
for the fight between the English and Scots.[1]   The Scots
generally (that is, the poorer sort) wear, the men blue
bonnets on their heads, and some russet; the women only
white linnen, which hangs down their backs as if a napkin
were pinned about them.   When they go abroad none of
them wear hats, but a party coloured blanket which they
call a plad, over their heads and shoulders.   The women
generally to us seemed none of the handsomest.   They are
not very cleanly in their houses, and but sluttish in dressing
their meat.   Their way of washing linnen is to tuck up
their coats, and tread them with their feet in a tub.   They
have a custom to make up the fronts of their houses, even
in their principal towns, with firr boards nailed one over
another, in which are often made many round holes or
windows to put out their heads.[2]   In the best Scottish
houses, even the king's palaces, the windows are not
glazed throughout, but the upper part only, the lower have
two wooden shuts or folds to open at pleasure, and admit
the fresh air.   The Scots cannot endure to hear their
country or countrymen spoken against.   They have neither
good bread, cheese, or drink.   They cannot make them, nor
will they learn.   Their butter is very indifferent, and one
would wonder how they could contrive to make it so bad.
They use much pottage made of coal-wort, which they call
keal,[3] sometimes broth of decorticated barley.   The ordinary
country houses are pitiful cots, built of stone, and covered
with turves, having in them but one room, many of them
no chimneys, the windows very small holes, and not glazed.
In the most stately and fashionable houses, in great towns,
instead of ceiling, they cover the chambers with firr boards,
nailed on the roof within side.   They have rarely any
bellows, or warming-pans.   It is the manner in some places
there, to lay on but one sheet as large as two, turned up

[1] Battle of Dunbar in 1650, when Cromwell defeated the Scots under Lesley.
[2] See p. 102 (above).   [3] Scotticé, *kail*.

from the feet upwards. The ground in the valleys and plains bears good corn, but especially beer-barley or bigge, and oats, but rarely wheat and rye. We observed little or no fallow grounds in Scotland; some layed ground[1] we saw, which they manured with sea-wreck. The people seem to be very lazy, at least the men, and may be frequently observed to plow in their cloaks. It is the fashion of them to wear cloaks when they go abroad, but especially on Sundays. They lay out most they are worth in cloaths, and a fellow that hath scarce ten groats besides to help himself with, you shall see come out of his smoaky cottage clad like a gentleman.

There hath formerly been a strong castle at Dunbar,[2] built on a rock upon the sea, but it is now quite ruined and fallen down. Yearly, about this time, there is a great confluence of people at Dunbar, to the herring-fishing; they told us, sometimes to the number of 20,000 persons; but we did not see how so small a town could contain, indeed give shelter to, such a multitude. They had at our being there two ministers in Dunbar; they sung their Gloria Patri at the end of the psalm after sermon, as had been ordered by the Parliament, in these words:[3]—

> Glore to the Father and the Sonne,
>   And to the Holy Gheast;
> As it was in the beginning,
>   Is now, and aye doth last.

There is in the church a very fair monument of the Earl of Dunbar, George Howme, made in King James's time.[4]

August the 19*th.*—We went to Leith, keeping all along on the side of the Fryth. By the way we viewed Tontallon Castle,[5] and passed over to the Basse Island;[6] where we

---

[1] Unploughed ground. A *lay* or *lea* is a meadow.

"A tuft of daises in a flowery *lay.*"—*Dryden.*

[2] The date of the erection of the Castle of Dunbar is uncertain; but for nearly four hundred years the history of the town centred round it.   [3] Episcopacy had been restored in Scotland at the Restoration in 1660.   [4] George Hume of Manderston, Lord High Treasurer of Scotland, and afterwards Chancellor of the Exchequer in England. It was upon him that James VI. chiefly relied in his attempts to introduce Episcopacy into Scotland.   [5] Tantallon.   [6] The Bass Rock.

saw, on the rocks, innumerable of the soland geese. The old ones are all over white, excepting the pinion or hard feathers of their wings, which are black. The upper part of the head and neck, in those that are old, is of a yellowish dun colour. They lay but one egg apiece, which is white, and not very large: They are very bold, and sit in great multitudes till one comes close up to them, because they are not wont to be scared or disturbed. The young ones are esteemed a choice dish in Scotland, and sold very dear (1s. 8d. plucked). We eat of them at Dunbar. They are in bigness little inferior to an ordinary goose. The young one is upon the back black, and speckled with little white spots, under the breast and belly grey. The beak is sharp-pointed, the mouth very wide and large, the tongue very small, the eyes great, the foot hath four toes webbed together. It feeds upon mackrel and herring, and the flesh of the young one smells and tastes strong of these fish. The other birds which nestle in the Basse are these: the scout, which is double ribbed; the cattiwake, in English cormorant; the scart; and a bird called the turtle-dove, whole footed, and the feet red. There are verses which contain the names of these birds among the vulgar, two whereof are:—

> The scout, the scart, the cattiwake,
> The soland goose sits on the lack,
>   Yearly in the spring.

We saw of the scout's eggs, which are very large and speckled. It is very dangerous to climb the rocks for the young of these fowls, and seldom a year passeth but one or other of the climbers fall down and lose their lives, as did one not long before our being there. The laird of this island makes a great profit yearly of the soland geese taken; as I remember, they told us £130 sterling. There is in the isle a small house, which they call a castle; it is inaccessible and impregnable,[1] but of no great consideration in a war, there being no harbour, nor any thing like it.

---

[1] In this connection it will be remembered that the Bass Rock was the last place in the country to surrender to the government of William III., and that only want of provisions compelled the garrison to capitulate after holding out for nearly three years.

The island will afford grass enough to keep 30 sheep. They make strangers that come to visit it burgesses of the Basse, by giving them to drink of the water of the well, which springs near the top of the rock, and a flower out of the garden thereby. The island is nought else but a rock, and stands off the land near a mile; at Dunbar you would not guess it above a mile distant, though it be thence at least five. We found growing in the island, in great plenty, *Beta marina*, *Lychnis marina nostras*, *Malva arborea marina nostras*, and *Cochlearia rotundifolia*. By the way also we saw glasses made of kelp and sand mixed together, and calcined in an oven. The crucibles which contained the melted glass, they told us, were made of tobacco-pipe clay.

At Leith we saw one of those citadels [1] built by the Protector, one of the best fortifications that ever we beheld, passing fair and sumptuous. There are three forts advanced above the rest, and two platforms. The works round about are faced with free-stone towards the ditch, and are almost as high as the highest buildings within, and withal, thick and substantial. Below are very pleasant, convenient, and well-built houses for the governor, officers, and soldiers, and for magazines and stores; there is also a good capacious chapel, the Piazza, or void space within, as large as Trinity-College (in Cambridge) great court. This is one of the four forts. The other three are at St Johnston's, Inverness, and Ayre. The building of each of which (as we were credibly informed) cost above £100,000 sterling; indeed I do not see how it could cost less. In England it would have cost much more.

At Edinburgh we went to the principal public buildings; those are:—1. The castle, a very strong building, on a precipitous solid rock. It is one of the king's houses, but of no very great receipt; in it are kept the Crown and Scepter of Scotland. There was then lying in the castle yard an old great iron gun, which they called Mounts Meg,[2] and some, Meg of Berwick, of a great bore, but the length is not answerable to the bigness. 2. Heriot's Hospital, a square

---

[1] Built in 1650.   [2] Mons Meg is reputed to be the oldest piece of ordnance in Europe with the exception of one in Lisbon.

stone building, having a large turret at each corner. It
hath very spacious and beautiful gardens, and is well
endowed. There is a cloister on both sides of the court,
on each hand as one goeth in, and a well in the middle
thereof. At our being there it maintained threescore boys,
who wore blue gowns; but they told us it was designed for
other purposes. It would make a very handsome college,
comparable to the best in our universities. Over the gate,
within side, stands the figure of G. Heriot the founder
thereof, and under him this verse:—

Corporis hæc, animi est hoc opus effigies.

3. The college, for the building of it but mean, and of no
very great capacity, in both comparable to Caius College
in Cambridge. Most of the students here live after the
fashion of Leyden, in the town; and wear no gowns till
they be *laureat*, as they call it, that is, commence. At our
being there (being the time of the vacancy) there was not
a student in town; the Premier [2] also, as they call him, was
absent at London. In the hall of this college the king's
commissioner, Middleton, was entertained by the citizens
of Edinburgh. 4. The Parliament House, which is but of
small content, as far as we could judge, not capable of
holding 200 persons. The Lords and Commons sit both in
the same room together. There is also a place which they
call the Inner House, in which sit 15 Lords,[3] chosen out of
the House, as it were a grand committee. There is an outer
room like the lobby, which they call the waiting room;
and two other rooms above stairs, where commissioners sit.
We saw Argyle and Guthry,[4] their heads standing on the
gates and toll-booth. At the time we were in Scotland,
divers women were burnt for witches, they reported, to the
number of about 120.

August the 21st.—We went on northward as far as

---

[1] Heriot's Hospital was designed solely for the maintenance and education
of the sons of decayed burgesses. During Cromwell's presence in Scotland the
hospital was used for his wounded soldiers. [2] Principal, who at this time
was William Colvill. [3] The Lords of the Articles. [4] James Guthrie, a
Covenanter of the most uncompromising type, was executed on a charge of
high treason in 1661. His name occurs in the lines on the Martyr's Monument
in Greyfriars' Churchyard, Edinburgh.

Sterling, 24 miles. By the way we saw the king's palace at Lithgow, built in the manner of a castle, a very good house, as houses go in Scotland. There is a small lough or standing water on two sides of the house. This lough formerly was never without swans: but Mr Stuart, one of the bailiffs of the town, told us a strange story of those swans, which left the lake when the house was taken and garrisoned by the English; and although two were brought on purpose for trial, yet would they not stay there; but at the time of the king's coming to London, two swans, *nescio unde sponte et instinctu proprio*, came thither, and there still continue.[1] This Stuart hath nourished in his garden divers exotick plants, more than one would hope to find in so northerly and cold a country; some such as we had not before seen, viz., *Archangelica, Fumaria siliquosa, Carduus lacteus peregrinus flo. albo, Verbas-cum 4 Matth. angusti folium, Anchusæ species flo. parvo nigricante, Alcea surrecta lœvis flo. amplo rubro et albo*, as we then named them. Sterling is an indifferently handsome town, hath a good market-place, two palaces, one of the Earl of Marr,[2] the other of the Marquis of Argyle.[3] But the castle is most considerable, and hath been, and, with little cost, may be again made, a very magnificent house. It hath an hall longer, if not broader, than Trinity-College Hall in Cambridge. The building, added by James V., contains many very stately rooms both for lodging and entertainment, in many of them very good carved wood-work on the roofs. There is also a chapel built by James VI. at the birth of his eldest son, in which we saw a model of Edinburgh Castle, and the ship in which they served up the meat into the hall, when Prince Henry was baptized. This castle stands on an high and steep rock; under the building are many vaults cut out of the rock, and one under another. The castle, on our being there, was garrisoned with 200 English. The

---

[1] This story is related in the *Mercurius Caledonius* of 8th January 1661. According to this account, it was a garrison planted in the town by Cromwell that occasioned the flight of the swans, which returned to their habitat the very day of the coronation of Charles II. at Scone. [2] Now known as Mar's Work—the remains of a palace built by the Earl of Mar in 1570. [3] Now known as Argyll's Lodging to the south-east of the Esplanade. It was built by the Earl of Stirling in 1630.

commissary told us that the greatest inconvenience of that castle, in case of a siege, was, that upon the discharging of the great guns, the water in the wells would sink, and the wells become dry; of which it is easy to render a probable reason. Sterling-Bridge is considerable for nothing, but that is a pass. The river here, Mæander like, takes circuits, and almost meets itself again, and that for a considerable space, both on the one and the other side of the bridge; so that what is by land but 4 miles, is by water 24.

From Sterling we went, August the 22nd, to Glascow, which is the second city in Scotland, fair, large, and well built, cross-wise, somewhat like unto Oxford, the streets very broad and pleasant. There is a cathedral church built by Bishop Law;[1] they call it now the High Kirk, and have made in it two preaching places, one in the choir, and the other in the body of the church; besides, there is a church under the choir, like St Faith's under Paul's, London; the walls of the church-yard round about are adorned with many monuments, and the church-yard itself almost covered with grave stones; and this we observed to be the fashion in all the considerable towns we came into in Scotland. The bishop's palace, a goodly building, near to the church, is still preserved. Other things memorable in this town are: —1. The college, a pretty stone building, and not inferior to Wadham and All Soul's Colleges in Oxon. The Premier, Mr Gelaspy, was removed by the Parliament there.[2] Here are (as they told us) most commonly about 40 students of the first year, which they call Obedients;[3] near so many of the second, which they call Semies; and so proportionably of the third, which they call Baccalors; and the fourth, whom they call Laureat or Magisters. It being the time of vacancy, we saw not the habits which the students use. 2. A tall building[4] at the corner, by the market-place, of

[1] See above, p. 150.   [2] The Scottish Estates (25th September 1660) accused Patrick Gillespie and others of having subscribed a dangerous and seditious paper tending to the disturbance of the kingdom, and sequestrated their stipends (*Munimenta Alme Universitatis Glasguensis*, ii. p. 327 *et seq.*). [3] *Bajan*, of course, is meant, a term derived from the mediæval universities of the Continent. The French was *bijaune*, or *bejaune*. The designations of the other three classes were—Semi, Tertian or Bachelor, and Magistrand, each being named from the degree to which it immediately led.   [4] The New Tol-booth already more than once mentioned.

five stories, where courts are kept, and the sessions held, and prisoners confined, &c., upon the door whereof is this distich :—

> Hæc domus odit, amat, punit, conservat, honorat,
> Nequitiam, pacem, crimina, jura, probos. [1]

3. Several fair hospitals, and well endowed; one of the merchants, now in building.[2] 4. A very long bridge of eight arches, four whereof are about fifty feet wide each ; and a very neat square flesh-market, scarce such an one to be seen in England or Scotland.

August the 23rd.—We rode to Douglas, 20 miles. We passed through Hamilton, by the way, an handsome little market-town, where is a great house of Duke Hamilton's. The country all thereabout is very pleasant, and in all respects, for woods, pastures, corn, &c., the best we saw in Scotland. At Douglas there is a castle[3] belonging to the Marquess Douglas, half a mile distant from the town; which, though it be a free burgh, and without doubt of great anti-quity, yet is a pitiful, poor, small place, scarce an house in it which will keep a man dry in a shower of rain. In the church[4] we saw some old monuments of the Douglasses, with two hearts wrapped up in lead,[5] which it seems were of two of that family that died in France, and were sent over hither.

August the 24th.—We rode to Dumfreis, or (as they spelled it) Drumfrese, 28 miles, and in the way saw lead mines, at a place called the Lead-Hills,[6] which will in time, it is likely, increase to a good considerable town. We also passed over much hilly ground ; the highest place was called Anderkin-Hill,[7] upon the top whereof the air was sharp and

---

[1] This house hates evil, loves peace, punishes crime, preserves the laws, honours the good.   [2] Hutcheson's Hospital.   [3] Douglas Castle. This is the Castle Dangerous of Scott.   [4] The Kirk of St Bride, dating from the thirteenth century, was the burying-place of the Douglases.   [5] The tradition is that the heart of Sir James Douglas, who was slain fighting against the Moors in Spain, was brought to this church ; but there is no satisfactory evidence of this. It is uncertain whose heart is contained in the leaden coffer to which Ray refers.   [6] The mines at Leadhills have been actively wrought since Ray's time ; but it cannot be said that his prediction has been fulfilled. In 1769 the population of Leadhills was 1500 ; in 1881, 1023. [7] The Enterkin Burn and Pass well known from Dr John Brown's paper. Ray was mistaken in the height of the surrounding hills. That on the left, Therstane Hill, is 1895 feet high ; Stey Gail or Steep Gable, on the right, 1875.

piercing, when in the level it was warm and gentle: neither
yet were we on the highest apex of it, by the ascent of near
half a mile, as we guessed. This hill we judged to be higher
than any we had been upon in England or Wales, Snowdon
itself not excepted. This is a dangerous passage in winter
time, the way being narrow and slippery, and a great precipice
on the one hand, besides the descent steep, so that we led
our horses down about a mile. At Dumfreis they have two
ministers, one a young man named Campbell, related (as we
were told) to Marquis of Argyle, the other, an elder man, by
name Henderson, who has married his daughter to the younger.
Campbell prayed for the preservation of their church government and discipline, and spake openly against prelacy and its
adjuncts and consequences. Here, as also at Dunbar, and
other places, we observed the manner of their burials, which
is this: when any one dies, the sexton or bell-man goeth
about the streets, with a small bell in his hand, which he
tinkleth all along as he goeth, and now and then he makes
a stand, and proclaims who is dead, and invites the people
to come to the funeral at such an hour. The people and
minister many times accompany the corpse to the grave at
the time appointed, with the bell before them, where there
is nothing said, but only the corpse laid in. The minister
there, in the public worship, doth not shift places out of the
desk into the pulpit, as in England, but at his first coming
in, ascends the pulpit. They commonly begin their worship
with a psalm before the minister comes in, who, after the
psalm is finished, prayeth, and then reads and expounds in
some places, in some not; then another psalm is sung, and
after that their minister prays again, and preacheth as in
England. Before sermon, commonly, the officers of the town
stand at the church-yard gate, with a join'd stool and a dish,
to gather the alms of all that come to church. The people
here frequent their churches much better than in England,
and have their ministers in more esteem and veneration.
They seem to perform their devotions with much alacrity.
There are few or no sectaries or opinionists among them ;
they are much addicted to their church government, excepting
the gentry, who love liberty, and care not to be so strictly
tied down. The country abounds with poor people and

beggars.   Their money they reckon after the French manner.
A bodel (which is the sixth part of our penny) they call
tway-pennies, that is with them two-pence ; so that, upon
this ground, 12 pennies, or a shilling Scotch (that is, six
bodels), is a penny sterling.   The Scotch piece mark'd with
XX, which we are wont to call a Scotch two-pence, is twenty-
pence Scotch, that is, two-pence sterling, wanting two bodels,
or four pennies Scotch ; the piece with XL is four-pence
sterling—4 bodels; and so one shilling sterling is 12 shillings
Scotch.   Thirteen pence half-penny English, a mark Scotch.
One pound Scotch, 20*d*. sterling.   One bodel they call tway-
pennies (as above), 2 bodels a plack, 3 bodels a baubee, 4
bodels 8 pennies, 6 bodels 1 shilling Scotch.

JAMES BROME

(1669).

JAMES BROME, a clergyman of the Church of England, visited Scotland in 1669, and published the account of his visit in 1700 under the title of *Travels over England, Scotland, and Wales*. From his preface we learn that his narrative had been published without his knowledge in 1694 with the title, *Historical Account of Three Years' Travels over England and Wales*. In 1712 appeared another volume by Brome giving an account of his travels through Portugal, Spain, and Italy. He died in 1719. As will be seen, Brome was an intelligent and fair-minded observer. His remarks on the Universities of Edinburgh and Glasgow, it may be said, are of special interest.

THREE YEARS' TRAVELS OVER ENGLAND, SCOTLAND, AND WALES. BY JAMES BROME. (p. 194).

BUT to return now again to our journy, passing through some part of the country of March, which lies upon the German Sea, we came to Lothien, called from the Picts formerly Pict-land, shooting out along from March into the Scottish Sea, and having many hills in it, and little wood, but for fruitful corn-fields, for courtesie and civility of manners, commended by some above all other countries of Scotland; about the year 873, Edgar, King of England (between whom and Kenneth, the third king of Scots, there was a great knot of alliance against the Danes their common enemies), resigned up his right to him in this country, and to unite his heart more firmly to him, he gave unto him some mansion houses in the way, as Cambden observes out of Matthew Florilegus, wherein both he and his successors in their coming to the kings of England, and in their return homeward might be lodged, which unto the time of King Henry the Second continued in the hands of the Scotch king.

The first town of any consequence, that offered it self unto us, was Dunbar, famous formerly for a strong castle, being the seat of the Earls of March, afterwards styled Earl of Dunbar; a fort many times won by the English, and as oft recovered by the Scots. And in the reign of Edward the Third, the Earls of Salisbury and Arundel came into Scotland with a great army, and besieged the castle of Dunbar two and twenty weeks, wherein at that time was black Agnes the Countess; who defended the same with extraordinary valour, one time, when the engine called the sow, was brought by the English to play against the castle, she replyed merrily, that unless England could keep her sow better, she would make her to cast her pigs; and indeed did at last force the generals to retreat from that place. The town stands upon the sea and hath been fenced in with a stone wall of great strength, though by the frequent batteries it hath of late years received, 'tis much impaired and gone to decay; the houses here (as generally in most towns of Scotland) are built with stone and covered with slate, and they are well supplyed with provision by reason of a weekly market which is held here. The inhabitants are governed by a mayor and aldermen, and talk much of great losses and calamities they sustained in the late civil wars, for in this place was that fatal battle fought betwixt Oliver Cromwell and the Scots, wherein he routed and cut in pieces twenty thousand Scots, with twelve thousand Englishmen, and obtain'd so strange and signal a victory, that the very thoughts of it do to this very day still strike a terror into them; when e'er they call that bloody day to remembrance, and think what great havock and spoil was made amongst them by the victorious success of the English forces.

Our next quarters we took up at Edinburgh, which is the metropolis of Scotland, and lies about twenty miles distance from Dunbar. 'Tis situated high, and extends above a mile in length carrying half as much in breadth, it consists of one fair and large street with some few narrow lanes branching out of each side, 'tis environed on the east, south, and west with a strong wall, and upon the north strengthened with a loch; 'tis adorned with stately stone buildings both private and publick, some of which houses are six or seven stories high which have frequently as many different apartments and shops, where are many families of various trades and calling, by reason of which 'tis well throng'd with inhabitants, and is exceeding populous, which is the more occasioned by the neighborhood of Leith which is a commodious haven for ships, and likewise, because as 'tis the seat of their kings or vice-roys, so 'tis also the oracle or closet of the laws, and the palace of justice.

On the east side or near to the monastery of St Cross,[1] that was a holy rood, is the king's palace, which was built by King David the First, but being much ruinated and impaired in the late unhappy broils betwixt the two kingdoms, it hath been since enlarged and beautified, and is now become a stately and magnificent structure : And not far from this house, within a pleasant park adjoyning to it, riseth a hill with two heads called of Arthur, the Britain Arthur's Chair.

A little further stands the college founded and endowed by that most famous favourer of learning, the wise and learned King James the Sixth, though afterward the magistrates and citizens of this place proved likewise very considerable benefactors to it, and upon their humble address to the same prince, it was made an university, A.D. 1580,[2] but the privileges hereof were not fully confirmed and throughly perfected till the year 1582, and have been since the same with those of any other university in this kingdom.

The dignity of Chancellor and Vice-Chancellor doth reside in the Magistrates and Town Council of Edenburgh, who are the only patrons; neither was the dignity, they say, as yet ever conferred upon any simple person:[3] the persons endowed were a Principal or Warden, a Professor of Divinity, four Masters or Regents, for so they are called, of Philosophy,

---

[1] The Abbey of Holyrood is styled by Fordun "Monasterium Sanctae Crucis de Crag." [2] The College of Edinburgh was first styled a university in an Act of the town council of date 24th March 1685. [3] It may be pointed out that this statement of Brome, together with that of Morer (p. 284), is of some importance in the history of the University of Edinburgh (see Grant, *The Story of the University of Edinburgh*, i. p. 234).

a Professor or Regent of Humanity or Philology: Since the first foundation the town hath added a Professor of Hebrew, 1640, and the city of Edenburgh hath since added a Professor of Mathematicks.[1]

The library was founded by Clement Little, oneof the officials or comissaries for Edinburgh, A.D. 1635,[2] since which time it is much increased both by donatives from the citizens, as also from the scholars, who are more in number, than in any other college in the kingdom; and here were presented to our view two very great rarities, the one was a tooth taken out of a great scull being four inches about, and the other was a crooked horn taken from a gentlewoman of the city who was fifty years old, being eleven inches long, which grew under her right ear, and was cut out by an eminent chirurgeon then living in the town who presented it to the college.

About the middle of the city stands the cathedral, which is now divided into six sermon houses, for which service there are seven other kirks set apart besides, and not far from the cathedral is the Parliament House, whither we had the good fortune to see all the flower of the nobility then to pass in state, attending Duke Lauderdale who was sent down High-Commissioner.[3] And indeed it was a very glorious sight, for they were all richly accoutred and as nobly attended with a splendid retinue, the heralds of arms and other officers, that went before were wonderful gay and finely habited, and the servants that attended were clad in the richest liveries; their coaches drawn with six horses, as they went ratling along, did dazle our eyes with the splendour of their furniture, and all the nobles appeared in the greatest pomp and gallantry; the regalia, which are the sword of state, the scepter, and the crown were carried by three of the antientest of the nobility, and on each side the honours were three mace-bearers bare headed, a nobleman bare headed with a purse, and in it the Lord High Commissioner's commission, then last of all the Lord High Commis-

---

[1] The Chair of Hebrew was founded in 1642. Mathematics were separately taught by the first James Gregory in 1674 (*ibid.*, pp 212, 215.) [2] It was in 1580 that Clement Little, advocate and commissary, made the first grant of books to the College of Edinburgh. [3] This fixes the date of Brome's visit. Lauderdale was Lord High Commissioner in 1669.

sioner with the dukes and marquesses on his right and left
hand: it is ordered that there be no shooting under the
highest penalties that day, neither displaying of ensigns, nor
beating of drums during the whole cavalcade: The officers of
state not being noblemen, ride in their gowns, all the members
ride covered except those that carry the honours, and the
highest degree and the most honourable of that degree ride last.

Nor is their grandeur disproportionate to their demeanour,
which is high and stately, but courteous and obliging, having
all the additional helps of education and travel to render
it accomplish'd, for during their minority there is generally
great care taken to refine their nature, and emprove their
knowledge, of which when they have attain'd a competent
measure in their own country, they betake themselves to
foreign nations to make a further progress therein, where
they do generally become so great proficients, that at their
return they are by this means fitted for all great services
and honourable employments, which their king or country is
pleased to commit to their care and fidelity, and are thereby
enabled to discharge them with great honour and applause.

On the west side a most steep rock mounteth up aloft
to a great height every way save where it looks towards the
city, on which is placed a castle built by Ebrank the son of
Mempitius, as some write, though others by Cruthneus
Camelon the first king of the Picts about 330 years before
the birth of our Saviour; 'tis so strongly fortified both by
art and nature, that it is accounted impregnable, which the
Britains called Myned Agned, the Scots the Maiden Castle,
of certain young maids of the Picts royal blood, which were
kept here in old time, and which in truth may seem to have
been that Castrum alatum, or castle with a wing before
spoken of: In this castle is one of the largest canons in
Great Britain, called roaring Megg, which together with two
tire of ordinance besides planted upon the wall, can command
the city and all the plains thereabouts: but most famous is
it, in that Queen Mary was brought to bed here of a son,
who was afterward christened at Sterling, and called James,
who at last became the happy uniter of the two crowns;
and in that chamber in which he was born are written upon
the wall these following verses, in an old Scotch character :—

James (6. Scot.) (I. England).

Laird Jesu Christ, that crownit was with thorns,
Preserve the birth quhais badgie here is borne,
And send hir son succession, to reign still
Lange in this realm, if that it be thy will,
Als grant (O Laird) quhat ever of hir proceed,
Be to thy glory, honour, and praise, so beed.

July 19, 1566.

A little below the castle is a curious structure built for an hospital by Mr Herriot, jeweller to the aforementioned King James, and endowed with very great revenues for the use of poor orphans, and impotent and decrepit persons, but by the ruinous and desolate condition it seem'd at that time to be falling into, it became to us a very doleful spectacle, that so noble a heroick design of charity should be so basely perverted to other evil ends and purposes, contrary to the will and intention of the donor.[1]

The city is governed by a Lord Provost, who hath always a retinue befitting his grandeur; and for the punishing delinquents there is a large tolbooth, for so they call a prison or house of correction, where all malefactors are kept in hold to satisfie the law as their offences shall require.

Within seven miles round the city there are of noble and gentlemens palaces, castles, and strong builded towers and stone houses, as we were inform'd, above an hundred, and besides the houses of the nobility and gentry within it, here dwell several merchants of great credit and repute, where because they have not the conveniency of an exchange as in London, they meet about noon in the High Street, from whence they adjourn to their changes, *i.e.*, taverns, or other places where their business may require them to give their attendance.

The fortune of this city hath in former ages been very variable and inconstant ; sometime it was subject to the Scots, and another while to the English, who inhabited the east parts of Scotland, until it became wholly under the Scots dominion about the year 960, when the English being overpowered and quite oppressed by the Danes were enforced

---

[1] See above, p. 236 (note).

to quit all their interest here, as unable to grapple with two such potent enemies.

A mile from the city lies Leith, a most commodious haven hard upon the river Leith, which when Dessry [1] the Frenchman for the security of Edenburgh had fortified very strongly by reason of a great concourse of people, which after this flocked hither in abundance, in a short time from a mean village it grew to be a large town : In the reign of our King Henry the Eighth, the sufferings and calamities both of it and its neighbours were grievous and inexpressible, being both burnt and plundered by Sir John Dudly, Viscount Lisle, Lord High Admiral of England, who came hither with a puissant army, and broke down the peer, burning every stick thereof, and took away all the Scotch ships that were fit to serve him, which kind of execution was done likewise at Dunbar ; [2] afterward when Francis, King of France, had taken to wife Mary, Queen of Scots, the Frenchmen who in hope and conceit had already devoured Scotland, and began now to gape for England, A.D. 1560, strengthened it again with new fortifications : But Queen Elizabeth solicited by the nobles, who had embraced the Protestant religion, to side with them, by her wisdom and prowess so effected the matter, that the French were enforced to return into their own country, and all their fortifications were laid level with the ground, and Scotland hath ever since been freed from the French, and Leith hath become a very opulent and flourishing port, for the peer is now kept up in so good repair, and the haven so safe for ships to ride in, that here commonly lieth a great fleet at anchor which come hither richly laden with all sorts of commodities.

After we had spent some time in this city, we went from hence through Linlithgow, a town beautified with a fair house of the king's, a goodly church, a pleasent park and a loch, a lake under the palace wall full of fish (of which lake it seems to have derived its name, lin in the British tongue signifying a lake), to another town called Falkirk famous for the notable battle which was fought here betwixt King Edward the First and the Scots, wherein were slain no less

[1] The Sieur d'Essé.   [2] The invasion referred to is that of 1544 under the Earl of Hertford.

than two thousand men : not far from which place likewise upon the river Carron was formerly situate the famous city of Camelon,[1] chief city of the Picts, founded by Cruthneus Camelon before the birth of Christ 330 year, which was destroyed by King Kenneth the Great about the year of Christ 846, and what was left was afterward swallowed up by an earthquake, where the void place is now filled with water.

At last we came to the renowned city of Glasgow, which (lying in Liddisdail[2]) was indeed the farthest of all our northern circuit; 'tis situated upon the river Glotta, or Cluyd, over which is placed a very fair bridge supported with eight arches, and for pleasantness of sight, sweetness of air, and delightfulness of its gardens and orchards enriched with most delicious fruits, surpasseth all other places in this tract; the buildings in this town are very large and beautiful; and the tolbooth itself so stately a structure, that it appears rather to be a palace than a prison : This has formerly been the see of an archbishop, and in the year 1554 an university,[3] which consists of one college, was founded here by Archbishop Turnbill for a rector, a dean of faculty, a principal or warden to teach theology, and three professors to teach philosophy : Afterwards some clergymen professed the laws here, being invited to that profession rather by the convenience of a collegiate life, and the immunities of the university, then by any considerable salary. King James the Sixth, A.D. 1577, did establish twelve persons in the college, viz., a principal, three professors of philosophy, called regents, four scholars called bursars, an œconomus or provisor, who furnisheth the table with provisions, the principal's servant, a janitor and a cook.[4]

The cathedral is a very fair ancient fabrick, built by Bishop John Achaian, A.D. 1135.[5] It oweth thanks to the memory of King James the Sixth; and which is most remarkable, to the mob itself at that time, for its preservation from ruine; for the ministers here having perswaded

---

[1] A western suburb of Falkirk is still called Camelon. [2] This should, of course, be Clydesdale. [3] Glasgow University was founded in 1451 by Bishop Turnbull. [4] This is known as the "New Erection," and was the work of the Regent Morton. [4] See p. 150 (above).

the magistrates to pull it down, and to build two or three
other churches with the materials thereof, and the magistrates
condescending, a day was appointed and workmen ready to
demolish it, but the common tradesmen having notice given
them of this design, convene in arms, and oppose the magistrates, threatening to bury the demolishers of it under the ruines
of that ancient building, whereupon the matter was referred to
the King and Council who decided the controversy in the
tradesmens favour, and reproving very sharply the magistrates
for their order, so that it still continues with four other
churches here beside for the exercise of their religion.[1]

The city is governed by a Mayor, and is very eminent for
its trade and merchandize, and is noted upon record for being
the place, where William Wallace, the renowned champion of
Scotland, was traitourously betrayed by Sir John Menteith,
and delivered up to our King Edward the First, by whose
order he was afterward publickly executed in Smithfield.

Passing away hence by Hamilton, a famous palace then
belonging to Duke Hamilton, which hath a fair and spacious
park adjoyning to it, we had two days journy very doleful
and troublesome, for we travelled over wide meers and
dangerous mountains in the company of some Scotch gentlemen, who were going that way for England, where the
weather was ill, the ways worse, and the long miles with
their way-bits[2] at the end of them worst of all, where our
lodging was hard, our diet course, and our bodies thin, that
it might easily be decerned how we had lately pass'd through
the territorys of famine, who reigns very potently over that
cold and pinching region.

But coming at length to Dumfries in the County of
Nidisdail[3] it made us some amends, for being situate
between two hills upon the mouth of the river Nid,[4] over

---

[1] Spottiswoode is the source of the history related in this paragraph, which
has been so constantly repeated as almost to have become an accepted fact.   Dr
M'Crie, however, has proved that it is entirely without foundation, and that
the magistrates of Glasgow, so far from wishing to injure the church, showed
anxiety for its preservation.   In support of this statement, M'Crie quotes an
entry from the Town Records of Glasgow, which leave no room for doubt in
the matter (M'Crie, *Life of Andrew Melville*, p. 39, edit. 1856).   [2] Brome,
like his countryman Guy Mannering, had evidently been exasperated by the
Scotch "mile and a bittock."   [3] Nithsdale.   [4] Nith.

which is laid a bridge of large fine stones, it appears to be
one of the most flourishing towns in this tract, notable no
less for its ancient castle and manufacture of cloath, then for
the murther of John Cummins,[1] one of the most renowned
personages for his retinue and equipage in all this kingdom,
whom Robert Bruce, for fear he should fore-stal his way to
the crown, run quite through with his sword in the Fryars
Church, and soon obtain'd his pardon from the Pope, though
he had committed so great a murder in so sacred a place.

After this we came to Anandale[2] at the mouth of the
river Anan in the County of Anandale, bordering upon our
own nation, which lost all its glory and beauty upon the
war, which was raised in Edward the Sixth's days ; in these
two last-named counties have been bred a sort of warlike
men, who have been infamous for robbery and depredations,
for they dwell upon Solway-Frith, a fordable arm of the
sea at low water, through which frequently they have made
many inroads into England to fetch home great booty's, and
in which they were wont after a delightful manner on horseback, with spears to hunt salmons, of which there are in these
parts a very great abundance.

[1] The Red Comyn.   [2] Annan.

THOMAS KIRKE

(1679).

THE following work was first published at London in 1679, under the title, *A Modern Account of Scotland by an English Gentleman*. It has since been frequently reprinted. All that is known of the book and its author is thus stated by Sir Egerton Brydges (*Censura Literaria*, vol. vi. p. 373): "This curious work was written in so splenetic a disposition, and contains many circumstances of so singular a nature, that the author naturally confined its circulation by not permitting it to be published, and also concealed his name from prudential motives. This omission, however, has been supplied in MS. in the copy from whence this description is taken, and 'the English gentleman' appears to have been Thomas Kirke, of Crookwige in Yorkshire." [1]

Though Kirke is a splenetic and perverse observer, he seems to have been well acquainted with Scotland, and he reports facts not noticed by other travellers. His bias is evidently due to his political leanings, and to his disgust at the proceedings of the Scots in connection with Charles I. and Charles II. From the style of his narrative we may conclude that Kirke had Sir Anthony Weldon before him as his model.

A MODERN ACCOUNT OF SCOTLAND BY AN ENGLISH GENTLEMAN (1679).

IF all our European travellers direct their course to Italy, upon the account of its antiquity, why should Scotland be neglected, whose wringled surface derives its original from

---

[1] Brydges printed certain portions of the *Modern Account* in his *Censura Literaria*. It is here printed in full with the exception of a few passages too distinctly in the taste of the author's time.

the chaos ?   The first inhabitants were some stragglers of the fallen angels, who rested themselves in the confines, till their Captain Lucifer provided places for them in his own country.   This is the conjecture of learned criticks, who trace things to their originals ; and this opinion was grounded on the devils brats yet resident amongst them (whose foresight in the events of good and evil, exceeds the oracles at Delphos) the supposed issue of those pristine inhabitants.

Names of countries were not then in fashion, those came not in till Adam's days, and history (being then but in her infancy) makes no mention of the changes of that renowned countrey, in that interval betwixt him and Moses, when their chronicle commences ; she was then baptized (and most think with the sign of the Cross) by the venerable name of Scotland, from Scota, the daughter of Pharaoh, King of Egypt.[1]   Hence came the rise and name of these present inhabitants, as their chronicle informs us ; and it is not to be doubted of, from divers considerable circumstances ; the plagues of Egypt being entailed upon them, that of lice (being a judgment unrepealed) is an ample testimony, those loving animals accompanied them from Egypt, and remains with them to this day, never forsaking them (but as rats leave a house) till they tumble into their graves.   The plague of biles and blains is hereditary to them, as a distinguishing mark from the rest of the world, which (like the devils cloven hoof) warns all men to beware of them.   The judgment of hail and snow is naturalized and made free denison here, and continues with them from the sun's first ingress into Aries, till he has passed the 30th degree of Aquary.

The plague of darkness was said to be so thick darkness, as to be felt, which most undoubtedly these people have a share in as the word σκοτιὴ (darkness) implies ; the darkness being applicable to their gross and blockish understandings (as I had it from a scholar of their own nation). Upon these grounds this original is undeniably allowed them, and that the countrey itself (in pyramids) resembles Egypt, but far exceeds them both in bulk and number ; theirs are

---

[1] According to the legend accepted by the early historians of Scotland, Gathelus, the successor of Moses, and his wife Scota, were the founders of the Scottish nation.

but the products of men's labours, but these are Nature's own handy work; and if Atlas would ease a shoulder, here he may be fitted with a supporter.

Italy is compared to a leg, Scotland to a louse, whose legs and engrailed edges represent the promontories, and buttings out into the sea, with more nooks and angles than the most conceited of my Lord Mayor's custards;[1] nor does the comparison determine here: A louse preys upon its own fosterer and preserver, and is productive of those minute animals called nitts; so Scotland, whose proboscis joyns too close to England has suckt away the nutriment from Northumberland.

The arms of the kingdom was anciently a red lyon rampant in a field of gold, but *anno dom.* 787 they had the augmentation of the double tressure, for assisting the French King;[2] but his Majesties arms in Scotland is a mere *hysteron proteron*, the pride of the people being such, as to place the Scots arms in the dexter quarter of the escutcheon, and make a unicorn the dexter supporter, with the thistle at his heels, and a suitable motto, *Nemo me impune lacessit*, true enough: whosoever deals with them shall be sure to smart for't: The thistle was wisely placed there, partly to show the fertility of the country; nature alone producing plenty of these gay flowers, and partly as an emblem of the people, the top thereof having some colour of a flower, but the bulk and substance of it, is only sharp and poysonous pricks.

Woods they have none, that suits not with the frugality of the people, who are so far from propagating any, that they destroy those they had, upon this politick state maxim, that corn will not grow in the land pestered with its roots, and their branches harbour birds, animals above their humble conversation, that exceeds not that of hornless quadrupeds; marry, perhaps some of their houses lurk under the shelter of a plump of trees (the birds not daring so high a presumption) like Hugh Peter's puss[3] in her Majesty, or an owl in

---

[1] Dr Johnson describes custards as "a food much used at city feasts."
[2] According to the early Scottish heralds, the tressure was granted by Charlemagne to Achaius, King of Scotland, to symbolise that in all time coming the French cities would be the defence of the Scottish lion. In point of fact, however, the tressure first appears on the seal of Alexander III.
[3] For an explanation of this reference the curious reader may consult *The Tales and Jests of Mr Hugh Peters* (Lond. 1660), jest vii.

an ivy bush.　Some firr woods there are in the Highlands, but so inaccessible, that they serve for no other use than dens for those ravenous wolves with two legs, and they prey upon their neighbourhood, and shelter themselves under this covert; to whom the sight of a stranger is as surprising as that of a cockatrice.　The vallies for the most part are covered with beer or bigg, and the hills with snow; and as in the northern countries the bears and foxes change their coats into the livery of the soyl; so here the moor fowl (called termagants)[1] turn white, to sute the sample, though the inhabitants still stand to their Ægyptian hue.

They are freed from the charge and the incumbrance of inclosures, the whole being but one large waste, surrounded with the sea: Indeed in many places you may see half a rood of land divided by an earthen bank, into many different apartments, according to the quality of the beasts that are to possess them.

The whole country will make a park, forest, or chase, as you'll please to call it; but if you desire an account of particular parks, they are innumerable, every small house having a few sodds thrown into a little bank about it, and this for the state of the business (forsooth) must be called a park, though not a pole of land in't.

If the air was not pure and well refined by its agitation, it would be so infected with the stinks of their towns, and the steams of the nasty inhabitants, that it would be pestilential and destructive; indeed it is too thin for their gross senses, that must be fed with suitable viands, their meat not affecting their distempered palates, without it have a damnable hogœ,[2] or musick their ears, without loud and harsh discord, and their nostrils (like a Jew's) chiefly delight in the perceptible effluviums of an old Sir R———.

Fowl are as scarce here as birds of paradise, the charity of the inhabitants denying harbour to such celestial animals, though gulls and cormorants abound, there being a great sympathy betwixt them.　There is one sort of ravenous fowl amongst them that has one web-foot, one foot suited for land, and another for water; but whether or no this fowl (being particular to this country) be not the lively picture of the inhabitants, I shall leave to wiser conjectures.

---

[1] Ptarmigans.　　　[2] From the French *haut goût*.

Their rivers, or rather arms of the sea, are short, few places in Scotland being above a day's journey from the sea; but they are broad, deep and dangerous, pestered with multitudes of porpuses and sharks (some of them perhaps amphibious too, that live more on land than water) which destroys their salmon, the great commodity of this country; which being too good for the inhabitants, are barrel'd up and converted into merchandise, &c. Their banks and borders of these rivers (especially near their towns) are adorn'd with hardy amazons, though inverted, their valour being (chiefly) from the waste downwards, which parts they readily expose to all the dangers of a naked rencounter.

The exercise of their arms, I shou'd say feet, is much about linen; sheets are sufferers, a fit receiver is provided (not unlike a shallow pulpit to mind them of their idol sermons) wherein foul linen is laid to suffer persecution, so they turn up all, and tuck them about their wastes, and bounce into buck-tub, then go their stock, and belabour poor lint till there be not a dry thread on't. Hence came the invention of fulling-mills, the women taught the men, and they put in practice.

The country is full of lakes and loughs, and they well stockt with islands, so that a map thereof, looks like a pillory coat bespattered all over with dirt and rotten eggs, some pieces of the shells floating here and there, representing the islands.

Their cattle are only representatives of what are in other countreys, these being so epitomized, that it is hard to know what class they relate to. Their horses are hardy and not without gall (as some say other horses are) using both tooth and nail to mischief you; that they may not use more state than their masters, they go bare-foot, which preserves them from the gout; and if Hudibras's horse had been of this race, he had not needed a corn-cutter;[1] their furniture or harness is

---

[1] Butler describes Hudibras's horse as

> . . . . . Yet so fiery he would bound
> As if he grieved to touch the ground ;
> That Cæsar's horse, who as fame goes,
> Had corns upon his feet and toes,
> Was not by half so tender hooft,
> Nor trod upon the ground so soft.
>
> *Hudibras,* pt. i. canto ii. l. 431.

all of the same matter, all wood from head to tail, bridle,
saddle, girths, stirrups, and crupper, all wood; nothing but a
withy will bind a witch, and if these be called witches, I
shall not oppose it, since by their untoward tricks one would
guess the devil to be in them; their bridles have no bitts,[1] but
a kind of musroll [2] of two pieces of wood; their crupper is a
stick of a yard's length, put cross their docks, both ends
thereof being tyed with woven wood to the saddle. Their
bed and board too is all of the same dry straw, and when
they heave it up, whip on harness and away. Their neat
are hornless, the owners claiming the sole propriety in those
ornaments, nor should I deny them their necklace too, for
methinks that hoisted wood wou'd mightly become them.
Their sheep too have the same preferment, they are coupled
together near their masters palace. Some animals they have
by the name of hogs, but more like porcupines, bristled all
over, and these are likewise fastned to the free-hold by the
former artifice; all their quadrupedes (dogs only excepted, in
which sort they much abound) are honoured with wooden
bracelets about their necks, legs, or arms, &c.

Their cities are poor and populous, especially Edenborough,
their metropolis, which so well suits with the inhabitants,
that one character will serve them both, viz., high and dirty.
The houses mount seven or eight stories high, with many
families on one floor, one room being sufficient for all
occasions, eating, drinking, sleeping, &c. The other cities
and towns are copies from this original, and therefore need
no commentators to explain them; they have seven colleges, or
rather schools, in four universities; the regents wear what
colour'd cloaths or gowns they please, and commonly no
gowns at all, so that it is hard to distinguish a scholar from
an ordinary man, since their learning shines not out of their
noses; the younger students wear scarlet gowns only in term
time; their residence is commonly in the town, only at school-
hours they convene in the college, to consult their oracle
Buchanan; their chief studies are for pulpit preferment, to
prate out four or five glasses with as much ease as drink
them; and this they attain to in their stripling years, com-

---

[1] It will be remembered that Æneas Sylvius noted this.   See p. 27 (above).
[2] Musrole, the nose-band of a horse's bridle.

mencing Master of Arts (that is meant onely Master of this Art) before one wou'd judge them fit for the college; for as soon as they can walk as far as the school (which they will do very young, for like lapwings they run with shells on their heads) they are sent thither, where they find no benches to sit on (only one for the master) but have a little heath and fadder strewed for them to lye upon, where they litter together, and chew the cud on their fathers horn-books, and in good time are preferred to the bible; from this petty school away with them to the grammar school, viz., the college, where in three or four years time they attain to (their *ne plus ultra*) the degree of A. Mag., that is, they can extempore coin graces and prayers for all occasions; if you crack a nut, there is a grace for that, drink a dish of coffee, ale or wine, or what else, he presently furnishes you with a grace for the nonce; if you pare your nails, or any other action of like importance, he can as easily suit you with a prayer, as draw on a glove; and the wonder of all is, that this prayer shall be so admirably framed, that it may indifferently quadrate with any occasion, an excellency no where so common as in this country. Thus you see the young man has commenced and got strength to walk to the kirk and enter the chair, where we find him anon, after we have viewed the outsides of their kirks, some of which have been of antient foundations, and well and regularly built, but order and uniformity is in perfect antipathy to the humour of this nation, these goodly structures being either wholly destroyed (as at St Andrews and Elgin, where by the remaining ruines you may see what it was in perfection) or very much defaced; they make use of no other quires, those are either quite pulled down, or converted into another kirk, for it is common here three, four or five kirks under one roof, which being preserved entire, would have made one good church, but they could not then have had preaching enough in it; out of one pulpit now they have thirty sermons per week, all under one roof plenty of spiritual provision, which gusts[1] much better with a mixture of the flesh; as you may guess by their stools of repentance in every kirk, well furnished with whore-mongers and adulterers of both sexes. In Venice

[1] Tastes.

the shadows only of curtezans are exposed to publick view only in the Effigie, but here the whore in person, has a high place provided her in the view of the whole congregation, for the benefit of strangers, who (some think) need not this direction, but may truck for all commodities with the first they meet with. They use no service-book, nor whore of Babylon's smock (as they term a surplice) nor decency, nor order in their divine or rather contumelious service. Wou'd a king think himself honoured by subjects, that petitioned him without bonet vailed, but cockt his cap the while his request was granting; while precious Mr Presbyter grimaces, prays or houls, the monster-rabble vails; but as soon as the text is taken, blew-bonnet takes place again, and this pulpit-prater is esteemed more than God's ambassadour, having the Holy Spirit at his beck, to prompt him every word he speaks, yet not three sentences of sense together, such blasphemy, as I blush to mention.

Their christnings (as all other things) are without form, only water is poured on the infant, and such words used as) Sir John's Mephistophilus supplies him with, and so the child commences Christian, as good (or better) than the best of them. Some think marriage an unnecessary thing amongst them, it being more generous and usual amongst them to take one anothers words; however, 'tis thus performed, the young couple, being attended with tagrag and bobtail, gang to kirk, where Mr Scruple (like a good Casuist) controverts the point in hand to them, and schools Mr Bridegroom in his lesson, then, directs his discourse to Mrs Bride, who being the weaker vessel, ought to have the more pains taken with her; he chalks out the way she is to walk in, in all its particulars, and joyns their hands, and then let them fall to in God's name: Home they go with loud ravishing bag-pipes, and dance about the green, till they part by couples to repetition, and so put the rules in practice, and perhaps Sir Roger follows Mrs Bride to her apartment, to satisfie her doubts, where he uses such pungent and pressing arguments as she never forgets as long as she lives.

When any one dies, the bell-man goes about ringing their passing-bell, and acquaints the people therewith, in form following, "Beloved brouthrin and susters, I let you to wot that thir is an fauthful broothir lawtli departed awt of this prisant varld, aut thi plesuir of Aulmoughti Good (and then he vails his bonnet) his naum is Volli Voodcok, third son to Jimoy Voodcok a cordinger; he ligs aut thi sext door vethin thi Nord Gawt, close on thi Nawthwr Rawnd, and I wod yaw gang to hus burying on Thrusdau before twa acloak, &c." The time appointed for his burying being come, the *bell-man* calls the company together, and he is carried to the burying-place, and thrown into the grave (as Dog Lyon was) and there's an end of Volli.   Few people are here buried in their kirks (except of their nobility) but in the kirk-garths, or in a burying-place on purpose, called the hoof, at the further end of the town (like our Quakers) enclosed with a wall, so that it serves not only as a burying-place, but an exchange to meet in; perhaps in one part of it the Courts of Judicate are kept; in another are butts to shoot at for recreation. All agree that a woman's tongue is the last member she moves, but the Latin proverb, *Mulieri ne credas*, &c., seems to prove it after death; I am sure the pride of this people never leaves them, but follows them to their long homes (I was about to have said, to the devil), for the meanest man must have a grave-stone full fraught with his own praises (though he was the vilest miscreant on earth) and miserable *memento moris*, both in English and Latin, nay Greek too, if they can find a Greek word for cordinger, the calling he was of, and all this in such miserable Scotch orthography, that 'tis hard to distinguish one language from another.

The castles of defence in this country are almost impregnable, only to be taken by treachery or long siege, their water failing them soonest; they are built upon high and almost inaccessible rocks, only one forced passage up to them, so that few men may easily defend them.   Indeed, all the gentlemens houses are strong castles, they being so treacherous one to another, that they are forc'd to defend themselves in strong holds; they are commonly built upon some single rock in the sea, or some high precipice near the mid-land, with many towers and strong iron grates before their windows (the lower part whereof is only a wooden shutter, and upper part glass), so that they look more like prisons than houses of reception; some few houses there are of late erection, that

are built in a better form, with good walks and gardens
about them, but their fruit rarely comes to any perfection.
The houses of the commonalty are very mean, mud-wall and
thatch the best; but the poorer sort live in such miserable
hutts as never eye beheld; men, women, and children pig
altogether in a poor mouse-hole of mud, heath, and some such
like matter; in some parts, where turf is plentiful, they
build up little cabbins thereof, with arched roofs of turf,
without a stick of timber in it; when their houses are dry
enough to burn, it serves them for fuel, and they remove to
another. The habit of the people is very different, according
to the qualities and places they live in, as Low-land or
High-land men. The Low-land gentry go well enough
habited, but the poorer sort go (almost) naked, only an old
cloak, or a part of their bed-cloaths thrown over them. The
Highlanders wear slashed doublets, commonly without
breeches, only a plad tyed about their wastes, &c., thrown
over their shoulder, with short stockings to the gartering
place, their knees and part of their thighs being naked; others
have breeches and stockings all of a piece of plad ware,
close to their thighs; in one side of their girdle sticks a
durk or skean, of about a foot and half a yard long, very
sharp, and the back of it filed with divers notches, wherein
they put poyson; on the other side a brace (at least) of brass
pistols; nor is this honour sufficient, if they can purchase
more, they must have a long swinging sword.

The women are commonly two-handed tools, strong-posted
timber, they dislike English men because they have no legs,
or (like themselves) posts to walk on; the meaner go barefoot and bare-head, with two black elf-locks on either side
their faces; some of them have scarce any cloaths at all,
save part of their bed-cloaths pinn'd about their shoulders
and their children have nothing else on them but a little
blanket; those women that can purchase plads, need not
bestow much upon other cloaths, these cover-sluts being
sufficient. Those of the best sort that are very well habited
in their modish silks, yet must wear a plad over all for the
credit of their country.

The people are proud, arrogant, vain-glorious boasters,
bloody, barbarous, and inhuman butchers. Couzenage and

theft is in perfection among them, and they are perfect English haters, they show their pride in exalting themselves, and depressing their neighbours.

The nobility and gentry Lord it over their poor tenants, and use them worse than gally-slaves; they are all bound to serve them, men, women, and children; the first fruits is always the landlord's due. Those of his own name that are inferior to him, must all attend him (as he himself must do his superior, of the same name, and all of them attend the chief) if he receives a stranger, all this train must be at his beck armed as aforesaid; if you drink with them in a tavern, you must have all this rubbish with you; and if you offend the laird, his durk shall be soon sheathed in your belly, and, after this, every one of his followers, or they shall suffer themselves that refuse it, that so they may be all alike guilty of the murder. Every laird (of note) hath a gibet near his house, and has power to condemn and hang any of his vassals;[1] so they dare not oppose him in any thing, but must submit to his commands, let them be never so unjust and tyrannical. There are too many testimonies of their cruelty amongst themselves in their own Chronicles, forty of their kings have been barbarously murthered by them, and half as many more have either made away themselves for fear of their torturing of them, or have died miserably in strait imprisonment. What strange butcheries have been committed in their feuds, some of which are in agitation at this day, viz., Argill with the Macclenes, and Macdonnels about Mula Island,[2] which has cost already much blood, and is likely will cost much more before it will be decided; their spirits are so mean, that they rarely rob, but take away life first; lying in ambuscade, they send a brace of bullets on embassy through the travellers body; and to make sure work,

---

[1] This feudal jurisdiction carrying with it the power of life and death, was not taken from the Scottish nobility till after the union of the Parliaments. On the occasion of his visit to Scotland in 1617, James VI. did his best to put an end to this system, offering to compound with the barons for the surrender of their claims. None accepted the offer, and only in the succeeding reign did one lord, the Earl of Huntly, barter his jurisdiction (Gardiner, *History of England*, vol. iii. p. 225-6). [2] For the cruelties exercised by Argyll and Lesley on the Macleans, see Brown, *History of the Highlands*, ii. pp. 5, 6, 95.

they sheath their durks in his lifeless trunk, perhaps to take off their fine edges, as new knives are stuck in a bag pudding. If an highlander be injured, those of his own name must defend him, and will certainly have satisfaction from the offenders. A late instance whereof was at Inverness (a considerable town) where one of the Macdonnels was slain, but shortly the chief of his own name came down against the town with 1500 men of his own name, and threatned to fire the town, but the inhabitants compounded with them for 2000*l.*

Their cruelty descends to their beasts, it being a custom in some places to feast upon a living cow, they tye in the middle of them, near a great fire, and then cut collops of this poor living beast, and broil them on the fire, till they have mangled her all to pieces; nay, sometimes they will only cut off as much as will satisfie their present appetites, and let her go till their greedy stomachs call for a new supply; such horrible cruelty as can scarce be parrallel'd in the whole world.[1] Their theft is so well known, that it needs no proving, they are forced to keep watch over all they have, to secure it; their cattle are watch'd day and night, or otherwise they wou'd be over-grown by morning. In the Highlands they do it publickly before the face of the sun. If one man has two cows, and another wants, he shall soon supply himself from his neighbours, who can find no remedy for it. The gentry keep an armory in their own houses, furnish'd with several sorts of fire-arms, pikes, and halberts, with which they arm their followers, to secure themselves from the rapine of their neighbourhood. The Lowland language may be well enough understood by an English man, but the Highlanders have a peculiar lingue to themselves, which they call Erst,[2] unknown to most of the Lowland men, except only in those places that border on them, where they can speak both. Yet these people are so currish, that if a stranger enquire the way in English, they will certainly answer in Erst, and find no other language than what is inforc'd from them with a cudgel. If Cornelius Agrippa

---

[1] I have been unable to discover any other authority for this statement of Kirke. It will be remembered that James Bruce was mercilessly ridiculed for relating that this custom prevailed among the Abyssinians.   [2] Erse.

had travelled Scotland, sure cookery had been found in his vanity of sciences, such is their singular skill in this art, that they may defie the world to rival them; King James's treat for the devil, that is a poll of ling, a joll of sturgeon, and a pigg, with a pipe of tobacco for digestion, had been very compleat, if the ordering thereof had been assigned to a cuke of this countrey, who can sute every dish with its proper hogœ, and bring corruption to your table, only to mind men of mortality. Their meat is carrion when 'tis killed, but after it has been a fortnight a perfuming with the aromatick air, strained thro' the clammy trunks of flesh flies, then it passes the tryal of fire under the care of one of those exquisite artists, and is dish'd up in a sea of sweet Scotch butter, and so cover'd and served hot up to the table. O how happy is he that is placed next to it, with a privilege to uncover it, and receive the hot steams of this dainty dish, almost sufficient to cure all distempers. It will be needless to instance in particulars so plain and evident to all that have travell'd through the countrey, that they may certainly bear away the bell from all their neighbouring nations, or indeed from the whole world. Their nobility and gentry have tables plentifully enough furnish'd, but few or none of them have their meat better order'd. To put one's head into their kitchen doors, is little less than destructive; you enter Hell alive, where the black furies are busied in mangling dead carcases and the fire and brimstone, or rather stew and stink, is ready to suffocate you, and yet (which is strange) these things are agreeable to the humours of the people. The poorer sort live on haddock, whiting, and sower milk, which is cryed up and down their streets (whea buyes sawer milk) and upon the stinking fragments that are left at their laird's table. Prodigious stomachs, that, like the gulon,[1] can feed on their own excrements, and strain their meat through their stomachs, to have the pleasure of devouring it again.

Their drink is ale, made of beer-malt, and tunned up in a small vessel, called a cogue; after it has stood a few hours, they drink it out of the cogue, yest and all; the better sort brew it in larger quantities, and drink it in

---

[1] The glutton (*Gulo*)? The most extraordinary stories of the voracity of this animal used to be current.

wooden queighs, but it is sorry stuff, yet excellent for preparing birdlime; but wine is the great drink with the gentry, which they pour in like dishes, as if it were their natural element; the glasses they drink out of, are considerably large, and they always fill them to the brim, and away with it; some of them have arrived at the perfection to tope brandy at the same rate; sure these are a bowl above bacchus, and of right ought to have a nobler throne than a hogshead.[1]

Musick they have, but not the harmony of the sphears, but loud terrene noises, like the bellowing of beasts; the loud bagpipe is their chief delight, stringed instruments are too soft to penetrate the organs of their ears, that are only pleased with sounds of substance.

The high-ways in Scotland are tolerably good, which is the greatest comfort a traveller meets with amongst them; they have not inns, but change-houses (as they call them) poor small cottages, where you must be content to take what you find, perhaps eggs with chicks in them, and some lang cale; at the better sort of them, a dish of chap'd chickens, which they esteem a dainty dish, and will take it unkindly, if you do not eat very heartily of it, though for the most part you may make a meal with the sight of the fare, and be satisfied with the steam only, like the inhabitants of the world in the moon; your horses must be sent to a stablers (for the change-houses have no lodging for them) where they may feed voluptuously on straw only, for grass is not to be had, and hay is so much a stranger to them, that they are scarce familiar with the name of it.

The Scotch gentry commonly travel from one friend's house to another, so seldom make use of a change-house; their way is to hire a horse and a man for two pence a mile; they ride on the horse thirty or forty miles a day, and the man, who is his guide, foots it beside him, and carries his luggage to boot. The commonality are so used to worship and adore their lairds, that when they see a stranger in any tolerable equipage, they honour him with the title of laird at least. 'An't please you, my laird such

[1] It is worth noting that by none of our travellers is whisky mentioned as a drink of the country.

a one,' or 'An't please you, my laird Dr,' at every bare
word forsooth.

The nobility show themselves very great before strangers,
who are conducted into the house by a many servants
where the lord with his troop of shadows receives them
with the grand law, then enter into some discourse of their
countrey, till you are presented with a great queigh of
syrup of beer, after that a glass of white wine, then a
rummer of claret, and sometimes after that a glass of sherry
sack, and then begin the round with ale again, and ply you
briskly; for its their way of showing you'r welcome, by
making you drunk. If you have longer time to stay, you
stick close to claret, till bacchus wins the field, and leaves
the conquer'd victims groveling on the place where they
receive their overthrow. At your departure you must
drink a *dougha doras*, in English a stirrup-cup, and have
the satisfaction to have my lord's bagpipe (with his loud
pipes, and his lordship's coat armor on a flag) strut about
you, and enchant you with a loath to depart.

Their money is commonly dollars, or mark-pieces, coined
at Edenbrough, but the way of reckoning is surprising to a
stranger. To receive a bill of £100 in one of their change-
houses, when one wou'd not suppose they had any of the
value of a hundred pence; they call a penny a shilling, and
every twenty shillings, *viz.*, twenty pence, a pound; so the
proportion of their pound to ours is twelve to one.
Strangers are sure to be grossly imposed upon in all their
change-houses, and there is no redress for it. If an Englishman shou'd complain to their magistrates, they wou'd all
take a part against him, and make sure to squeeze him.

THOMAS MORER.

(1689).

THE title of Morer's book, from which the following extracts have been taken, tells us all that appears to be known of its author. "A short account of Scotland; being a description of the nature of that kingdom, and what the constitution of it is in church and state. Wherein also some notice is taken of their chief cities and royal boroughs. With an appendix, 1. about the king's supremacy, 2. the difference of the Scotch and English liturgy, 3. the revenue and expense on the civil and military list, according to a late establishment. Written by the late Rev. Mr. Thomas Morer, minister of St. Ann's within Aldersgate, when he was chaplain to a Scotch regiment. Lond. 1715, 12mo. First printed without a name, 1702, 8vo."

Of all the accounts of Scotland here brought together, Morer's indubitably stands first in historic interest and value. Indeed, Morer's book, which consists only of some pages, cannot be neglected in any study of Scotland during the latter half of the 17th century. By the breadth of his interests, his intelligence, and justness of mind, Morer should rank high among English travellers; and his book well deserves to be reprinted in the interests of Scottish history. Here we produce only those parts of it which are of most general interest.

A SHORT ACCOUNT OF SCOTLAND. By THOMAS MORER
(London, 1715).

THE soil of the country seems to the eye very indifferent, and tho' they have many fine valleys, which might be improved into a competitorship with our English meadows, yet for want of sufficient industry and care they become almost useless, on the account of frequent bogs and waters in such places. Whence it is, that they have little hay in

that kingdom.   And tho' there is a competency of grass
daily exposed to sale in their towns and villages, yet being
cut out of the intervals or little spaces between the ridges
of corn, sometimes very distant from one another, they think
it more profitable to sell the grass, than to make it into hay
for winter; at which time their horses feed for the most
part on straw and oats, which are sold in their markets at
tolerable rates.   And this is the reason likewise why their
arable ground is very considerable; and 'tis almost incredible
how much of the mountains they plough, where the declen-
sions, I had almost said the precipices, are such, that to our
thinking, it puts 'em to greater difficulty and charge to carry
on their work, than they need be at in draining the valleys.

Their harvest is very great of oats and barly, which is the
more common and flourishing grain of the country, the straw
whereof is very serviceable to 'em for the support of the
cattle.   Not but they have beans, pease, and some wheat
likewise, but the oats and barly are most in request, as on
which they chiefly depend: on the first for bread, on the
other for drink, which is sometimes strong enough to arm
'em against the coldness of the climate.   And of their barly
there are two sorts; one of which has double ears, and they
call it beer: This they make their malt of, and may be a
reason for giving the drink that name.[1]   But that which
employs great part of their land is hemp, of which they have
mighty burdens, and on which they bestow much care and
pains to dress and prepare it for making their linen, the most
noted and beneficial manufacture of the kingdom.

We seldom meet with inclosures; either because being a
corn country, they would be injured as little as may be by
birds which harbour in the hedges; or being without those
long and kind leases the tenants of England have, they are
not encouraged by their lords in that and some other
improvements;[2] or that there is want of industry in this,
and the like cases: So it is, that their fields are open, and
without fences, unless here and there they raise out of the
road some little continued heaps of stone in the nature of a
wall, to secure their crops from the incursions of travellers.

[1] Skeat (*Etymological Dictionary*) is disposed to accept this etymology of
beer in preference to that which connects it with *bibere*.   [2] *Cf.* p. 42 (note).

The Highlands.

Scotland is distinguished into High-lands and Low-lands. The people of the first were anciently called Brigantes (a name the Irish sometimes go by, of whom they are supposed. to be descended), from Briga or Bria, a Bray, a word still in use with 'em to signifie an high place; as when they say, the Bray of Athol, they mean the mountainous part of that country. But now mostly High-landers, whether because they lie more northerly than the rest of the kingdom, or because they dwell in the hilly part of it, is uncertain. But heretofore this was the main of the Scotch King's territories till the Picts were expelled, who had Edinburgh in possession, and the better part of the Low-lands, where about five miles from that city there are a row of hills, called Pictland Hills,[1] in which those distressed princes frequently sculked in convenient refuges or rooms hew'd out of the rocks, till they had fresh opportunities to try their fortune, and recover their country: But were at last, in the reign of Kenneth 2nd (about the year 839),[2] so intirely routed, that the name is now extinct as well as the kingdom.

The High-landers are not without considerable quantities of corn, yet have not enough to satisfie their numbers, and therefore yearly come down with their cattle, of which they have greater plenty, and so traffick with the Low-landers for such proportions of oats and barly as their families or necessities call for.

They are in great subjection to their lords, who have almost an absolute power over 'em. So that whenever they summon'd 'em, they immediately got together, and attended them whithersoever they went, tho' to the loss of their lives and the little fortune they had. But of late years the scene is changed; and tho' at this day there are divers instances to be seen of that power of their lords yet their present case is much better, and the yoke easier than it was before.

Nor are they more obedient to their lords than affection-

---

[1] Pentland Hills. [2] The Union of the Picts and Scots took place in 843, under Kenneth MacAlpin. It is perhaps unnecessary to say that Morer's history must be taken with large reserves.

ate to their clans, and the heads of their tribes, or families whom they usually have so great a regard to, that they will not, as far as lies in them, suffer 'em to sink under any misfortune. But in case of·a small estate, they make an honourable contribution on their behalf, as a common duty or concern to support the credit of their houses.

Their religion, as to outward profession, is for the most part after the establishment of the kingdom; yet too many not only retain the Irish language, but the Irish religion; and not a few profess no religion at all, but are next door to barbarity and heathenism. However, in the general, they have so great a veneration for ministers, or men in holy orders, that notwithstanding their natural roughness, and perhaps rudeness to other sort of travellers, these persons coats are a sufficient protection and passport to them throughout that part of Scotland. Which respect is grounded on a principle they have, that should they in the least injure such a man, they must not expect to prosper all the days of their life. 'Tis true, at the skirmish at Brechin, some of Colonel Barclay's Dragoons found in one of their sacks, among other things, a minister's gown; and 'twas a hot report at that time, while we were in sight of their camp, that they used a clergyman hard by very ill both as to goods and person. But then this is imputed to the villainy of the Irish join'd 'em a little before, and who are remarkable enemies to men of this profession. For I was well assured by an old divine at Perth, who had spent many years among 'em, that this was not the way of the High-landers themselves who reverenced gown-men to a degree, not much short of superstition.

They are constant in their habit or way of clothing; pladds are most in use with 'em, which, tho' we English thought inconvenient, especially for swordsmen in times of action, and in heat of summer, as when we saw 'em; yet they excused themselves on these accounts, that they not only served them for cloaths by day in case of necessity, but were pallats or beds in the night at such times as they travelled and had not opportunities for better accommodation, and for that reason in campaigns were not unuseful: The Low-landers add, that being too often men of prey, by this means they cover their booty the better, and carry it off without the owner's knowledge. These pladds are about seven or eight yards long, differing in fineness according to the abilities or fancy of the wearers. They cover the whole body with 'em from the neck to the knees, excepting the right arm, which they mostly keep at liberty. Many of 'em have nothing under these garments besides wastcoats and shirts, which descend no lower than the knees, and they so gird 'em about the middle as to give 'em the same length as the linen under 'em, and thereby supply the defect of drawers and breeches.[1]

Those who have stockings make 'em generally of the same piece with their pladds, not knit or weaved, but sow'd together, and they tie 'em below the knee with tufted garters.

They wear a sort of shooes, which they call brocks,[2] like our pumps, without heels, of a very thin sole, and affording little security from the wet or stones, which is their main use and chiefly intended for.

They cover their heads with bonnets or thrum-caps,[3] not unlike those of our servitors, tho' of a better consistence to keep off the weather. They are blue, grey, or sad-colour'd, as the purchaser thinks fit; and are sometimes lined according to the quality of their master.

The quarrels and animosities between their great ones made it always necessary in elder times to be very well armed, and the custom continues to this day; so that you shall seldom see 'em, tho' only taking the air, without sword and dirk, which is a short dagger. In war, they had formerly bows and such kind of arrows as once entered the body could not be drawn out without tearing away the flesh with 'em: But now they carry muskets and other fire-arms; and when they are on the defensive part, they depend much on the targes or targets, which are shields of that form the Latines call by the name of Clypeus, round and æquidistant from the center, and are made of the toughest wood they can get, lined within and cover'd without with skins, fenced with brass nails, and made so serviceable that no ordinary bullet, much less a sword, can penetrate to injure them or their masters, who have such an artificial way of

---

[1] This is a description, not of his philabeg or kilt, but of the older Highland "belted plaid."   [2] Brogue, Gael. *brog*.   [3] Caps made of coarse yarn.

twisting themselves within the compass of these shields, that 'tis almost a vain attempt for their enemy to seek to annoy 'em. And indeed they fight with too much odds, when they come so near us, because they not only have the protection of their bucklers, but are withal very expert at their swords, which consist of the best blades now in being, and were therefore much sought after by our officers and souldiers, who were very well furnished with 'em before wee left the High-lands.

Once or twice a year, great numbers of 'em get together and made a descent into the Low-lands, where they plunder the inhabitants, and so return back and disperse themselves. And this they are apt to do in the profoundest peace, it being not only natural to 'em to delight in rapine, but they do it on a kind of principle, and in conformity to the prejudice they continually have to the Low-landers, whom they generally take for so many enemies.

The Lowlands.

The Low-lands are so called by way of comparison, and as they relate to the High-lands I just spoke of. Not but that the mountains here are both numerous and lofty, and we pass not many miles without climbing some of 'em (so that this track of ground, independently taken, might be very well named the hill-country). Yet, considering its neighbourhood to the Northern Provinces, whose mountains are more contiguous and of greater number, it may (in some measure) justifie the distinction ; though I should chuse rather to make the difference between 'em on the account of the language, garb, humour, and spirit of the people, than the strict etymology of the word or situation of the country.

We take the Low-landers to be a Medley of Picts, Scots, French, Saxons, and English, as their language and habit insinuate, which is the reason why the High-landers, who look on themselves to be a purer race, cannot affect 'em ; but on the contrary deal with 'em as a spurious degenerate people. And indeed the Low-landers abate much of that true courage anciently and deservedly given their forefathers. Whether it be that they degenerate in their kind, or become soft and effeminate by their daily converse with politer nations, we know not ; but certain it is, they fall short of their ancestors' spirit (whether Picts or Scots), and in case of a breach, the High-landers think it advantage enough if they have only these men to fight with. An instance of which we had at the Battle of Gilliecranky, where, upon the approach of the High-landers, the Scotch forces on our side scoured away, and left one only regiment, that of Colonel Hastings, to bear the charge and fury of the enemy.

The Low-landers have plenty of most sorts of grain, especially oats and barley. And as for cattel, though they have large herds and hags of their own, yet their plenty of this kind depends much on the yearly descent of the High-landers, who come hither with considerable droves to exchange for corn, when their own is spent at home.

Their habit is mostly English, saving that the meaner sort of men wear bonnets instead of hats, and pladds instead of cloaks ; and those pladds the women also use in their ordinary dress when they go abroad, either to market or church. They cover head and body with 'em, and are so contrived as to be at once both a scarf and hood. The quality go thus attired, when they would be disguised, and is a morning dress good enough when some hasty business calls them forth, or when the weather disheartens 'em to trick themselves better.

Their language is generally English, but have many words derived from the French, and some peculiar to themselves. They are great criticks in pronunciation, and often upbraid us for not giving every word its due sound, as when we call *enough* " enow " or " enuff," without making it a guttural, but neglecting the *gh* as if not written. Wherein, however, they are as faulty themselves, as I shew'd 'em by divers examples in their daily discourse ; particularly their neglect of vowels is very remarkable, which being few, ought to be pronounced with greater care. As when *o* happens to terminate the word, especially monosyllables, they change it into *a*, as *wha* for *who*, *twa* for *two*, &c., and if in the middle, they say *steans* for *stones*, *mare* for *more*, &c., all which they no other-wise excused than by custom and usage of speech, which is our apology for the like misrepresentations in words objected to us. They have an unhappy tone, which the gentry and nobles cannot overcome, tho' educated in our schools, or

never so conversant with us; so that we may discover a
Scotchman as soon as we hear him speak : Yet, to say truth,
our Northern and remote English have the same imperfection.

They have the advantage of their brethren in the North,
as to trade and merchandice, which is the reason why they
are more factious than the rest of the kingdom, the spirit of
schism usually reigning in such places where the people are
rich to reward their teachers.

This is all that occurs at present concerning the Low-lands,
as before distinguished. What I add more, treats of the
Scotch in common.

Their ordinary women go barefoot, especially in the
summer. Yet the husbands have shoes, and therein seem
unkind in letting their wives bear those hardships without
partaking themselves. Their children fare no better when
scarce able to go. But, what surprised me most, some of
the better sort, lay and clergy, made their little ones go in
the same manner, which I thought a piece of cruelty in them,
that I imputed to the others poverty. But their apology
was, the custom of the country, grounded on an ancient
law, that no males were to use shoes till fourteen years of
age, that so they might be hardened for the wars when their
Prince had occasion for their service.[1]

Their bread, for the most part, is of oat-meal, which, if thin
and well baked upon broad irons or stones for that purpose,
is palatable enough, and often brought to gentlemen's
tables. But the vulgar are not so curious, for they only
water the meal into a convenient consistence, and then
making 'em into thick cakes, called bannocks, they set 'em
before the fire to be hardened or toasted for their use.
These people prepare the oats after this manner,—they take
several sheaves, and setting fire to 'em consume the straw
and chaff to ashes, which, after a convenient time, they blow
away, then gathering up the grain sufficiently parched, they
bruise it into meal.

Their flesh is good enough, yet I confess it will not keep
as long as that in England, which they say proceeds from
the largeness of the pores, exposing it more than elsewhere
to the air and weather.

[1] I have found no trace of such a law in the Acts of the Scottish Parliament.

Their cheese is not the best, nor butter, made in part of
ewes-milk, which did not relish with us, yet we could not
tempt 'em to forbear that mixture.

Their drink is beer, sometimes so new that it is scarce
cold when brought to table. But their gentry are better
provided, and give it age : yet think not so well of it as to
let it go alone, and therefore add brandy, cherry-brandy, or
brandy and sugar, and is the nectar of this country at their
feasts and entertainments, and carries with it a mark of
great esteem and affection. Sometimes they have wine (a
thin-bodied claret) at 10d. the muskin, which answers our
quart, but is no more than half of the Scotch pint; and
thereupon they tell us, that if their drink be not so good as
ours, yet their measure is better. But the difference lies
only in the terms, for the proportions are alike, and we paid
as much for their chopping as for the pint here, containing
the same quantity.

They have poultry and fowls in convenient plenty.
Among the rest there is the solon goose, a large bird, but
tastes more of fish than flesh, because accustomed to the sea,
and feeds there oftener than in other places. The inhabitants say that the manner of its production is this : She
lets fall her egg according to the season on the side of a
rock, which, having a slimy, glutinous matter about it, fastens
itself to the place where it happens to fall, nor can it be
removed without danger of breaking it to pieces. And
sometimes the egg is so untowardly fix'd that there is no
more room for the bird to come at it than with one of her
feet, which she spreads on the upper part of the egg, rests
on it with her whole body, and in time, with the heat of her
foot, produces the young one, which from this way of hatch-
ing takes its name, and is called solon, *quasi* "sole on,"[1] from
the sole of the dam's foot, which after this manner gives it
being. But whether so or no I am not sure; you have the
relation.

The houses of their quality are high and strong, and
appear more like castles than houses, made of thick stone
walls, with iron bars before their windows, suited to the
necessity of those times they were built in, living then in

[1] *Solan* is now connected with the Icelandic *sula.*

a state of war and constant animosities between their families. Yet now they begin to have better buildings, and to be very modish both in the fabrick and furniture of their dwellings: Tho' still their avenues are very indifferent, and they want their gardens, which are the beauty and pride of our English seats. The vulgar houses, and what are seen in the villages, are low and feeble. Their walls are made of a few stones jumbled together without mortar to cement 'em: On which they set up pieces of wood meeting at the top, ridge-fashion, but so order'd that there is neither sightliness nor strength; and it does not cost much more time to erect such a cottage than to pull it down. They cover these houses with turff of an inch thick, and in the shape of larger tiles, which they fasten with wooden pins, and renew as often as there is occasion; and that is very frequently done. 'Tis rare to find chimneys in these places, a small vent in the roof sufficing to convey the smoak away. So that, considering the humility of those roofs, and the gross nature of the fuel, we may easily guess what a smother it makes, and what little comfort there is in sitting at one of their fires. However, in their towns and cities the case is otherwise: but of them when I come to particular places. 'Twas matter of wonder at first that so great a corn-country as Scotland is should not be able to afford 'em straw enough to thatch the houses: But calling to mind their want of hay, which makes 'em employ the straw in feeding their horses as well as foddering their other cattel, I was quickly satisfied as to this point, and thereupon chose rather to pity their poverty than charge 'em with ill contrivance in the covering of their cells.

Orchards they have few. And their apples, pears, and plumbs are not of the best kind; their cherries are tolerably good. And they have one sort of pear, large and well tasted, but seldom had. Wall-fruit is very rare. But of gooseberries, currans, strawberries, and the like, they have of each; but growing in gentlemen's gardens, and yet from thence we sometimes meet with 'em in the markets of their boroughs.

They have excellent pit-coal, so bituminous and pitchy that it burns like a candle, and is both pleasant and useful.

But this is chiefly for their gentry and boroughs; the common people deal in peat and turff, cut and dried in the summer, and would be no bad fuel, but that at first kindling it makes a very thick and offensive smother.

They are fond of tobacco, but more from the snush-box than pipe. And they have made it so necessary, that I have heard some of 'em say, that should their bread come in competition with it, they would rather fast than their snush should be taken away. Yet mostly it consists of the coarsest tobacco, dried by the fire, and powdered in a little engine after the form of a tap, which they carry in their pockets, and is both a mill to grind and a box to keep it in.

The women of Scotland are capable of estates and honours, and inherit both as well as the males; and therefore after marriage may retain their maiden name; but one disadvantage they lie under, that in case the husbands die without a will, they claim no thirds, which is a consideration awes 'em a little, and makes 'em more obsequious to their husbands.

Most of their titles of honour are derived from England, brought thence into Scotland in the second century by Malcomb the Third, who had been a great while a guest in our Prince's court. But one degree seems peculiar to themselves concerning their lairds; which, tho' some compare to our freeholders with independent tenures, yet, being masters of royalties, they cannot be less than the English lords of mannors; and from these regalities they assume to themselves titles, as many do among us, both here and in Wales.

The water is good, and they have several considerable rivers; the chief whereof, which fell within my knowledge and are navigable, were the Fryth,[1] the Tay, and the Clide. The first runs from Leith to Sterling, and further upwards with tide. The next from Dundee to Perth, and the last from the Irish Sea to Glasgow. Three very serviceable currents, and would contribute much to enrich the bordering places if they had sufficient shipping.

This makes the trade of this kingdom inconsiderable, having, as was said, very few ships, and those of light burden. With these they fetch their wines from France, and some

---

[1] Forth.

other commodities had from thence and Ireland. But other merchandice comes at second hand from the citizens of London and Bristol.

Money of their own coining they have little, for want of bullion; and therefore make use of all foreign stamps, especially the Elector of Cologne's, which by reputation or weight pass current among 'em. The Spanish cobbs, half cobbs, and quarter cobbs, are commonly put in the scales, and so were formerly dollars of all sorts. But now to save trouble, they divide 'em into two sorts, the rix-dollar at 4s. 10d. and the leg-dollar [1] at 4s. 8d., and so in proportion for the lesser pieces.

The coins properly Scotch consist of these pieces, crowns coined in the minority of King James the Sixth, having the arms on the one side, and a sword on the reverse with that treasonable circumscription, *Si mereor pro me, si non in me,* made by Buchanan, his preceptor.[2] There are three lesser pieces of this impression, 1s. 3d., 1s. 8d., and 2s. 11d., which is all I saw of that coin. They have likewise crowns, half crowns, marks, and nobles of King Charles II.'s; ten groat pieces, ten penny, and three pence half pennies of King James VII.'s, but shillings and sixpences they have none peculiar to the nation, nor any current gold but what is common with England, which they advance and give sixpence more for every jacobus or guinea.

They show some vanity in the stile of their money, for they call a bodel twa pennies, tho' no more than the sixth part of our penny. So that should they have occasion to mention three half pence or two pence half penny, they chuse rather to call the one 18 pennies, and the other 30. Each of our pence is with them a shilling, and so our twenty pence is a Scotch pound. Their mark is 13½d. of our money,

---

[1] Leg Dollar or Leggat, so called from Liège, its place of coinage. Its value was £2, 16s. ; whereas that of the Rix-dollar was £2, 18s.   [2] I have found no satisfactory authority for this statement, but it is certainly consistent with the whole tenor of Buchanan's political teaching. In the famous speech which he puts in the mouth of the Earl of Morton on his return from an embassy to Queen Elizabeth, he makes the Earl tell the story of Trajan handing the sword to the prefect of the City with the words, "Use it for me or against me, as I shall deserve." As the coin was struck at the coronation of James VI., the legend was in all probability the suggestion of Buchanan.

and the half of that is their noble; and by the number of these pieces it is they reckon the estates and fortunes of their people.   As when a man is supposed worth 50*l.* per annum sterling, they call it near 1000 mark, which bears a bigger sound, tho' it adds nothing to the substance of the party.

They have many bridges for the ease and safety of travellers, very strong and well built, sometimes consisting but of one mighty arch, whose height and breadth deserves admiration.

Stage coaches they have none, yet there are a few hackneys at Edinburg, which they may hire into the country upon urgent occasions.   The truth is, the roads will hardly allow 'em these conveniences, which is the reason that their gentry, men and women, chuse rather to use their horses. However, their great men often travel with coach and six, but with so much caution, that, besides their other attendance, they have a lusty running footman on each side the coach, to manage and keep it in rough places.

But this carriage of persons from place to place might be better spared were there opportunities and means for the speedier conveyance of business by letters.   They have no horse-posts besides those that ply 'twixt Berwick and Edinburg, and from thence to Port Patrick, for the sake of the Irish packets; and if I forget not, every town the post passes through contributes to the charges.   But from Edinburgh to Perth, and so to other places, they use foot-posts and carriers, which, tho' a slow way of communicating our concerns to one another, yet is such as they acquiesce in till they have a better.

EDINBURGH.—Edinburgh is in Lothien; and it was first called Ageda from ἀγὴ, a rupture or broken rock, meaning the place where the castle was built from which the town took its name.   The northern Scotch term'd it Duned, from whence probably the Latines had their Edinum and Edinodunum.   But the moderns say Edinburgh, or the city near the Winged Castle, because the Castle, which was built before the town, stands between two eminent rocks, like two wings, one whereof is called [Arthuri Sedes] Arthur's Stool, and is a steep rock on the south of the castle.   It is now the royal city, having the King's Palace, the courts of justice, and the Parliament House, which was before the reign of King James the V., held indifferently at Perth, Sterling, or Forfar.[1] It is seated on an hill, and consists chiefly of one fair street from west to east, about a mile long, from the castle to Hall-rood-House[2]; but then we include Cani-gate, or Canon-gate, tho' a distinct corporation; and, in strictness, is rather the suburbs of Edinburgh, than any part of the city itself, like London and Westminster, and has the name of Cani-gate, from a society of Canons who formerly dwelt in it. The street is wide and well paved, and the Scotchman is apt to say that it is sike another as Cheapside; It swells in the middle, the kennels being made on each side, so that 'tis commonly very clean, and is thereupon their parade, tho' the natural descent, and its situation on an hill contributes more to keep it so, than any industry or care of the people.

Their old houses are cased with boards, and have oval windows (without casements or glass), which they open or shut as it stands with their conveniency. Their new houses are made of stone, with good windows modishly framed and glazed, and so lofty, that five or six stories is an ordinary height, and one row of buildings there is near the Parliament Close with no less than fourteen. The reason of it is, their scantness of room, which, not allowing 'em large foundations, they are forced to make it up in the superstructure, to entertain comers, who are very desirous to be in, or as near as they can to the city.

Most of the houses, as they are parted into divers tenements, so they have as many landlords as stories; and therefore have no dependence on one another, otherwise than as they stand on the same foundation, so that in this respect they may be compared to our students' apartments at the Inns-of-Court, which are bought and sold without regard to the chambers above or below 'em.

Their stairs are unsightly and inconvenient: for, being built out of the street for the service of every story, they are sometimes so steepy, narrow, and fenceless, that it requires care to go up and down for fear of falling. But in their

[1] The town records of Forfar prove that Parliaments were held there by William the Lyon, Alexander II., and Robert II. [2] Holyrood.

new houses the contrivance is better; and the staircase, being made within the yard, or foundation of the building, the ascent and descent is more decent and easie, and rids the street of an incumbrance, which cannot be avoided in the other houses.

On the south-side of Edinburgh was heretofore a lough or lake, but is now drained, and a narrow street built upon it, which they call Cow-gate. Between which and the High Street there are many little lanes of communication, but very steepy and troublesome, and withal so nasty (for want of bog-houses, which they very rarely have), that Edinburgh is by some liken'd to an ivory comb, whose teeth on both sides are very foul, though the space between 'em is clean and sightly.

The city is govern'd by a Lord Provost and four bailiffs, who, with the assistance of some substantial citizens, in the nature of our Common Council, manage all publick affairs relating to the benefit of the Corporation, or peace of the city.

The pride of Edinburg is the Parliament-Yard or Close, as they call it. In the midst whereof is the effigies of King Charles II. on horse-back, a well-proportioned figure of stone, and natural enough. The Yard is square and well-paved, beautified with good buildings round about it; and the only fault is, that it is no bigger, the height of the houses bearing no correspondence to the dimensions of the area. Its western boundary is the Parliament House, a large room and high roofed. Over the entrance is the Scotch arms, with Mercy and Truth on each side, like two supporters, and this inscription—*Stant his Felicia Regna*—These Vertues make Kingdoms happy. Under the arms was, *Unio Unionum*, "The union of unions"—meaning not only the union of the two kingdoms, but that to the uniting of kingdoms good advice is necessary, which is the business of that place. Within the room on the south of it is an high throne, and on each side several benches one above another, the uppermost whereof is level with the throne, and the lowest reaches the pit, well furnished with forms, for the conveniency and ease of the members. Opposite to the Throne, and without the area, is a pulpit, for sermons in sessions of Parliament, upon special occasions. Behind the pulpit is a large partition, where strangers stand and hear the sermon; and sometimes the delater of the house, which to my thoughts were not managed with gravity enough, but was next door to wrangling.

East of this House, but south of the Square, is the Privy-Council Chamber, and not far from it the Royal Exchange, made up of a double row of shops, very small and meanly furnished. There is also another Exchange, inferior to this, but both above stairs, and without any piece of magnificence to distinguish them from the other buildings.

In the first floors level with the Yard are three or four booksellers, and as many goldsmiths, whose shops are sufficiently stockt, to let us see their occupations and trades.

The northern boundary is the wall of the High Church,[1] which, with a few shops joining to it (leaving room for coaches to pass to the Parliament House) concludes the figure of this close, the beauty of their City.

On the west of the High Street and a musket-shot distance from the houses stands the Castle, built near 2020 years ago, *Castrum alatum* (said Ptolemy), the Maiden Castle (say the Scotch), because the Pictish kings kept and educated their daughters in it. On the west, south, and north it is a rock very steepy, yet not inaccessible (as they called it) for upon the bombarding of it[2] 'twas so batter'd, that with the fall of the walls and some other rubbish, it was brought to that pass, that the soldiers with little difficulty might have clamber'd up, but that it was timely surrender'd. On the east towards the town, 'tis guarded with an half-moon, and has on its battlements eight pieces of cannon, with a wide trench, and draw-bridge, and then a thick wall lined with guns for its better security from the assaults of that quarter. The Castle is certainly a strong building, both from art and nature, well stored with ordinance and other conveniences to bear a siege, provided it be well man'd, as it was not when the Duke of Gourdon deliver'd it up.[3] There is a little room in the Castle where they say King James VI. was born, and thence in a little

---

[1] The Church of St Giles.   [2] In 1573, when Kirkaldy of Grange and Maitland of Lethington held it for Queen Mary, the Regent Morton, with the assistance of English troops, bombarded the castle, and forced the garrison to surrender.   [3] At the Revolution in 1689.

time removed to Stirling, which occasions some authors to assert that he was born at Stirling. Whereas the verses writ over the chimney-piece in that chamber, which they there apply to him, otherwise give out in this language and spelling.[1]

South of the Castle, and not far distant from it, we have the beautiful front of a large hospital, built by one Hariot, a goldsmith, for the education of 40 boys, who, if they take learning, and go to the College, have an exhibition, each of 7*l.* sterling or thereabouts ; if put to trades, about 200 marks or about 11*l.* sterling, for the incouragement of their masters.

South of the Cow-Gate, and on a rising stands the College, consisting of one small quadrangle, and some other lodgings without uniformity or order, built at several times, and by divers benefactors, who thought probably to be better distinguished by this variety of forms and situations in those buildings. In the midst hereof is the library, a large and convenient room made about 60 years ago for that purpose. The roof is covered with lead, and is neatly kept within ; well furnish'd with books, and those put in very good order, and cloister'd with doors made of wire which none can open but the keeper, and which is thought a better way than our multitudes of chains incumbering a library,[2] and are equally troublesome and chargeable to us. It has (as all other publick libraries) many benefactors, whose books are distinguish'd by their several apartments, and the donors names set over 'em in golden letters.[3] A device, grateful and honourable enough for the parties concern'd, encourages others to follow their examples ; such especially who may be charmed to the doing of a good work, tho' not always upon a principle of goodness. Over the books are hung the pictures of divers Princes, and most of the reformers, as Luther, Melancthon, Zuinglius, Calvin, &c., and near them Buchanan's scull,

---

[1] The lines have already been given by Brome (p. 246).   [2] Alberti, visiting Oxford about the middle of the eighteenth century, found this chaining of books still in practice there, and makes the same complaint as Morer, *Briefe betreffend den allerneuesten Zustand der Religion und der Wissenschaften in Gross-Britannien* (Hanover, 1752), iii. 794.   [3] The only separate collections of books now in the library of the University of Edinburgh are those of Clement Little (mentioned above) and Drummond of Hawthornden.

very intire, and so thin that we may see the light through it, and that it is really his appears from hence, because one, Mr Adamson, principal of the College, being a young man of 24 years of age, when Buchanan was buried, either out of curiosity or respect to the dead, brib'd the sexton sometime after to procure him the skull, which being brought he fastened these[1] verses to it, and at his death left it and them to the College.

The east end of the great street of Edinburgh brings you to the royal palace, formerly an abbey, but converted into this use by King James V., yet still retains its old name, and is sometimes called the Abbey, and Hali-rood House. It is a noble structure, built of stone, well carved and beautified, in the fashion of a square, with a piazza or gallery under it, from whence by several staircases they ascend to such apartments as their respect or business ingage 'em. The gallery above is very fine, extended to a considerable length, and set out with the pictures of their 112 kings, and hath also a billyard table for the diversion of the house. The lodgings are stately enough, and not meanly furnished. The house is guarded from surprize by a large court where the souldiers draw up when they relieve one another.

Adjoining to the palace is the shell of the old abbey, and by the common yard for burials, which is ill situated on the account of the king's house, but very convenient for the ease and health of the citizens who have no vacant ground within the walls for such an use, and who thereby lose the scents which must needs attend such places.[2]

[1] This is the earliest notice I have found regarding Buchanan's skull now in the Anatomical Museum of the University of Edinburgh. In a MS. catalogue, prepared (about 1697) by Robert Henderson, Librarian of the University, there is an entry to the same effect as the above account as to how the skull was obtained (Irving, *Memoirs of Buchanan*, p. 311, note, edit. 1817). The same story is again told by Sir Robert Sibbald, *Commentarius in Vitam Georgii Buchanani*, p. 62 (Edin. 1702). Morer's testimony, therefore, carries us still further back ; and as he must have had his information from persons connected with the University, it must have been the received belief that the skull was that of Buchanan. The Latin verses to which Morer refers may be found in Sibbald.

[2] In 1566 Queen Mary granted to the Town Council of Edinburgh the yards and site of the Greyfriars' Monastery for the purpose of a public burying-place, as "being somewhat distant from the town" (Wilson, *Memorials of Edinburgh*, p. 73, edit. 1866).

On the north of the city in a bottom, is the physick-garden with 2700 sorts of plants, as the keeper of it told me. But then this variety of plants is all its beauty, having no walks, and but little walling or good hedges to recommend it; and is (to my thinking) the rudest piece of ground I ever saw with that name.

The manager of it, I suppose, guest at my thoughts, and told me that he was taking a much more convenient field a little farther off, which he designed to fence with a large brick wall, and, removing his plants thither, digest 'em into such a method as might make it a pleasant as well as useful garden. He had for his incouragement a small sallary allowed by the apothecaries of the town, which he adds to by the sale of such goods.[1]

Before we leave Edinburg, we ought to number their churches. They are seven, (1) the High Church,[2] divided into three parts, the Old, the New, and the Tolbooth Church, (2) the Trone Church, (3) the Friary,[3] (4) the Abbey, (5) the College Church, (6) the West Church, (7) the Lady Esther's Church,[4] which with the castle chappel are all the churches they have; and of these some are not used, and the rest thin, excepting the Trone and High Church.

There is no Cathedral, and tho' there be a chapter when there is a bishop, yet the prebendaries are little more than nominal, the stipends being deduced out of the bishops' revenue, which being not great in itself, very ill affords those defalcations. And tho' the prebendaries demand not above 8 or 10*l.* yearly each of them, yet are seldom paid,

---

[1] The Physic Garden was established in 1675, mainly through the action of Sir Robert Sibbald and Dr R. Andrew Balfour. Mr James Sutherland was its first curator, and he still retained his charge at the time of Morer's visit. The first site of the garden and that of which Morer speaks so disparagingly was the ground adjoining Trinity Hospital, which stood a little to the east of what is now the North Bridge. The object of the garden was to discover "what *materia medica*, in the way of herbs, Scotland was capable of producing." The garden proved a success; for, under date 1695, there is an entry in the Town Council Records, to the effect that "the Physic Garden is in great reputation both in England and foreign nations." From the Physic Garden sprang the present Botanical Garden of Edinburgh (Grant, *Story of the University*, vol. i. pp. 218–220). [2] St Giles. [3] Church of the Trinity, on the site of the North British Railway Station. [4] Lady Yester's Church, built in 1644, stood at the corner of the High School Wynd.

and thereupon sometimes murmur.   But the reason of that neglect I take to be this, that because these prebends are not given by the kings, or bishops, but are appendages to the neighbouring benefices, and follow the presentation to such living, therefore the bishop thinks he is not bound to take that notice of 'em, as he might otherwise do, were they creatures of his own.   And so much for Edinburg.

A mile from Edinburg is Leith, a mart town, at the mouth of the Fryth, having a fine piere stretching itself a great way into the sea, and serves for the safety of the vessels, and the pleasure of those who walk on it.   It may be called the warehouse of Edinburgh, to supply the merchants and other citizens.   It was formerly a great check to Edinburg, when King James VI. was there, who often threaten'd 'em to remove his palace and courts of judicature thither, to keep the citizens in better obedience.   It is a thriving town, having a double advantage, the sea-trade and the citizens' recreation to inrich it ; for thither they flock by foot or in coaches to divert themselves, having no play-house, musick meetings, or spring-garden to tempt them to those superfluous expences.

The second city of Scotland is Perth, or St John's town, because St John is its tutelar saint or guardian.   It stands on the bank of the river Tay, and not being above twenty miles from the sea, is every day saluted with the tide which brings up vessels thither.   There are two long spacious streets, besides others of less moment, for intercourse, which being well paved, are at all times tolerably clean.   The houses are not stately, but after the Scotch way make a good appearance.   The most remarkable building, is that where the Gowries had like to have murder'd James VI. to revenge their father's death, executed in the King's minority.[1] But the person hired to dispatch him at that instant refusing, and one of the Gowries not being able of himself to do it, succour came in, the King escaped at that time, and returned safe to Sterling.

Here are only two churches ; but one of 'em so big that

---

[1] The site of the Gowrie House, of which nothing now remains, is occupied by the County Buildings.

it looks more like a cathedral than parish church, kept in good repair, and decent within.[1]

The trade of the town depends chiefly on linen, which the Highlanders bring thither, and which they export to the value of 40,000*l.* sterling per annum. It was in former days the seat of divers parliaments, is a county town govern'd by a Lord Provost and Bailiffs, has the stile of royal borough, with the honours and privileges of the most eminent places of Scotland ; and the inhabitants speak very big whenever they have occasion to mention the city, as we may see in the instrument of burgess-ship given us, and which is a civility and honour they confer on strangers.

While we staid at Perth, our curiosity led us to visit Scone, being a walk of pleasure, or short mile thither. It was formerly a monastery, tho' now made a lay-mansion, belonging to my Lord Stormond, and has a few houses about it to the bulk of a country village, but hardly fit to be called a town. The honour of the place is a little chappel, where the kings of Scotland are usually crowned, and where King Charles II. took the covenant when he was in that kingdom. From hence the stone was brought to Westminster Abbey by King Edward I. whereon the Scotch princes anciently received their crowns, and concerning which there is this kind of prophecy—

Si verum est fatum, Scoti, quocunq ; locatum
Invenient lapidem, regnare tenentur ibidem.

The Scots shall brook the realm as natif ground,
If wierds fail not, whaire'ere this stane is found

which is thought to be accomplish'd in the late race of kings, from King James VI. downward.

From Perth we march'd northerly to Forfar, a place of no great noise, saving that it is a country town, a royal borough, and anciently the seat of several parliaments, govern'd by a Provost and Bayliffs, and had once the King's Palace,[2] though now we scarce see the ruins of it.

While we quarter'd here, we took the air so far as Dundee,

---

[1] The Church of St John already more than once referred to.   [2] The castle of King Malcolm on a rising-ground to the north of the town.

a very pretty town, seated at the bottom of an hill, almost at the mouth of the river Tay, which runs up to Perth; 'tis furnish'd with two or three small piers for the conveniency of shipping, and the buildings are such as speak the substance and riches of the place. It is a royal borough, and considerable for its trade, wherein it has supplanted St Andrews on the other side the river, and about seven miles from it. Here we were handsomly treated at the charges of the corporation, who complimented us with burgess-ships.

Returning back to Perth, we received orders to march to Glasgow; and in our way thither we pass'd through Dunblain, a bishop's sea, but a very ordinary town, without anything worthy remembrance but Bishop Leighton's new library;[1] a large church much abused by the wild Cameronians; and the late bishop's kindness, whose name is Douglas, a very reverend and hospitable gentleman, and entertained me courteously.

About four miles farther was Sterling, a fine town, and in two instances a copy of Edinburgh, as standing on a considerable rising, and having a strong castle to defend it, built on a steep rock, and by a great river, over which is a long stone bridge, and a strong gate. 'Tis a town of good trade, having the benefit of the Fryth to bring up vessels to it. 'Tis a royal borough, was formerly the king's palace, and seat of Parliaments, is well built and continues still in much reputation and honour. But I only pass'd through it, and can say no more.

Twelve miles hence, and the midway between Sterling and Edinburg, is the town of Linlithgow, a royal borough, with a large building called the Castle, and was formerly the residence of several princes. It is still own'd forthe king's house, but used by my Lord Leviston,[2] and consists of a stately quadrangle, in the midst of which is a fine fountain. About the quadrangle are divers niches or places for images to stand in, but not one figure left besides

---

[1] Archbishop Leighton, who died in 1684 (five years before Morer's visit), bequeathed a library of over 1500 volumes for the use of the clergy of the diocese of Dunblane. The library still exists, and is known as the *Bibliotheca Leightoniensis*, which is inscribed on the present building.   [2] From the reign of James VI., Linlithgow Palace had been little more than the occasional residence of the Earls of Livingstone.

the Pope's, which affords matter of reflection.   There are many such conveniences about the church wall, but there is no effigies besides that of St Michael the archangel, the protector or tutelar angel of the church and town, whose common seal is gartered with this inscription—

Sancte Michael ora pro nobis.

The church is large and has an handsome gallery and a seat for the king.   One of its ministers formerly served at Iver in Buckinghamshire, by name Mr Seaton, who studies divinity and physick together.

'Tis from Linlithgow to Glasgow 24 miles, and we go through Falkirk and Kelsyth, two boroughs of royalties, but there is nothing remarkable in 'em, nor in all the way to Glasgow, excepting the sight of grey crows, which are very numerous in this country.

Glasgow is a place of great extent and good situation; and has the reputation of the finest town in Scotland, not excepting Edinburgh, tho' the royal city.   The two main streets are made cross-wise, well paved and bounded with stately buildings, especially about the centre, where they are mostly new, with piazzas under 'em.   It is a metropolitane sea, and at the upper end of the great street stands the archbishop's palace, formerly without doubt a very magnificent structure, but now in ruins, and has no more left in repair than what was the ancient prison, and is at this time a mean dwelling.   A little higher is the church, a great fabrick, with a lofty steeple, built by St Mungo, who lies buried between four pillars in that part of the church they call the baronie; for it is divided into three parts, the upper, the lower, and the baronie, which is assigned the country people thereabouts for their use, and the town has nothing to do with it.   This cathedral, with one large church more in the heart of the city where the magistrates attend, are all the places of publick worship at Glasgow, the nest of fanaticism, and the most factious town in all that kingdom. The yard belonging to the cathedral is the common burial-place, and the fence or wall consists of continued monuments, or stones erected for the memory of the dead, a pretty device and useful. From hence to the river the city reaches, a mile in length, the half of which is upon a declension. This river is a great current, called the Clyde, and conduces much to the riches of the inhabitants, and makes it the most considerable town of that nation. Here are several hospitals, or houses of charity, and many spires more for ornament than use: And a tolbooth or common-hall very magnificent (as most of 'em are in the towns of Scotland) for publick entertainments, or city business.

Glasgow is as factious as it is rich. Yet the most considerable persons for quality, are well disposed to the church. But the disaffected make up that defect with number, and sometimes call the hill men or field conventiclers to assist 'em.

Over the river Clyde is a very fine bridge, with a great number of arches;[1] and on the other side is a little town,[2] which is the suburbs of Glasgow, and is as Southwark to London. The sight of the river and arms of Glasgow (being a fish with a ring in his mouth), put me in mind of this story, as the inhabitants report it.[3]

A young lady being courted by a gentleman living not far from Glasgow, was presented with a ring, which after marriage, going over the river, she accidentally let fall into the water. A while after, the husband missing the ring grew jealous, and suspected she had given it to some other man whom she fancied better. This created great discontent, nor could the archbishop himself reconcile 'em, tho' he earnestly and often endeavour'd it; till one day walking in a green by the river-side, and seeing the fishermen drawing their nets, it so happened that the bishop made a purchase of the draught, and in the mouth of one of the fishes found the ring, which had occasioned so much animosity and quarrels between the man and his wife. The bishop immediately carries the ring to the husband, convinces him of his wife's innocency, and so without much difficulty reconciles 'em again. And from the strangeness of the

---

[1] Erected in 1350, and widened and modernised in 1770. [2] The Gorbals.
[3] Morer here gives a version of the well-known legend of St Mungo and Langneth, queen of Strathclyde, invented to account for the salmon and ring, which make part of the arms of the city of Glasgow.

event, from this time forward, was made the arms of the town.

We went from Glasgow to Ayre, a country-town, and royal borough, situated near the Clyde, the same river that runs up to Glasgow, from whence it is distant 24 miles. Here are seen the ruins of a citadel, built by Oliver Cromwell about the year 1652, and was demolish'd after the Restauration. In this town King William and Queen Mary were first proclaimed, and own'd for their sovereign. The town is pretty enough, and had formerly a very great trade, but is much impair'd of late years by the losses they have sustained; so that now they give way to the success of Glasgow, and chuse rather to freight other men's ships, than be at the hazard to build any of their own. There is a small river runs by the town side into the Clyde, with a good bridge upheld by four arches.[1] Here I had the sight of a manuscript in much repute, and of which I had heard before, tho' I could not come at it, when I had more leisure to peruse it. The Bishop of Dunkell was the author. It is an historical account or narrative of all the transactions during the late civil war, wherein being himself a concern'd party, he was better able to do such a work.[2]

[1] The 'Auld Brig' of Burns. [2] Henry Guthrie or Guthry was made Bishop of Dunkeld in 1665, and died in 1677. " He wrote *Memoirs of Scottish Affairs from the year 1637 until the Murder of good King Charles I*."—Keith, *Catalogue of Scottish Bishops*, p. 99 (edit. 1824). Guthrie's manuscript, to which Morer refers, was published at London in 1702, and afterwards at Glasgow in 1747.

INDEX.

ABERBROTHOCK = Abbey of Burbro-do-ché, 5.
Abercarny, Lord, 115.
Aberdeen = Dabberden, 5; Aberdyne, 20; described by De Beaugué, 66; 112, 151; bridge at, 152; 163; described by Tucker, 172–4; described by Franck, 203–5; 218.
Aberdour, 169.
Abernethy, 218.
Acherson, James, 126.
Ailsa Craig = Ellsey, 153.
Albany, Duke of, 44, *note.*
Allan Water, 194.
Alloa = Alloway, described by Tucker, 168.
Alloa Tower, 117.
Almond, the, 171.
Angus, 19.
Annan, the River, 107.
Annan, 250.
Anstruther, 169, 170.
Apples, 275.
Arbroath, Abbey of Burbro-do-ché, 5; Arbroith, 20; Arbroth, 172.
Archbishoprics, number of, 45.
Archibalds, John, 118.
Ardmillian, 180.
Ardoch, Bridge of, 196.
Armour, use of, 74.
Army, Scottish, in 1498, 48; 52.
Arnet, William, and his inn at Cockburnspath, 127.
Arran, Island of, 153, 179.
Artillery, 48.
Assynt, 176.
Atholl = Athill, 20.
Atholl—Erle of Acelelles, 3; Earl of, 124.
Auchmuchty, James, 113.
Auchterarder = Entrearde, 4.

Auldhame = Adam, 127.
Ayr, 21, 23, 151, 163; described by Tucker, 179; 290.
Ayton = Aton, 81; Aten, 144; Aiton, 228.

BADENOCH = Bedvaasok, 3; Baden-asshe, 4, 5; hunt in, 123.
Badgers, 87.
Bag-pipes, 99, 258, 265.
Balcary, 180.
Baledgarno = Balygernathe, 5.
Baliol and Edward I. at Montrose, 4.
Ballantry = Ballantrae, 180.
Ballo Castle = Castle Grant, 123.
Balvenie, 5.
Banff = Banet Castle, 5, 152, 173.
Baptism, ceremony of, described, 101, 146, 258.
Barley, grown on the islands, 46; in Scotland, 86, 232.
Barnacle geese, 26, 56–7, 202–3.
Bass Rock, described by Swave, 55; by De Beaugué, 67; by Taylor, 126–7; by Brereton, 135; 216; by Ray, 232–4.
Baylie, James, 127.
Baylye, Will, 157.
Bears in Scotland, 60, 254.
Beaufort Castle = Lovet, 200.
Beer, 74; home-brewed, 89; brewery in Edinburgh, 141; made without hops, 228; 263.
Benavon, 120.
Benoit, Réné, xv.
Bergenroth's *Simancas Papers*, 39.
Berner's *Froissart*, 8.
Berteville, Jean, xii.
Bervie = Barvye, 20.
Berwick on Tweed = Barwyk, 2; siege of, 3, and *note;* Barwik, 6; Berwike

17 ; Barwyke, 23 ; and Æneas Sylvius, 28, 29; fortress at, 53 ; bridge by Henry VII., 53, and *note;* described by Moryson, 81, 86 ; by Taylor, 128; by Brereton, 132–3 ; 163, 165, 227 ; by De Rocheford, 229; by Ray, 230–1.

Bishoprics and Abbacies, revenue from, in 1498, 42 ; number of, 45; 83, 100.

Blacknesse, 17, 167.

Blaeu's Atlas, xxvi.

Blare, James, of Irvine, 154.

Blythe, 108.

Boece, Hector, x.

Boghall Castle, 186.

Bog-of-Gight Castle, 125.

Bo'ness = Bowne, 17; 163, 167.

Bordeaux, wine from, 78.

Bothwell, James, Earl of, 76.

Bowyer, Sir William, 128.

Box-beds, 89.

Braemar, 120.

Brahan Castle, 200.

Brantôme, xvi.

Bread, oatmeal of, 273.

Brechin = Breghem, 5 ; Brichan, 20 ; Breekin, 118 ; the Water-Poet at, 125; 152, 218.

Brereton, Sir William, xxii, 132.

Bridge at Berwick, 132, *note ;* in Scotland, 152.

Brimstone and butter, 103.

Brome, James, xxii, 241.

Bronkhorst, Arnold, xxiv.

Broom, 75.

Buchan—therle of Bochan, 4 ; Earl of, 120.

Buchanan, George, 256, 282–3.

Buckle's Sketch of Scottish History, 16.

Bullets of gold, value of, 112.

Burgundy, Duke of, 13, 30; wears the Cross of St Andrew, 49.

Burntisland = Brutelan, 69; 112, 113, 125, 163, 169, 170, 212, 213.

Bute, 178.

CABBAGE, 88.

Cadder, 221.

Cairn-o'-Mount, 125.

Caithness = Chatnesse, 20.

Calderwood, David, 138.

Callis, William, lodging-house, 136.

Cambuskenneth = Camskinelle, 18.

Camden, xxv.

Campbell, John, 56, 58.

Camphire = Campvere or Vere, 87.

Cantlow—Sir John Cantelow, 5.

Capua, Prior of, 66, and *note.*

Cardan, Jerome, xiii.

Cardross, 193.

Carlisle = Carlill, 22 ; Carelyl, 22 ; Carlile, 107.

Carrick = Carryct, 21; 23; cave of, 149, 156; 179.

Cars, the, of Prestongrange, 82.

Cartelok (Kirkintilloch) Castle, 221.

Cassanate, William, xiii.

Cassillis, Lord, 154.

Castelton, 4.

Caudwel, Domine, anecdote regarding, 195.

Chappell, the (Stranraer), 180.

Charles VI. of France, 13.

Chastaigner, Louis, xvi.

Chastellard, xvi.

Cheese, 61.

Church, the government of, 143 ; service, 146, 239, 258 ; training for, 257.

Churches, highly ornamented, 79 ; in Edinburgh, 284.

Clackmanan = Clakmannan, 18.

Claret, 265; price of, 274.

Climate of Scotland in 1598, Fynes Moryson, 86.

Cluny = Clony Castle, 4.

Clyde, the, 23, 163, 176, 219, 276, 289.

Coaches in Edinburgh, 140.

Coal, given in alms, 26, and *note;* 61, 75 ; sea-coal, 87 ; mines, 98 ; at Culross, 115, *note,* 116, 117; price of, 148 ; at Tranent, 227; 275.

Cockburnspath, 127, 228.

Cockles, 214.

Cocks, non-crowing, 57.

Codfish, caught in moats, 78, 214.

Coldingham = Coldynghm, 3; 6, 22.

Coldstream = Calderstreme, 2.

Colewort, red, 88.

Compass of straw, 211.

Comyn, Sir John, of Badenoch, 3, and *note,* 4.

Conies, 87.

Constable, Marmaduke, family of, 57.

Contareno, Peter Francis, xii.

Cookery, primitive, 8–9 ; bread, 79 ; on a deer hunt, 122 ; 263, 273.

Cormorants, 233, 254.

Corn, method of sowing and cutting, 44 ; 86, 87 ; plenty of, 98.

Cowie = Cowy, 20.

Crabs, 214.

Crail, 169, 171, 212.

Cramond, 163, 166.

Cranston, David, 77, and *note.*

Crawfish, 214.

Craycross = Creke Crosse, 22.

Crighton, Master, 115.

Cromarty, 175, 176, 218.

Crows, 27, and *note.*

Cuffabouts, 167.

Culross = Cooras, 115.

Cupar-Fife, 211.

Curlew, 214.

Currants, 275.

Customs in 1498, 42.

Dalkeith, castle, 8 ; 10, 82, 216.

Danes, 53.

Darnaway Castle = Tarnaway, 124.

David I. of Scotland, 8.

D'Angers, Sir Aubert, death of, 9.

De Ayala, Don Pedro, xi, 16, 39, 50, 51, 54.

De Beaugué, Sire Jean, xii, 63.

De Charny, Sir Geoffry, 10.

Dee, the, 20, 204.

Deer hunt in Braemar Forest, 120–3.

De Lalain, Jacques (1448), 30–8.

De Longueville, Madame, 75, and *note.*

De Medina, Sir John, xxiv.

De Meriadet, Hervé, 32.

Denmark, Anne of, 94.

De Rocheford, Jorevin, 217.

De Rohan, Henri, Duc, *Travels,* 91–5.

De Thermes, Monsieur, 78.

De Vienne, Sir John, 11, 12.

De Witt, James, xxiv.

Dickson, Rev. David, 155.

Dirt of the houses, 97.

Distances travelled by the Scottish army, 8.

Dogs, used for hunting, 61.

Done (Don) Bridge, 152.

Donglasse, 22, 67.

Dornoch, 202.

Dornock, 218.

Douglas—Lord William Dowglas, 3 ; Sir William, 8 ; Earl of, 9, 12 ; William, Earl of, 30, and *note ;* Douglas and Burgundy, 32–8.

Douglas, 238.

Dozay, Monsieur, 76.

Dress, 47, 121, 140, 142, 231–2, 260, 269–70, 272.

Drink, different kinds of, 274.

Drinking, habits of, 90.

Drip (Ford of) = Tirps, 18.

Drummond = Dromon Castle, 195.

Drummond of Hawthornden, xx, xxi.

Drummond, David, 113, 129.

Dryburgh = Treborch, 56.

Du Bartas, Guillaume de Salluste, xvii.

Duck, 214.

Dumbarton = Dumbertayne, 21 ; Domberterand, 75, 78, 151, 163, 177, 207, 218.

Dumfries, 21, 22, 151, 179, 184, 238, 239, 249.

Dunbar, Earl of—Erle Patrik, 3, and *note.*

Dunbar, Earl of = George Hume, 232.

Dunbar, Castell of Dunbarre, 3, 10, 17, 22, 23 ; De Beaugué's description of, 67 ; 75, 78, 81, 112, 127, 134, 152, 165, 227 ; described by Ray, 231, 232 ; 239, 242.

Dunblane, 191, 193, 194–5, 287.

Dundee, 5, 20, 55, 58, 67, 112, 125, 151, 163, 171, 172, 208–9, 287.

Dunduff = Dundufmull, 180.

Dunfermline = Donffremelyn, 6 ; 10 ; Domfarmelin, 94 ; palace and church, 115, 148 ; 212.

Dunfermline, Earl of, 102.

Dunglass Castle, 134.

Dungyrdloch = Drumgarloch, 180.

Dunkeld, 171, 218.

Dunnotter Castle, 206.

Dunrobin, 175.

Dunskey Castle, 158.
Dunure, 180.
Durham—Bishop of Dwreysm, 5.
Durris = Downes, 5.
Dysart = Disert, 18, 112, 170.

EAGLES, 214.
Earls, Scottish, and their soldiers, 45.
East Linton, 227.
Edinburgh = Edenbrough, Edward I.'s
    visit, 4, 6 ; French Army in, 9 ;
    described by Froissart, 10; 23, 47,
    56 ; Ennebroc, 75 ; Lislebourg, 78 ;
    walls of, 84, and *note ;* described by
    Fynes Moryson, 82–4, 86 ; by Duc
    de Rohan, 92–3; 99; Taylor's visit
    to, 108–12, 125, 126 ; described
    by Brereton, 136–42; 151 ; Howell
    writes from, 159; Tucker's account,
    164–5; Franck's, 215; 218; described
    by De Rocheford, 221–6; by Ray,
    234–5 ; by Brome, 242 ; by Morer,
    278–85.
Edinburgh Castle, siege of, 4; 83,
    93, 99, 109–10, 138–9, 215, 234,
    281.
Edinburgh, High Street, 83, 110, 139,
    215.
Edward I., voyage of, in 1295, 1–6.
Edward VI., 71.
Edzell, 119.
Eel, 214.
Ehingen, Georg von, x.
Elgin, Earl of, 120.
Elgin = Deigm, 5 ; Elgen, 124, 152,
    257.
Elizabeth, Queen of Bohemia, 94.
Elphinstone, Sir George, 152.
Elphinstone, 168.
Ely, 169, 170.
Emigration to Ireland, 154.
Enterkin, the, described by John
    Ray, 238.
Enzie = Lannay, 5.
Erskine Ferry, 177.
Erskine, Lords of, 86,
Esk, the, 107.
Ettrick = Etryke, 22.
Ewes-dale = Ewysdale, 22.
Execution of a criminal, 225.
Exports, 87.
Eyemouth = Esmons, 67, 165, 166.

FALKIRK, 148, 221.
Falkland, 18, 85, 212.
Farms, value of, in 1498, 41.
Farro Islands, 217.
Fast Castle = Fauxcastel, 67.
Fasting-man, account of, 56.
Fenton, John, 115.
Ferdinand and Isabella, 39.
Fernell = Fernovell, 4.
Fife = Fiffe, 18, 45, and *note,* 85, 210–
    11.
Findorne, 174.
Fish, dried and salted, 87.
Fisheries in 1498, 43 ; rent from, 43.
Fisherrow = Fisherawe, 82.
Flemish, the arrival in Scotland of
    the, 43, and *note.*
Floating Island of Lochlomond, 57 ;
    of Loch Ness, 196.
Food, of the common people, 27 ; in
    1598, 88; 231.
Forests in Scotland, scarcity of trees,
    13, and *note ;* no trees, 26, and
    note ; well-timbered oak, 60.
Forfar Castle, 4, 125, 286.
Forth, the Frith of = Scottish se, 4 ;
    Foorth, 17, 18, 19, 23, 193–4
    windings of, 237; 276.
Foxes, 60, 254.
Fox's *Journal,* xxiii.
France, young Scotchmen well
    received in, 48, 102.
Franck, Richard, xxii, 182.
Fraserburgh, 173, 174.
French in Scotland, 9, 85, 93.
Friars Observant, 40, and *note.*
Froissart, Jean, his acquaintance
    with Scotland, 7 ; different trans-
    lations of, 8.
Fruits, 44.
Funerals, 101, 239, 259.
Futtie, 173.
Fyvie = Fyuin Castell, 5.

GAELIC, the language in the " wooded
    region," 27; James IV.'s knowledge
    of, 39 ; in the islands, 48 ; 174,
    262.
Galloway, 21, 22 ; name for Scotland
    south of the Forth, 45, and *note,*
    157, 179.
" Galloways "—horses, 8.

Garioch = Garioth, 20.
Garmouth, 174, 176.
Garran, 180.
Garvilland, Port, 180.
Gatehouse of Fleet, 180.
Geese, 28 ; salted, 88, 214.
General Council, 46.
Geographical position of Scotland described, 25–6, 48, 50, 59, 72, 217.
Gibel, John, 115.
Gipsies, 28.
Girven, 180.
Glasgow = Glasgo, 21, 23 ; Brereton's visit to, 150–4 ; bridge at, 152 ; 163, 176–7, 179, 191–3, 218–9, 219–21, 537, 248, 288–90.
Glass, made of kelp and sand, 234.
Gleenfoote, 180.
Glenbervie = Glowberwy, 5.
Glenesk, 119.
Glutton, the, 263.
Gold-mines, 61.
Gooseberries, 275.
Gosford, 126.
Gos-hawks on Ailsa Craig, 154.
Gossander, 214.
Gowrie—The Kerse of Gowry, 19.
Graham—Lord Patrik of Greahm, 3, and note.
Grahame, Sir John, 149.
Grahames Wall, 149.
Grampians, 19.
Grangemouth, 167.
Greenock, 178, 219.

HACKET, Laird of—Hauket, 32 ; Haguet, 32.
Haddington = Hadyngton, 3, 6 ; Haddyngtoune, 17 ; Edimton, 67 ; Hadirington, 82 ; 152, 216, 227.
Haddock, 214, 263.
Hamilton, 238 ; palace, 249.
Hamilton, Duke of, 76 ; Marquis of, 138, 153.
Hardyng, John, 16 ; Chronicle of, 17–23.
Hares, 60, 225.
Hastings—Sir John Hastynges, 5.
Hawick = Hawike, 22.
Hawks, 214.
Hay, 98 ; price of, 150 ; scarcity of, 264, 267.

Hay, Robert, 113, 129.
Hay, Sir George, Earl of Kinnoul, 102, and note.
Heath-game, 214.
Hebrides = Ebudes, 217.
Henderson, James, 126.
Henry, Prince, son of James VI., 94.
Heralds, 99.
Heriot's Hospital, 141, 246, 282.
Herrings, great quantities exported, 44; fisheries, 87, 214, 217; at Dunbar, 232.
Highlands described, 218, 268.
Hogs, 60.
Holyrood Palace = Holy Crosse, 83: 110, 215, 283.
Horse-post, 278.
Horses, of the Scots, 8; value in 1367, 12; management, 27; breed, 60, 86; wild, 121; harness, 255; hire of, 264.
Hospitality, treatment of foreigners, 44, 52, 60.
Hostility to the English, 60.
Houses, construction of, 27, 47, 52, 74, 84 ; state of, 140, 142, 190, 195, 231, 260, 274–5, 279 ; sheep grazing on top, 186.
Howell, James, 96 ; Familiar Letters, 159.
Hume, Lord, 81.
Huntly, Marquis of, 120, 125.
Hutton, Berwickshire—Hatton, 2.

IMPORTS, 87.
Inchgarvy, 167.
Inchkeith = Isle Dieu, 69 ; Isle aux Chevaux, 78.
Inhabitants of Scotland characterised, 27, 51–2.
Innerquharanche = Interkeratche, 5.
Innerwick = Anderwick, 134.
Inns in Scotland, 89, and note.
Interest on money, "in kind," 77, 81.
Inverbreakie, 201.
Inverkeithing = Ennerkethen, 19, 169.
Inverness, 152, 163, 174, 176, 199, 262.
Inverqueich = Entrecoit Castell, 4.
Iron, none in Scotland, 11.
Irvine, 151, 154, 178, 179.

Islands, number of inhabited, 45, 163.
Isle of Man, 54.
Italian's, an, account of Scotland in 1500, 50.

James I. described, 25.
James IV. described by Pedro de Ayala, 39–41 ; government of the Highlands, 46.
James V., "Navigation round Scotland," xi ; and Peder Swave, 54 ; at Melrose, 57.
James VI., 92 ; visit to Scotland, 98–9.
Jasper, columns of, in Melrose, 58.
Jedburgh = Gardeford, 4; Gaydeford, 4; 22 ; Jeduart, 56, 58 ; Jedard, 186.
Jonson, Ben, xx ; and Taylor the Water-Poet, 104 ; in Edinburgh, 126.
Jorevin, xxii.

Kale, 210, 231.
Keeling, 214.
Kelburn, 178.
Kelso, 10.
Kendrick, Sir Alex. of Cullen, 156.
Kennedy, Joan, mistress of James IV., 41.
Kennett, 168.
Kildrummy = Kyndroken, 5.
Kilmalcolm, 218.
Kilmarnock, 188.
Kilpatrick, 177.
Kincardine = Kyncarden, 5; Kynge Carden, 5; Kincarne, 168.
Kinclavin = Kyne Colowen Castle, 4.
Kindroghit Castle, 121.
Kinghorn = Quincornes, 78; 85, 112; well at, 113; 125, 169, 170.
King's places of residence, 46.
Kintore = Kyntorn, 5.
Kirkcaldy, 112, 169, 170, 212.
Kirkcudbright, 179, 180.
Kirke, Thomas, 251.
Kirkwall, 175.
Kittiwake Gull, 233.
Knighthood, order of, conferred by James II., 32.
Kyle = Kile, 23, 179.

Lammermore, 22.
Lanark = Lamarke, 23.
Lapwings, 257.
Lauder = Lowedere 3 ; Lowdere 4 ; Lader, 22 ; Ladres, 67.
Lauderdale = Lawdendayle, 22.
Law, administration of, in 1498, 42.
Leadhills, 238.
Lead-mines, 61.
Le Grange, David, xxiv.
Leith, 17 ; Petit Lict, 69, 84 ; Lits or Petit Lict, 93 ; exports from, 112; 142, 163, 167, 214, 215, 218 226, 234, 247, 285.
Lennox, Duke of, 138.
Lenox, 20.
Lesley, Bishop, xii, xxvi.
Leven, 169, 170.
Levingston, Henry, 126.
Liddesdale = Lyddis-dale, 22.
Lindores = Loundos, 6.
Lindsay, Barnard, 112.
Ling—heather, 134.
Linlithgow = Lunsta, 4 ; Lansen, 6 ; Lithko, 17; Lythko, 23, 45; Lescow, 94; Light-Goaw, 148, 151 ; Lynlithquo, 167, 221; 236, 247, 287.
Linnen cloathes, 87.
Livingstone, Earls of, 287.
Livingstone, Sir William, 158.
Lobsters, 214.
Loch Leven, 19.
Lochlevyne, Laird of, 32.
Lochlomond, xxii ; floating island, 57, and note, 149, 199.
Loch Ness, 174, 197.
Lodgings of the French in Edinburgh, 10; difficulty to procure, 76 ; at Blythe, 108 ; at Edzell, 119 ; at Brechin, 125 ; at Cockburnspath, 127 ; at Berwick, 134 ; at Edinburgh, 136, 145; at Glasgow, 152 ; at Irvine, 155 ; at Hugh Boyde's house, 158 ; at a country cottage, 186, 264.
Lonquhards = forest huts, 121.
Lord High Commissioner's procession, 244.
Lord's Supper, sacrament of, 147.
Lords, the, in Scotland, 100.
Lord Provost of Edinburgh, 246, 280.
Lowlands described, 271.

MACHANY, 194, 196.
Mackrel, 214.
Maidens, the = Maidenhead, 180.
Malcolm, King of Scot, 53.
Mallard, 214.
Map, ancient, of Scotland, xxv.
Map of Scotland, 13th century, author unknown, xxv.
Mar—Earl of Marre, 4, 5, 115, 120.
Mar, district of, 20, 45, *note*.
Markinch, Merkynch, 6.
Marnock, the, 190.
Marriage, without the ring, 101 ; ceremony, 258.
Martens, 87.
Marvels in Scotland, barnacle geese, 26, 56 ; floating island, 57.
Master of Arts, training for, 257.
Maxwell, John, and the Water-Poet, 109, 126.
Maxwell, Mr, of Anderwick, 134.
May, Isle of, De Beaugué's description of, 69 ; 136.
Mearns = Marnes, 5 ; Morenue, 5 ; Meernes, 20.
Melrose, 22 ; Jemoers, 57, 58.
Melville's, James, *Diary*, xvii.
Menteith = Menteith, 18.
Mercator's Atlas, ix.
Metal, temper of, 190.
Mice, none in Ross, 201.
Moffat = Mophot, 107, and *note*.
Monasteries or abbeys, number of, 45.
Money, value in 1498, 42 ; scarcity of, 79 ; value, 240, 265, 277.
Mongavile, Laird of, 32.
Mons Meg at Edinburgh Castle, 110, 245.
Monteith—erle of Monetet, 3.
Monteith, 45, *note*, 194.
Montigny, Messire Simon de Lalain, Lord of, 32.
Montrose, Duke of, 44, *note*.
Montrose = Monorous, 4 ; Monrosse, 20 ; 66, 172, 173, 207.
Moor Fowl, 214.
Moray, Earl of, 9, 12.
Moray = Mureffe, 20 ; 45.
Morer, Thomas, xxii, 266.
Morrison's Haven, 166.
Morton, Earl of, 82.

Moryson, Fynes, 80–90.
Mount Keen = Skeene, 119.
Mull, Island of, 261.
Murray, Bishop of, 124.
Murray, Captain, 113.
Murray, Earl of, Banquet, xii.
Murray, Earl of, 121, 124.
Murray, Sir Patrick, 124.
Murray, Sir William, 115, 120.
Murray, 152.
Music, 264.
Musselborough, 82, 136, 148, 166, 216, 227.
Mussels, 214.
Mutton, salted, 88, 214.
Mynour, artist, xxiv.

NAVY in 1598, 86.
Neal's Craigs, 214.
Newark, 178, 218.
Newbattle = Abbey of Neubattaill, 4.
Newburgh, Aberdeen, 173.
Newcastle, 29.
Newhaven, 166.
Newport = South Ferry, 169, 171.
Niddrie, 227.
Nith, the = Arnotus, 185, 249.
Nithsdale = Nithysdayle, 21.
Norham Castle, 29, *note*.
Nucius Nicander, 59–62.

OAK FORESTS, 60, 61.
Oat Cakes, 9, 89, 157, 186.
Oatmeal, chief fare, 98.
Oats, 86 ; price of, 150 ; 232, 267.
Ochills = Oyghylles, 18 ; Oyghles, 18, 221.
Oil of Bays, 103.
Organ in Holyrood Chapel, 98, *note*.
Orkney Islands, 26, 45, and *note*, 54, 174, 176.
Ortelius's Atlas, xxvi.
Otters, 87.
Oxen, without horns, 60–61.
Oysters, size of, 27, 214.

PAISLEY, 218.
Panton, George, xii.
Paris, Matthew, xxv.
Parliament House, Edinburgh, 137, 160, 280.

Partridge, 210, 214.
Payment in kind in 1598, 88.
Pearls, exported, 27, and *note*.
Pears, 275.
Peas, 267.
Peat, 26, *note*, 150, 276.
Peebles = Pebles, 23.
Pennyless Pilgrimage, 107-31.
Pentland = Pictland Hills, 268.
Perch, 214.
Perlin, Estienne, 71.
Perth, xxiii ; Saynt Johns, 4 ; Saint John of Perte, 5 ; Saynte Jhons Towne, 18, 19, 20, 66, 118, 151, 152, 171, 218, 285-7.
Peterhead, 173, 174.
Peter's Pence, 58, *note*.
Pewter Pots, 143.
Pheasant, 210, 214.
Physic Garden in Edinburgh, 284-5, and *note*.
Piccolomini, Æneas Sylvius, 24.
Pidgeon. 214.
Pigs, 256.
Pike, 214.
Pinkerton = Pikelton, 6.
Pistols, cost of, 145.
Pittenweem, 169, 170, 212.
Plaice, 214.
Plover, grey and green, 214.
Plums, 275.
Poland, emigration to, 88.
Police, 47.
Pope Pius II., 24.
Population of Edinburgh in 1636, 141.
Pork, 214.
Porpoises, 255.
Porridge, 88.
Portincragge, 19.
Port Patrick, 149, 158, 180, 278.
Prelates, 46.
Prestonpans, Prestongraung, 82, 166, 216.
Principatus Gallovidiæ, 45, and *note*.
Principatus insularum, 45, and *note*.
Privy Council, Edinburgh, 46, 137.
Provisions, price of, 73.
Ptarmigans, 254.

QUART MEASURE, 107.
Queensferry, 167.
Queens of Scotland, possessions of, 47.

RABBITS, 225.
Ransom, claimed by the Scots for damage done by the French army, 14-15.
Rats, none in Ross, 201.
Ray, John, 230.
Red Castle, near Montrose, Balygernatthe, 5.
Red-shankes, 120, and *note*.
Religion, 100-1, 269.
Renfrew, 177, 179, 219.
Rents in kind, collection of, 47.
Revenue in the time of James IV., 41.
Ringing Rock, near Port Patrick, 149.
Roads, 264.
Robert II., 10.
Rochelle, wine from, 78.
Rollock, Principal of Edinburgh College, 146.
Ross, Duke of, 44.
Ross—Roos, erle of, 3.
Ross = Rosse, 20, 45, *note*, 575.
Rothes = Rosers Maner, 5.
Rothesay, Duke of, 44, *note*.
Rowlands, Samuel, 105.
Roxburgh, Lord, 135.
Roxburgh (Rokesbrough)—Castell, 3 ; Graie Freres, 4 ; Roussebroa, 67.
Rycks pennynck, 58.
Rye, 232.
Ryngwodfelde, 22.

SABBATH EXERCISE, 101.
St Andrew, patron saint of Scotland, 49.
St Andrews, Archbishop of, John Hamilton, xiii.
St Andrews, Archbishop, richest man in Scotland, 76, and *note*, 137-8.
St Andrews, xviii, xxii, 6 ; Saynte Andrewes, 18, 65, 74, 77 ; Sainct Andrè, 78 ; 85, 101, 112, 151, 169, 171, 211-2, 218, 257.
St Catherines, oil well of, 57.

St Giles' Cathedral, Edinburgh, 83, 100, 244, 281.
St John, Sir Hugh, 5.
St Margaret's Hope, 19.
St Monance, 169, 170.
St Mongo's Shrine, 20.
St Patrick = S. Patryke, 21.
Salmon, great quantities, 44 ; caught in moats, 79 ; at Berwick, 81, 128, 133, 134 ; in the Spey, 174–5 ; in the Forth, 193 ; servants' stipulation, 194; 214, 217; at Dunbar, 227.
Salt, 87.
Saltcoats, 178.
Salt-pans, 136, 148.
Sanquhar = Zanker, 187.
Scaliger, the younger, xvi.
Scart, the, 233.
Scone, 19, 148, 212.
Scots, characterised, 8, 43, 44, 47, 64, 74, 95, 163, 231, 264, 269.
Scots and French, *disagreement* at Edinburgh, 10.
Scott, John, a hermit, 56, and *note*.
Scott, Sir Walter, on Froissart, 8.
Scottish mile, 107.
Scout, the, 233.
Seaports, number of, in 1498, 45.
Serpents near Dundee, 59.
Seton Castle, 82, 136.
Sharks, 255.
Sharpe, Dr, 138.
Sheep, immense flocks of, 44, 46, 60, 61.
Sheep-stealing, punishment for, 61.
Sherley, James, 146.
Sherry, sack, 265.
Shetland, 175.
Shooting, near Edinburgh, 224, 225.
Signets, 214.
Silver-mines, 61.
Simson, Simon, a doctor, 77, and *note*.
Sinclair—Saintler, Sir William, 3.
Siward—Sir Richard Suard, 3.
Solan Geese, 57, 67, and *note*, 126 ; on Ailsa, 154; on the Bass, 55 ; habits of, 135–6, 233, 274.
Soles, 214.
Southerness = Satternis, 180.
South Esk, 207.

Soutra = Soltray, 23.
Speed's Atlas, xxv.
Spencer, Sir Hugh, 5.
Spey, 213.
Sport—James IV. hunts in the mountains, 41; hunting bears and wild boars, 61 ; near Edinburgh, 224 ; spearing salmon, 250.
Spottiswoode, Sir Robert, 137.
Spynie, 124.
Stag, Scots hunting the, 57, 60.
Stage-coaches, 278.
Stewart, of Bute, 144.
Stirling = Estrevelyn, 4 ; Strevelyn, 6, 17, 18, 21, 23 ; tournament at, 32–8; 45, 94, 115, 148, 151, 163, 168, 193, 218, 236–7, 287.
Stirling Castle, 118, 236.
Stock fish = stoque fix, 43.
Stonehaven, 173.
Stool of repentance, 144, 185, 257.
Stow = Stowe, 22.
Stranraer, 180.
Strathbogie, 125.
Strathearn—Earl of Stradern, 4.
Strathearn = Strathren, 19, 45.
Strathnavar, 202.
Strathnaverna, 176,
Strawberries, 275.
Stuart, John, 126.
Summer, day, length of, in, 61.
Sunday, observance of, 40.
Sutherland, 20, 45,
Sutors, the, 175.
Swans on Linlithgow Loch, 236.
Swave Peder, xi ; 1535–55, diary of, 55–8.
Sylvius, Æneas, Pope Pius II., visit to Scotland, 24.

TAIN, 175, 202.
Tantallon Castle = Tinton, 78 ; 232.
Tarbert, Lochfyne, 177.
Tay = Taye, 18; 19, 56, 171, 218, 276.
Taylor, the Water-Poet, xxi, 104–31.
Tayport = Portincragge, 20.
Teal, 214.
Tempest's, Nicholas, house, 129.
Teviotdale = Tyvydale, 22.
Thistle, the fairest flower in Scotland, 98, 253.

Thornback, 214.

Thurso, 175, 176.

Tin-mines, 61.

Tinto Hill, 186.

Tobacco, 263, 276.

Todrigg, George, 126.

Topographical description, 43, 60, 218, 241, 253, 266.

Torrie, 173.

Torryburn, 168.

Tranent = Trenat, 227.

Traquair, Earl of, 145.

Trees in Scotland, scarcity of, 13, and *note;* none, 26, and *note;* the wooded region, 27 ; oak forests, 60 ; not one for Judas to hang himself, 97–8; fir, 123 ; at Seaton, 136 ; want of, 150, 254.

Trevisano, Andrea, xi, 50.

Trout, abundance of, 187 ; 214 ; in the Tyne, 227.

Tucker, Thomas, xxii, 162.

Turbot, 214.

Turnberry, 180.

Turtle-dove, 233.

Tweed, the = Twede, 2, 23, 28; Tivida; 53 ; 58, 128, 132.

Tyrie, Captain, 113.

Ubaldini, Petruccio, xiii.

Urr, 180.

Vansoum, Adrian, xxiv.

Vassals, time of service, 47.

Veal, 214.

Venison, 214.

Volcano, near Edinburgh, 57.

Wanlockhead, lead-mines, 187.

Wards, revenue from, in 1498, 42.

Warfare, Scottish mode of, 64,

Warham, Sir Thomas Worhne, 5.

Wark on Tweed, 23.

Washing clothes with the feet, 135, 143, 231, 255.

Weapons, 270.

Wedale, 22.

Weldon, Sir Anthony, 96.

Wemyss, 169, 170.

Wheat grown in Scotland, 60, 232.

White Kirk = Wiel, 4 ; Whitekirk, near North Berwick, Æneas Sylvius's pilgrimage to, 25, *note*.

Whithorn, 180.

Whiting, 263.

Wick, 175.

Widgeon, 214.

Wigton (Weghkton), Earl of, 150.

Wigton, 180.

Wild ducks, 225.

Windows in houses, 231.

Wine, drinking of, 264.

Wine, white, 265.

Winter in Scotland according to Æneas Sylvius, 25 ; length of day, 25, 27.

Winton, Earl of, 136.

Witherington, Sir Henry, and the Water-Poet, 113–5, 129.

Wolves, 27, and *note*, 60, 121.

Wood-cocks, 225.

Yarn, 87.

York, 129.